SECURING THE STATE

T0386771

DAVID OMAND

Securing the State

HURST & COMPANY, LONDON

First published in the United Kingdom in 2010 by
C. Hurst & Co. (Publishers) Ltd.,
41 Great Russell Street, London, WC1B 3PL
© David Omand, 2010
Editors' introduction and translation
All rights reserved.
Printed in India

The right of David Omand to be identified as the author
of this publication is asserted by him in accordance with
the Copyright, Designs and Patents Act, 1988.

A Cataloguing-in-Publication data record for this book
is available from the British Library.

ISBN: 9781849041881

www.hurstpublishers.com

For Liz

CONTENTS

Abbreviations   xiii
Preface   xvii

Introduction: A Lesson from the Fourteenth Century   1
The importance of security   1
... And a warning from the fifteenth century   6

1. Securitas: The Public Value of Security   9
The meaning of security today   9
From Secret State to Protecting State   9
The first shift: protection from major disruptive events   11
The second shift: an emphasis on the value of anticipation   11
The third shift: towards building national resilience   12
Future security challenges   13
The current takfiri jihadist terrorist threat   16
Developing the risk management approach   17
The politics of security   19

2. Sapientia: The Public Value of Intelligence   21
A short dance around the subject and a definition   21
The uses of intelligence   24
The nature and types of intelligence reporting   28
Classic intelligence   29
Open sources   31
PROTINT: the electronic traces we all leave behind   32
The different types of intelligence product   34
*The professionalization of intelligence: The Joint
    Intelligence Committee*   36
*The professionalization of intelligence: The UK Joint
    Terrorism Analysis Centre*   41

CONTENTS

An introduction to secrets, mysteries and complexities   46
The legitimacy of intelligence work   49

3. Fortitudio: The Public Value of Resilience   57
    The fragility of living in cities   57
    Organizing for resilience   58
    The role of good government in managing crises   61
    Critical National Infrastructure: a framework for
      resilience planning   66
    Into cyberspace   70
    Second generation resilience   73
    Moving on to third generation adaptive resilience   75
    The limits to protection   79
    Paying for the security of the critical national
      infrastructure   80

4. Civitas: The Public Value of Civic Harmony   85
    Living under the shadow   85
    Assessing strategic success   87
    The strategy for maintaining normality   92
    The first 'P': Pursuit   94
    The second 'P': Prevent   101
    The tension between liberty and security   106
    The tension between security and privacy   108

5. The Intelligence Cycle: From Whence Owe
   You This Strange Intelligence?   113
    From whence owe you this strange intelligence?   113
    The intelligence cycle   117
    Access   119
    Elucidation   122
    Dissemination   126
    Need to know or requirement to provide   129
    Action-on   131
    Direction   132
    Spy versus counter-spy: recognizing the race
      between offence and defence   133
6. Elucidation: Ye Shall Know the Truth, and the Truth
   Shall Set You Free   139
    The validation of single-source reporting   139

CONTENTS

Degrees of truth	142
Sharing the outcome of validation with analysts and users	144
Judging the likely customer interest in a single-source intelligence report	146
The analysis of single-source reporting	149
The place of all-source intelligence assessment	149
A hierarchy of intelligence analysis	151
The nature of intelligence assessment	153
On dealing with fragmentary and incomplete information	157
The inductive fallacy, the Achilles heel of analysis	158
How to go about solving a problem	160
Ye shall know the truth, and the truth shall set you free	164
7. Analysts and Policy-Makers: Idealists and Realists	171
The sources of failure	171
Idealists and realists	178
Setting requirements: marketing versus sales models	182
Readers, users, customers, or consumers: push and pull	185
The view from the top: Prime Ministers and Presidents	189
Writing for policy-makers	193
Potentialities, possibilities and probabilities	196
Fuzzy logic but plain speaking	200
8. Intelligence Failures: On Not Being Surprised by Surprise	209
The three watchful faces of Prudentia: observing past, present and future	209
What is surprise?	210
The lessons of military surprise	213
Terrorism, surprise and shock	219
Acquiring foreknowledge to counter surprise	220
Living with surprise	221
Warning fatigue and handling residual risk	223
An example of how using foreknowledge might help generate security	224
Reducing the risk of bias	225
Setting thresholds for response: indicators, warning and alert states	230
The example of the Yom Kippur War	233
The coastline of the future	236
The benefits of hindsight: intelligence gaps and intelligence failures	237

CONTENTS

Uncovering secrets and mysteries as ways of
reducing surprise   243
Linking the intelligence model to the policy world   247
Practical ways of reducing surprise   249

9. *In Medias Res*: Security and Infotainment   251
Peering through Hollywood's lenses   251
Secrecy and intelligence: the smile on the face of
the Cheshire cat   253
The lure of covert action   254
Putting secret intelligence into the public domain   256

10. Ethical Issues: The Good of the City and the City
of the Good   261
The justification for secret means   261
The Theseus syndrome   262
Oversight   264
The level of public understanding of what collecting
secret intelligence involves   265
Just intelligence   268
Distinguishing good from bad government   270
Intelligence and security as a regrettable necessity   277
The absence of an international legal framework   279
A distinctive British experience: the importance of ethos   281
Underlying dilemmas of counter-terrorism   285

11. Intelligence Design: Building Intelligence Communities   289
The need for change   289
The requirements of national security strategy   290
The requirements of being a modern 'knowledge industry'   291
Openings and barriers to change   294
The state of development of national intelligence
communities   296
The issue of trust: circles of cooperation   300
The case for stronger leadership, not just coordination
of the community   302
Further pressures for fundamental intelligence reform   304

12. A Fresco for the Future   309
Assembling the picture   309
Harnessing all the talent   310
Learning from history   312

CONTENTS

National security and intelligence models	315
At the strategic level	316
At the operational level	318
At the tactical level	319
The 'big picture' implications	320
Towards a grand understanding	323
Envoi	325
Notes	327
Index	339

ABBREVATIONS

ABMT	Anti–Ballistic Missile Treaty
ACCINT	Accoustic Intelligence
ACPO	Association of Chief Police Officers (UK)
ALARP	As low as reasonably practicable risk management
ANPR	Automatic [automobile] number plate reader
AQ	Al-Qa'ida
BSS	British Security Service (MI5)
CBRN	Chemical, Biological, Radiological and Nuclear
C	Initial by which the Chief of SIS is traditionally known (UK)
CCA	Civil Contingencies Act 2004 (UK)
CCC	Civil Contingencies Committee of UK Cabinet
CCS	Civil Contingencies Secretariat, UK Cabinet Office
CCTV	Closed circuit television
CHIS	Covert human intelligence sources
CIA	Central Intelligence Agency (US)
CIG	Current Intelligence Group (UK)
CNI	Critical National Infrastructure
COBR	Cabinet Office Briefing Rooms (UK)
COMINT	Communications Intelligence
CONTEST	Counter-terrorism strategy (UK)
COS	Chiefs of Staff (UK)
CPNI	Centre for the Protection of National Infrastructure (UK)
CREVICE	Codeword for investigation of UK terrorist network
CSIS	Canadian Security Intelligence Service
CSOC	Cyber Security Operations Centre (CSOC) (UK)
CX	Digraph denoting SIS intelligence report (UK)

DCI	Director of Central Intelligence (US)
DCRI	*Direction Centrale du Renseignement Intérieur* (France)
DDOS	Distributed Denial of Service cyber-attack
DEFCON	Defense Readiness Condition (US)
DF or D/F	Direction finding
DG	Director-General
DGSE	*Direction Générale de la Sécurité Extérieure* (France)
DIA	Defense Intelligence Agency (US)
DIS	Defence Intelligence Staff (UK)
DNI	Director of National Intelligence (US)
DoD	Department of Defense (US)
DST	*Direction de la surveillance du territoire* (France)
ELINT	Electronic Intelligence
FBI	Federal Bureau of Investigation (US)
FISA	Foreign Intelligence Surveillance Act (US)
GC&CS	Government Code and Cypher School
GCHQ	Government Communications Headquarters
GEOINT	Geographical and mapping intelligence
GRU	Military intelligence directorate of the Soviet General Staff
HUMINT	Human Intelligence Sources
IC	Intelligence Community
IED	Improvised Explosive Device
IISS	International Institute for Strategic Studies (London)
IRPTA	Intelligence Reform and Prevention of Terrorism Act of 2004 (US)
JCS	Joint Chiefs of Staff (US)
JIC	Joint Intelligence Committee (UK Cabinet Office)
JTAC	Joint Terrorism Analysis Centre (UK)
J-2	Military staff intelligence function
KGB	Soviet state security and external intelligence service
MACV	Military Assistance Command (US, Vietnam)
LOCINT	Target location intelligence
MASINT	Measurement and Signature Intelligence
MI	Military Intelligence
MOD	Ministry of Defence (UK)
NATO	North Atlantic Treaty Organization
NCTC	National Counterterrorism Center (US)
NIE	National Intelligence Estimate (US)

ABBREVATIONS

NIWS	NATO Intelligence Warning System
NPG	Nuclear Planning Group of NATO
NSA	National Security Agency (US)
NSS	National Security Strategy (UK)
OCS	Office of Cyber Security (UK)
ORCON	Originator controlled intelligence
OSINT	Open source intelligence
OSS	Office of Strategic Services (US)
OVERT	Codeword for investigation of UK terrorist network
PDA	Personal Digital Assistant
PDB	Presidential Daily Briefing (US)
PFIAB	President's Foreign Intelligence Advisory Board (US)
PIRA	Provisional Irish Republican Army
PJHQ	Permanent Joint Headquarters (UK)
PLA	People's Liberation Army (China)
Pol-mil	Politico-military affairs
PROTINT	Data-protected personal information
RCMP	Royal Canadian Mounted Police (Canada)
RHYME	Codeword for investigation of UK terrorist network
SAS/SBS	Special Air Service/Special Boat Service (UK)
SIA	Single Intelligence Account (UK)
SIGINT	Signals Intelligence
SIS or MI6	Secret Intelligence Service (UK)
SOCA	Serious Organized Crime Agency (UK)
TTW	Transition to War
UKUSA	UK–US Security Agreement
UN/ISDR	United Nations/International Strategy for Disaster Reduction
WMD	Weapons of mass destruction

PREFACE

Why did I set out to write this book?

My first job in the public service was in the Government Communications Headquarters (GCHQ), the UK agency responsible for signals intelligence (an activity that the organization sought to conceal until the very last stage in the process of my recruitment). That was in 1969, at a time when the very purpose of that organization was unacknowledged and its activities were a state secret. My last tour of duty in 2002–5 was in the Cabinet Office coordinating the UK intelligence and security community, working with intelligence agencies that were avowed, subject to parliamentary statute and oversight, and increasingly in the public eye as a result of the controversy over the Iraq war and the measures taken to counter Al-Qa'ida. My experience over the intervening years, in the Ministry of Defence as a policy-maker and regular user of foreign intelligence, and then in the Home Office as Permanent Secretary with strong links to the Security Service, left me with a conviction that there is a pressing need for a better public understanding of what modern national security involves and the modern role of secret intelligence in supporting it.

We now rely upon the intelligence community to help with very hard decisions on national security, the first responsibility of government. We know that the absence of reliable intelligence and understanding at times of security threats will limit the options open to government in trying to protect the public. Intelligence does also have inherent limitations that need to be understood, as well as bringing in its wake moral hazards and dilemmas over the methods used to produce it and their potential impact on our personal privacy. These are not new issues, but they are ones that have added point due to our increased consciousness of the threats we face.

If security and intelligence work is to be accepted as a legitimate function of government, then we have to change the way we look upon it; and those who inhabit the secret world have to recognize that times have changed and some of the old habits have to give way in the interests of securing public support for their work. These are also issues that are often confused in the public mind, since it is hard to shake off the way that the fictional representations of the secret world in cinema and print unconsciously shape our interpretation of events. The reality of the world of security policy and intelligence is that it is inhabited by people very far removed from either the guilt-ridden characters of Greene or Le Carré or the muscular ex–special forces operatives of 24 or Mission Impossible. So I wrote this book to encourage thinking sensibly about national security and its essential support, secret intelligence, as acknowledged but unique functions of government—and necessary ones.

This book has been written for those, like myself, who are grappling with the paradoxes of national security and intelligence. How can security, the first duty of good government, be maintained at a bearable and sustainable cost? How do we avoid becoming obsessed with security risks, and how do we avoid the benefits of security turning to the taste of ashes in our mouth if the methods used to deliver security, and the essential intelligence that underpins it, were to turn out to have undermined and even violated the very values we seek to defend? These are questions that will in the future increasingly separate what we will recognize as the signs of good government from those of bad government. The analysis in this book is offered in the hope that it will help academics and practitioners alike, politicians and journalists, believers and sceptics, think more clearly about where the balance of interests is best struck in matters of security and help signal where the shoals and reefs of bad government are likely to lie and how to navigate between them.

Security strategy is no different from any other form of strategy; it consists of linking ends, ways and means. Security is thus an 'end' that public policy has to secure, for which both resilience and intelligence are 'means'. In the last couple of centuries, national security would have been seen primarily in terms of protection of the state from invasion, or from foreign ideas (including from religion) inspiring subversive threats to the constitution and parliamentary democracy. We might label that view of 'national security', as it was seen during the Cold War and before, as the freedom from armed conflict, in the same way as the post-war generation welcomed Beveridge's call for freedom from want, ignorance, disease, squalor and idleness. On the other hand, personal security at an individual and family level, in the sense of absence of fear as we walk out in the street at night or travel to work, would have been seen as largely a matter for action at a community level, for which we would expect operationally independent police services to be locally accountable for results. That remains the case with the renewed emphasis now seen on neighbourhood policing but with the added complication, however, that in a society with the motor-car and now the internet much local trouble—and news of it—travels to and from the area. The need for national policies is inescapable. The same is true for other forms of threat and for the major hazards that can seriously disrupt the life of the citizen. Increasingly today troubles have their roots overseas, such as in the narcotics trade, terrorism, proliferation or pandemics, which means that even purely national solutions are unlikely to be sufficient.

The core of this book is based on articles published and lectures given at King's College London after my retirement from public service and appointment as a visiting professor in the Department of War Studies. I am very grateful to Professor Sir Lawrence Freedman and Professor Mervyn Frost and his colleagues in the department for their welcome and support for my introduction to academe. I have benefited greatly from the stimulus of a series of seminars for government intelligence analysts that I have run with Dr Michael Goodman of King's College on behalf of the Professional Head of Intelligence Analysis in the UK Cabinet Office. We examined together how we could understand intelligence better through looking at it from four different perspectives: from the functional view of the intelligence cycle showing how intelligence is now accessed and its meaning elucidated; from the organizational view of the position of intelligence agencies within government; through looking at the historical view of their past activities; and finally by asking what public value is added by secret intelligence and what difference secret intelligence has actually made to events. Each of these different viewpoints opens up insights into a subject that is subject to rapid change under the pressure of events, not least combating international terrorism and understanding the present flux of international events.

I am grateful to Demos, for their support in making these ideas more widely known through their security programme and for inviting me to deliver the 2006 Demos annual security lecture, 'In the National Interest: Organizing Government for National Security'. The Institute of Public Policy Research invited me to be a member of their 2008/09 National Security Commission and I have gained much from the debate on these issues with fellow-commissioners and in preparing for them the material on the modern intelligence cycle that forms chapter 5 of this book. In writing this book I have been conscious of the example of Michael Herman, one of my first bosses when I started work at GCHQ so many years ago, as a practitioner turned academic at Nuffield College, Oxford, and of the value an insider can bring when writing for a wide audience about these subjects. Finally, I should like to acknowledge the contribution to my own thinking made by so many colleagues recently retired or still serving and therefore for now nameless. The opinions expressed in this book are however my own, and should not be read as expressions of government policy or as implying any endorsement by Her Majesty's Government.

It has come as something of a surprise to me since retirement to discover how much material bearing on intelligence and security has been released by governments into their national archives on both sides of the Atlantic to be disinterred and analyzed by academics in the literature of intelligence studies, much more than is generally recognized by those with heads down hard at work within the intelligence community. My own journey in writing this book parallels that the intelligence community itself is undertaking as it recognizes that the public interest will benefit from practitioners debating matters of key public interest and using to the full the open sources that are now available. At the same time there needs to be greater recognition on the outside that the effectiveness of security and intelligence work fades if its sources and methods are exposed to the light. I have been able to present the arguments in this book drawing on open sources, tempered of course by my own experiences of what it is really like to work on the inside, but without being tempted to fresh indiscretions about matters that genuinely deserve protection. As far as I can judge there are no new secrets revealed in these pages, and those seeking revelations should look elsewhere.

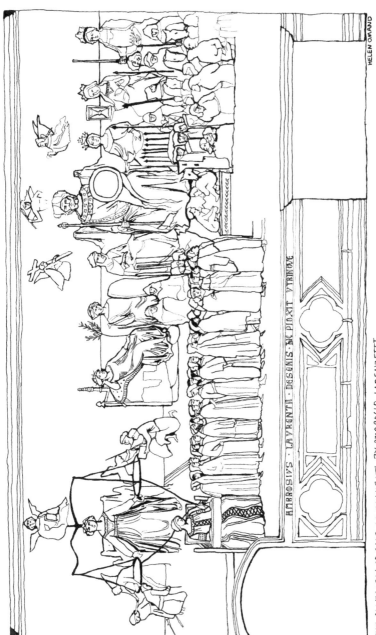

THE ALLEGORY OF GOOD GOVERNMENT BY AMBROGIO LORENZETTI

HELEN OMAND

INTRODUCTION

A LESSON FROM THE FOURTEENTH CENTURY

The importance of security

What makes the difference between good and bad government? The ruling council of the prosperous city-state of Siena in the late fourteenth century would have had a daily reminder as they glanced up proudly at the frescoes on the walls of their town hall, the Palazzo Pubblico. In what became known as the Hall of Peace is Ambrogio Lorenzetti's great three-part fresco cycle: on the facing wall as they entered the room they would have seen an awful warning, a huge representation of all the Effects of Bad Government; and opposite, on the wall behind them, they would have contemplated the beneficial Effects of Good Government on the life of the City and the surrounding countryside. On the best-lit wall opposite the large windows, and situated between these two depictions of good and bad government, is the fresco that was intended as a very public reminder to the ruling council of the city of what makes the difference. This Allegory of Good Government is what I can best describe for a modern readership as the fourteenth century equivalent of a PowerPoint slide. The rulers of Siena were being given a constant visual reminder of the ideal relationship they should aspire to create between the necessary components of Good Government so that inhabitants of city and countryside can live together in harmony, security and prosperity.

Let us start as we enter the room with that vivid reminder of the terrifying conditions—as relevant today as in 1353—that bad government can create. The prevalent emotion is insecurity and fear. Bands of hungry and diseased citizens roam the clearly violent city. Not only the city

1

walls are crumbling, leaving the city vulnerable to its enemies, but the very internal fabric of the town is decaying. The message directed at Siena's rising merchant class (and now to our own) is that insecurity makes investment hazardous. The representation of good government on the opposite wall shows, on the other hand, that under the stability brought by good government new buildings are under construction and corn is being delivered to be ground in well-kept mills, key components of the critical infrastructure of the Middle Ages that could only be justified by conditions of stability in both town and country.

In his fresco Lorenzetti provides a dramatic warning that bad government flows principally from the fear that comes from exercise of arbitrary power. The figure of Tyranny, shown as a dark, horned, sabre-toothed figure, lords it over the city. As his inspiration, winged figures float above him representing pride, avarice and vainglory, and seated beside him are representations of the vices that accompany bad government: cruelty, betrayal, fraud, terror, internal discord and conflict. The fresco illustrates how insecurity is borne of inability to maintain borders, failure to deal effectively with internal discord and unwillingness to administer impartial justice (represented as a bound and tethered figure captive at the bottom of the painting). The citizens themselves are shown subject to poverty, disease, arbitrary arrest and torture.

We can also readily recognize, in our world as in the fourteenth century, the depiction on the opposite wall of the desired Effects of Good Government: peace, stability and security, prosperity, and culture. Cheerful townspeople and country folk are shown in the spring and summer, working in harmony and going freely about their affairs transporting their goods on well-kept roads or sowing in the weed-free fields. Builders are hard at work developing the city. The watchtowers are well kept and manned. Maidens dance in the street and the aristocracy, it may be seen, is shown blamelessly employed in the countryside in hunting and falconry, whilst the business of city government is left to the hard-working merchants. The fresco of good government shows this blessed state of affairs as flowing from the hovering presence of Securitas, or Security. Shown as a winged figure, Security holds an emblem of justice administered. Watching over town and country, Security also holds up a scroll on which is written the promise that all can live in safety, and without fear: the words eerily presage the aim of CONTEST, the UK government's twenty-first century counter-terrorist strategy, 'so that people can go about their normal business, freely and with confidence'. In her other hand, however, Security holds a model of a gibbet, a stern warning to those who might seek to undermine the peace of the city or the countryside.

How did the fourteenth century Sienese imagine that this utopian ideal of Security could be maintained and the evils of Tyranny be avoided? The answer is provided in the central fresco of the cycle, on the best-lit wall opposite the window, depicting the Allegory of Good Government. Lorenzetti explains in graphic images what the art of good government consists of and what the governing council of Siena needed to understand and to act upon to bring about this utopian state of Good Government. The leading citizens would thus be reminded of their duty in running the City every time they entered the town hall.

At the centre of the fresco, inspired by the winged figures of the theological virtues of faith, hope and charity hovering above him, is a dominant figure. It is a calm, bearded, mature man (this is the fourteenth century), representing wise government. He is the representation of Common Good: the Good of the City and the City of the Good, to which private interest is subordinate. Figures representing the cardinal virtues sit alongside the Common Good in support. The eye is artfully drawn to the first of these figures, the desirable Peace, depicted as a reclining, relaxed, shapely woman in a light dress holding an olive branch and with a garland of olive leaves. A closer examination shows that Peace sits on the arms and armour of the vanquished as a reminder to the rulers of the city that peace rests on strong defences and must be continually fought for. Peace, like the figure of Security in the depiction of good government, is dressed in white and centrally placed, emphasizing the link between them. By the side of Peace sits the stern figure of Fortitude, with shield and baton and armed mounted escort at the ready, as well as a thoughtful Prudence no doubt ready to provide strategic notice of dangers to come. On the other side of the central figure of the Common Good are representations of the virtues to be encouraged in the City (ours as well as theirs) of temperance, magnanimity and justice upheld.

All that symbolism in itself would be a remarkable iconographic drawing together of advice to government. There is however a much larger and more fundamental message than that, a message that is also as relevant to us as it was to the council of fourteenth century Siena. On the left, and placed symbolically apart from the representation of the Common Good, is a connected group of large figures. The striking figure of Justicia, depicted with her scales of justice, is administering the law to the citizens kneeling before her. By being set apart from the group of figures representing the government of the city, Lorenzetti thus symbolizes the ability of justice to act impartially and independently from the executive. Below Justice is another large (and therefore considered to be important) attractive female figure: Concordia, whom we might interpret loosely as civil harmony and a sense of civic responsibility. She is looking upwards towards Justice, and is connected directly to her by cords attached to the pans of the scales of justice. The message is an important one, for communities in Britain today as much as the citizens of the rivalrous *contrada* or districts of fourteenth century Siena, that civil harmony is dependent on confidence in the proper administration of impartial justice.

As if that message were not enough, at the foot of the fresco the twenty-four members of the ruling council process towards the feet of the figure of the Common Good each holding on to a single rope that connects them back to the female figure of Concordia, or civil harmony. So the full message to be derived from this part of the fresco is clear. From the protection offered by exercise of independent justice we can have civil harmony and civic responsibility which, mediated through the representatives of the citizens, leads to wise government that can deliver the common good through peace and security. This lesson for the governing body of fourteenth century Siena is equally valid as a message to ourselves today.

In the Allegory of Good Government, Peace and Security are twin concepts. Peace herself rests on strong defences and Security on justice firmly exercised. In the next chapter we examine what 'Security' should mean for us today in describing a state of public confidence in the management of threats such as terrorism and natural hazards such as flooding or pandemic disease that threaten to generate insecurity and to disrupt normal life.

To animate these relationships, there is a winged figure at the very top of the fresco above Justice and above civil administration and the common good. The figure represents Sapientia, intelligence and understanding, illuminating and guiding those below. To reinforce this message (although now hidden by the effects of later restorations), at the same level as Sapientia, the original fresco also had a symbol of the Sun. As a neo-Platonist symbol the meaning would have been clear to the ruling council of Siena. The sun represents intellectual illumination.

Intelligence and understanding is in this view the starting point (although of course very far from sufficient) to make good government possible, through both justice and security. But the misuse of knowledge, or its use without respect for the balancing interests of Justice and Civil Harmony, is a road that leads eventually to Tyranny, as illustrated by the figures on the opposite wall. The dilemmas involved in maintaining balance between these extremes are eternal challenges to our earthly attempts to generate security for ourselves in an inherently unpredictable world.

Sapientia herself, with Prudentia in chorus of support, would at this point insist on some words of caution about the risks of exaggerating to the public what government can deliver by way of security. Life is uncertain, that is what distinguishes it from death. That would have been all too obvious a point in the fourteenth century. Today we dignify it by saying that delivery of security is an exercise in risk management. Secret intelligence can deliver only an improved probability of forestalling threats to security, not certainties. Lorenzetti as a neo-Platonist would also have understood that intelligence of this world must be seen as a product of human reason and therefore fallible and incomplete, shadows on the wall of the room.

Secret intelligence would have been very familiar to the rulers of Siena as they struggled to predict the moves of their neighbouring city-states. Ultimately they failed, and the power of Siena waned in relation to that of Florence. Of course, not only is it necessary to have the intelligence but also the willingness and ability of policymakers to make good use of it. If, as a result of resistance on the part of government to pay heed to bad news or unwelcome advice, Prudence is blinded at times of national danger, then we must expect trouble to follow.

In Lorenzetti's central fresco, the figure of Fortitude, representing the public's willingness to accept hardship and soldier on, sits alongside Peace and supports Civil Good. Today we have a modern interpretation of public fortitude based on 'resilience', the ability of the nation to absorb a shock and bounce back quickly into shape. The fourteenth century certainly suffered all the consequences of having national infrastructure liable to disruption: inability to sow seed in the spring due to war or pestilence would mean famine the following winter. Life today, especially in large cities, is however in so many ways much more complicated than in the Middle Ages, and with complexity comes an increased likelihood of breakdown under stress.

...And a warning from the fifteenth century

The Sienese Allegory of Good Government is a collection of ideals. Not far away, in the rival city-state of Florence, a more realistic not to say cynical view was to develop in the following century through the advice that Niccolo Machiavelli was giving to a new Medici administration, that in aspiring to deliver good government the ruler should exhibit publicly all the virtues and relationships so valued by Lorenzetti, whilst behind the scenes being prepared to authorize activities in the dark that he would not be prepared to admit to in the light. The ruler who aspires to provide public security and good government must be prepared to compromise on his own values so that...

'...taking everything into account, he will find that some of the things that appear to be virtues will, if he practices them, ruin him, and some of the things that appear to be wicked will bring him security and prosperity.'[1]

(Machiavelli, The Prince)

But if the ruler pursues Machiavelli's advice too far, then at some point he risks tipping over into the tyranny that was for the Sienese the hallmark of bad government. Niccolo Machiavelli's advice was the *realpolitik* of a senior civil servant in the Florentine Chancery trying to help guide his state through unstable years borne of a combination of external threats and internal unrest. Powerful government based on internal unity was his remedy for revived fortunes. His ideal ruler would have a carefully cultivated public reputation for compassion rather than cruelty, but above all, however, the wise ruler would recognize that his behaviours, whether liable to earn praise or condemnation, must above all be calculated. Machiavelli too did not, however, have to contend with 24/7 news media and demands through freedom of information that his private advice to the ruler (and the ruler's response) be published.

Machiavelli justifies his hard-headed advice: 'Many have dreamed up republics and principalities which have never in truth been known to exist; the gulf between how one should live and how one does live is so wide that a man who neglects what is actually done for what should be done learns the way to self-destruction rather than self-preservation.' And that dynamic explains the perennial attraction of secret agency for rulers down the ages: the secret world provides the means to do in hidden ways what is judged necessary for the interests of the state but which cannot be admitted to. Machiavelli must have seen himself as the wise counsellor of Princes, capable of speaking truth about power unto power. That capacity to penetrate the fond conceits and policy illusions of the decision-maker is of course part of the ideal equipment of the senior intelligence analyst, but not easy to sustain without in turn entering into a collusive relationship with the ruler, a danger that we explore in chapter 9.

The British also learnt generations ago that obtaining pre-emptive information does matter when it comes to national survival, as they tried to navigate amidst the shifting alliances of European nations and their imperial ambitions. From time to time obtaining that advantage involved a degree of Machiavellian deception as well as skill and art, and even of cheating by way of seeing through the backs of the opponents' cards. The justification for secret intelligence is in the end an empirical one: it reduces the risks from decisions that governments decide have to be taken in the national interest. What has changed in the last decades is the growing perception amongst most nations that they can no longer protect their publics by national efforts alone, whether from the consequences of instability, violence and extremism or the activities of international terrorist and criminal gangs. The realization has grown that sharing intelligence on these threats is in their mutual interest. The world of secret intelligence amongst nations is no longer a zero-sum game.

It may seem quixotic to pick as my starting point the view of security taken in Siena in the early fourteenth century. But we see there the intimate relationship between internal and external security, between collective and personal security, between security and privacy, and the impact of hazards such as weather and disease as well as the threats of internal disorder or external aggression. In that world, as in ours, the welfare of the citizen still depends upon the presence of wise government, impartial justice and civil harmony within society. Security, as a sense of public confidence that it is safe to go outside, work and play and get on with one's life, is at the heart of good government. Government will be judged in that respect largely on its ability through sensible use of pre-emptive intelligence to anticipate trouble, heading it off or mitigating its impact, whilst maintaining public support. This book explores these issues and in the final chapter concludes that we would do well to encourage the creation of a new 'grand understanding' between governed and governors, setting out the relationships being sought between the eternal virtues of understanding and intelligence, justice, civil harmony and the actions of good government.

1

SECURITAS

THE PUBLIC VALUE OF SECURITY

The meaning of security today

'Security' and 'Intelligence' are two words that have tended, sometimes misleadingly, to be chained together. To an earlier generation, 'security' would have been regarded as an important part of intelligence work, keeping the adversary from knowing your plans and encouraging him in false beliefs about your intentions. Today it is the other way round. Security has become itself a key objective of public policy: *national security today should be defined as a state of trust on the part of the citizen that the risks to everyday life, whether from man-made threats or impersonal hazards, are being adequately managed to the extent that there is confidence that normal life can continue.* A state of public insecurity on the other hand is not hard to detect, whether caused by fear of attack by terrorists or criminals, fear of pandemic disease or by fear of unemployment.

From Secret State to Protecting State

A very different approach to national security was taken during the Cold War, an approach that has been labelled 'the Secret State'.[1] During the early days of the Cold War, national security for the UK had a relatively narrow compass. Maintaining the territorial integrity of the nation through membership of the collective North Atlantic Alliance (an attack on one is an attack on all) and countering communist subversion at home and in territories overseas were the principal preoccupations. There were threats that could not be defended against (such as the classic case considered in 1954 by the Chiefs of Staff[2] of a Soviet merchant vessel entering the Thames with a hidden nuclear weapon on board) and that could only be deterred by NATO's nuclear posture. The credibility in the eyes of the potential adversary of such a deterrent posture depended in turn on a belief in the ability of the NATO nuclear powers (and on their practical readiness) to be able to select an appropriate response option in every circumstance of aggression. The essential paradox of nuclear deterrence lay in the way in which certainty of response had to be surrounded by a protecting screen of uncertainty in the mind of the adversary. A consequence of the logic of deterrence was that the British public would have to be kept in the dark about the full extent of what was being done in their name, literally as well as figuratively under the surface. Of course, the UK had many other post-colonial preoccupations, and a serious terrorist campaign to counter in Northern Ireland, but the paradigm that guided the world of security and intelligence was that of the Cold War, being conducted through the hidden wiring of 'the Secret State', and most hidden was its intelligence component.

A major transformation started to take place, coincident with the end of the Cold War, in the amount that the public got to know about what government was doing in its name. Intelligence and security agencies were avowed and the results of their work seen in the arrests and trial of terrorists. Activities of the armed forces on operations overseas were broadcast by embedded journalists living with front-line units. Defence policy was recast. By the time of the shock of the Al-Qa'ida (AQ) attacks on 9/11, a distinctively British approach to modern national security strategy was beginning to crystalize, blurring the previous boundaries between the overseas and domestic theatres and broadening thinking about risks to include hazards as well as threats. Civil protection arrangements (whether against AQ terrorism, pandemics or floods) had to be explained to the public since individual, community and business participation and engagement became essential for their effectiveness. The paradigm was that of 'the Protecting State' not 'the Secret State'. Lorenzetti would have understood.

We can see three powerful shifts in thinking in the development of this modern approach to national security.

The first shift: protection from major disruptive events

The first shift is the reorientation and broadening of government's primary duty in respect of national security towards the protection of the individual and the daily life of the community. This focus on the security of the citizen leads naturally to thinking about protection from the full range of major disruptive events, not just from malicious threats such as from terrorism, proliferation and international crime, but civil protection from the impact of natural hazards such as pandemics. It is thus an all-risks approach, based on the principles of good risk management where risks have to be individually assessed in terms of the likelihood they will arise, the vulnerability of society to them, and the impact they will have if they do occur. It includes, but goes well beyond, the defence of territorial integrity or countering subversion aimed at overthrow of parliamentary democracy that were the preoccupations of the Cold War. The duty is to contribute to public security, defined as a state of mind that gives confidence that the risks ahead are being managed to a point where everyday life—and investment in the future—can continue. We should not underestimate the significance of this shift to an inclusive approach to national security where the aim is to manage the risks of natural hazards as well as man-made threats.[3]

The second shift: an emphasis on the value of anticipation

The second shift in security thinking has been an increased emphasis on the value of anticipation, in the proper sense of that word. Not just to be able to make predictive judgments about the future course of events, but to realize what the world would then look like so as to be able to identify and start to implement policies and partnerships now that would mitigate the risks to society of such trends. We should see the armed services, appropriately organized, trained and equipped for counter-insurgency warfare, as an essential component of the capability for anticipatory action when need arises. But to improve the capacity of troubled states to deliver sufficient security to enable economic development, and sufficient good governance to entrench that progress—no mean task in most circumstances—requires more than military intervention. Not only will armed forces need to be more capable of operations to counter insurgency and disorder, but a comprehensive approach will need contributions from most of the capabilities of civil government. That requires organization and strategic direction for which peacetime British government is so far not fully equipped.

'Clear and present dangers' will of course arise unexpectedly. Such dangers have to be faced nationally with whatever weapons, defences and allies are at hand at the time. That will always be the case, but it is more important now than for some time past that we look ahead and recognize what may lie ahead; preferably, when the prospect of danger is sufficiently clear to justify attention but before the danger becomes present; ideally, acting in advance so as to avert the problem altogether, but if not then reducing its likely impact on our lives; and certainly, preventing the needs of the moment crowding out the necessary preparations to face the future with confidence. And a similar statement can and should be made in respect of spotting opportunities when they are real enough prospects, and early enough to allow the necessary investment to capitalize on them. An anticipatory approach thus increases the importance of having the capability to produce pre-emptive operational intelligence as threats develop and materialize, a subject tackled in chapter 2. Maintaining community confidence in the actions of the state in that regard will become more important than ever in the years ahead. Good pre-emptive intelligence can reassure the community by removing the extremists and by disrupting potential attacks without having to fall back on the sort of blunt discriminatory measures that alienate moderate support within the community on which effective policing and counter-terrorism depends. The anticipatory approach also requires strategic notice of emerging trends relating to threat actors and threat domains. The nature of warfare for example has already changed significantly in the last twenty years, and further changes are only to be expected as new technology is applied and as potential adversaries alter their own tactics in response. The problems are acute for defence planners, and careful hedging strategies are needed that reduce the risk of irreversible decisions being taken on the basis of attempts to forecast future developments over a very long timescale, a problem described in chapter 7.

The third shift: towards building national resilience

Even given strategic notice and good intelligence, there will be some threats and hazards that cannot be headed off. The third shift in national security thinking has therefore been to see the value in investing in national resilience, so that the impact of disruptive events on the public can as far as possible be minimized, for example through better equipping and training of the emergency services. Resilience is an increasingly important element of any sound security strategy, since advanced societies are more vulnerable to disruption, especially as they become more networked and IT dependent. Even relatively modest means of attack can lead to significant cascading failures in interconnected networked systems, and in the future such attacks may well be delivered through cyberspace. Governments, in these conditions, must be urged not to continue with business as usual. We must work smarter: think strategically, prepare for the worst, ruthlessly target resources at risks and work with allies and partners to anticipate and prevent threats before they become real. This preparation is in itself a form of dissuasion as well as of defence. The shift towards thinking about the benefits of a more resilient society in turn has directed attention to the value of educating and increasing the self-reliance of communities and the value of extensive partnership working at home, with the private sector, with community groups and with citizens as individuals, issues addressed in chapter 3.

These shifts in thinking about domestic and external security and in resilience increase the importance of coordination of government effort that has to span many departments and institutions and integrate a wide range of policy instruments. This means adapting government structures; the strengthening of the ability to provide strategic direction at the centre of government and breaking down departmental stovepipes, coupled with the decentralization of the detailed formulation of the policies and tactics to deliver the strategy based on the evidence and experience of those closest to the front-line.

Future security challenges

Developments in the security environment that can be forseen appear to be reinforcing the need for these shifts in thinking about security strategy. We can all see the way that strong forces are changing the nature of power relationships, diluting the control of individual governments, deepening interdependence across borders and empowering a far wider range of actors emerging on to the world stage, not just states but also private companies, NGOs, terrorist organizations, and transnational criminal networks that corrupt state governance and facilitate and profit from violent conflict. The overall result is increased freedom for some to disrupt or destroy, together with reduced state dominance of the security environment. Disorderly, fragile and unstable states today outnumber strong, accountable and stable ones in the international system by more than two to one, and we are already seeing the effect of instability and conflict, including a resurgence of piracy. Human rights abuses from the effects of climate change, global poverty and inequality must be expected. In addition we have yet to see the working out of the gradual diffusion of economic power eastward towards the Asia Pacific region, and the emerging concerns over future access to energy and raw materials.

These powerful forces are reshaping the international security environment.[4] Global communications will amplify their effect, and lead to unexpected correlations between them. It is clear that no modern state today can isolate itself or provide for its security needs by acting alone, a central conclusion for any national security strategy. Modern societies are also inherently more vulnerable to shocks and disruptions as technology becomes more complex and dependent on global interconnections. It is also evident that the aftershocks from the 2008 financial confidence and liquidity crisis have narrowed, at least for some years to come, the options open to address these needs.

How are such general observations to be operationized and priorities for action selected? One approach emerging from the UK Cabinet Office in the 2009 National Security Strategy[5] is to see these major forces of change as 'drivers' of future threat. One such driver, for example, is the risk that new hostile ideologies will emerge. Other drivers include the way that non-state actors will further threaten our interests, that developments in science and technology (including in cyberspace) will be misused and that global issues such as demography, poverty and climate change will create fresh insecurities to which modern societies will be, unless action is taken, increasingly vulnerable. These drivers then animate 'threat actors' be they traditional states (where the judgment is that although 'no state directly threatens the UK at present' there is the 'realistic possibility' of malign influence, through disrupting trade, energy, cyber or other attack on critical infrastructure or subversive influence), failing states or non-state actors such as terrorist or criminal groupings. Security policy is complicated by the evident recognition that these actors can operate in very different 'threat domains', from nuclear technology to cyberspace, and from maritime piracy to public information. Running through such analysis is the common thread that effective security action is going to require greater emphasis on building stronger multilateral financial and diplomatic arrangements.

It is a truism that no modern state today can provide for its security needs by acting alone. The UK has benefited over many years from being part of a collective defence alliance, NATO, based on shared democratic values embodied in the principle that an attack on one is an attack on all. At a time of global shifts in power the case for retaining the North Atlantic Alliance at the heart of UK security strategy—thus linking the security of Europe to that of North America—should hardly need arguing. But there are wider preoccupations and dangers to security to be faced for both North America and Europe. The best strategy to maintain a strong and relevant Alliance would in my view be to pursue a major strengthening of European defence and security cooperation, not as an alternative to NATO but to produce a re-invigorated transatlantic alliance based on deeper and more effective European cooperation and a more equal relationship between Europe and the United States. A major increase is needed in levels of multilateral cooperation to achieve a partnership approach in relation to the full range of risks arising overseas. Such wider cooperation must be a strategic priority for the UK and its allies, even when this sometimes means compromising on short-term national preferences. In a world where problems and destinies are shared, measures to promote international peace and stability and address fragile political climates will often be the best course of action in our own defence. Well targeted conflict prevention policy, based on a good understanding of the dynamics of emerging problems, saves money, lives and political relationships. In so doing, demonstrating and establishing legitimacy of state action is a strategic imperative in current conditions, since in a world where the partnership and cooperation of others will be required, legitimacy will be central to securing it. Sharing risks with others introduces reciprocal obligations that inevitably will constrain national freedom of action to use resources for purely national purposes. The benefits of alliances have to be paid for.

The current takfiri jihadist terrorist threat

One major source of insecurity today on which such analysis can be tested is the globalized takfiri ideology that spread as a result of the formation of Al-Qa'ida and that has become a significant driver of international terrorism. It is no coincidence that 'national security strategies' were published in the years after 9/11 in Washington, Paris, Berlin, London, The Hague, Canberra, Singapore and elsewhere. On the one hand, governments have recognized their responsibility for providing a sense of security to their publics in the face of such dangers as terrorism and proliferation. On the other hand, the same governments are grasping for what it means to be secure in an interdependent world without a single dominant state adversary but with global interdependency and facing the serious threat of mass casualty terrorism. The issues this raises for domestic harmony are considered in chapter 4.

Counteraction over several years by the US and its partners, notably the UK, has gradually constrained the freedom of movement and operations of the AQ leadership and led to the death or capture of a significant number of experienced terrorists. It is possible that the global high water mark of the rising tide of AQ-related terrorism has been reached. On present showing they face strategic failure and gradual decline in influence. AQ ideology remains however an internal threat to security in many European countries, especially the UK. Individual networks of extremists will for some time to come be able to carry out terrorist attacks. The murky waters in which these extremists swim remain deep. The terrorists have shown a capacity to innovate and to adopt effective counter-security precautions. So far they appear to have placed more emphasis on certainty of effect by choosing well tried methods of attack such as bombings, shootings and hijacking rather than the much more uncertain worlds of chemical, biological or radiological attack. Under-appreciated perhaps are the vulnerabilities generated by rapid advances in information- and bio-technologies, making more likely cyber-crime, cyber-terrorism and new forms of chemical and biological attack, all threat domains that would be a more dangerous possibility given global urbanization. The overall risks from terrorist attack would worsen greatly if terrorists or other non-state criminal groups were to obtain a new safe haven, or succeed in acquiring significant means of mass disruption, as they might if international action is not mobilized to stop further proliferation. So tackling this threat in future is going to have to be guided by a security strategy that embodies these post-Cold War shifts in national security thinking towards focusing on the protection of the citizen, anticipation of risks and building enhanced societal resilience.

Developing the risk management approach

I have argued that national security should now be seen in terms of a state of confidence on the part of the citizen that normal life can continue, despite the dangers to individuals, families and businesses from man-made threats or impersonal hazards. Applying the principles of risk management to security therefore seems eminently sensible. There can be no absolute security, but fatalism or trusting to chance will expose the public to avoidable danger. As Juvenal[6] put it, *Nullum numen habes, si sit prudentia*. If men would act prudently and wisely, we would hear no more of good or ill luck—the goddess Fortune would no longer be a divinity in the eyes of mortals if they were themselves prudent and careful in the management of themselves and their affairs.

There is also a heavy responsibility on government in pursuing security not to deceive itself or the public about what is feasible, affordable and sustainable in a free society. It makes sense given the inherent complexity of this security environment for government to level with the public about the limitations of its security measures and about the residual risks that will have to be accepted. The political implications need however to be understood. Risk management is about taking managed risks to achieve desired objectives. In chapter 7, the risk paradox is explored that in many circumstances a bold rather than a hesitant move often reduces not increases the risk. Business recognizes the truth of the old saying, without risk there is no profit. When things do not work out, however, the natural media reaction is to conclude that government miscalculated the risks, and to express political dissatisfaction accordingly. But government may well not have miscalculated. Government may have calculated all too well, but it is in the nature of taking a risk that there is a finite possibility of the dice rolling against you, and that is what has been experienced. Government may succeed in transferring some financial risk to other parties, and sharing risks through alliances and reciprocal obligations, but the final 'business risk' in the security domain will always rest with government. Having (one hopes) assessed the risk, and implemented measures to manage it down to a reasonable level within the risk appetite of the government, the rest is up to fate.

Even if the risks are assessed as tiny, improbable things do happen. This requires stoicism on the part of government and public. You accept the possibility of failure as well as the expectation of success when you manage a risk. I recall listening in 1982 to the First Sea Lord explain in the Chiefs of Staff Committee what his expectation in terms of the loss of naval ships was as the Fleet was readied for sea for the campaign just launched, against the odds, in the South Atlantic to repossess the Falkland Islands. His estimate was put to the government of Margaret Thatcher, who accepted the likelihood of such losses as part of the risks of achieving the recovery of the Islands. Sadly, Admiral Sir Henry Leach's estimates proved very close to the mark, but he knew from the outset that the Task Force had been launched on that clear understanding of the risks involved. Today we have counter-terrorist operations that all involve risk-management: for example letting a surveillance operation run whilst evidence is gathered and networks uncovered, or not closing down air traffic or a city centre when a piece of fragmentary threat intelligence arrives, or allowing a participating informant with knowledge of crimes being committed to continue inside a proscribed terrorist organization when that individual might commit further crimes. On balance, the public interest lies in encouraging government and its security authorities to feel confident that they can take calculated risks in order to uncover and neutralize the threats to public security. In the end, however, the public has to have confidence in the security authorities' ability to make those risk judgments. Government therefore has to explain through the media the rationale for the strategy it is following and convey a sense of where and why it is balancing the benefits from additional security with all the costs of providing it. Government has as a result to provide sufficient background information about its intelligence and security organizations and the kinds of people involved in them to engender the needed trust in operational security decisions.

There is a potential contrast that might be drawn here between the adoption of risk management of security as a principle and much of the present approach by government to policy-making. It is inherent in risk management that the decision-taker accepts that the risk may not pay off, and explains that clearly to those who may be affected. Every patient who has talked to their surgeon knows the feeling. Strong advice may be given that this is the procedure that is most likely to result in effective treatment of the condition, but it will be explained that there are known risks that have to be accepted in advance that it may not work. In my own cancer treatment some years ago the then relatively new stem cell procedure on which my life depended had an 80 per cent success rate. Excellent odds in advanced medicine—but a procedure that was liable to fail 1 in 5 patients. In medicine, informed consent has to be given to show that the patient understands the risk. Compare with the normal assertion by ministers of the rightness of the policy being introduced, and the equal vehemence with which the opposition parties dispute this. No doubts are allowed on either side. The public is then led to expect that the target outcome will be delivered. Where risk management then comes in is at one or two levels below in the technical details of the delivery plan; but of the rightness of the policy decision itself there is to be no doubt. In matters of security at least, there should be no such assertion of certainty over public safety.

Since there is no absolute security to be had at an acceptable financial or moral cost in this world, at every stage a balance must be maintained within the framework of human rights based on the time-honoured principles of proportionality and necessity. All strategies involve making choices over ends, ways and means. Central to sound strategy is having a clear statement of principles and values to inform the inevitable trade-offs and to highlight what cannot be compromised: the importance of human rights, including the absolute ban on torture, justice and the rule of law, legitimate and accountable government, and the maintenance of freedoms of assembly and speech. The words 'freely and with confidence' in the present UK government's own strategic security aim[7] ('so that people can go about their daily lives freely and with confidence, in a more secure, stable, just and prosperous world') are both significant qualifiers and significant reassurance to all sections of the community that in seeking security governments hold to their fundamental values.

The politics of security

A theme running through the arguments in this book is that it matters how governments choose to categorize issues of public policy. Take defence. During the Cold War the emphasis was on collective defence of the state through an alliance with like-minded democratic nations, NATO. That remains important: nation states have not withered away. Strong defence forces are still needed. Today, however, the analysis has to be of how armed force can also be a means towards achieving a wider sense of security.

Such use of the category 'security' matters, when it comes to government priorities and the allocation of effort and resources, and to what the public is told is being done in their name to protect them. But categories here are contested. I have described national security in terms of a state of public confidence that the risks are low enough or are being managed sufficiently that normal life can continue. Some commentators have written of the dangers of over-securitization. If every problem looks like a security issue then ministers will be conditioned to see the response in terms of seeking more security, through seeking military solutions overseas and threatening further restrictions domestically on individual liberty and privacy. Care is thus needed that a subliminal message does not become reinforced that Good Government is just about security. We can, however be reasonably confident that Bad Government will be marked by its neglect.

A common feature of many of the problems encountered by government in trying to take a modern approach to national security is the quality, or lack of it, in the strategic notice that governments had of trouble brewing. How wise governments should address that need is what we now move on to consider in chapter 2.

2

SAPIENTIA

THE PUBLIC VALUE OF INTELLIGENCE

A short dance around the subject and a definition

How should we best think about secret intelligence and its use to support government as it seeks to provide public security? Reflecting on examples from diplomatic and military history the natural approach is to think about decision advantage. The Zimmermann telegram was deciphered by British cryptographers in 1917 and the outrage following its publication in the American press contributed to the United States' declaration of war against Germany and its allies. Being in ignorance of the real position of the Japanese aircraft carriers, the US discounted the possibility of an attack on Pearl Harbor. Being able to control German agents in the UK and read German cypher traffic, the UK was able to mount an effective deception plan that materially reduced the risk of the 1944 Normandy landings. Absence of intelligence warning of the Soviet invasion of Czechoslovakia in 1968 faced Western allies with a *fait accompli*. We can apply the same approach to today's circumstances. Having secret intelligence on the activity of AQ suspects enabled the discovery and disruption in 2006 of a major plot to bring down a number of airliners over the Atlantic (the so-called airlines plot, Operation Overt). The Metropolitan Police were however forced to apologise earlier that year for a massive but fruitless raid on a house in Forest Gate in London after intelligence had indicated that a chemical device was being stored there. Intelligence is not always going to be up to date.

Well-known examples such as these illustrate both the value and limitations of intelligence across the domains of warfare, international affairs and diplomacy, terrorism and public safety. They suggest defining intelligence by purpose: *the most basic purpose of intelligence is to improve the quality of decision-making by reducing ignorance.* Thus we improve the odds of acting in line with our goals beyond what we would have achieved had we simply tossed a coin to decide between courses of action, acted on hunch or wrong information, or allowed events in the absence of decision to decide the outcome.

Much of the information that goes into making an intelligence assessment is available openly if you know where to look, or comes from normal diplomatic and military reporting. There is, however, an additional characteristic that defines *secret intelligence* as intelligence that others are seeking to prevent you knowing, often with formidable security barriers and violent sanctions against those who cooperate with intelligence officers. Obtaining such secret intelligence is usually the result of a specialized and hazardous process. Thus defined, secret intelligence is an end product that may be oral, written, visual, technical or digital. It results from a set of activities that characterizes what is known as the intelligence cycle. The cycle starts with an original requirement for intelligence on the part of a customer and proceeds through collection by an agency, analysis and assessment and finally distribution of the product back to the customer. The cycle is described in detail in chapter 4. In this book I shall as shorthand usually refer to 'intelligence' rather than 'secret intelligence', reserving the latter term for when it is necessary to emphasize that it includes information that has been obtained covertly, whether by human or technical means, as against open sources (including these days commercial satellite imagery) or normal diplomatic and military reporting.

As individuals we use fresh information every moment to alter our assumptions about the risks involved in decisions, from crossing the road to proposing marriage. We do not always do so by extracting all the information content available to us: faulty peripheral vision and love alike can temporarily blind us. But the assumption we usually make is that the more we know the better off we will end up being. In his 1971 novel *The Dice Man*, Luke Rhinehart creates the opposite world: a principal character who embarks on the experiment of taking all life's decisions, large and small, simply at random on the roll of the dice, with results both picaresque and amusing, but as might be expected eventually ending in tragedy. The world of national security and intelligence takes a strongly rationalist stance based on the assumption that more information will lead to less ignorance, thus better informed decisions can be taken that have a higher chance of being favourable and hence can lead to better outcomes: the steps connecting these statements are however not always obvious or straightforward, and are critically examined in chapters 6 and 7. Possessing secrets does not always confer advantage, nor is it always possible to act upon them. Secret knowledge is not always comfortable for government. An analogy is perhaps with a patient who accesses their genetic profile, revealing a predisposition to serious disease in years to come about which they can do nothing, but the knowledge of which may fundamentally change their life.

The hope is nevertheless that an intelligence assessment will make a difference and result in improved decisions. There are of course times when all that good intelligence will give is the sure knowledge of the inexorable working out of a historical process that governments are powerless to stop. The decline of the British Empire, for example, involved economic and social changes too large to be susceptible to the tactical manoeuvring of successive British governments, although that may not have been apparent to the rulers of Britain at the time.

The rationalist approach should produce outcomes that on average should result in better odds for the government concerned. Policymakers and military commanders will nevertheless still make some poor decisions, sometimes because they are led astray by faulty evidence, or because an absence of evidence misleads, and sometimes just because. Experience shows too that it is in the nature of the world that it is often when the situation is about to change most dramatically and governments are about to be faced with major surprises that the evidence and analysis base is most likely to let the policy-makers down. As we shall see in chapter 7, there is some basis for this casual observation in the prevalence of inductive thinking and of certain forms of analytic error. The more important the decision, the more the analyst and decision-taker alike are liable to be influenced by subconscious desires. The lesson for any decision-taker is to apply scepticism about the evidence base and their understanding of it in proportion to the likely importance of the decision.

The uses of intelligence

It is important in considering the role that intelligence can nevertheless play in improving decision-making on security issues to recognize that any piece of secret intelligence may be used to reduce uncertainty (or ignorance, as I prefer to think of it) in three distinct ways.

The first use, and by far the greatest in terms of volume of effort involved, is what I term *building situational awareness*. Take an example of a plausible intelligence judgment.[1] 'The first of the new class of Chinese ballistic missile carrying submarines, the Jin-class, has entered its sea trials' is an example of an intelligence judgment that policy-makers might receive based on a range of open and closed sources and that would contribute to situational awareness of the development of the Chinese strategic nuclear programme. In chapter 6 we examine in detail how an intelligence community might come to make such a judgment and the degree of certainty that they might attach to it (it might for example be an inference from a long series of naval attaché reports, open statements by senior Chinese officers, satellite photographs of dockyard activity, new communications patterns and the assessment based on previous intelligence that such a step is now to be expected in the submarine building programme). A later intelligence report might judge that the trials had been successfully concluded. The key word there is 'successfully', representing a judgment of all the evidence, some of which may well conflict. What such specific intelligence would do is help to build up awareness of a domain of interest to the policy-maker—in the case of the Chinese example a situation likely to be of considerable interest to arms control experts trying to craft long-term global strategic arms control proposals. Individual intelligence reports can be seen as building blocks, but it would be misleading to think of the purpose of such intelligence effort as being just to heap up presumed facts in data bases and lists. Individual reports contribute to overall situational awareness. Some reports will turn out to be the missing pieces in the jigsaw that transform awareness of the whole situation and thus can have considerable value-added to the policy-maker, military commander or senior police officer, for example where the identification of a new insurgent or terrorist group then causes revision of the judgment of the overall level of threat.

The second use of intelligence in supporting decision-making can best be described as *explanatory*. To extend the Chinese example above, there might be parallel evidence that, in addition to developing a submarine-based missile system, the Chinese People's Liberation Army (PLA) is also developing a long-range strategic road-mobile missile system. Taken together such intelligence suggests a PLA desire to have a more survivable nuclear deterrent, and that in turn suggests explanations for the Chinese programmes in terms of fears of growing vulnerability of existing silo-based missiles to the latest US conventional hi–tech precision attack capability and to future US anti–ballistic missile defences. Intelligence can therefore be used to build an explanatory theory of past and present Chinese military behaviour, and thus help explain why for example the Chinese tested an anti–satellite missile capability, which might be, for example, to put China in a position in a crisis to take advantage of US dependence on satellite systems. Such explanatory theories are important in understanding, and more importantly not misunderstanding, the behaviour of foreign states, for example, whether the Chinese developments described above should be taken as indicators of essentially defensive or offensive intent.

There are obvious dangers, which are discussed further in chapter 7, of over-interpreting evidence, particularly if analysts and policy-makers share implicit assumptions about the country concerned or the motivations of its leaders. Even if they do not recognize that they are doing it, decision-makers take for granted significant assumptions about the way the nations interact, about the motivations of insurgent or terrorist groups or the military doctrine of an opponent. As Keynes famously said of city financiers and businessmen in his 1936 *General Theory of Employment, Interest and Money*: 'Practical men, who believe themselves to be quite exempt from any intellectual influences, are usually the slaves of some defunct economist.' In the security domain there are defunct thinkers too. Good intelligence assessment has explanatory value in helping deepen real understanding of how a situation has arisen, the dynamics between the parties and what the motivations of the actors involved are likely to be.

The third use of intelligence is both potentially the most valuable, and the most fraught, and that is for *prediction*. From the Chinese example already cited it is but a small step to use the explanatory theory of the rationale for their strategic nuclear programme to predict their likely attitude to new arms control initiatives, or to US defence technology developments, and to make forecasts about the future size and shape of Chinese nuclear forces and the development of the doctrine for their employment.

Prediction is the end product of much intelligence activity. It could be a single intelligence report from inside a terrorist group that allows prediction of the intended target of a terrorist attack on a crowded place triggering anticipatory security action that saves scores of lives. It need not be a 'point estimate' (often a highly speculative undertaking) but could also be the forecasting of a limited range of outcomes that would still usefully focus down the options for the policy-maker. It could be a predictive assessment based not on specific intelligence reporting but on judgments made about a developing situation in an unstable country overseas that extends the explanatory into the predictive. Much of the discussion by commentators and scholars of both explanatory and predictive intelligence assessments has tended to focus on developments in international affairs, often after failure to predict sufficiently (or at all) the discontinuities of war (such as the Yom Kippur war of 1973 or the Falklands invasion in 1982) when active deception or high levels of secrecy had to be penetrated. In the case of failure to predict revolutionary change (such as in Iran in 1979 and in Berlin in 1989) what is likely to matter more is the 'feel' that the analyst has for the developing situation based on news reports and diplomatic reporting rather than specific secret intelligence. As we shall explore in chapter 7 the record of forecasting the course of events in complex security situations is mixed, and there are real limits to how far it can be improved, but the effort to shift the odds has to be made in the interests of public security—but made with eyes wide open.

Is the track record of government intelligence assessment in such complex international circumstances that much better than the best of journalism? The sceptic might argue that being able to assess a developing situation is a capability that can be achieved by good journalists from their open sources and private contacts. There are however differences in the intelligence role of government and of the media, as *The Economist* itself recognized when it wrote on the retirement in 1966 of Sir Kenneth Strong as UK Director-General of Defence Intelligence:

'Modern intelligence has to do with the painstaking collection and analysis of fact, the exercise of judgment, and clear and quick presentation. It is not simply what serious journalists would always produce if they had time: it is something more rigorous, continuous, and above all operational—that is to say, related to something that someone wants to do or may be forced to do.'

That quotation reminds us too that good intelligence has an operational purpose to help government secure its objectives. It has to tell governments what they do not know, and sometimes perhaps what they would rather not have to know, about approaching threats. In 1982, when the first warning signs of trouble in the South Atlantic arose following the landing of Argentine scrap metal merchants on the British island possession of South Georgia, the Secretary of State for Defence, the Chief of Defence Staff and the senior officials were all in Colorado Springs, USA for the NATO Nuclear Planning Group (NPG). With the UK purchase of the Trident D5 nuclear missile system uppermost in ministerial minds, it would be fair to say that the initial reports of events in the remote South Atlantic did not get the full immediate attention that hindsight shows they should have been given. On the other hand, I have the enduring memory of working with the Secretary of State in the House of Commons a few days later on his speech to announce the purchase of Trident D5 when specific signals intelligence reports arrived via the Defence Intelligence Staff unambiguously recording that the Argentine military had carried out beach reconnaissance at landing sites on the Falkland Islands; then the penny did certainly drop, and we raced down the corridors to find Prime Minister Margaret Thatcher in her room to tell her the bad news that having suffered a failure of intelligence assessment, intelligence now indicated an invasion was now almost certain, but also that we were militarily powerless to stop it.

After the re-possession of the Falkland Islands, and the subsequent inquiry led by Lord Franks, the arrangements for intelligence assessment and ensuring its independence within government were tightened up by the practice of appointing a senior public servant with no Foreign Office or other departmental responsibilities to the chair of the British Joint Intelligence Committee (JIC), and giving the Chairman of the JIC a personal responsibility in the JIC terms of reference for providing early warning: 'to monitor and give early warning of the development of direct and indirect foreign threats to British interests, whether political, military or economic, and to keep under review threats to security at home and overseas.' 'Speaking truth unto power' is a basic responsibility of officialdom; the intelligence community in particular recognizes that sometimes the truth comes cloaked in lies and has to be unmasked, and sometimes it will have to shout louder to be heard through the background noise of other events.

Under Franks' recipe for greater JIC independence, Sir Anthony Duff, a distinguished former wartime submarine commander and diplomat then serving as Intelligence Coordinator in the Cabinet Office, was appointed in 1983 JIC chair as well (his second tour as chair). He was followed by another senior diplomat, Sir Percy Cradock, who combined the chairmanship with serving as Prime Minister Thatcher's foreign policy adviser, a combination of roles also followed by his successor, Sir Roderick Braithwaite. The subsequent four JIC chairs combined the role with that of head of the relevant Cabinet Office Defence and Overseas Secretariat. After the JIC's failure in 2002 to assess correctly Iraq's programmes of weapons of mass destruction, the subsequent inquiry led by Lord Butler produced an even tighter formula: the JIC chair should not be combined with other posts and should be held by a senior official who is 'someone with experience of dealing with Ministers in a very senior role, and who is demonstrably beyond influence, and thus probably in his last post'.[2]

The nature and types of intelligence reporting

There is an important defining characteristic already referred to that is crucial for understanding why we have the intelligence machinery we do and how it operates in support of national security. If, as argued, the point of intelligence generally is to enable action to be optimized by reducing ignorance, then secret intelligence achieves this in respect of information that others positively do not want you to have and may go to very considerable lengths to stop you acquiring. That characteristic determines the secrecy that surrounds intelligence sources and methods, and those that carry out intelligence work. On the other hand, it is not just the secretly acquired piece of information that justifies protection. Secrecy can rightly surround an overall intelligence assessment that was based largely on information gleaned from open sources if it reveals information about the limits of government understanding or government intention that could be of use to a potential adversary. Nor is the dividing line clear-cut between secret intelligence and other forms of hard to get open source information.[3] For those investigating a terrorist, proliferation or other criminal network, there is also likely to be much sensitive information of interest to be accessed from public or private sector databases containing information that is data protected but is otherwise unclassified about the individuals of interest.

• An illustrative list of the uses to which intelligence might be put in the area of counter-terrorism shows how wide the range of information would ideally need to be:

- The identities, and aliases, of those suspected of supporting or engaging in terrorism and their past personal history and criminal record
- Biometric details identifying the root identity of terrorist suspects
- The location of terrorist suspects
- Their patterns of behaviour and association
- The aspirations and operational planning of suspected terrorists
- Their modus operandi for attacks
- Their counter-surveillance understanding and measures they take
- The movements of suspected terrorists
- The logistics, training and financing of their networks
- Uncovering their target reconnaissance and target selection
- Recruitment and communication activities including active use of the internet
- The belief systems of terrorist groups
- The attitudes and policies of other relevant countries
- Mutations, developments and fissures in the threat

For completeness, therefore, at this stage in our dance round the world of intelligence, we can note that the intelligence requirements of those designing and implementing modern national security measures will be met by accessing three very different types of information: traditional or classic secret sources, open sources, and a third category that has recently risen considerably in importance, that of protected personal data. We look briefly at each in turn.

Classic intelligence

The traditional heart of twentieth century secret intelligence lay in the recruitment of human sources (HUMINT) and the interception (and where necessary decyphering) of communications (COMINT)and their patterns and modes that together with radar and electronic intelligence (ELINT) makes up the broader category called signals intelligence (SIGINT). The technologies may have changed over the years (internet steganography not microdots, public key cyphers not one time pads) but the principles have remained. And to the original HUMINT and SIGINT there are now many other 'INTs': there is imagery from satellite and photo-reconnaissance (IMINT), acoustic intelligence (ACINT) measurement and signature intelligence (MASINT), geographical intelligence (GEOINT), location intelligence (LOCINT) and so on. Essentially, these categories provide the organizational structure for specialized recruitment, skill development and organizational structure for national intelligence communities.

Nations have differed in whether some or almost all these intelligence 'INTs' have been under the wing of national defence or of chancelleries, diplomatic or interior ministries. But the basic organizational structures based on classic type of source remain similar. That for the UK is shown in Figure 1. There are three UK civilian secret agencies: the Secret Intelligence Service (SIS) otherwise known as MI6 collecting human intelligence overseas; the Government Communications Headquarters (GCHQ) collecting signals intelligence; and the British Security Service (BSS), otherwise known as MI5. The Foreign Secretary is accountable to Parliament for SIS and GCHQ and the Home Secretary for the Security Service. The Prime Minister traditionally accepts overall responsibility for secret intelligence matters. All three secret agencies are funded from the Single Intelligence Account (SIA) for which special arrangements are made for audit and scrutiny of spending by the chair (a senior member of the main opposition party) and deputy chair of the Parliamentary Public Accounts Committee. The Ministry of Defence has its own Defence Intelligence Staff (DIS) which in addition to performing the normal defence staff (J-2) role in the MOD provides essential intelligence support for military operations and has the responsibility for providing imagery across the community, for delivering most scientific and technical intelligence analysis and for managing Defence Attachés and Advisers around the world.

Figure 1: UK Secret Intelligence Agencies

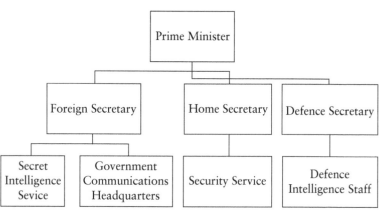

Consideration of the many possible operational purposes of intelligence should also remind us that government—its policy-makers, diplomats and armed forces—need information in fine detail as well as broad sweep. Like the bulk of an iceberg, the value of secret intelligence in all three dimensions of use that I have described above is mostly hidden below the surface, in the detailed technical weapons specifications, radio-nucleide analysis, radio and radar frequencies, internet sites, covert financial dealings, identification of a suspect's photograph and all the other fine texture of intelligence.

Open sources

The volumes of information provided by those secret sources are, however, now dwarfed by the availability of open sources of information (sometimes referred to as OSINT). Before the internet age OSINT provided a valuable cross-check and supplement to all-source secret intelligence assessment, for example though monitoring of overseas radio and then TV and now internet broadcasts and print media. Now vast quantities of information about target groups and countries, their economies, culture, physical geography, climate and so on are available not just centrally but at any point of access to the internet, which is anywhere on the planet. Self-regulating internet tools such as an adaptation of the Wikipedia approach have found application, at least within the US intelligence community.[4] And intelligence targets also use the internet, as seen by the imaginative use by takfiri jihadists of websites to promote radicalization and recruitment, maintain contact within networks and disseminate information about targets, tactics and weapons. A whole branch of intelligence work is having to be created to access (not a straightforward matter), monitor and exploit such internet-based material.

The private sector has discovered the open source intelligence market, both for due diligence and market intelligence for commercial clients and as outsourced suppliers of analysis to government. This information revolution does not, for the reasons given earlier, supplant the need for more traditional secret intelligence obtained from secret sources—but it is no longer the poor relation. Like the wire services such as PA and Reuters that media outlets have long used, intelligence agencies themselves now subscribe to many of the daily or weekly private sector 'intelligence' reports that represent a cost-effective way to

31

keep up with the news. Non-profitmaking organizations such as the RAND Corporation[5] offer web-based services such as collated databases of terrorist incidents (an initiative started in RAND by the scholar Brian Jenkins in 1970, continued by Bruce Hoffman when at St Andrews University in Scotland and now by the University of Maryland, supported by the US Homeland Security Department[6]). Institutes such as the IISS[7] in London offer extensive collated data on international conflict and on relevant literature, as do many university international affairs departments. Serious publications such as *The Economist* have extensive searchable databases online of past articles. This wealth of information now provides the principal means for government to acquire contextual and situational awareness.

The problem is that there is far too much potentially relevant open source material to be digestible (drinking at a fire-hose is the usual expression). Search engines such as Google and MSN have helped sort the material for the user by applying logical (Boolean) operations, sorting and classifying by page content (although there is now a small industry devoted to advising on how website owners can beat the system and optimize their ranking in response to a search). More advanced versions of such search engines now use link analysis, thus taking the structure of the web itself into account. So called third generation tools are promised that will draw on past user preferences, collaboration, collective intelligence, clustering of results in folders and other ways of making information more productive. Nevertheless there will still be the problem that quality control of external sites cannot be relied upon unless prior steps have been taken by government, for example through contracts to supply specific classes of information, and once incorporated into a government product the limitations of the original source can easily be lost sight of. The most egregious example of such dangers was the unattributed use of material from an academic paper[8] in the public information document (quickly labelled by the media as the dodgy dossier) on Saddam's Iraq issued to the media in 2003 by Alistair Campbell as the Prime Minister's Director of Communications.

PROTINT: *the electronic traces we all leave behind*

To the huge changes happening in the world of OSINT must be added the growth of a third category of information from which intelligence for national security may be derived, one that might be labelled 'protected information' or, as I might term it, PROTINT. This is personal information about us as individuals that resides in databases of both the public and private sectors, for example covering passport and biometric data, immigration, identity and border records, criminal records, airline bookings and other travel data, financial and telephone and other communications records, credit ratings, shopping habits and much more. Such information may be held in national public and private sector records covered by national Data Protection legislation, but also offshore by other nations with different legal frameworks, or by multinational companies. Carmen Medina of the CIA has described to me what she terms the 'electronic exhaust' that we all leave behind us as we purchase online, use credit cards, loyalty cards, electronic season tickets and all the rest, and as we are increasingly captured on CCTV cameras, automatic number plate readers (ANPR) for parking or congestion charging and so on. The commercial world is far ahead of government in storing information about the citizen because that data can be used to extract consumer preferences and thus competitive advantage. Access to such information, and in some cases the ability to apply data mining and pattern recognition software to databases, may well in terrorist cases be the key to effective pre-emption. Data of interest for security purposes may be, or more often may not yet be, subject to international agreement on sharing.

Such PROTINT sources as bank accounts and passport details have of course always been accessible, with right authority, to traditional law enforcement officers seeking evidence against a named suspect where the search is justified by reasonable suspicion of having committed a crime. Having the material stored electronically makes such search easy and quick, and that in itself carries some danger that private information will be accessed when it is not strictly necessary. Application of modern data mining and processing techniques does, however, open up very different forms of intelligence investigation before the fact, rather than police investigation after the fact. To take a simple example, most people wishing to fly from A to B (say from Karachi to New York) will simply book a suitable flight. Some will make a dog-leg via another airport (for example Heathrow or Schiphol since that combination of flights and airlines might happen to be cheaper, and there are advertised websites that will readily do the price comparisons). But some people may take unusual routes with several stops before ending up on a popular route into New York, raising the suspicion that they are trying to avoid drawing attention to their point of origin. There will be perfectly innocent explanations in almost all cases—but the intelligence analyst is looking for the exception, and by running overlays of different kinds of information may narrow down the search. More traditional investigation (such as questions by an immigration officer) can then follow, and could provide the initiating clue that triggers a major counter-narcotics or counter-terrorism investigation. Thus such techniques involve examination (at least through sorting of data by a computer) of the innocent as well as the suspected to identify patterns of interest for further investigation.

The most developed PROTINT area accessed by law enforcement is in the examination of communications billing information, the metadata held by the telecoms companies that enables them to bill customers by knowing who called whom, when and for how long. Another example already in use is the use of specialist software[9] by the major banks to examine accounts to try to identify closed loops of transactions that could be the sign of so-called 'ring fraud' or of money laundering. Such data mining will become much more prevalent as the risks of identity and other forms of fraud increase in cyberspace. The criminal investigation potential is considerable. Obtaining international agreement on the sharing of such data also becomes very important to ensure future regulated access to these vital sources, and there has been a vigorous debate in the European parliament, for example, over whether EU governments should have the power to require telecoms operators to retain communications data for a specified period. Privacy issues also arise over other sources of information on the movements and activities of individuals, revealed by technology such as CCTV or ANPR, again with future potential for smart recognition software to be applied to mine such data for intelligence and law enforcement purposes. Some ethical implications of these developments are considered in chapter 9.

The different types of intelligence product

Up to this point, however, we have largely considered secret intelligence as an undifferentiated product in the form of value-adding information delivered to decision-takers in government, the armed services and law enforcement for purposes that range from the grand strategic to the very tactical. If we were, however, to drop in on any regular British user of intelligence in Scotland Yard, the military Permanent Joint Headquarters (PJHQ), the Home Office, Ministry of Defence or the Foreign Office (or elsewhere in Whitehall) we would see on the desk (or nowadays the electronic equivalent on a screen) on the one hand a heap of intelligence reports from single sources issued by the controlling intelligence agencies and on the other hand a smaller pile of all-source reports that have been compiled by drawing on multiple sources to produce an integrated assessment.

It is best to avoid thinking of types or sources of intelligence themselves as being 'strategic' (centrally controlled) or 'tactical' (locally controlled) since high level national intelligence gathering controlled centrally can generate intelligence for local tactical purposes (such as the WWII breaking of the Enigma cypher providing information on which convoys in the Atlantic could be rerouted away from U-Boat packs) and tactical collection can have strategic effect (documents found on a captured terrorist courier for example that reveal the strategic plans of the enemy). What matters is the level of command, and the level of decision needing to be made by command. There is, in looking at the uses to which intelligence can be put, a rough parallel therefore with the military distinction between planning at the tactical, operational and strategic levels. At the tactical level, there is a flow of detailed reporting going to inform activity on the ground, whether domestic security, criminal investigation or military operations overseas. Single-source reporting forms the bulk of the material informing tactical level decisions (but noting as recognized above that some high-grade single-source reporting has strategic impact, such as that from the SIS agent Oleg Gordievsky, the KGB head of London station, during the latter stages of the Cold War). Examples of tactical use of single-source reporting might include, for example, the monitoring of a conversation between terrorist suspects planning an attack, real-time intelligence being passed to police officers at a port on the movements of a criminal suspect; and a report from an agent overseas (such reports from SIS are traditionally referred to as CX reports) describing the intentions of a local warlord to attack a security force base. Such single-source reporting is intended to be read by those who have to take action, drawn from a wide group of customers in police forces and law enforcement agencies, government departments and military headquarters as selected by the originating agency.

The professionalization of intelligence: The Joint Intelligence Committee

Democratic governments are elected to govern on behalf of all the people, not just those that voted for them. It is their responsibility to take decisions based on their view of the national interest and to be accountable to the electorate for the consequences. In governing, they may seek information and advice from any quarter inside or outside government, and there are many professional associations, think tanks and institutes that exist to provide channels to inform and influence government from outside as well as a bewildering array of lay opinions from lobbyists and media. There are also plenty of organizations and groupings inside to which ministers can turn, ranging from departmental policy and strategy units to experts of all kinds. The heads of profession, the Treasury Solicitor, the chief medical officer, the chief scientific adviser, chief economists and statisticians, heads of armed services, occupy special places since they are the pinnacle of expertise bound by the professional ethics and methodologies of their particular grouping. Ministers have no obligation to follow the advice from their professional bodies, as there may well be wider considerations to be weighed, but in coming to decisions ministers must have considered what the professionals had to say. They will be open to legitimate criticism if they cherry-pick from the advice, selectively quote from it or send it back with instructions to alter their views to fit the policy. Independent advisory bodies have to be protected from political and other interference with their work. Professional judgment is what it says it is, take it or leave it. Secret intelligence assessment by bodies such as the JIC must fit into that ethical framework.

In the case of secret intelligence work, since the origins of MI5 and MI6 in 1909, followed in 1919 by the establishment of a single cryptanalytic and signals interception agency (known since 1946 as GCHQ) there has been increasing formalization of intelligence staffing and processes within government that amounts to professionalization. For intelligence reporting from an individual agency, the head of that agency takes responsibility for quality control of all the intelligence issued, thus providing the equivalent of a professional endorsement. There are processes laid down by which a report is validated that involve auditing the integrity of the steps by which it was produced, the coherence and consistency of what it says, and there are standards to which staffs have been trained, and the equivalent of a professional body's code of conduct. When problems arise it is therefore against the ideal of a professional standard that lapses are examined, as was done in the case of intelligence bearing on Iraqi WMD programmes in 2003.[10]

The JIC provides the strategic (and grand-strategic) levels of assessment, drawing on all available sources of information, open and secret. The readership of JIC papers includes Her Majesty the Queen, the Prime Minister, senior ministers and officials, and Chiefs of Staff and senior commanders. The output of the Joint Intelligence Committee as the UK's most senior assessment body has the status of professional advice to government. Much of the public outrage over the intelligence background to the 2003 intervention in Iraq stemmed from a feeling that government had interfered with the process of producing that professional advice in order to end up with an assessment for public consumption that bolstered its policy case. Subsequent detailed independent inquiry revealed significant flaws in the underlying intelligence reporting on Iraqi WMD and in the way the inherent limitations of the intelligence material was described for public consumption, but not that the JIC itself had allowed itself to be improperly influenced.

The position of the JIC as a professional body is particularly interesting in this respect since, as described below, a majority of its members are not intelligence professionals. When founded in 1936 as a sub-committee of the Chiefs of Staff Committee, the Joint Intelligence Committee consisted of the Heads of the Service Intelligence Branches of the (then) three Service Departments: Admiralty, War Office and Air Ministry. By the start of the Second World War the JIC had developed into a committee chaired by the Foreign Office (by default since the Service Directors could not agree that any one of them—and the Navy was in the senior position—should chair) and with the Secret Intelligence Service and Political Warfare Executive represented. Later in the war, the Director-General of the Security Service and the Director of the Government Code and Cypher School (the forerunner of GCHQ) joined. The subsequent development of the JIC added on the intelligence side the Chief of the Assessments Staff in the Cabinet Office and (in 1967) the Intelligence Coordinator. After a unified MOD had been created in 1964 the Service Intelligence Directors were replaced with the single Director-General of Defence Intelligence (a retired senior officer) and the three-star uniformed post of Deputy Chief of the Defence Staff (Intelligence). On the policy side, senior officials joined the JIC from the Foreign Office, the Colonial Office and Commonwealth Relations Office (merged into the Foreign and Commonwealth Office, FCO, in 1966) and HM Treasury, the Cabinet Office Head of Defence and Overseas Policy Secretariat, the Department of Trade and Industry (given the interest in export controls, sanctions and proliferation) and latterly the Home Office (given the terrorist threat). Other senior officials from departments concerned with particular subjects can be invited to attend. The JIC is now (2010) chaired by a senior official, based in the Cabinet Office and reporting directly to the Prime Minister (see Figure 2).

Figure 2: UK Central Intelligence Machinery

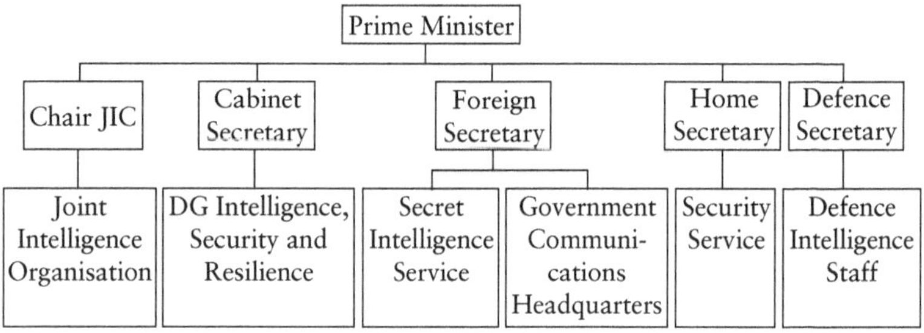

Source: Cabinet Office, as at September 2009

Drafts of papers for the JIC are written by the Cabinet Office Assessments Staff (very exceptionally, for highly technical subjects the first draft can be written by the DIS experts). A Current Intelligence Group (CIG), chaired by a senior member of the Assessments Staff, is then called with country and subject experts from the agencies and relevant departments. It is in the expert CIG that the detailed (often very vigorous) debate will take place over the analysis of all the available intelligence on a topic, including open source material. Only when the CIG is satisfied (which may take several redrafts) will the paper be forwarded to the JIC itself. JIC discussion will then focus on points of contention identified in the CIG, or on how key judgments are best framed to be understood by the senior readership. The present practice is for JIC papers to include statements about the depth and adequacy of the intelligence base behind the paper, and will start with a set of key judgments (rather than a summary) drawing out for the policy-maker the conclusions reached by the JIC, usually with a predictive flavour ('It is likely that…' etc.). Just occasionally the JIC will fail to be persuaded of the case made out by the CIG and send the subject back for further analysis and redrafting. More usually, the Chief of the Assessments Staff will offer to refine the wording in the light of the JIC discussion and clear a subsequent final draft out of committee

The Heads of the Intelligence Agencies (SIS, Security Service and GCHQ) are members of the JIC but, as described above, so are senior policy-makers from the departments most concerned, and the latter form the majority on the Committee. The collective judgments reached by the JIC (examples of which are given in chapter 6) are nevertheless treated by ministers as the 'professional' conclusions of the UK *intelligence* community. Thus, and this can be seen as the genius of the UK system (as well being as its most puzzling feature to those brought up in the US tradition), the judgments of the JIC are treated by UK government as having the same status as professional advice.

The policy-makers on the JIC are therefore exercising more of a 'non-executive director' role, bringing outside expertise to bear rather than behaving (as they would have to in the US system, being political appointees) as policy-makers with a duty to promote the policies of their ministers and departments. The fact that they are politically aware but yet politically impartial senior public servants and not political appointees makes it possible for them to work in this way and to be seen to subscribe to collective judgments that may be highly unwelcome to the policy community without pressure being then brought to bear on them. All have to dip their hands in the blood of the collective judgments, however unwelcome they may be. This feature is, as far as I know, unique around the world. The intelligence professionals' task is to keep judgments anchored to what the intelligence actually reveals (or does not reveal) and to keep in check any predisposition of policy-makers to pontificate. The policy-makers in turn ensure that the judgments actually try to address the issues that need answering rather than just those on which their intelligence sources are richest, and help the professionals couch any warnings justified by the intelligence, without their seeming to attack the policy itself and thus risk compromising the neutrality of the JIC. Having senior policy officials participate in the JIC debate makes it much less likely that intelligence warnings will go unnoticed.

There is one other clear advantage that the UK system has: forcing top, and very busy, intelligence chiefs and policy officials to work actively together in the JIC on key judgments for an afternoon most weeks of the year generates a sense of pol-mil community that is uniquely well informed about each others' likely positions and attitudes on an issue and that generates high levels of mutual understanding and trust. That is, for example, likely to be one reason why the UK has been able to work across domestic/overseas and policy/intelligence organizational boundaries on counter-terrorism and serious crime and promote closer operational working within the UK intelligence community in ways that other nations with their more compartmentalized intelligence and police structures have not yet achieved.

The range, type and form of reporting that is circulated under JIC authority has evolved over the years, for example through the invariable practice now of having the JIC reach 'key judgments' for the busy reader in its main assessments rather than simply include a summary of the intelligence material. It has always been the practice of the JIC to argue through to consensus so that the readership is given the best professional advice of the community. One potential disadvantage of the JIC approach is that differences of opinion could be submerged or blurred in the process of fine drafting around a sensitive point, or adopting 'on the one hand, on the other hand' language. There could be times when it is important for readers of assessments to know of significant minority views rather then have judgments watered down or omitted for lack of consensus. It is open to the chair of the JIC to add comment to accompany a JIC paper, on his or her own authority, to flag up for senior readers important divergences of opinion, or highlight where JIC reports are altering past judgments on the basis of new intelligence. Further evolution in the presentation of intelligence to ministers is to be expected, including greater use of maps and graphics.

The British JIC system can only cope in committee with a very small number of subjects at a time, leaving single-source reporting from individual agencies as the main vehicle by which intelligence reaches customers. When need arises, such as in times of military operations or impending conflict, the JIC authorizes the Chief of Assessment Staff to issue directly on its behalf to the JIC readership all-source assessments as current intelligence products. These current assessments will be noted retrospectively by the next JIC meeting, when if necessary further JIC comment could be circulated. The JIC does also have an important formal responsibility for providing government with early warning of trouble, a topic discussed in more detail in chapter 7.

The professionalization of intelligence: The UK Joint Terrorism Analysis Centre

After 9/11 it became evident to the Security Service that the existing arrangements could not hope to process the volume and type of terror-ist-related intelligence reporting that the UK was able to access. The JIC system operated well, but at the strategic level and supported by a very small staff. The terrorism analysis function itself was being car-ried out in different places, principally by the Security Service, the Metropolitan Police and the Defence Intelligence Staff, but also in the other Intelligence Agencies, the Home Office and the Foreign Office. It became evident to the Director General and to me as UK Intelligence and Security Coordinator looking across the community that we should build upon planning by the Security Service for expansion of their analytic capability to bring together all those concerned in the government with analysing and assessing intelligence on terrorism at home and overseas, and thus be able to generate all-source operational assessments and warnings and decide upon alert states. The upshot was to create in June 2003 a new joint all-source body, the UK Joint Terrorism Analysis Centre (JTAC).

JTAC is located in the Headquarters of the Security Service but is a genuine multi–agency body with an Oversight Board, chaired by the Cabinet Office, to ensure that JTAC meets the requirements of all its many customers. It sets threat levels and issues warnings of threats and other terrorist-related subjects for customers from the police service, the military, civil government and the Foreign Office. Where single-source reporting is likely to have strategic impact then it would be likely to be followed quickly by an all-source assessment, in the case of terrorism by JTAC, and for counter-insurgency operations overseas by the Defence Intelligence Staff. Pursuing the parallel with military planning, we can think of such intelligence assessment as being at the level of the 'operational art'. Such all-source assessments will be produced by the Defence Intelligence Staff on military topics, for example on the char-acteristics of weapons likely to be used against British forces, including improvised explosive devices (IEDs), and on weapons programmes that can guide research and development effort. JTAC will for example issue reports on terrorist tactics to guide protective security planning.

The establishment of JTAC brought together counter-terrorist exper-tise from the Security Service, the police, key government departments and the other intelligence agencies each with access to their own organization's databases of intelligence. Collaborating in this way now ensures that information is analyzed and processed on a shared basis, with the involvement and consensus of all relevant departments, and with the assurance that there is unlikely to be information relevant to a particular threat lurking unknown inside an agency stove-pipe. The result is a stream of intelligence reporting at the tactical and operational levels including in-depth reports on trends, terrorist networks and capabilities.

JTAC decisions on the appropriate terrorist threat alert level (ranging from 'low' through 'moderate' and 'substantial' (the level early in 2010) to 'severe' and 'critical') have the status of professional advice, for the quality control of which the Director-General of the Security Service is responsible. The government has thus accepted in advance that it would expect to follow the JTAC decisions on threat levels. Ministers would not therefore see themselves as responsible for those professional judgments, only for accounting for their own decisions on how to respond. This approach had a practical test in 2005 when, three weeks before the 7/7 bombings on the London transport system, JTAC lowered the threat level from 'severe' to 'substantial'. There was subsequently media criticism of this decision after the surprise of 7/7. The response of government was that JTAC was following the logic of its methodology, given the lack of specific evidence then available of the existence of any group with both capability and intent to attack the UK. JTAC had not aimed off to take account of presentational calculations. In that it can be seen to be following the old US intelligence analysts' adage[11] that 'it is better to be wrong for the right reasons than right for the wrong reasons' since following reasoning that is flawed, or failure to follow a coherent methodology, can lead next time to judgments that may turn out to be disastrous. This paradox is explored further in chapter 6.

UK ministers are therefore given the considered collective professional views of 'the intelligence community' through the JIC and JTAC, but they then have the right not to be swayed in their policy response by intelligence reporting if they so choose, although in that case they would be wise to bear in mind the advice of 'the father of US intelligence analysis', Sherman Kent: 'An Estimate … should be relevant within the area of our competence, and above all it should … be credible. Let things be such that if our policy-making master is to disregard our knowledge and wisdom, he will never do so because our work was inaccurate, incomplete, or patently biased. Let him disregard us only when he must pay greater heed to someone else. And let him be uncomfortable—thoroughly uncomfortable—about his decision to heed this other.'[12]

In the US, the National Counter-Terrorism Center (NCTC) parallels the UK JTAC. At the strategic level, the nearest US equivalent to the JIC assessment is the National Intelligence Estimate (NIE), although the latter tends to be longer and more detailed, and presenting at times alternative views when these are held by some but not all members of the US intelligence community. The aim is, as the then Director of Central Intelligence Walter Bedell Smith put it in 1950 in relation to the US: 'A national intelligence estimate ... should be compiled and assembled centrally by an agency whose objectivity and disinterestedness are not open to question ... Its ultimate approval should rest upon the collective judgment of the highest officials in the various intelligence agencies ... [It] should command recognition and respect throughout the Government as the best available and presumably the most authoritative estimate. ... It is ... the clear duty and responsibility of the Central Intelligence Agency under the statute to assemble and produce such coordinated and authoritative Estimates.' That responsibility for the US now rests with the US Director of National Intelligence (DNI) and for the UK remains with the chair of the JIC.

Should there be joint organizations in the UK comparable to JTAC for other intelligence topics, such as counter-proliferation? For defence-related topics, such as weapons system characteristics, the Defence Intelligence Staff already provides an all-source assessment capability, as the Defense Intelligence Agency (DIA) in the Pentagon does for US

Figure 3: Levels of Explanation

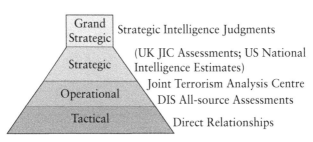

Grand Strategic — Strategic Intelligence Judgments

Strategic — (UK JIC Assessments; US National Intelligence Estimates)

Operational — Joint Terrorism Analysis Centre / DIS All-source Assessments

Tactical — Direct Relationships

customers. The US has recently moved further than the UK in setting up centres for intelligence analysis, for example for counter-proliferation. So far in the UK the view has been taken that the scale of effort is too small to be able to justify pulling people out of the agencies and departments into a central organization. Instead there is virtual networking between the analysts concerned who come together to form inter-agency groups to issue reports drawing on all available sources on such matters as the working of proliferation networks. The Serious and Organized Crime Agency (SOCA) does the same for international criminal routes for narcotics or people smuggling, and so on. Those planning operational capability will thus ideally have up to date all-source assessments to guide them in deployment, training and investment decisions (see Figure 3).

The great advantage of the UK/USA system of giving policy staffs considerable access to single-source intelligence is that they get the detail and the granularity that is inevitably missing from most all-source strategic assessment. It is, however, the invariable practice in the UK for the originating single-source agencies not to use different kinds of intelligence to help illuminate the meaning of their reporting, thus mixing HUMINT and SIGINT or vice versa. In that way the risk is minimized that readers might get the impression that they are being given multiple and thus potentially confirmatory reports when it is simply the same information appearing in different reports. This restriction places a greater premium on readers having timely assessed all-source intelligence from the JIC, the DIS on defence subjects or from JTAC on terrorism that can distil the meaning of all the information available on a given topic.

What every inquiry after an alleged failure of warning intelligence points out afresh is that readers of secret intelligence did not sufficiently recognize that it is usually, some would say always, incomplete, often fragmentary and may bear more than one interpretation. Individual single-source intelligence reports clearly carry the danger of being interpreted out of context by the lay reader. Readers of intelligence cannot (and should not) expect to know about the sources and methods by which the intelligence was obtained. They must be able to rely on the originating agency to have validated the product to guard against deception, exaggeration, mistranslation or misunderstanding of the subject by the source (whether oral or written—not every document circulating inside government department or agency (even those of HM Government) is to be wholly relied upon!). It is a heavy responsibility on individual intelligence agencies to validate the intelligence product they circulate. The agencies must have the capability through independent scrutiny by experienced officers to test lines of reporting and to make sure officers are not portraying all their geese as swans (something that in the case of intelligence on Saddam's Iraq was found to be a contributory reason behind the intelligence failures). Readers of intelligence need to remember that individual intelligence reports may mislead as well as enlighten. Reports may well convey only a snapshot of a fast moving situation, and the sources may not be able to keep up with the pace of events. They may well be an accurate expression of the views of a senior individual in the government or military headquarters of the country concerned, but that person may be someone who is not 'in the loop' on the secret planning that will lead to the surprise attack. The agent may be reporting information gleaned from sub-sources to whom the controlling intelligence officer does not have access. The reporting by individual agents may be coloured by what they think will best please or by motivations of their own. It is therefore always salutary to reflect on how a foreign intelligence service would report on whatever happens to be the policy issue of the day in one's own government: when some new policy is being hatched, how many people in political life and the civil service or military would really be in the know as against being all too willing to re-circulate gossip and rumour? Documentary evidence such as a copy of the relevant operational order, technical manual or transcripts of intercepted conversations that the parties believed to be secure are likely to be the strongest form of intelligence.

Policy-makers should certainly routinely question the secret reporting they receive when that is likely to be of significant relevance to national security decisions. What is the degree of confidence in the report? Is there other confirmatory intelligence? Does this intelligence assessment match earlier reporting? Is there a possibility of being taken in by a deception operation? Questions such as these must be asked, and the intelligence community must be ready to answer honestly and not defensively. There comes a point, however, when aggressive, sustained challenge of the work of the intelligence community by policy-makers upset that intelligence does not conform to their expectations will discourage honest answers, and create a danger of 'politicization' of the intelligence process, an issue discussed further in chapter 6.

An introduction to secrets, mysteries and complexities

This is an appropriate point at which to introduce a fundamental distinction that is often used in the world of intelligence and was first popularized by Professor R. V. Jones, the founder of modern scientific intelligence, and that is the difference between secrets and mysteries. A secret is best thought of as information that exists, although it may be carefully hidden and protected, but which at least in theory is capable of being found out by an effective intelligence agency. The characteristics of foreign weapons systems, the locations of opposing enemy military formations or missile silos, the location or real name of a terrorist leader, are all examples. A mystery on the other hand is highly desirable information concerning intentions not yet crystallized into decisions or predictions of the outcome of events that have not yet taken place. Thus whether a dictator will order his forces to cross the border and invade his neighbour in the next week, whether the mob will overthrow the dictator or a terrorist group will attempt to develop chemical weapons are all questions to which there is no factual answer, yet intelligence assessors will be pressed for their best judgments on such matters, and the fate of nations and regimes may thereby hang in the balance.

The discovery and assessment of secrets is clearly core business for the intelligence community. But should the intelligence community be tasked by government to make judgments about mysteries if, by definition, there can be no definitive secret intelligence on the matter? There is a school of thought that would hold that it is better for the intelligence world to stick to secret reporting, as factual as possible, and leave crystal ball gazing to those in the policy world. Such a course would certainly be less hazardous for the reputation of the JIC and other intelligence assessment bodies. On some subjects, diplomatic reporting, including from the Ambassador on the spot, may be as good as it can get. On the other hand, the intelligence analysts and assessors have well-defined methodologies, checks and balances and peer review procedures that make it less likely that the answer will end up unconsciously biased to conform to the received wisdom of the day or to the prejudices of the policy customer (accepting that intelligence processes are not themselves always infallible in that respect either). On balance, both US and UK governments expect their strategic intelligence assessment bodies to have a stab at divining mysteries where these are relevant to major policy questions, but of course to make it clear (and clearer than it was, for example, in the case of the 2002 Iraqi WMD assessments) when the judgments in question rest on past assessments together with experience and feel and not on up to date specific secret intelligence.

The classification of an intelligence report or assessment is usually an indicator of how hard it was to obtain (such as by clever cryptography, recruitment of a very sensitively placed source or deployment of a sensitive high–tech sensor). But classification is no guide to the added value the intelligence can provide. It is often alleged that ministers are intoxicated by reading Top Secret (and higher) classified reports and give them undue weight over more mundane sources of information such as diplomatic or media reporting. There is some truth in this from my own observation, and the secret world is not above playing to the inherent theatricality of intelligence procedures. When, for example, a minister or senior official is indoctrinated, as the term has it, into a particularly sensitive line of reporting, elaborate arrangements will be made so that the material can be read in total security, and a stern warning will be given that the material may only be discussed with those on the list provided by the intelligence agency or department concerned. But ministers quickly learn where value added is to be found, and their Private Offices learn accordingly to be selective in the paper they send in to the minister. A greater danger is that busy ministers may not read carefully enough, if at all, regular strategic intelligence assessments and thus register that trouble is brewing until the signs of impending crisis become very evident and are reported in headline terms. These conflicting interactions between senior customers and the secret intelligence world deserve their own more detailed analysis, to be found in chapter 6.

A further level of complexity that is often present when assessing mysteries is the (quite normal) situation where the prediction of how a mystery itself will unfold depends upon assumptions by the intelligence analyst about the responses of one's own or allied governments. The timing and likelihood of the attack being threatened by the dictator on a neighbouring country may well depend upon whether he will be deterred by the fear of reprisals, and that in turn will depend upon his intelligence assessment of the likelihood that one's own government will respond, and that in turn may depend upon precautionary actions and messages of support to the threatened state that one's own government may not yet have decided upon. Such complexities represent the most difficult challenges for intelligence analysts. Thus, for example, it is likely that the Argentine junta brought forward their plans to invade the Falkland Islands in the spring of 1982 as a result of Argentine intelligence misperceptions of media reports of a UK submarine sailing from Gibraltar as meaning that it was heading for the South Atlantic (it was in fact secretly heading for northern waters). The UK JIC had previously correctly assessed the Argentine capability to undertake an invasion, an accurate assessment of a secret, and predicted a window of danger in autumn 1982, a good assessment of a mystery, but failed to recognize the Argentine leadership's misreading of the submarine report and thus failed to assess that in Argentine eyes the invasion window was closing. The UK was thus caught by tactical surprise, a failure to unravel a complexity.

Governments should not expect to receive a flow of pre-emptive intelligence that would allow them virtually to eliminate risk in their policies, for example in detecting and disrupting preparations for terrorist attacks or in launching a diplomatic initiative over some trouble-spot overseas, nor should the public be led to believe that this may be possible. There can be no perfect foreknowledge. Secrets are hard to find out, mysteries are hard to assess, and complexities involve second-guessing the moves of one's own side. Attempts to reduce or transfer risk may simply cause it to pop up unexpectedly elsewhere. It may be better to leave some risks where they can be assessed and managed rather than eliminated, such as keeping an eye on intelligence activity in London by overseas governments where this is not directed against British interests. Even with plentiful secret intelligence, properly analyzed and acted upon, unexpected events will nevertheless sometimes intervene and produce surprising outcomes. Chapter 7 is therefore devoted to the problems for government of living with, and not being surprised by, surprise.

Maintaining a serious intelligence community is an expensive continuing investment for a nation. It is hard for governments to judge when the point of diminishing returns is being approached from the considerable expenditure involved. Secret intelligence is intended to add value to the quality of important areas of decision-making in government, whether in helping decide what is the best course of action to deal with threats, civil and military, or in helping construct sounder policies to manage future risks. It follows that intelligence (secret or otherwise) is information that has value to decision-takers, and that is how its value is conventionally assessed by the agencies in customer feedback. But that is only part of the story. Intelligence capability is also by way of being an insurance policy that the necessary intelligence support will be there when it comes to be most needed. Given the time taken to develop technical systems and recruit and train the right personnel and build networks of trust overseas, if at least the core capability is not in being on which expansion in a crisis can be built, then governments will be caught flat-footed. The same argument applies to continuity of coverage, so that there is an evidence base of understanding of the issues, people and culture requiring study when the call comes. The problems in obtaining reliable intelligence before the US-led intervention into Iraq in 2003 dramatically illustrated the problems that arise when, as happened after the first Gulf War, coverage is scaled back for financial reasons when an immediate crisis is over.

The legitimacy of intelligence work

There has been a shift in most countries towards regarding secret intelligence as a legitimate and therefore avowed part of government, encouraged in the case of many emergent democracies by support from UK agencies helping them establish a proper constitutional and legal basis for intelligence activities. Intelligence remains, however, a rather special part of government given the steps—covertly observing troop movements, running agents, obtaining confidential documents, and all the rest—that have to be taken in order to circumvent the obstacles to collecting it. The very intrusiveness of the methods of assessing secret intelligence, both traditional and using modern technology, and their potential use by civil government and by private industry for purposes well beyond the confines of national security can create problems of public acceptability. As explored in chapter 10, those special steps often involve moral hazard for those involved, and that inevitably brings ethical issues into play: the world of secret intelligence is not, at least in the UK, seen as an ethics-free area of government activity.

There is a long history of informers and agents, intercepted letters and despatches being collected on behalf of military commanders and rulers from earliest recorded history, but not usually as an openly acknowledged activity. In the second half of the fifteenth century King Henry VII of England set up his own personal intelligence system after his victory at Bosworth Field in 1485, which was developed by succeeding monarchs into an effective intelligence gathering apparatus. Such were the precarious circumstances of the reigns of Charles II and James II that their attention was on countering domestic subversion, and not the rise of foreign competition, in particular the development of the Dutch navy. After the disaster of the war with Holland, parliament resolved in 1689 that a fixed sum of money should be paid for the acquisition of overseas intelligence. That was the beginning of the Foreign Secret Service Fund or Secret Vote (today known as the Single Intelligence Account, or SIA), a device of great convenience whereby the government would be voted the funds to pay for secret intelligence without having to account for it in detail or to acknowledge the existence of those conducting the activity itself.

In the late nineteenth and early twentieth centuries intelligence on enemy dispositions and capabilities became an essential input for the military and naval staffs then being created in European capitals. A practice emerged, notably in France after the defeat of the Franco-Prussian war, followed by the United States and most of the rest of the world, to specialize the collection of intelligence about foreign powers into the hands of separate agencies of government rather than leave this activity to personal contacts and informal networks. The German invasion scares of the first few years of the twentieth century led to further developments in both France, with a reactivation of the Deuxième Bureau (that had fallen on hard times after the scandal of the Dreyfus affair) and the founding of the Renseignements Généraux, and in Britain, with the creation (1909) of a British Secret Service Bureau. As a Foreign Office minute of 1909 put it, it was 'most important that the Admiralty and the War Office should rely on their own secret sources of intelligence, the organization of which should be as highly developed and efficient as possible'. The British Secret Service Bureau was to provide secret intelligence for the Admiralty and the War Office, to be funded from the Secret Vote, but quickly separated into the external MI6 or Secret Intelligence Service and domestic MI5 or Security Service. Shortly after the end of the First World War the Government Code and Cypher School had joined them as the UK cryptographic department, responsible to the Chief of SIS but operating as a separate organization. It was later re-established after the Second World War as the separate UK SIGINT Agency, Government Communications Headquarters (GCHQ). Those three agencies still define the core of the UK intelligence community and similar functions in respect of the collection of intelligence to be found across most of Europe. Notwithstanding slightly different national arrangements, in particular the strength of the links to defence and the extent of involvement in signals intelligence, the existence of domestic security and external HUMINT agencies is widespread and legitimized by national legislation.

A key issue for many countries is whether secret intelligence by espionage should be confined to activities and intentions of foreigners who threaten national security or whether these capabilities should be available to be directed inwards towards domestic targets that threaten the state. Most nations have chosen to restrict their secret intelligence services to the collection of foreign intelligence, plus for some the ability to conduct covert paramilitary operations overseas, and have wished to have separate arrangements for intelligence and security work related to domestic threats such as uncovering intelligence penetrations of government by foreign powers and countering domestic subversion. The FBI Director J. Edgar Hoover prohibited the US wartime Office of Strategic Services (OSS) from conducting any domestic espionage activities,[13] and when in 1947 the US Congress legislated to set up the CIA, the subject matter of the agency was specifically designed to be 'foreign intelligence' and 'counterintelligence'. The term 'foreign intelligence' is defined in the US Statute to mean information relating to the capabilities, intentions or activities of foreign governments or elements thereof, foreign organizations, or foreign persons, or international terrorist activities. The term 'counterintelligence' covers information gathered, and activities conducted, to protect against espionage, other intelligence activities, sabotage, or assassinations conducted by or on behalf of foreign governments or elements thereof, foreign organizations, or foreign persons, or international terrorist activities. A similar approach was taken much later by the UK parliament in legislating in 1994 to put the Secret Intelligence Service onto a statutory footing. The functions of SIS are similarly focused externally: to obtain and provide information relating to the actions or intentions of persons outside the British Islands, and to perform other tasks relating to the actions or intentions of such persons (including disrupting their plans as, for example, was seen in the successful work to neutralize the AQ Khan proliferation network).

A number of reasons can be adduced as to why nations have chosen to keep domestic and external intelligence work separate, given what would at first sight seem to be the efficiencies from having a single organization. One good reason rests on the suspicion of the political influence that a single agency, privy to so many secrets, might be able to deploy. The career of J. Edgar Hoover in the US makes the point, and his responsibilities were domestic. Another, a distaste for the act of spying on one's own citizens and therefore the need to have greater domestic accountability, something naturally falling to the Justice or Interior Minister (in the case of the UK, the Home Secretary) of the day, than would be necessary for overseas operations for which the Foreign Minister would carry the can in case of diplomatic embarrassment. Yet another reason might be (mostly) benign operating conditions domestically as against having to collect intelligence in a potentially hostile nation overseas, leading to rather different recruitment and operational requirements. A more fundamental strand of thinking would also lay emphasis on the difference between an 'intelligence' and a 'security' agency. The primary task of the former is as we have seen to collect foreign intelligence that will add value to the decisions taken by government. Such intelligence is, amongst other things, a means towards the end that is national security. The primary function of a domestic service was traditionally not to collect and distribute to policy customers intelligence on domestic enemies (although that may well happen) but to neutralize domestic threats to the state. Domestic intelligence is therefore collected in the UK by the Security Service to drive its own security operations, supported by the police, against threats that the Service itself determines require disruption, in its statutory role (sometimes described as its 'self-tasking' role).

The Canadian experience is illuminating since it both clarifies the differences between intelligence and law enforcement work and illustrates how countries are having to adapt to ways in which the dividing line between the domestic and overseas domains has become porous to international threats such as from Al-Qa'ida. Until 1984 domestic security and intelligence work in Canada was conducted by a branch of the Royal Canadian Mounted Police (RCMP). Under pressure from a succession of espionage cases, and terrorist and subversive activities, a separate organization was set up: the Canadian Security Intelligence Service (CSIS) whose 'proactive role contrasts with the reactive one of law enforcement agencies such as police forces, which investigate crime and collect evidence to support prosecutions in courts of law', to quote the official CSIS line. In recent years, given the international nature of terrorism, CSIS, although a domestic service, has had to operate overseas, and to acknowledge that fact, in order to be able to obtain intelligence to prevent terrorist acts from being planned in Canada, from occurring on Canadian territory and from affecting Canadian citizens and assets abroad.

Whatever the reasons to explain the past, almost universal, separation of national arrangements for domestic and foreign intelligence, it is today in the nature of national security work against threats such as international terrorist and other criminal networks that the targets span the domestic and overseas spaces. However intelligence and security services are organized, there needs to be a very high degree of cooperation between domestic and external agencies. This theme, of the demands of modern national security strategy on national intelligence communities, is developed in chapter 11.

There are also some distinct national differences in the relationships between security and intelligence agencies and law enforcement (that is, organizations staffed by officers with police powers including the power of arrest). US and UK practice diverges sharply, for example when it comes to the collection of secret intelligence on domestic threats. Secret intelligence in respect of domestic threats has in the US always been seen as a law enforcement function for which, in the most serious of cases, Federal authority would be exercised by the Federal Bureau of Investigation, the FBI. When the CIA, outside its mandate, engaged in Vietnam war related domestic surveillance of the political activities of US citizens, the result was scandal. The 1975 Senate 'Church Commission' of Inquiry into US intelligence activities followed the revelations of the Watergate era and concluded that intelligence activities had undermined the constitutional rights of US citizens and that they had done so primarily because checks and balances designed by the framers of the Constitution to assure accountability had not been applied. The Committee did not question the need for lawful domestic intelligence and that certain intelligence activities serve perfectly proper and clearly necessary ends of government. Catching spies and stopping crime, including acts of terrorism, were judged essential to ensure 'domestic tranquility' and to 'provide for the common defense'. The question was over what should be the effective restraints and controls over the power of government to conduct proper domestic intelligence activities. One outcome was the creation of the Senate Select Committee on Intelligence and the passing of the Foreign Intelligence Surveillance Act and setting up the Foreign Intelligence Surveillance Court to warrant intrusive interception operations. The attacks on 9/11 triggered a renewed policy debate across the US as to whether the Church findings had generated too restrictive an environment for collecting intelligence on terrorists and whether there would be value in having an internal domestic purely intelligence gathering and analysis body separate from the FBI (which has law enforcement powers). It turned out that there was little public appetite for domestic espionage, a topic that raised deep hostility as being contrary to the founding spirit of the Republic.

In the UK on the other hand no special police powers for investigation or arrest were given to the officers of the Security Service, which legally did not exist until 1984. The only government codification of the remit of the Security Service was in an administrative charter governing the Security Service's work, the so-called Maxwell-Fyfe Directive—named after the Home Secretary who issued it in 1952. This brief document emphasized the role of the Service in the 'Defence of the Realm' as a whole, from external and *internal* dangers arising from attempts at espionage or sabotage, or from actions of persons and organizations, whether directed from within or without the country, which may be judged subversive of the State'[14] (my emphasis). The story of the decision to put the Security Service onto a statutory footing is told in chapter 10. Here it is worth noting that its statutory aims (Section 1 of the 1989 Act) are the protection of national security, including (but not limited to) protection against threats from espionage, terrorism and sabotage, and from the activities of agents of foreign powers, and 'counter-subversion', i.e. 'actions intended to overthrow or undermine parliamentary democracy by political, industrial or violent means'. In addition, both SIS and the Security Service have the function to safeguard the economic wellbeing of the UK from external threats and (under the Security Service Act 1996) to assist in the prevention or detection of serious crime—supporting but not taking the lead from law enforcement.

For the signals intelligence and interception organizations, in both the United States and the UK, there are subtly different distinctions between the authority they have domestically and against overseas targets. For the UK the essential legal distinction is between interception of a communication originating in the UK to a recipient in the UK, that is a domestic call of some sort, and a communication with at least one participant overseas. For domestic interception (whether of

British nationals or foreigners) a strict domestic legal regime applies requiring a warrant signed by a Secretary of State. For the case where there is overseas interception (at least one party is overseas and the target of interception is outside the UK) there is a more general Secretary of State authorization which requires that the interception is in accordance with purposes set out in statute, notably in the interests of national security. All interception (domestic and overseas) must be adjudged to be necessary and proportionate by the Secretary of State and those carrying out the interception. In the case of the United States, on the other hand, the approach is to have the strictest regime of authorization applying to the interception of communications of US citizens wherever they may be in the world, with a more general authorization applying to the communications of foreign nationals, wherever they may be.

Taking anticipatory action may also involve measures out of the public eye using the secret knowledge the intelligence community has acquired. The ability to pursue policies in the dark, which nations cannot afford to be seen to be doing in the light, has however sometimes proved too tempting because it appears to be an easy win, like a surprise attack in warfare, and so it may prove in the short term as temporary advantage, whether from covertly equipped forces, secretly acquired intelligence or subverted malcontents, is pressed home. But once the surprise is over, the laws of war and diplomacy reassert themselves and the long-run outcome may not be favourable. As Machiavelli described the fifteenth century prospects for taking over France by subversion:

'You can easily invade if you win over one of the barons. There always exist malcontents and those who want a change. These, for the reasons explained, can open up the state to you and facilitate your victory. But subsequently, when you want to maintain your rule, you run into countless difficulties, as regards both those who have helped you and those you had subjugated. Nor is it enough for you to have destroyed the ruler's family, because there still remain nobles to raise insurrections; and being able neither to satisfy them nor to destroy them you lose the state as soon as their opportunity presents itself.'[15]

3

FORTITUDIO

THE PUBLIC VALUE OF RESILIENCE

The fragility of living in cities

We glimpsed in chapter 1 a vivid depiction of the fears of fourteenth century Siena of what bad government might allow, in the form of insecurity, diseased citizens roaming a crumbling and dangerous city, with the enemy at the open gate. In that era there would have been a profound sense among the civic leaders that urban life was fragile. The systems of support (what today we would call the 'national infrastructure') were easily disrupted, whether by natural hazards, a bad harvest, extreme weather, earthquake, or disease, or by threats created by warring neighbours. Hence the emphasis on the effects of Good Government, deliberately creating the conditions to allow the citizens to go about their daily business freely and with confidence, with the granaries full, the wells clean, the walls and streets of the city kept in good repair and the watchtowers manned with guards alert. The motivation for government attention to these issues today is no different. The UK definition of an emergency is a situation or series of events that threatens or causes serious damage to human welfare, the environment or security.[1] Being able to cope with emergencies that threaten these domains of health, welfare and personal security is now regarded as a principal task of government today. It was no accident that the figure representing Good Government in Siena was flanked by Fortitude and Prudence, and overseen by the winged figure of Security. We need their support as much today.

The city today has regained comparable importance in the life of the nation as in the era of Renaissance city-states. About one-third of the UK population lives in seven large urban agglomerations. It is impossible now to imagine a purely agrarian and pastoral Western society. The last such visions, never pursued to their conclusion, were Gandhi's intention for an independent India to be an agrarian society shunning modernization, and the 1944 Morgenthau proposal for post-Nazi Germany to be not only de-militarized but de-industrialized to prevent a resurgence of the capacity to wage war. Cities now dominate industrializing as well as industrialized nations, with the mega-city with a population of tens of millions common and over half of the world's population living in urban areas. Urban life on that scale can only continue through the maintenance of highly complex social and technical systems, ranging from the supply of food and water and the disposal of waste to the provision of shelter, heating and light, the ability to clear financial transactions, and mass transit systems to move people to and from work.

The ability to produce and distribute electric power is central to all these social systems, including supporting the electronic data communications that are today the nervous system of the body politic. All those systems are vulnerable to disruption, whether by natural hazards or malicious threats, and once disrupted can cause cascading failures throughout other essential services. The widespread use of internet technology to pass data globally between systems has now also created new vulnerabilities in cyberspace, where an attacker 'outside the walls of the city' can penetrate to its heart, perhaps assisted by supporters inside who can metaphorically open the gates to the intruder, and create confusion or worse by disrupting the flow of information between citizens, commerce and government.

Organizing for resilience

A government seeking to create future security for its citizens must therefore seek to reduce the risks created by urban fragility. How is that to be done? We can calibrate attempts to reduce the risks to public security from disruptive events by examining the product of four factors, measuring the value of the expected outcome as the product.

Expected value of risk = (likelihood) × (vulnerability) × (initial disruption × duration) often written more simply as

Risk = (likelihood) × (vulnerability) × (impact)

The first factor in this equation upon which government can work is the likelihood of the risk arising in the first place. Sound external policies and vigorous law enforcement domestically can reduce (although almost certainly not guarantee the elimination of) threats such as from terrorism or serious crime. Such anticipatory action will rely upon good intelligence and pre-emptive action by the security authorities, as was discussed in the previous chapters. Natural hazards are by their nature less amenable to prevention, but provided that sufficient notice can be provided of their arrival then mitigation may be possible. Having a tsunami warning system will significantly reduce the expected number of casualties when such events arise, as they did causing huge casualties in the Indian Ocean and South Pacific region in 2004, and again in 2009.

The second factor in the equation is vulnerability, recognizing that the first factor, the probability of threats and hazards arising, cannot be reduced to zero or near zero. By examining the vulnerability of the workings of the city and its systems to disruptive events, measures can be designed to make the city and its population (and of course by extension the wider nation) a harder target through protective security affecting people, physical infrastructure and information, and through building in redundancy into critical systems.

The third factor, recognizing that there will be both unexpected events arising and remaining vulnerabilities that can be exploited, is impact—the scale of the effect on society. By preparing in advance to be able to respond effectively when untoward events happen, lives can be saved and property protected and the impact of the event blunted. A key here is the maintenance or restoration of essential services and dealing effectively with the human and material damage caused by a successful attack or other disruption. Examples of what can be done include building up the emergency services and ensuring that they are ready and trained to manage disruptive challenges; encouraging business continuity planning in the private and public sectors; and equipping health services with vaccines and stocks of anti–viral agents.

The severity of any disruption will also be related to its duration. The longer a disruptive event lasts, the more damage it is likely to cause. Anticipating the types of challenge and taking steps to be able to restore services quickly can materially reduce the damage likely to be done, for example by ensuring that inventories of replacement components and spare parts are available for critical facilities, such as power transformers or natural gas pumping equipment whose loss would produce severe dislocation. In assessing potential disruption, the initial effect and its possible duration are often for convenience lumped together under the heading 'impact'.

There are obvious links between measures to reduce vulnerability and impact (or as they are termed in the UK counter-terrorist strategy, measures to 'protect' and to 'prepare'). Together they make up what has been termed *national resilience*, strengthening the overall ability of society to bounce back as quickly as practicable into the patterns of normal life after a major disruption. Resilience is a term borrowed from the metallurgists, as originally meaning the capacity of a material to withstand an impact and bounce back again into shape quickly. Pursuing this metaphor, an impact delivers kinetic energy to the material, which deforms under the blow. If the material is resilient then little of the energy is absorbed into the inner structure, and thus little internal damage is done, and most of the energy is returned as the material flexes back into its original shape.

How then to make the city more resilient? An obvious necessary step is creating the capacity in government to lead work on resilience planning and to be able to manage effectively the response to a disruptive challenge. This is activity that is going to involve all parts of government and all sectors of society. Modern government, however, is so complex that we cannot hope centrally to plan and coordinate all the contributory activities to building resilience. Even at the domestic level, a coherent approach to resilience is going to involve government working through many independent organizations in the private sector, at local level and even at voluntary community level. Many of these contributing organizations are not, and short of wartime conditions cannot be, 'under command'. Instead, the approach must be to establish consensus over the threats and hazards to be faced and the strategic objectives to be secured, to build strategic partnerships to work together, but all the time recognizing that what is being sought is the freely given alignment of independent actors working to a shared purpose and inspired by the same goals. Internationally, it is even more essential to apply the same approach, given cultural differences and national sensibilities.

Along with the analysis of risks and vulnerabilities arising overseas goes the parallel consequence that solutions too require international action. The activities to that end are likely to be more mutually reinforcing if their various decisions are guided by understanding of and general sympathy for the 'Grand Strategy' being followed. For the UK, this has significant implications for national leadership, for the framing of strategy and for the international presentation of the shared values that underlie it. The strategic paradigm must be the 'Nelsonian' rather than the 'Napoleonic' model of leadership. For the United States, in particular, this represents a challenge under President Obama to rebuild 'soft power' and moral leadership,[2] as well as having the capacity and will to deploy hard power when national interests demand it. Next, however, let us examine the capacity of government to respond effectively when under challenge, whether from man-made threats or natural hazards.

The role of good government in managing crises

The UK's current arrangements for protecting the public from a terrorist incident date back to a set of inter-departmental arrangements that were made after the terrorist attack on Israeli athletes at the Munich Olympics in 1972, to ensure that teams of specially trained and equipped British armed forces from the Special Air Service (SAS) and the Special Boat Service (SBS) would be available on standby in case of a terrorist hostage-taking or hijacking, and to develop the doctrine of 'aid to the civil power' to allow their deployment at the request of and under the operational direction of a Chief Officer of Police. A Cabinet Office conference room was turned into a specially equipped Cabinet Office Briefing Room (COBR, or COBRA as it is now popularly known) to allow government ministers, as the civil power, to link with the relevant police Chief Constable and the military command chain. This essential command and control arrangement was used not long after it was set up during the siege of PIRA terrorists in Balcombe Street, London in 1975 and in the ending of the terrorist hostage taking at the Iranian Embassy in 1980, as well as dealing with several aircraft hijackings during that period. COBR was subsequently developed into a purpose-built situation centre with the capacity to house teams of senior officials with their secure communications from the main government departments, the intelligence community and the police. COBR thus became the focal point for inter-departmental liaison and for obtaining ministerial strategic direction for counter-terrorist and defence operations.

Governments do not, however, normally like to use publicly the word 'crisis' in referring to their arrangements, preferring terms such as 'emergency' or, most recently, 'disruptive challenge', for fear that the mention of crisis may evoke in the citizen the critical thought that government is expecting to lose control and will be unable to provide protection. Returning in 1979 to a strike-torn Britain after a summit in Guadeloupe, Prime Minister Callaghan remarked, 'I promise you that if you look at it from outside, and perhaps you're taking rather a parochial view at the moment, I don't think that other people in the world would share the view that there is mounting chaos.' The *Sun* newspaper memorably summed up his point in their headline the following day: 'Crisis, what crisis', a phrase that acted as the obituary of the Callaghan government.

There has been a committee of the British Cabinet nominated to deal with emergencies in one form or another since the General Strike of 1926. Currently called the Civil Contingencies Committee, it has the remit 'to consider, in an emergency, plans for assuring the supplies and services essential to the life of the community and to supervise their prompt and effective implementation where required'. The focus of attention for most of its existence has been on mitigating the effects of civil disruption caused by industrial (in)action, notably the miners' strikes of 1972, 1974 and 1984/5 and the dock strike of 1989. The Committee has the ability to activate emergency legislation to provide additional powers for the government to keep the country running in a major emergency, the latest version of which is the Civil Contingencies Act 2004. The committee is a mixed group of ministers and senior officials, police and military officers with the Home Secretary as Chair of this committee and a senior official in the Cabinet Office the Deputy Chair.

In parallel, during the Cold War, the UK central government funded local government to make arrangements for civil defence (that is, arrangements in order to minimize the inevitable casualties should the nation come under attack, as against 'home defence', the term used to describe the protection of the ability of the nation to prepare for war and resist direct attack). Vestigial structures were retained from the massive civil defence arrangements of the Second World War (the capacity, for example, to sound alerts by siren, to have a few emergency planners in each local authority, and to maintain essential communications with the seat of government), but in the knowledge that there could be no effective protection of the population from nuclear attack. National security rested on deterrence through NATO of armed aggression. A small team in the Home Office coordinated the civil defence arrangements, but after the end of the Cold War the funding for these activities was further run down to the point where they ceased to provide an effective national structure, although still maintaining local capacity to plan for disasters such as major industrial pollution incidents and transport accidents.

This lack of national preparedness for crisis was brutally exposed by a series of civil calamities that affected much of the UK around the turn of the twentieth century involving severe flooding, a serious fuel shortage caused by disruption to the supply chain, and an outbreak of animal (foot and mouth) disease. The major disruption of fuel supplies within the UK in September 2000 in particular revealed how potentially serious the consequences for normal life would be if domestic fuel supplies were interrupted.

That crisis was the first time that a UK government had recognized the extent to which a modern economy was dependent on complex supply chains and how 'just-in-time' value engineering had reduced the buffering that stocks of goods and work in progress would have provided in a previous era. Most people ran their motor cars less than half full of fuel; the hint of a shortage and everyone filled up, and in a prosperous age of multi–car families that was enough in many areas to empty the fuel distribution system overnight. Traditional measures, such as wartime fuel rationing systems to choke off demand and to channel supply to priority users, begged the question of who, in a modern peace-time economy, was a priority user. An inconclusive traditional meeting of the Civil Contingencies Committee chaired by the Home Secretary at the start of the emergency revealed widespread confusion in government over what measures might be applicable. 'This is shaping up to be a disaster. How are we going to manage this?' asked the Home Secretary, and my reply as the Deputy Chair of the committee was that we should run the emergency response as we would for a major terrorist incident, through the Cabinet Office Briefing Room (COBR), using procedures for counter-terrorist information management and decision-taking in which ministers, officials and police had all been trained. Adapting the CT procedures to a civil emergency proved straightforward in principle but time-consuming in practice. Eventually representatives of the oil companies were installed, with their laptops linked to their company logistic systems, in the COBR under the directions of a senior Home Office official and a Chief Officer of Police, to make the best use of the fuel available to keep the country running. Their work and the discipline associated with the 'battle rhythm' of COBR helped restore confidence and buy extra time for a political solution to the dispute to be found, which was just as well since it proved a close-run thing.

The inevitable inquiries after the 2000 fuel crisis and the other emergencies of the period confirmed that major gaps had developed in emergency communications, especially between central and local government, and proved the wisdom of building much stronger central capacity in government to provide strategic direction in an emergency, with a properly equipped situation centre in which a recognized information picture could be developed and presented to decision-makers. It was recognized—a turning point in thinking about resilience—that modern urbanized economies are inherently fragile, and the critical infrastructure upon which ordinary life depends does itself rest on the availability of power and modern telecommunications. The concept of resilience was taking shape. The residual Home Office civil emergencies capability was transferred to the centre of government in the Cabinet Office, and a larger dedicated team, the Civil Contingencies Secretariat, started work to plan national resilience in July 2001, including planning new UK civil contingencies legislation. The work was thus just getting into its stride when the terrorist attacks in New York and Washington on 9/11, 2001 changed everything.

After the 9/11 attacks in the US, urgent arrangements were made to complete the bringing of civil contingency planning and counter-terrorist response planning together under a single operational doctrine, reflecting the reality that the consequences of any serious cascading disruption, such as loss of electricity supply, would have to be managed regardless of whether the cause was accident, natural hazard or malign intent through terrorism or sabotage. By 2003, the UK government had its counter-terrorist strategy, CONTEST, with four strategic campaigns: Pursue (near term) and Prevent (longer term) to reduce the likelihood of terrorist attack; Protect to reduce the vulnerability of the public and of national infrastructure to attack; and Prepare to reduce the impact and duration of disruption from attacks should they take place, integrating all the work done on civil contingencies and ensuring that the arrangements are well exercised. In the United States, 'homeland security' was the term used to describe the protection of the public after the attacks of 9/11, but that was a term not much liked in UK security circles, who saw the creation of the giant US Department of Homeland Security as a precedent not to follow. The UK already had the Home Office, and the Security Service with its protective security role, and a focus on 'homeland' defence run counter to the increasing recognition that the domestic and overseas threats were intimately linked.

Despite the existence of a proactive function at the centre of UK government to drive work on this US concept of 'homeland security', the fundamental principle in the UK was that the structure of emergency management should remain decentralized.[3] Whilst central government would need in an emergency to be able to provide central strategic direction, finance and, when appropriate, legislation, the command of the emergency services on the scene would rest with the police. It was recognized that there are many incidents whose scale or complexity are such that they can be perfectly well handled at a local level without activating COBR and central government. All emergencies are in the end local, and 'blue light' services and local government and voluntary organizations are always the first on the scene and the ones who carry the burden of protecting the public, providing rescue, emergency shelter, clothing, food and water.

For major incidents in Great Britain, the framework of management of response and recovery under the strategic direction of COBR is organized into three levels, which differ from each other based on their functions rather than rank, grade or status. 'Bronze' level is the description of the management of immediate 'hands-on' work undertaken at the site(s) of the emergency or other affected areas. Responders and agencies working at this level on the scene must act together and coordinate with all other agencies in order to sustain integrated effort. 'Silver' level commanders at the next level up will coordinate and integrate the activities of Bronze commanders in order to achieve maximum effectiveness. The Silver commander would be expected to form an incident command point located close to the scene. At the strategic level, the 'Gold' commander is a senior police officer, who forms a Strategic Coordinating Group (SCG) to bring together the senior

(Gold) commanders from Fire and Rescue, Ambulance, Public Health, Power services and other utilities, local government and appropriate organizations and agencies. Once they come together they establish the operational framework within which Silver commanders will work. Usually the police will provide the lead in the SCG, though the UK doctrine provides for other agencies to be able when necessary to take the lead, such as in public health emergencies and animal disease outbreaks.

One value of having this formal hierarchy below COBR, regardless of the type of incident, is that it emphasizes the devolved nature of emergency response. In a crisis, as in war, there is fog and friction, and no central authority can possibly have sufficiently up-to-date information to make operational and tactical decisions. Within the framework of established and practised doctrine, the immediate operational response can be left to those closest to the action, with government providing the necessary back-up and strategic direction as it looks beyond the immediate priorities of saving lives and property. As Lt.-Gen. Rupert Smith, one of the UK's most experienced commanders, has put the point,[4] 'As a general rule, the further away you are from the point of execution in time and space, the less likely you are to know all the facts and figures, and therefore you can't give any kind of detailed orders, therefore you must state what it is you wish to achieve rather than what others are to do.'

Critical National Infrastructure: a framework for resilience planning

In my three years as Security and Intelligence Coordinator in the Cabinet Office I worked on the development of the concept of the Critical National Infrastructure, or CNI. The origins of the concept lie in the Cold War, when arrangements were made to engage local authorities in planning to minimize casualties and disruption should war break out (for example, using the emergency powers given by the Civil Defence Act of 1948 to commandeer civil assets). As knowledge of Soviet capabilities was built up during the Cold War, national 'key points' were identified as potential targets for enemy sabotage. These key points included transport nodes and key communications facilities that were essential to national survival and would have to be protected from disruption caused either by sabotage by subversive elements or by direct attack by Soviet special forces, the infamous *spetznatz*. Many of the key points related to the ability of the UK as a NATO member to move smoothly from a peacetime posture to a mobilized war footing (the so-called transition-to-war (TTW), or, as the senior civil servant Michael Cary for whom I later worked as a Private Secretary called it, the deadly gavotte). Taken together, the mapping of these key points provided a first crude indication of the vulnerabilities of the UK's infrastructure. In the 1970s and 1980s, the Provisional IRA mainland bombing campaigns created a new need for the Security Service to identify vulnerabilities of a different kind and to plan systematically for the protection of the public in crowded places such as railway stations and shopping centres. Protective security measures included personnel security and vetting arrangements; physical hardening through the installation of shatter-proof glass; relocation of car parking; and regular evacuation exercises. The intent was to reduce the severity of an attack and improve the ability if attacked to recover quickly—what is now termed resilience. For the key infrastructure nodes, whether transport hubs, power stations or telecommunications facilities, primary responsibility for planning security was given to the facility operator, which meant increasingly—given the privatization of most previously state-owned infrastructure—private sector operators. The role of the state was redefined to be the provision of security and technical advice and suitably sanitized intelligence, keeping the list of key points up to date, and providing reinforcing physical security when needed. The Security Service set up with the police an information clearing-house and advice centre, now known as the Centre for the Protection of National Infrastructure (CPNI), to include personnel and cyber security aspects as well as physical security. Individual government departments were designated as 'lead departments'[5] through which the operators of sectors of the infrastructure such as energy, communications and transport could connect to government planning.

That remains the basic UK model for the protection of the CNI, regarded as those assets, services and systems that support the economic, political and social life of the UK whose importance is such that any entire or partial loss or compromise could cause large-scale loss of life; have a serious impact on the national economy; have other grave social consequences for the community, or any substantial part of the community; or be of immediate concern to the national government. Drawing any neat distinction between those parts of the national infrastructure of the economy that are 'critical' to national survival and those that are not is, however, far from simple.

In a modern economy everything is connected in supply chains, many layers deep. As a child I remember that butter came in large rounds from which the grocer could cut off the amount required, pat it into shape and wrap it in paper. Today the supermarket sells it pre-weighed and pre-packaged from the factory in specialist plasticized or metallized wrappings, or already homogenized in plastic tubs to be more easily spreadable or pre-loaded with additional vitamins. To take a completely different example, a modern hospital operating theatre works on the basis that the necessary dressings, swabs etc. for each type of operation come pre-prepared in sterilized packages provided by commercial suppliers. In one instance during the 2000 fuel dispute, hospital operating theatres were threatened with closure, not because of lack of staff (since the emergency arrangements had been made to get them to work), nor lack of power (since emergency generators had been supplied), but because the company that supplied the packs of dressings for operations had run out of sterilized wrapping and the sub-contractor that supplied the rolls of wrapping had no access to motor fuel under the emergency rationing arrangements. Ministers discussed at length whether, for example, taxis should be considered essential vehicles to be put on the list of those entitled to priority access to fuel, or whether taxi rides were to be treated as luxury items to be done without at a time of national austerity. The latter view won the day, but had to be reversed within a few hours when it became clear that hospitals and schools had contracted already with local taxi firms to bring their essential staff to work given the disruption to public transport. After the crisis was over, I discovered in one of the volumes of the UK *Official History of the Second World War* that in 1940 government had debated the same point and made the same mistake.

The existence of supply chains makes cascading disruption more likely. There are nevertheless some fairly obvious elements of 'single-point failure' within national economic life whose loss or severe disruption would produce significant dislocation to normal life. There are also elements that if damaged will take a long time to repair or replace, prolonging the disruption to normal life. On any definition, it is not hard to imagine some of the types of facility that must be on the UK government's current list as comprising the heart of the nation's critical national infrastructure. The loss of a major fuel pipeline, communications hub, electricity substation and other such facilities are obvious examples of what must be guarded against. A modern reading of critical infrastructure would have to be much broader, responding to the way that everyday life requires the support of the essential services delivered by the communications industry, and financial systems to allow settlement of payments (90 per cent of UK high street purchases are now made with 'plastic cards', not cash). A striking example of vulnerability, that caused shock waves through the British establishment, was the uncovering by the UK security authorities in 1996 of a Provisional IRA plot to attack simultaneously a ring of six electricity substations serving London and the south-east of England. Had the attack been successful (the plot was disrupted and the terrorists convicted and given lengthy jail sentences), then cascading system failures would have meant millions of people would have been without electricity for months, with social consequences appalling to contemplate. At the trial of the PIRA gang, it was claimed that their leader had based his plan on a map of the electricity network from the annual *Electricity Supply Handbook* which he had taken from Battersea public library in London. Urgent action was taken to protect such facilities and to re-engineer networks to frustrate any future attempt to cause such damage, as well as restricting information that the public can access that might allow system weaknesses to be pin-pointed.

The UK now treats nine 'sectors' of economic, political and social activity as having such critical elements of infrastructure (the CNI). They are:

• Communications
• Emergency Services (police, fire and rescue, ambulance, maritime/ coastguard)
• Energy
• Finance
• Food
• Government and Public Service
• Health
• Transport
• Water

Clearly not every activity within these nine sectors would be essential to national survival: life can go on without cold-pressed olive oil and black peppercorns, although for many it would be less piquant.

Application of the concept of identifying the critical activities and paths can, however, in the government's own words, assist government and managers within each sector to identify where best to concentrate protective security effort. That encompasses physical security measures, personnel security for those insiders who have the key knowledge, and now the added dimension of cyber security as well. And, as is often pointed out, most of the relevant facilities and processes of the CNI are nowadays owned and managed by the private sector through commercial markets (even in the government sector of the CNI, there are key processes managed by contractors). If, for example, the logistic systems of the major supermarket chains were to suffer simultaneous disruption, then the effect on daily life would be significant since the UK's 'big four' (Tesco, Asda, Sainsbury's and Morrisons) are estimated to account for more than three-quarters of the grocery market.

Into cyberspace

There is one very significant transformation going on in all advanced economies that has a material effect on national resilience, and that is the increasing dependence of all sectors on networked information technology. Modern economic and social life depends on information flows and on databases, many of which must not under any foreseeable circumstances be allowed to become unreliable. Daily life is now dependent on information assurance regarding the information systems and data, control systems, networks and protocols (not just the internet protocol but others that control Border Gateways and Domain Name Systems) that support, facilitate or control critical global infrastructure. Obvious cases include international aviation systems; emergency positioning systems and satellite communications; the need for adequate records of the 100 million people who cross the UK border each year; and the identity databases underlying the social security and national registration processes.

Such 'information infrastructure' has not so far been treated as a separate sector, although it now has its own UK national cyber security strategy[6], and can better be thought of as a set of golden threads running through all the CNI sectors. The long expected convergence between computing and communications has now arrived, creating 'cyberspace', a domain that encompasses all forms of networked, digital activities transforming the content and effect as well as the form of modern information. The economic opportunities of this revolution are self-evidently huge, but so are the opportunities that are created for malicious exploitation by hostile states, terrorists and criminals, as well as the latent risks of cascading failures rippling through the economy when problems arise. Network connectivity through the internet enables attackers 'outside the city walls' to penetrate to its heart and disrupt daily life. As the dependence of modern economies upon cyberspace increases so does the need to provide improved electronic defences. The UK government has set up an Office of Cyber Security (OCS) to provide strategic leadership for government in this domain as well as a multi–agency Cyber Security Operations Centre (CSOC) hosted by GCHQ to monitor actively the health of cyber space and coordinate the response to incidents.

The leading edge of the cyber threat at present comes from crime creating a malicious e-marketplace. With the sums accessible in electronic transactions, that is hardly surprising. The threat landscape is coming to be dominated by emerging phenomena such as customizable modular malicious code and networks of computers being remotely controlled by criminals and used to mount mass denial of service attacks. Targeted attacks on individuals by 'phishing' attacks to divulge personal account details, or on web applications and web browsers, are increasingly becoming the focal point for cybercriminals. An offence/defence race is underway between the criminals and the suppliers of anti–virus products and other security software. Criminal gains are considerable: it has been estimated that there were over 250,000 cases of online financial fraud in the UK in 2007, generating losses of some £535 million; global online fraud was estimated by the UK police as generating revenue of £52 billion in 2007. An estimate of UK identity fraud alone is that it costs £1.3 billion a year, and there are considerable additional costs for the citizen affected: it can take 300 hours of work to put personal records in order after a case of stolen identity.

At the same time, the most sophisticated forms of attack are those launched by states for the purpose of penetrating government and private sector networks for intelligence gathering purposes or, it is suspected, in order to plant malicious computer code that could be activated when needed in order to cripple the defences and armed forces capability at a time of tension or conflict. Some states also encourage and benefit from so-called 'patriotic hackers' who attack

71

foreign systems to uncover vulnerabilities or to disrupt activities, safe in the knowledge that they will not be prosecuted in their home country. Examples of offensive activity included the use of large numbers of infected computers (botnets) of unsuspecting users to launch tens of thousands of messages a second at Estonian government, banking and internet systems in April and May 2007, severely disrupting normal life. Similar Distributed Denial of Service (DDOS) attacks took place on Georgia at the time of its conflict over South Ossetia with Russia in 2008. Military forces are naturally extremely interested in cyber-warfare as a way of disrupting enemy defences. It was, for example, alleged that Israeli cyber-attacks on Syrian air defence networks assisted the Israeli airforce attack on a nuclear construction facility in September 2007. The South Korean government has claimed that North Korea has trained over 500 hackers through a five-year university course teaching methods of cyber-attack and that they have been the subject of DDOS attacks orchestrated from the north. The shape of such warfare is thus becoming clear. Such attacks can however be bounced off many intermediaries, using false flags, creating great difficulties in attributing cyber-attacks back to the originator sufficiently reliably to justify counter-measures in self-defence.

It would seem only a matter of time before neo-jihadist terrorists acquire and use cyber-attack capabilities, possibly by buying the services of criminal hackers, although so far they have preferred more traditional high explosives and guns. Terrorists have, however, mastered the internet as a medium for covert and overt communications, propaganda and training. The cyber-domain seems bound to become a battleground for counter-terrorism.

The information and communications industry naturally focuses on cyber-threats that use the technology itself as the vector. With malicious cryptography and crypto-virology, armoured viruses that are resistant to counter-measures or mutate to avoid detection, and other dangerous exotica in the cyber-zoo, the offence/defence race has become all but incomprehensible to the non-expert. But terrorist use of high explosive, or anthrax, against the critical infrastructure—especially if supported on the inside (a clear parallel with the world of conventional criminality)—could be just as devastating to the functioning of the information architecture supporting business and government alike. For many companies, however, physical security is organizationally and culturally entirely separate from personnel security and from those thinking about the technology vectored cyber-threats. And of course the role that the insider can play in guiding the attackers through the cyber-defences is often downplayed, because doing something about it may be seen as costing competitive edge—until, that is, disaster strikes. The Home Office in their publication *Business as Usual*, which looked at the aftermath of terrorist attacks on the economic infrastructure in the UK with especial reference to the bomb that devastated the centre of Manchester in 1996, state that research has shown that 80 per cent of small businesses without business recovery plans fail within one year of a major disruption. The London Chamber of Commerce and Industry has highlighted[7] that many UK businesses do not have plans for recovery after an incident, and in the event of a data failure 90 per cent would go out of business.

Inside the term 'critical national infrastructure', however, it is possible to sense that there are different meanings struggling to get out. The term CNI inescapably carries traces of its historical origins in key point protection described earlier, with a bias inevitably towards defence, and civil-defence, related installations. The whole subject was therefore for many years shrouded in special arrangements for security reasons with, for example, only cleared personnel in certain listed companies receiving classified briefings on the physical and personnel threats to their installations. The less said to the public the better. A very different approach is now appropriate if we are to have what I have described elsewhere[8] as 'the new protecting state' in which the active participation of individuals, communities and companies needs to be sought to reduce the overall level of risk.

Second generation resilience

The concept of resilience can be given a moral as well as a physical component if we think of the ability of society to face dangers with fortitude in order to to continue with normal life and to hold fast to cherished values, constitutional practices and the rule of law. Security in cities is not just a matter of physical protection, but rests upon civic harmony that in turn rests on consent by the governed. What makes great cities tick is an indefinable quality of human relationships and implicit conventions that make it possible for very large numbers of people to live, work and travel cheek by jowl yet preserve good humour and a village sense of belonging to a neighbourhood. These intangibles are precious assets to be cultivated, and care needs to be taken by those responsible for maintaining public order that unwritten boundaries are not crossed, for example in the way that demonstrations and peaceful protests are policed or intelligence is gathered. How much such stress can individuals and communities undergo when subject to disruptive challenge before the normal bonds break down? The UK has a self-image as a tolerant and robust society, yet it was only a week or so without running water in the west of England following heavy flooding in 2007 that put pictures on British televisions screens of grown men fighting in the street over access to an emergency water standpipe. Fortitude is an old-fashioned and much under-appreciated attribute, and those exhibiting it need to be praised. A collective ability to get on with life, despite the difficulties, is a huge national asset. It is debatable whether government can itself do much to create a high state of national morale; an unexpected win by a national sports team may do rather more. Exceptional leaders in exceptional times can perhaps stiffen national will. But poor government, uncaring bureaucracy and insensitive policing can quite easily dent national confidence.

Crying wolf by exaggerating possible threats only makes matters worse. Preparing the public with a realistic view of matters is an important duty of government. But we should ask ourselves how far we actually believe on the basis of the best evidence that we are in for more, or more severe, emergencies than in the past, thus justifying more attention to the consequences of both major threats, such as terrorism, and major hazards from natural causes. Resilience is also not just an issue in the domestic space; hazards and threats alike do not respect international boundaries. Government has a duty to 'horizon-scan' beyond our shores and spot dangers to the public when they are real prospects but before they become present dangers.

A worst case that governments must examine is the possibility that terrorists could come to pose a risk of undermining confidence in our ability to live safely in cities, for example through using means that might include chemical, biological or radiological attacks and cyber-terrorism. We know that terrorists boast of seeking such means (bin Laden called acquiring them 'a duty'); but it is not inevitable that they will succeed, given sufficient international cooperation and vigilance. Governments would nevertheless be foolish to ignore the possibility when making plans for public protection. Additionally, our vulnerability to certain classes of natural disaster does seem to be increasing, including effects from global communicability of disease and weather pattern changes. Investing in greater resilience is a sensible response in the face of such dangers, especially if we are all to have the confidence to get on with our normal lives, despite the risks. The challenge of course for all involved in government and industry is how to ensure that prophylactic measures do not end up creating worse symptoms than the diseases we are seeking to avert. It is possible to have too much of the wrong sort of security.

Such are the vulnerabilities of increasingly inter-connected and close-coupled systems that cascading failures of essential services may well, however, not be predictable and avoidable. Nor can there be complete defence against natural disaster (or indeed catastrophic terrorism, were it to occur). All crises are local in their impact, and in extreme circumstances the weight of response will fall upon communities and individuals helping each other. It is reasonable to expect communities that are strong in other ways to be effective in collective self-help in the face of floods, snow, black-outs and other disasters. High resilience systems,[9] when individuals and their groups see their interests as compatible with the collective interest, can be contrasted with low resilience systems, where the risks are borne disproportionately by some groups and narrow self-interest and conflict can therefore be expected to predominate. Pursuing such a 'second generation' programme of building societal resilience at household and community level, in parallel with the continuing work on the 'first generation' work to reduce vulnerabilities in the key essential services, should be an important part of any national security strategy. It would certainly be a key feature of a true 'protecting state'. So calculated investment in resilience—the ability of a prepared society to absorb deforming shocks and to bounce back into normal shape as quickly as possible—where the risks justify this seems a necessary part of national security strategy.

Moving on to third generation adaptive resilience

Addressing the psychological dimension of resilience leads me to a further question we should ask. How far would governments be right to heed higher expectations on the part of the public that they will enjoy greater protection than in the past by themselves promoting greater long-term investment in infrastructure that is itself more resilient?

It would be a natural development of thinking about the psychological dimension of fortitude in the face of adversity to create what we might call a state of 'adaptive resilience'. Such adaptive resilience would be seen in the readiness of the public to recognize the need not only to take individual steps, but to insist on work as communities to *anticipate* changes in their future environment. The metaphor of resilience can therefore be extended further into what I term 'third generation' resilience, moving from the 'bounce back as quickly as possible' physical analogy of resilience of materials to an organic societal metaphor of healthy communities able to adapt to changing circumstances. The United Nations International Strategy for Disaster Reduction (UN/ISDR)[10] has adopted the term resilience and defined it with reference to natural hazards as: 'The capacity of a system, community or society to resist or to change in order that it may obtain an acceptable level in functioning and structure. This is determined by the degree to which the social system is capable of organizing itself and the ability to increase its capacity for learning and adaptation, including the capacity to recover from a disaster.' The significant words in this international definition are 'its capacity for learning and adaptation'. At its crudest, after a flooding disaster would it be wise to allow rebuilding of the electricity substation on the same flood plain? How best are lessons to be learned in order to build the capacity to learn and adapt to the likely circumstances of the future? A more resilient society is also one capable of learning from circumstances. At this point, we might recall Charles Darwin's tenet of evolution that it is not the strongest of the species who survive, nor the most intelligent; rather, it is those most able to adapt to changes in their niche.

Should we therefore see the concept of the CNI itself as the central organizing principle for resilience? Up to a point, perhaps, although as we have just seen even the modern reading of CNI has a limitation, since it is essentially still largely about increasing protective security of critical infrastructure. Taking a wider approach to the CNI represents part of that fundamental shift to a citizen-centred view that was described in chapter 1 as being at the heart of modern approaches to national security. It should include the capacity to mobilize effort at a local level to keep things going, including using the voluntary sector to the full. It should also include the ability to ensure that the CNI is seen not just as elements of infrastructure to be protected but as networks to be strengthened, and whose adaptive development is to be encouraged in ways that will provide greater security in the future.

What is needed therefore is not just the physical hardening of the key nodes and facilities of the nation, encasing them in thicker concrete to extend the metaphor, or in the vetting of their staff, or in their cyber-security, important as these are. It is also going to be increasingly important to identify the vulnerabilities of these networks to a wide range of possible future disruptions, paying particular attention to the interfaces between networks, the boundaries between organizational responsibilities, and the connections with the public being served by these services; identifying where fresh investment or greater redundancy in capacity (for example, of a mobile telephone network) or duplication of key facilities (such as power transformers or water bowsers) would keep services going in circumstances where they would otherwise have failed, thus enabling a flexible response in time of crisis; and ensuring that the supply chains supporting national infrastructure and those who operate them can also function under adverse conditions.

If we revert for a moment to the original requirement to protect the key nodes and facilities of our national infrastructure, government is right to start with those in the nine sectors listed above, including the capacity to ensure the continuity of government itself in an emergency. There is an obvious test that can be applied in judging such criticality, which is how long it would take to reroute the service satisfactorily or to replace damaged or lost infrastructure. In some cases it would take months, or even years, to rebuild lost plant and machinery. Such cases clearly will warrant major investment in protection in the first instance, both in terms of on-site security and in supporting security measures and capacity to enhance security in an emergency. What in essence is being followed is then a 'mini–max' strategy, to borrow a term from the games theorists: identifying the worst that the opponent (and I count floods and animal disease as such, as well as terrorists) can do, and minimizing the maximum damage by selectively reducing individual spikes of risk.

We are entitled to ask, however, whether we can be sure that all the relevant components and critical nodes can be identified in this way? Or will we find in each fresh emergency that unexpected and damaging difficulties emerge each time? There are at any one moment always going to be some outstanding gaps that have been identified but where we have to accept that solutions are expensive in investment and take time, such as extending the coverage of emergency communications systems over the whole of the London Underground. Likewise the surge capacity of mobile telephone networks is known to be inadequate, as we see each time there is a serious incident, but it is hard to fix. Modern economies have a great deal of infrastructure. It is not affordable, or feasible, to provide security sufficient to give full protection for the totality of mass rail and road transport systems in the way that key facilities can be secured. The inter-connections between systems are complex and hard to map. So an additional approach is advisable, one we might call 'maxi–min': maximizing the minimum level of assurance that can be given to the general public as we all go about our business, keeping the floor of confidence sufficiently high to keep most of normal life working.

That is not a simple exercise. It is a feature of a modern economy that it functions through a highly developed set of relationships, what Geoff Mulgan, formerly head of the Prime Minister's Policy Unit, has described as a state of connexity,[11] when complexity and connections intertwine beyond the point where they can easily be disentangled and laid out as a logical map. So surprising inter-connections are liable to appear when the system is put under strain.

Connexity can be a positive virtue. It can bring much greater resilience to modern systems, given the ability of networks to rebalance and even in advanced cases the ability of some electronic systems to self-heal, finding automatically new pathways when others are blocked. But some dependencies only show up when the system is severely tested, and are much harder to spot in advance. Close-coupled complex systems without adequate buffering are particularly prone to failure. Attempts to build in additional safety systems may make matters worse by creating new and unmapped inter-connections in an emergency, leading to so-called 'normal failures' which we discuss in chapter 7 in the context of intelligence failures. Dependencies may be located several levels down the supply chain. These realizations alter the nature of the 'critical infrastructure' exercise. It is not just about locating the key facilities and advising on protecting or duplicating them, but also about getting the operators of services to provide assurance that they have checked out the supply chain supporting their key services, and the interdependencies between such services in an emergency.

This is a responsibility principally for the owners and operators of the components of the national infrastructure services, not for government. The level of connexity is too great to imagine that any central group can have the detailed information necessary to know where to advise investing in material stocks, redundant capacity, or dormant contracts or in protection, or in preparation and training down individual supply chains. So a distributed model of infrastructure protection and preparation seems sensible, leaving it to private sector organizations overseen by their regulators to apply the concept of total corporate resilience within their own areas of responsibility, with government sharing its assessments of vulnerability and risk and providing relevant planning assumptions against which resilience can be judged.

In some cases analysis is likely to reveal a sound national cost-benefit case for investment in reducing the risk of system failure in an emergency, for example by creating redundancy in the form of greater capacity, emergency stocks, or standby facilities that can be brought into operation. We should not be surprised if the financial returns on such investment and the potential impact on the competitive position of the company may look rather less encouraging from the point of view of a private sector board representing the interests of shareholders. It may be sufficient in some cases when opportunities for renewal of facilities come up to rely on a combination of public spirit in the boardroom, plus the legitimate commercial interest in avoiding the reputational damage to the company concerned if it were to be its service that failed in crisis. There will, however, be other cases when the public interest demands greater certainty for the sector as a whole than an individual company would see justified in terms of its competitive position. This is a classic example of what the economists would call an external benefit. As in other parts of the economy, in circumstances where from the national point of view we face a market imperfection or failure, the government will then need to consider intervening.

The limits to protection

There are limits to what government can reasonably do to protect the public. Care will continue to be needed not to fuel an illusion that life can ever be made risk-free. Risk avoidance is not an option, but good risk management is. There may be a parallel here with the continuing debate about over-zealous attitudes to health and safety. Fresh examples are reported regularly of the absurdities caused by lack of confidence on the part of those in authority and in business in common sense risk management, largely driven by exaggerated fears of health and safety legislation, or the supposed impact of human rights law. Let us not unconsciously add security fears to that list of reasons for not getting on with life.

One of the key requirements is to identify how to improve the treatment by government of risk, and how it can best be communicated to the public. The cleavage between government and governed about the reliability and truthfulness of 'official' and 'expert' opinion, and the reluctance of the citizen to accept government information at face value, is well established. As the UK Cabinet Office Strategy Unit concluded, for government effectively to discharge its responsibility in communicating risks, it needs to have a track record of openness and reliability. A Strategy Unit report cites the Bovine Spongiform Encephalopathy (BSE) outbreak and the Measles, Mumps and Rubella (MMR) vaccine as examples of particularly difficult risk communications to the public. There are signs that government is beginning to realize that there is a real problem here, and that the involvement of the public in prioritizing risks is crucial to the validity and acceptability of the process. Two-way communication is of paramount importance. How effective this two-way communication will be, and far it can act as a vehicle for strengthening resilience, is difficult to predict given the inevitable tendency of the media, particularly the newspapers, to seek out the sensational and affective in every story in the interests of keeping up circulation. Public distrust is deep, and both government and the local response agencies will have to work hard if they are to convince the public of the wisdom of their actions. Government and industry need therefore to take care not to over-promise on the subject of security. At the same time, the public must be confident that government does see care for public security as a defining duty.

Paying for the security of the critical national infrastructure

Who should pay for that care for public security? Additional costs will be incurred in the public good if government decides to mandate higher standards for security and resilience in the CNI sectors. Examples include relocating infrastructure away from flood plains, insisting as part of the planning process that new shopping centres or office buildings incorporate higher security standards, or building in redundancy into networks or preventing commercial considerations closing down standby facilities or alternative transport routes. Given the importance of cyberspace for the effective functioning of the CNI, government will in future, for example, have to consider listing certain suppliers or nations whose products the security authorities would be

FORTITUDIO: THE PUBLIC VALUE OF RESILIENCE

happy to see embedded in the CNI and those they would not, even if they may be significantly cheaper. Government may also have to discourage incorporation of products from other countries whose future bona fides towards the UK we could not guarantee. Does security of their part of the CNI become a key objective for the different economic regulators, extending their role considerably? The answer so far has been no, and there are doubts about whether that would survive a competition law challenge in Europe. But the upshot is that society may be developing systemic vulnerabilities as companies invest in new generation networks—not just creating the vulnerabilities that would allow a foreign power to turn the lights out, metaphorically as well as literally, in a period of international crisis, but also vulnerability to criminal attack. But if it is in the general interests of society to be more secure, who should pay for the extra protection? The consumer of the service or the general taxpayer?

There are some government-run services where the future investment patterns are funded directly by public expenditure and can be made more resilient if the executive so chooses. But these cases are the minority. What are the levers that government has in relation to incentivizing (or compelling) the private sector to invest in resilience? At least three obvious possibilities exist.

First, the ability to awaken the self-interest of the private sector, both generally in terms of the value of national resilience and keeping the economy functioning in an emergency, and more specifically through emphasizing the market advantage of corporate resilience. We can look on this as an extended version of traditional business continuity into a new concept of total corporate resilience for the organization itself.

The second lever that the government has is regulation, both through general legislation and sector-specific regulation. A debate is needed about the role that the regulators might play in future for their industries in respect of security and resilience issues as well as safety and security, investor protection and service target delivery. Such an approach has, for example, traditionally been taken in the conditions for granting licences for commercial operation of water supply on public health grounds, and for transport companies on safety grounds. The regulator for the industry concerned can then take that statutory position into account. The time may have come for the government then to apply such an approach on the grounds of the public interest in security as well as safety, and thus mandate intervention by the regulator if required standards of resilience and redundancy are not being met, and allow security considerations for CNI facilities to be part of the consideration of the conditions to be applied to the granting of licences to operate in that industry, with costs being passed on to the customers.

A third lever is direct subsidy or grant. It is open, at least in theory, for government to subsidize the delivery of a service or provision of buffer stocks where the market level would fall below the optimum level, taking account of the public value of the additional capacity in a crisis. It was long accepted, for example, that government should subsidize the capacity to maintain transport links to the Scottish islands. No government is, however, likely to welcome the additional expenditure involved, especially given the economy-wide aspects of resilience, and there would be the obvious risk of companies seeking government support for services that they would in any case have profitably provided. It is also hard to prevent subsidies to specific companies leading to market distortions. But there may nevertheless be some exceptional cases.

For completeness, there is an 'emergency cord' that governments can pull when crisis looms, and that is to call on the armed services. In countering terrorism, and responding to floods, fire strikes and foot and mouth, the value of the disciplined command and control and planning capacity of defence has been vividly demonstrated. But given the many other calls on defence, a 'subsidiarity principle' should apply so that civil society should shoulder the responsibility to provide services to the public, unless there is likely to be a clear public value to having armed forces undertake the task. There are already a few such cases, and an important part of the rethinking of national security strategy should be to look afresh at where that boundary might need to shift, for example in preparing against the unlikely but nevertheless potentially devastating effect of terrorist use of novel, chemical or biological weapons.

Harnessing for civil purposes the technologies developed by the defence industrial base is going to be increasingly important in resilience, as it is in supporting modern security and intelligence capability. It is highly encouraging that the relevant UK trade associations are working with government through the Resilience Industries Suppliers Council, RISC. The ideal is to imagine a tripartite series of confidential and private conversations between government, the operators of the critical national infrastructure and the security industry supply base so that there is a shared understanding of what future needs are going to be (and also what they are not likely to include), what new possibilities are opening up from science and innovation and where, globally, the best practice is to be found. Such a structure operated flexibly would do much to overcome the imperfections of the present highly fragmented UK market place.

All that said, the speed and effectiveness of response to an emergency will always depend upon the local reaction, the emergency services on the spot, the orderly good neighbourliness of people helping each other, and the commitment to voluntary organizations such as the local branch of the Red Cross, the Women's Institute or the St John's Ambulance Brigade. Such responses depend crucially on the degree of civil harmony, a theme that runs throughout this book.

4

CIVITAS

THE PUBLIC VALUE OF CIVIC HARMONY

Living under the shadow

I remember the morning in 1989 when the barriers were erected at the entrance to Downing Street after the Provisional IRA had intensified their terrorist campaign in Great Britain. Before that day, any passer-by in Whitehall could walk past the Prime Minister's front door taking a short cut to St James's Park or with children to be photographed standing by the police officer on the steps of No. 10 (once an essential photograph for the future Prime Ministerial memoirs). Ducking to the right, halfway along Downing Street, the tourist could walk down Cockpit Passage, underneath the Cabinet Office and the remains of Henry VIII's tennis court, emerging into the expanse of Horseguards Parade, one of the greatest urban panoramas in Europe. Today, giant iron gates bar every entrance to Downing Street; police officers with machine guns scrutinize the credentials of every official visitor. The day seems far away when the gates and barriers might come down. Can we ever return to what now seems an age of innocence?

There is more to life than security. Living within the national equivalent of a gated and barred community would not be most peoples' choice, when they come to weigh up the costs, and opportunities foregone, and when they recognize that every fence can in the end be scaled from the outside by those sufficiently determined to get in for criminal gain or simply to wreak havoc. The method chosen by PIRA in 1991 was to mortar Downing Street from across the street and they came very close to killing or injuring Mrs Thatcher's successor John Major and the entire British Cabinet (I watched helplessly from my office in the Ministry of Defence as the van the PIRA gang had used as a launch vehicle burst into flames when the home-made mortar bombs shot out of the roof). Adding ever more bolts and bars and living in fear behind them is no life. Which gives a clue to the puzzle of how to decide how much national wealth should be allocated to security, taking the wider definition of the concept of national security used in chapter 1. In the light of a realistic view of the nature and seriousness of the major risks facing the public we should look at what it would take to reduce those risks to the level at which we would all feel sufficiently confident to get out and get on with our normal lives, taking reasonable precautions for our collective safety but not such as to inhibit our sense of freedom and self-confidence.

That in a nutshell was my thinking as Security and Intelligence Coordinator when I launched work in November 2002 on a UK counter-terrorism strategy (that I called CONTEST: COuNter-TEerrorism STrategy). The strategy was later presented to Cabinet and adopted in 2003 but the details were not published by the government until 2006; an updated version, CONTEST2, was published in 2009. Terrorism associated with the ideology promoted by Al-Qa'ida was of course the threat that had dominated security thinking since the 9/11 attacks on New York and Washington. That threat was very real, with AQ threatening further attacks and intelligence revealing that there were indeed networks of radicalized violent extremists within British and other parts of European society, aided from outside, who were intent on carrying out that threat. The intervention in Iraq was further stoking up passions and attracting further supporters for the AQ world view. Top priority was naturally already going to uncovering and neutralizing the growing terrorist networks in the UK, including an emphasis on emergency counter-terrorist legislation to make it easier to charge and convict on terrorism-related offences. But was that going to be enough in the face of the audacity of the attacks and the worldwide nature of the phenomenon? The danger was that for every terrorist caught and taken off the street we might find two springing up willing to replace him.

Assessing strategic success

In playing chess it is always wise to consider the strategy being followed by your opponent and not just your own plans, however deeply laid. Denying the adversary what they most seek and blocking off their attempts at quick wins seemed in 2002 a good place to start. In the case of AQ strategists such as Ayman al-Zawahiri, had in their writings and broadcasts, made clear their long-term objectives and announced their intentions. The senior official responsible for counter-terrorist policy in the Home Office has explained[1] publicly how such radicals see themselves as the vanguard of a wider global movement. In crude terms, the strategy followed by Osama bin Laden and al-Zawahiri seems to be reasonably clear in terms of the ends they seek, the ways they have chosen by attacking 'the far enemy'[2] and the means they appear to have at their disposal. We can characterize this in terms of:

- *Ends*: to liberate and unite the global community of Islamic believers in a Caliphate covering all 'Muslim' lands (including the present state of Israel), free of Western influence, with religion and state unified in Shari'a, in line with the Salafist/Wahhabi interpretation of Islam.
- *Ways*: to weaken the 'Zionist and Crusader' enemy (as they characterize it), build strength through global alliances with existing terrorist organizations in the Middle East, Maghreb, East Africa and South-East Asia, and then return to local liberation struggles to overthrow 'apostate' regimes. To cast the US, Israel and the West as the 'crusading' and invading enemy (culturally as well as militarily). To diminish the perceived power, influence and moral stature of the US and its allies, forcing their retreat from 'Islamic' lands and thus remove their ability to frustrate AQ's ambitions for insurgency in those countries.
- *Means*: to use extreme and dramatic terrorism to expose weakness and decadence in the West, to create confidence that resistance to US influence is possible, and to inspire an 'awakening' of revolutionary consciousness in the *Ummah*. To take a longer view than the West and thus through the power of modern media to leverage Western public intolerance of casualties and foster new networks of converts using the internet.

It is instructive to look on an act of terrorism, and a suicide bombing in particular, as an ultimate form of communication, with multiple audiences in mind. There is the directly instrumental part: the population to be intimidated, or the government to be influenced into changing policy, such as terrorists trying to bomb their way to the conference table or to the early release of prisoners. But that may well not be the primary meaning. There is the audience of fellow conspirators, the group whose solidarity is to be enhanced or flagging morale boosted by the act. There is the wider audience of potential supporters to be convinced that the fight is serious and can be carried to the enemy. There are also the media as an important ever-present audience, with the terrorists intending that their attacks will produce coverage that will provoke governments to over-react to terrorist attacks for fear of looking weak and thus validate the message of the terrorists about the repressive and discriminatory nature of the state.

This last consideration is an ancient tactic. Professor Magnus Ransdorp has drawn attention in his writings to the expression 'propaganda by deed' to describe it, a term coined in 1878 by the French anarchist Paul Brouse and adopted in 1881 by the International Anarchists Conference. As Camus reminds us in his work *La Rebelle*, that late nineteenth century period saw an extraordinary upsurge of anarchist violence. Political assassinations were committed by individuals claiming, often in testaments left behind, that they had no alternative because only the shock of extreme violence would bring consciousness of the degree of state oppression or injustice being done. Anarchist violence against property, for example, was intended to force questioning of the conventions of property ownership and private profit; their descendants infiltrate anti–globalization protests in Davos or at G20 summits. Such violence may also be intended to question the omni–presence of the state itself, as in the case of Timothy McVeigh and the 1995 Oklahoma bombing, the most serious terrorist incident that the US had suffered prior to 9/11.

Threatening personal violence to intimidate is a tactic older than mankind; terrorist acts are intended to disrupt the normality of society itself. Terrorism becomes a battle of wills, as to who is psychologically stronger, terrorists or society, in those circumstances. UK counter-terrorism policy was therefore designed in 2002/3 as a five-year strategy to maintain normality by managing down the risk from terrorism to tolerable levels whilst at the same time fundamental prevention work was started to undermine the roots from which this form of terrorism springs and thus prevent the radicalization of a further generation of young Muslims in the UK. As we have seen in chapter 3, the management of the risk to normalcy was thus expressed as simultaneous action to try to reduce the components in the risk equation: *Risk = likelihood × vulnerability × impact.*

From the point of view of the jihadist movement, on the other hand, their aim can be seen to have been to alter the equation sufficiently in their favour by creating conditions of abnormality so that the government is regarded (by the media and public, by government itself and by the supporters of the jihadists) as impotent in controlling risk. If such pressure from the terrorists were to result in significant and sustained damage to the credibility of authority, then the prospect would be of reaching a tipping point at which the jihadist movement has the upper hand and government has to compromise on its foreign policy, with serious repercussions globally. Likewise, the UK would be vulnerable to the consequences to its policies were jihadists to succeed in destabilizing public confidence elsewhere in Europe. In the eyes of the terrorists, such developments would increase their chances of promoting successful insurgencies in the Middle East and elsewhere.

So far, despite being able to mount destructive and murderous attacks in the West and against Western interests, the AQ strategy has failed. It has not led to the fundamental changes in policy that it sought. By aligning themselves with sectarian killing between Sunni and Shia Muslims in Iraq and elsewhere, AQ has also alienated many potential supporters. Relentless US and allied military pressure on the AQ leadership, hiding, it is assumed, in the tribal areas on the Pakistan/Afghanistan border, has reduced its capacity to communicate and respond to changing circumstances. The election of President Obama makes the US global presence, cultural and military, less toxic. All these are factors that point to strategic decline for AQ as a movement. Nevertheless, we must assume that in the nature of their religious outlook they take the long view, and they have certainly stirred up passions with their ideology that will take a long time to cool. The year 2009 has seen a steady stream of would-be jihadist terrorists making their way from Europe, including from Britain, France, Germany and the Netherlands, to seek contacts and training from AQ sympathizers in Pakistan. Despite, therefore, the evident successes in eroding AQ leadership overseas and in bringing terrorists to trial in the UK, it remains the case that extremely violent jihadist views are shared by a significant number of radicalized individuals within the United Kingdom and elsewhere in Europe. Well publicized statements by successive Director-Generals of the British Security Service,[3] backed by evidence from subsequent trials of individuals charged with terrorist offences, have gone some way to remind the public of the extent to which the authorities do have reason to believe that the risk of attacks still remains substantial.

Looking back, the so-called 'war on terror' pursued by the Bush administration in the years from 2001 to 2008 brought security gains, in terms of disrupting terrorist training and infrastructure, capturing or killing leading AQ figures, and gaining significant intelligence on AQ's terrorist networks. The 'war on terror' also brought significant excesses, creating difficulties with allies such as the UK pursuing different counter-terrorism strategies and, more fundamentally, inadvertently playing into that part of the AQ objectives that involved inspiring a revolutionary consciousness in the Ummah. The impression gained ground among many young Muslims, including in the UK, that the US—and its allies such as the UK—were indeed part of a 'Zionist/Crusader alliance' (in the words of bin Laden) intent on oppressing the world of Islam.

The relationship between the benefits of security and intelligence operations and their impact on both the domestic and international audiences is important for government security planners to understand. Pre-emptive security and intelligence operations are central to controlling terrorism. Given the advent of mass casualty attacks, especially hard to protect against given the role of suicide in jihadist terrorist tactics, society cannot rely only on effective detection and prosecution after the event, nor even on long prison sentences acting as a deterrent to future would-be terrorists. Pre-emption is needed. For that, information is needed, much of which ideally will be volunteered by the community in rejection of the extremists and their ideology. Heavy-handed domestic security responses—police raids, house-to-house searches, movement restrictions, hasty legislation—can alienate the community and play to the terrorist agenda. Media reporting of operations by allies and partners overseas, and media exposures, for example of US coercive interrogation and extraordinary rendition during the Bush-era 'war on terror', are quickly reflected back into domestic perceptions, reinforcing the stereotypes of the terrorist narrative.

The ethics of state action are discussed in chapter 9, but at this stage of the argument we need only note that there needs to be a guiding sense of strategic direction so that operational options (such as large-scale stop and search tactics) and policy choices (such as draconian counter-terrorist legislation) can be assessed against the standard of not just whether they would deliver an immediate benefit but against long-term political sustainability in terms of the values of society that the government is seeking to defend from the terrorists. The front-line officer will often argue that he or she is taking considerable personal risks on behalf of society and should not be asked to do so 'with one hand tied behind their back'. The question that higher command must always ask is whether the proposed measures would be likely to take the overall campaign closer to or further from the strategic objective. It was for that reason that in 2002 we framed the overall aim of the UK counter-terrorist strategy as being to reduce the risks from terrorism so that people could go about their normal business freely and with confidence. Managing the risk according to such a strategy means that not everything that could be done should be done.

Such an expression of the power of normality would directly deny the terrorists part of what they most seek, which is to destabilize confidence in the authorities. Expressing the aim in risk reduction terms avoids the corrosive effect of impossible promises, such as to eliminate terrorism, and leads naturally into framing campaigns that can reduce the overall risk. And such an aim is measurable: it is possible to measure public confidence, and count the number of tourists visiting the country and using the Underground transport system in London.

It is also possible, although harder, to gauge whether valued freedoms have been eroded in the process of seeking security. We may regret the presence of the gates outside Downing Street, and hope that one day they will be able to be removed. We can however see the point of them, especially now after the terrorist attempt in 2007 to crash a car carrying gas cylinders into Glasgow airport. We learnt in 2009 of the reason for the tiresome restrictions on carrying liquids in hand-luggage onto airliners when we heard of the AQ bomb plot to bring down several airliners over the Atlantic in an attempt to achieve an impact comparable to 9/11, for which life sentences were passed on three young British Muslims at Woolwich Crown Court (the ringleader receiving forty-one years in prison).

After 9/11, the British government entered a derogation from the Human Rights Act 2000, justified on the grounds that 'there exists a terrorist threat to the United Kingdom from persons suspected of involvement in international terrorism. In particular, there are foreign nationals present in the United Kingdom who are suspected of being concerned in the commission, preparation or instigation of acts of international terrorism, of being members of organizations or groups which are so concerned or of having links with members of such organizations or groups, and who are a threat to the national security of the United Kingdom.'[4] When, however, the point was tested in the House of Lords[5] during the appeal in the case of the Belmarsh prisoners detained under immigration powers, one Law Lord, Lord Hoffman, (admittedly in a minority opinion and before evidence of the reality of the threat reached the courts, for example through the 2007 Crevice trial conviction of terrorists who had plotted mass murder by planning to detonate a huge home-made bomb in a crowded place such as a nightclub or shopping centre) held the derogation unlawful on the ground that there was no 'war or other public emergency threatening the life of the nation' within the meaning of Article 15 of the European Convention on Human Rights. Public sentiment at the time seemed to share the sceptical judgment of Lord Hoffman about the British government's attempts to use immigration legislation so that, in his words, 'The real threat to the life of the nation, in the sense of a people living in accordance with its traditional laws and political values, comes not from terrorism but from laws such as these. That is the true measure of what terrorism may achieve. It is for parliament to decide whether to give the terrorists such a victory.' That expresses well the 'freely and with confidence' qualification in the CONTEST aim that should modulate the security measures being enforced. Rallied by the retired Director General of MI5, Baroness Manningham-Buller, the House of Lords refused in 2008 to legislate to allow the detention of terrorist suspects for up to forty-two days before charges had to be brought, even with added safeguards of judicial review of cases. That, in the present perception of the threat, she felt would have been a step too far. That judgment is one that has, however, to be revalidated with each change in the threat, especially if the threat were to increase sharply, for example with a real prospect of commando-style attacks such as that in Mumbai in November 2008 or the use of radiological weapons by terrorists.

The strategy for maintaining normality

Lorenzetti had a clear conception in his fourteenth century fresco when he connected Justice through Civic Harmony to Good Government.

The first duty of government is to seek to protect the public. This is part of the unwritten understanding between governed and governors, in return for which the people provide government with a monopoly on the use of force and agree to be taxed to pay for it. The figure of Peace rests upon armed vigilance. Justice must, however, remain independent and impartial. Security measures such as control orders are not in themselves incompatible with justice; the police do need time to gather evidence before charge, especially when having to comb through large amounts of electronic data on seized PDAs and computers; and the police must have the authority to act swiftly if they fear an imminent danger to public safety. If, however, measures are presented and then enforced in an aggressive fashion, by emphasizing the language of fear, they will risk being felt as discriminatory and alienate precisely those from whom the extremists hope to gather support.

The UK counter-terrorism strategy contains an important implicit assumption, that there is no complete defence against modern determined terrorists, as they develop new ways of attack including sophisticated IEDs (improvised explosive devices) and suicide tactics. And neither is there a framework of deterrence that will guarantee peace. The aim has to be to take sensible steps to reduce the risk to the public at home and to our interests overseas, on the principle known in risk management as ALARP, to a level 'as low as is reasonably practicable'. What should be meant by 'reasonably' in such an approach? We might characterize the British response to the characterization of the AQ ends, ways and means analysis as given above by expressing the UK security strategy[6] in the following terms:

- *Ends*: to protect the UK and its interests from security risks, including from terrorism in all its forms, in order to enable people to go about their lives freely and with confidence.
- *Ways*: to work systematically to reduce the terrorism risk through concerted action by government domestically, and with allies and partners overseas, to exert downward pressure on all the contributing factors in the risk equation: the likelihood of terrorists mounting attacks, the vulnerability of the public and of daily life to such attacks, and the ability of society to respond swiftly and effectively to disruptive attacks to minimize the impact and return to normality as quickly as possible. From this we mapped the '4P' campaigns:

    Pursue: to stop terrorist attacks

Prevent: to stop people becoming terrorists, or supporting violent extremism

Protect: to strengthen protection against terrorist attack

Prepare: where an attack cannot be stopped, to mitigate its impact

- *Means*: to be seen to uphold human rights, the rule of law, legitimate and accountable government and the core values of justice and freedom. To work in partnership with allies and friendly governments overseas, and domestically across central and local government, the private and the tertiary sectors to mobilize the energy and resources to implement the '4P' campaigns. To have the means to acquire and use pre-emptive intelligence to inform all 4 'Ps', but especially the pursuit campaign to uncover, disrupt and bring to trial those engaged in or supporting terrorism. To have community support for the measures necessary to achieve the four campaigns and to use only such methods as are sustainable in public opinion.

The first 'P': Pursuit

The most obvious point to emerge from the murderous attacks on London transport on 7 July 2005 and the succession of British terrorist trials since 9/11 has been repeated confirmation that within British society there are disaffected young people who have been prepared to commit mass murder for their cause, and who have made the shift from extremist rhetoric to violent action. Several trials have revealed how terrorist networks had made preparations for assembling home-made bombs and that, significantly, most networks had been in contact with terrorist trainers and planners in Pakistan. In the case of the Crevice plotters they were put in touch by AQ-associated facilitators with a Canadian-based extremist to help them construct the detonation mechanism for their bombs. In the case of the airline bomb plotters, it was during terrorist training in Pakistan that they appear to have learned how to make home-made liquid explosives that could be smuggled onboard airlines in soft drinks bottles and with disposable cameras hiding their detonators. These cases therefore could be clearly seen by the public to exemplify the new type of international terrorism that had eroded traditional boundaries between domestic and overseas spheres of security and intelligence operations.

All the terrorism cases in the UK and elsewhere have also illustrated how the security authorities had had to work with counterparts overseas in order to frustrate the plots and to assemble evidence to bring those responsible to trial through intelligence and detective work on a scale never experienced before. Without that pre-emptive cooperative intelligence work by intelligence and police services enabling the plots to be uncovered, thousands would have lost their lives over the last few years. The importance for public safety of having the intelligence to guide pre-emptive security actions, using the rapier not the bludgeon of state power, has already been highlighted in chapter 2 and cannot be over-emphasized.

When the Crevice gang were given long sentences in 2007 for their terrorist offences, more alarming still than their plan to explode bombs in crowded public places, but surprisingly less publicly remarked upon, was the revelation that they had pursued an AQ plan to acquire from the Russian Mafia a radiological dispersal device, or 'dirty bomb'. That possibility turned out to be a criminal scam and the gang fell back on attempting to make home-made explosives. Although they were not successful in obtaining a radiological device, the evidence at the trial left little doubt that that was their intention and that had they succeeded they would have used such a device, with devastating consequences. This ever-present fear, of terrorists acquiring a viable means of committing mass murder and causing long-lasting disruption to life in a major city, haunts Western security authorities. It distinguishes the present terrorist campaign from any previous, and it conditions the counter-terrorist responses of governments. It does not, however, yet seem to be fully reflected in public perceptions of the threat. We should not be surprised, therefore, that there have been continuing tensions between government, parliament and public over what security measures should be considered both necessary and proportionate in the pursuit of terrorists.

The experience in the UK over the years since 9/11 has shown that terrorist networks are hard targets to penetrate, principally because of their flexibility, lack of formal structure and security awareness and reliance on personal introductions and contacts. On the other hand, they have to sacrifice effectiveness for security. The classic army command structure (with quartermasters, planners and so on) as used by the Provisional IRA has operational and logistic advantages, as does the cell structure adopted by most past terrorist movements. Networks are more easily hidden, but it is harder to sustain effect using them. So far, the few self-radicalized individuals in the UK who have tried to carry out 'lone wolf' attacks have not been effective.

Another factor that makes 'pursuit' of terrorists hard is that despite much research there is no reliable profile of a jihadist terrorist suspect. They come in all guises, men and women, young and old. We should not be surprised that many of the UK terrorist suspects arrested since 9/11 are well educated, in employment or higher education, and are not the most deprived in society. As with earlier, far-left, groups, it is those who have the advantages of education but who feel the outsider, who have a foot in different worlds, who can be open to be persuaded that the ills of one world can be redressed by the dreams of the other and are therefore most likely to be susceptible to extremist views. That is, they fall victim to the circular logic of the cult, where everything has an explanation consistent with the cult's beliefs and any contrary evidence can be explained away within the belief system.

Groups that share such belief systems can be very resilient in the face of security force pressure. There is, after all, no such thing as failure if you believe you are acting as the agent of divine will. Failed suicide bombers when captured in Israel have explained their failure in terms of God's purpose that the time was not yet right to accept their martyrdom, and that they have more work to do on Earth in support of the cause. That is certainly not to argue that many of the young people who are being radicalized today actually have a serious clerical understanding of the religious doctrine of the AQ leadership and how it draws selectively from, hijacks and distorts different strands of Islamic teaching. Anger, a sense of collective victimhood, a strong bonding with their fellow-radicals, a search for meaning in their own lives, and for some simply a search for excitement are no doubt more important factors, as they have been with recruits at other times to different forms of cult.[7] But we should not underestimate the power that the very existence of the salafist-jihadist doctrine gives the terrorist recruiter in being able to cast a cloak of apparent religious respectability over their violent ideology. The role of converts to the Muslim faith in recent plots is, I think, evidence of that.

There are important tactical as well as strategic lessons to be learned from experience since 9/11 in combating terrorism in circumstances where there is no regard on the part of the terrorist for the level of civilian casualties, for the concept of an illegitimate target, or worse where there is a takfiri outlook that the victims deserved to die on the grounds that those who are not wholeheartedly with us are against us. Suicide bombers are very hard to defend against, and counter-measures will be controversial with the general public, as the Metropolitan Police have found with their Operation Kratos which authorizes officers to shoot suspected suicide bombers in the head without warning if they are convinced that is the only option open to them to protect the public from imminent attack. Prior identification of those involved in terrorist planning will be hard. Outside the conduct of an actual terrorist operation, being a member of terrorist network is not an objectively discoverable condition that someone is in, like holding the Queen's Commission. It is defined by what people do, and they may do only part-time for a short part of the week. Otherwise they can be engaged for most of the time in what to the outside observer will appear to be normal hanging out with the peer group, or life with family, sports club, or work group. For the dedicated extremist, however, there will be a secret core existence to which they can retreat, out of sight, and which for them will involve an engagement in the cause with a passion and intensity lacking in normal life.

Even dedicated extremists have, however, at times been forced to take account of popular feeling. The Egyptian Islamic Group discovered this in 1997 when it killed fifty-eight tourists (predominantly Swiss) and 4 Egyptians at Luxor. That massacre proved to be the turning point in the counter-terrorist campaign in Egypt. Support for terrorist violence evaporated, and without the consent of the population, there was nowhere for them to hide. In the five years before Luxor, Islamist terror groups in Egypt had killed more than 1,200 people, many of them foreigners. After Luxor, the attacks by the violent extemists dwindled. The similar reaction of many militants to the bloody hotel attack that the AQ-associated terrorist al-Zarkawi mounted in Jordan, killing those from whom they might have hoped for support, suggests there is a realization that causing Muslim casualties will eventually impair their ability to operate.

In a society such as the United Kingdom, indiscriminate violent attacks, such as those on 7/7, will inevitably cause deaths and injuries to members of the Muslim faith. We could therefore speculate that if unconventional means come to be used by AQ and its associates, then these are most likely to be anthrax or low contagion or small-scale biological, chemical or radiological devices aimed at local dislocation and panic, with the intention of diminishing the perceived authority of Western governments, but without a catastrophic level of killing and damage that would risk serious problems for the extremists with Muslim communities. On the other hand, a few highly skilled engineers and scientists putting their knowledge and facilities to jihadist use would make it much more likely that AQ-related groups could eventually obtain high impact capabilities. If they had them, then we cannot in my view rule out catastrophic initial and indiscriminate use to demonstrate capability being followed by specific demands. This is speculation, and we must hope it will remain the stuff of bad films. The truth is we do not know how AQ capabilities will develop, and very probably neither do they. But we can reasonably reach the precautionary conclusion that security planning must take account of the possibility of such low probability but high impact developments, and security policy should seek to keep the international temperature down and avoid inflaming the perceptions of Muslim communities. As ex–President Bill Clinton has put it:[8] 'If you come from a wealthy country with open borders, unless you seriously believe you can kill, imprison, or occupy all your enemies, you have to make a world with more friends and fewer enemies.'

A 'criminal justice' paradigm as the basis of the 'Pursuit' part of counter-terrorism strategy certainly fits an aim of emphasizing normality in the face of terrorism. In Northern Ireland during the worst years of the PIRA campaign and the 'loyalist' terror gangs, there was a 'state of emergency' that justified exceptional criminal justice provisions: most notably from 1972 to 2007 the right to trial by jury for scheduled terorrist offences was suspended because of the risk of jury intimidation. That was the period when British ministers had indeed to insist that all terrorists and their attacks should be described only in the language of criminal justice, and that despite the huge part the British army played in maintaining basic security the policy was to be presented as police primacy so as to emphasize the rule of law and avoid giving the terrorists the status they themselves sought as legitimate defenders of their communities and, when captured, being treated as 'political prisoners'. Care is, however, needed not to over-simplify: the 'criminalization' approach in Northern Ireland may well initially have reinforced the impression in the local communities that London was on another planet and that the naïve Brits simply did not understand what 'the troubles' were really about. And more importantly, if all concerned on the British side had simply acted as if the problem were only one of law enforcement to punish those convicted and to deter future criminality, we would not have had the peace process and a political settlement.

International terrorism has forced most nations (including the UK in the Terrorism Act 2000) to extend the boundary of what constitutes an offence by criminalizing intimidation carried out for political, religious or ideological reasons. The European Union[9] has adopted this approach by agreeing that terrorist offences are serious offences against persons and property which

'given their nature or context, may seriously damage a country or an international organization where committed with the aim of: seriously intimidating a population; or unduly compelling a government or international organization to perform or abstain from performing any act; or seriously destabilizing or destroying the fundamental political, constitutional, economic or social structures of a country or an international organization.'

In the past it has been difficult to get universal international consensus on defining terrorism because of the difficulties of avoiding criminalizing independence movements, as the UN has found (e.g. applying a test of whether the ANC or the French resistance would have been caught by any proposed UN definition: Schmid and Jongman collected no less than 109 different definitions[10] of terrorism). There is, however, UN agreement on condemning the impact of terrorism: UN General Assembly resolution 49/60, adopted on 9 December 1994 is clear:

'Criminal acts intended or calculated to provoke a state of terror in the general public, a group of persons or particular persons for political purposes are in any circumstance unjustifiable, whatever the considerations of a political, philosophical, ideological, racial, ethnic, religious or any other nature that may be invoked to justify them.'

Countering serious terrorist campaigns needs the full attention of all parts of government. Risk management will, as we have seen, involve action on prevention, protection and resilience preparation as well as pursuit of terrorists. And within a 'Pursuit' campaign, criminal investigation of terrorist suspects themselves will have to be supplemented by disruption and denial operations to stop finance, weapons and other materiel falling into terrorist hands.

In particular, as identified in chapter 2, we can see secret intelligence as the key to pre-emption, and thus to keeping down the level of violence and reassuring the population, including dampening pressures that might lead governments into counter-productive measures that create sympathy in the communities from which the terrorists seek support. In some overseas jurisdictions, gathering intelligence on domestic issues is the responsibility of a secret police, a concept that has never sat well with British sensibilities. The British started down that road with the creation in 1883 of the world's first Special Branch (of the Metropolitan Police) to counter Irish 'Fenian' terrorism on mainland Britain. But from 1909 the Security Service provided the ability to gather intelligence and frustrate those threatening the state but, crucially, did so without police powers of arrest. In 1931, the Service gained formal responsibility for assessing all threats to the security of the UK, apart from those posed by Irish terrorists and anarchists, which remained the responsibility of the police until 1992 when the Security Service was given the lead in the overall intelligence effort. The Special Branch has since merged with Scotland Yard's anti–terrorist branch to form the police counter-terrorism directorate. So the British approach continues to depend upon the closest Security Service/ police cooperation in uncovering, disrupting and then arresting suspects. If the cooperation is close, as it is currently, then the result is highly professional intelligence and security operations combined with policing that is operationally independent of government in effecting arrests and enforcing criminal justice. It is striking how few jurisdictions overseas have been able to overcome tensions between intelligence and police cultures, between acting before and after the fact of a crime being committed, and between a secret organization and being a publicly accountable police service.

Having a domestic intelligence service in a democracy requires great subtlety. The legislation (the Security Service Act 1989) that now governs the relationship between the Home Secretary of the day and the Director-General of the Security Service was framed to reconcile two contrasting (some would say contradictory) requirements. On the one hand, parliament must be able to be hold accountable the agencies of the state for their actions, and under the unwritten British constitution that has to be through a Secretary of State, the Home Secretary of the day. On the other hand, the Secretary of State must never be in a position where suspicions could arise that he or she could have been tempted to try to misuse the domestic intelligence service, for example to investigate political opponents. The Security Service must therefore be clearly seen to be under a legal duty to refuse any such pressure as unlawful. So parliament in the legislation provides explicitly the Director-General of the Service with the authority to direct the activities of the Service, not making it, as would be the case for civil government, the responsibility of a Secretary of State. At the same time, the Home

Secretary is placed under the obligation to be accountable to parliament for the Service; a very British solution, that rests on restraint and understanding between Home Secretary and Director-General of where the boundaries of authority lie. It is also a solution that provides protection for a Home Secretary who may be called upon to render an account to parliament of the activities of the Security Service when they have come to public notice but who cannot be held personally responsible/be blamed for the operational decisions of the Service. The wiser Home Secretaries have recognized this.

The second 'P': Prevent

When work started on the UK CONTEST counter-terrorism strategy at the end of 2002, we felt that the immediate priority had to be given to expanding capacity to 'pursue' the terrorist networks and pre-empt attacks on the public. At the same time, it was clear that a longer-term effort would be needed to 'prevent' another generation falling prey to the violent extremism of the the AQ ideology. In the early stages of CONTEST the 'prevent' campaign was seen in probably over-simplistic terms as the combination of focused diplomacy and where necessary military intervention overseas to prevent AQ acquiring new safe havens in which their facilities destroyed in the allied intervention in Afhganistan could be rebuilt, and domestically the development of a 'counter-narrative' with Muslim community leaders to win back the hearts and minds of young British Muslims. These tasks turned out to be much more complex and difficult than we had at first thought, and it was only in 2008 that the UK government was able to publish a consistent and detailed account of a fully worked-up 'Prevent' strategy.[11]

The 'Prevent' strategy is intended to counter the appeal of *violent* extremism. The threat or use of terrorist violence is unacceptable in any civilized society and rightly attracts the most severe sanctions of the criminal law and the opprobrium of society. Holding radical views, provided that they are promoted in non-violent ways, is not in itself normally regarded as incompatible with membership of a democratic free society. Some extreme radical views associated with political Islam do, however, directly challenge the norms and values of secular society, and would be unacceptable to the majority over such issues as the role of religious teachings in prescribing law, and of the status of women and of sexual orientation. For government to seek to divert extremists from violence into such non-violent but nonetheless highly extreme groups might be thought to serve the ends of counter-terrorism in the short term, but is liable to undermine majority trust in the actions of government. Nor is there any certainty over whether and when a holder of extreme Islamist views might, if the circumstances arose, tip over into violent action. A democratically elected government is entitled, acting within the framework of human rights, to use its resources to identify those at risk from violent extremism and to support them. It is also entitled to challenge extreme views themselves, even where they fall short of supporting violence and are within the law but which reject and undermine fundamental shared values of society. Government is justified in encouraging the promotion of alternative outlooks, including emphasizing what it might mean to be British (for example in citizenship ceremonies). During the early Cold War, great efforts were made by the Labour government of 1945–51 to encourage trade unions and left-leaning intellectuals to see their future lying in a democratic and non-syndicalist route to socialism. In the extreme case of international communism, declaring a belief in communism (and fascism) incurred civil sanctions such as inability to join HM Forces, the police service or the civil service (and, it is alleged, the BBC), although the Communist Party was not banned and membership of it was not a criminal offence. In the United States, however, in the early Cold War period the McCarthyite pursuit of communists in government amounted to a witch-hunt, and there was subsequently a strong reaction against such excess. A number of governments in Europe are today under pressure from the majority to oppose radical Islamist views that challenge the secular basis of post-Enlightenment society. France has banned the public display of conspicuous religious symbols and the wearing of the hijab; Switzerland has banned the building of minarets on mosques. Civic harmony will be directly challenged by the clash of views over such measures, particularly when radicals come into direct conflict with counter-views from groups strongly opposed to such ideas. Causes as well as symptoms of terrorism have to be addressed, but all sections of society will need to recognize the commitment to human rights and the rule of law. A counter-terrorism strategy may well not be the best vehicle for government to use in promoting the values of a free and democratic society, and tackling the fundamental issues of the risks to civic harmony of dissenting but non-violent views.

As UK Security and Intelligence Coordinator after 9/11, I kept asking what we should call the global terrorist phenomenon led by Osama bin Laden. It was the first time that I could think of when we were under attack by an enemy we could not name. The media used the descriptor Al-Qa'ida or AQ terrorism but that was potentially misleading since AQ was as much an ideology and support mechanism for other groups as a traditional terrorist organization comparable to PIRA. Our discourse ranged over terms such as 'Islamist' terrorism (too easily confused in the public mind with Islamic); 'Jihadist' terrorism (a term I use in this book, accepting that it may give offence to some orthodox believers as conceding the very heresy that extremists were promoting); 'Salafist' or 'Takfiri' terrorism (closer, but not likely to be understood by the public). The UK government finally adopted in 2003 'international' terrorism as its preferred descriptor, a term that not only failed to convey any sense of what the terrorist campaign was about but was liable to mislead, given the rise of domestic home-grown terrorism.

In thinking strategically about tackling violent extremism it is helpful to see Al-Qa'ida as having a dual identity as an ideological movement in religious garb as well as the base for terrorist planners with a political agenda. An analogy is to recall the debates of the physicists in the 1920s over whether a photon of light was a wave or a particle. The best answer we have is that it has its own nature, it is what it is, a superposition of different states, and that it will reveal its particle nature when confronted with certain kinds of reality, such as a photographic plate, and its wave nature when faced with a different reality, such as passing through a lens. The answer depends upon the questions we are implicitly asking through our interaction with the phenomenon. So it appears to be with Al-Qa'ida.

Over the last few years, understanding has built up of the origins and nature of the violence we now face. To understand, of course, is not to condone. When, therefore, in 2009 a redraft of the counter-terrorism strategy, CONTEST 2,[12] was published, the government finally provided its explanation of the origins of AQ and its ideology and of the reasons for its global appeal. That was an important step in developing the current 'Prevent' campaign to counter violent extremism that is at the heart of the British counter-terrorism strategy.

New recruits to extremism appear to have been not hard to find in the years after 9/11; indeed, during the height of the campaign in Iraq it appeared that far from having to reach out to recruit new blood the experienced radicals were acting as gatekeepers to vet those who were pressing to join an extremist network in order, as they saw it, to express their solidarity and contribute their part to the global jihad. By the end of 2009 that peak seemed to have passed and the attrition of experienced extremists was beginning to take its toll on the capability of the networks; nevertheless JTAC increased in January 2010 the UK threat level from substantial to severe (that is, from 'a strong possibility' of an attack to one being 'highly likely'). That makes it all the more important that the waning global AQ movement is not given fresh impetus by new recruits.

Government has, however, found it very hard to get to the roots of radicalization, in part because of the problems of finding *interlocuteurs valables* from within the various Muslim communities from which the extremists seek to draw support and who are sufficiently in touch with often alienated young people to be credible in their eyes, for example in seeking to counter the terrorist justification for their actions as defensive on the basis that they consider that the West has been conducting a war on Islam itself. It has also become tragically evident that for the violent extremists the concept of an 'innocent' Western civilian in this struggle has no meaning, as they argue that it is in the nature of democracy that the people have chosen their government and paid their taxes and have thereby, in the minds of the extremists, allowed their governments to wage war on Islam.

We need to understand such thought processes better if we are to be able to decompress converts and break into their self-justifying self-referential mental frameworks in order to detach them from violence. Changing their attitudes to the US and its foreign policies is quite another matter, of course. In the words of Eliza Manningham-Buller[13] when Director-General of the UK Security Service, theirs

'is a powerful narrative that weaves together conflicts from across the globe, presenting the West's response to varied and complex issues, from long-standing disputes such as Israel/Palestine and Kashmir to more recent events as evidence of an across-the-board determination to undermine and humiliate Islam worldwide. Afghanistan, the Balkans, Chechnya, Iraq, Israel/Palestine, Kashmir and Lebanon are regularly cited by those who advocate terrorist violence as illustrating what they allege is Western hostility to Islam'.

That broad message is shared by very large numbers of people in the Muslim world, and more widely, who may well not share the same understanding of religion. As the then Director-General of the Security Service reminded us,

'if the opinion polls conducted in the UK since July 2005 are only broadly accurate, over 100,000 of our citizens consider that the July 2005 attacks in London were justified'.

We should pay particular attention here to the operational implications of the apocalyptic nature of extremist beliefs. They draw on powerful archtypes such as victimhood, the conviction that the adepts are the chosen ones, the few to whom the truth has been revealed, part of a persecuted group and for whom martyrdom is the highest goal. This sense of becoming someone special, a chosen one, seems at the heart of the radicalization process. That sense has of course its converse, that the 'other' is a lesser being, to be despised and whose life is of no intrinsic worth. The concept of *takfir* associated today with Al-Qa'ida extremists has deep roots in human psycho-pathology. Civilization survives in the middle ground; yet it is precisely that middle ground that is excluded by such extremist world-views. Indeed, the extremists see the victims of their violence as having only themselves to blame by their rejection of salvation—those immoral 'slags' drinking and dancing in clubs that the UK Crevice case bombers were overheard discussing as targets.

An indifference to death and destruction that is simply part of the fulfilment of a higher purpose is not a new phenomenon. We might cite the authority of the Inquisition, the triumph of the proletariat, or the security of the Empire. But the iconography that the jihadists deploy appears to portray psycho-social aspects of extreme violence at an individual and a group level that are not just about the pursuit by violent means of political ends. The act of violence (a beheading, for example) tells us something about the internal world of the militant.

Although thankfully the circumstances have not yet arisen, government planning must look ahead to the 'low probability but high impact' possibility that terrorists could equip themselves with serious means of mass disruption and destruction, not least owing to the spread of the underlying scientific and technical knowledge (*banalization*, as the French describe this phenomenon). We must take seriously the possibility that at some point a suicidal terrorist may come to see widespread urban fire, destruction and killing as a cleansing power, bringing closer a millenarian vision of a new society. Think here of the north European religious extremists of the early sixteenth century and the slaughter they inflicted in Munster in 1535 as they attempted to set up a theocracy based on the most extreme reading of scripture and its eschatological prophecies. Munster was to be the New Jerusalem, pure amidst the destruction of the world of the unbelievers. An apocalyptic vision can indeed drive people from reason to the extremes of violence to terrorize non-believers they declare damned and unworthy of human respect. Deterrence against such potential catastrophe is not in present circumstances a viable option since there is no central set of opposing power structures or assets that can be held at risk and whose loss the terrorist would regard as unacceptable damage.

The tension between liberty and security

The very heated debate in 2008 in which the UK government's proposals for extending the time that suspects may be held in police custody to forty-two days before charge[14] were heavily defeated in the House of Lords demonstrated the absence of consensus on how serious to judge the potential future threat from extremist jihadist terrorism and on what tools should be available—if needed—to the security authorities to combat it. Asailed by very much the same arguments, the UK government was forced in September 2009 to order an independent review of the working of their Control Order regime (involving electronic tagging and movement restrictions on suspects) following adverse judicial judgments. Public tolerance of further security measures (including tough counter-terrorism laws) will be dependent on an understanding of the necessity for them that rests on a considered appreciation of the dangers terrorism could pose—and that in turn depends upon a belief in the integrity of the assessments of the threat that government and police make publicly available. Intelligence assessment and policy advocacy do not comfortably coexist. Yet that is in essence the everyday dilemma facing the police, security authorities and ministers after every controversial counter-terrorist operation or new security measure or legislative proposal that has to be justified to a curious and possibly sceptical public. Government can of course, as we have seen, make the situation worse by appearing to be using the need to act tough on terrorism as a political device for outflanking the opposition. It is remarkable, and depressing, that unlike the long struggle against terrorism in Northern Ireland and the search for peace there, no British inter-party consensus has existed on policy towards jihadist terrorism.

In assessing how far to act in anticipation of events (particularly of low probability but high impact attacks), governments have to draw on the assessments of their intelligence communities, but are constrained in how much of that intelligence material can safely be put in the public domain and how. The intelligence and security services therefore find themselves not just in the front line in the fight against terrorism, where they would want to operate, but also in the associated front line of political and media controversy where they have no wish to be. Their actions, and the intelligence justification for those actions, are constantly under media scrutiny. In addition, the intelligence community in the UK, as in the US, has faced heightened media scepticism harking back to the problems of intelligence assessments on Iraqi WMD, and their use by government to make the case for the intervention in Iraq.

Government has therefore struggled within the confines of security and the sub judice convention to justify the tougher aspects of its counter-terrorist legislation and to explain new security measures, such as the ban on liquids being carried by airline passengers or the introduction of whole-body scanners using millimetric wave technology. The police have equally found it hard to explain their operations, such as the large-scale raid on a suburban house in Forest Gate, London that failed to find evidence of the suspected existence of terrorist cyanide dispersal devices or the hasty arrest of twelve suspects, none of whom was then charged, in what the Prime Minister declared to be the stopping of 'a major terrorist plot'. There is a natural tension here: bringing terrorists and their supporters to justice depends upon the deployment in court of highly sensitive material from secret sources, such as human agents (whose lives have to be protected), covert surveillance, electronic bugging or from overseas liaisons with countries whose methods may differ from those of the UK. Unlike other jurisdictions, however, telephone intercept is (under RIPA 2000) not admissable in UK courts but there is pressure on government from the prosecutors and from many politicians to legislate to allow this. The UK has a unique combination of advanced covert intelligence-gathering techniques, very close sharing of intelligence between intelligence agencies and law enforcement engaged in a high volume of joint operations, an adversarial common law justice system, and strict adherence to the European Convention on Human Rights (including Article 6, the right to a fair trial) incorporated into domestic law in the Human Rights Act 1998. No way has been found of reconciling the disclosure requirements in the interest of equality of arms between defence and prosecution with the need to protect sensitive techniques and to avoid placing impossible administrative burdens on the intelligence and security agencies. The advantages for criminal justice in the short term have to be balanced by the need to protect intelligence sources, methods and effort for the long term.

An ages-old dilemma has therefore been heightened as to how much of the hidden in a world of secret intelligence to reveal for the honest purposes of public safety and education and in the interests of justice. On the other hand, having access to good pre-emptive intelligence would become even more important were the threat to worsen significantly in order to manage the risk to the public without government being driven to consider extreme measures such as crude profiling based on ethnicity or religion, changing the rules of evidence, introducing house arrest or detention without trial for suspects, courts sitting without a jury or new offences such as association with known terrorists.

The tension between security and privacy

As demonstrated by a succession of terrorist trials, the extremists live and work amongst the general population. There is no simple profile that can be used to identify someone who holds extremist views and has decided to become an active member of a terrorist network. In order to identify suspects, the authorities have to be able to access the product of the various traditional intelligence activities: recruiting human agents, carrying out surveillance, examining the telephone records and other communications of suspects, receiving tip-offs and so on. This category includes of course information volunteered from sources within the community, thus reinforcing the point that the community must have confidence in the integrity of the intelligence and security authorities and confidence that the rights of individuals will be protected when action is taken on information provided. In addition, there is a huge amount of information that is available openly on thousands of extremist internet websites, used by jihadists for recruitment and propaganda, and in the public statements and videos emanating from terrorist leaders, all of which can produce useful insights into the causes, extent and nature of extremist activity.

As was noted in chapter 2, those investigating terrorist suspects also need access to data-protected personal information relating to individuals of interest (which I labelled with the acronym PROTINT by analogy with human intelligence, HUMINT, and signals intelligence, SIGINT). Such information is nowadays held on electronic databases such as mobile telephone call data, banking and credit card transactions, biometric border and passport data and many other examples. Modern computer technology provides sophisticated ways of analyzing and correlating such information and identifying clusters of associated data for further investigation by more traditional police methods. It has of course always been the case that authorized investigators can with probable cause obtain access to personal information about named suspects, but now the associations and connections of the suspect can be identified leading to new lines of investigation.

Another controversial area of technology that has already been exploited for counter-terrorism is the availability of cheap camera and video recording technology through extensive CCTV systems installed inside and outside public and commercial buildings, and in public spaces. Such capability has been of enormous help in the investigation of terrorist attacks such as 7/7 and the subsequent attempts to bomb the London Underground on 21/7 as well as high profile murder, abduction and assault cases. Future CCTV systems will employ active rather than passive technology, alerting operators to unusual behaviour. In future, we may well see the widespread application of advanced pattern recognition technology to provide automatic warning of anomalous or suspicious behaviour (such as leaving bags unattended) that can be detected on such systems. It is now feasible to use in future such technology to tag the image of a suspect so that the individual can then be tracked through a transport system and even, as the technology improves, we can expect systems to be able to recognize wanted individuals. Automatic vehicle number plate readers have over the last few years been widely installed in the UK on main roads, and provide the basis for congestion charging systems, such as that which covers central London. Such developments can then effectively identify the presence and location of any suspect vehicle. The prevalence of miniaturized video capability in mobile phones has however also generated a different phenomenon, that of the citizen reporter—able to send to the media real-time footage, for example of a police raid or the policing of a public demonstration.

A further cause for public concern has been the spread of the use of techniques of surveillance into other parts of government, for example by local authorities and by civil government agencies of the powers to authorize surveillance, at least at the less intrusive levels, provided for in the Regulation of Investigatory Powers Act 2000. Thus, some local authorities have conducted surveillance operations on families to check whether they live within the catchment areas of their chosen schools, to catch fly-tippers and environmental polluters, and even to reduce dog fouling on tourist beaches. The authority granted by parliament through the provisions of RIPA 2000 was intended to provide strict regulation of all intrusive investigation by public bodies, and in response to public concerns the Home Office[15] has proposed to raise the rank of those in local authorities who are allowed to authorize use of RIPA techniques, and is asking the public to consider whether or not it is appropriate for those people to be allowed to use those techniques to conduct investigations into local issues.

These developments in the possibilities of new technology, lumped together, have been criticized as evidence that the UK is heading to become a 'surveillance society'.[16] The total impact of individually justifiable measures may add up to an unwelcome capability of the state to access information on its citizens for undefined purposes, and thus to provide an unconscious chilling effect on everyday behaviours, freedom of association and expression. I would describe this nightmare as 'the Panoptic State': the all-seeing state where surveillance is so widespread as to provide a new form of social control. In his 1785 description of the design of his ideal prison, the Panopticon, Jeremy Bentham wrote of it providing 'a new mode of obtaining power of mind over mind, in a quantity hitherto without example',[17] what the French philosopher Michel Foucault[18] much later saw as a powerful metaphor for how modern societies exercise unconscious social control through surveillance. As Josephine Butler wrote in the late 1880s, 'the records of private and family life, gathered by espionage and treasured up in the secret cabinets of the police, constitute the instruments of an occult and immoral tyranny'.[19] As a vocal contemporary critic, Henry Porter, has described his fears: 'Who knows what conclusions will be drawn from innocent web searches, phone calls and emails? Who dares to predict the kinds of abuse by the government, which is already tracking legitimate protestors in real time with automatic number recognition cameras and infiltrating environmental groups with informers and spies?'[20]

There are counter-arguments that such developments are not an inevitable consequence of current trends in policy provided that adequate safeguards are put in place. As former Home Secretary John Reid[21] has put the case for government access to communications data: 'Used in the right way, and subject to important safeguards, communications data can play a critical role in keeping us safe. It helps investigators identify suspects and solve life-threatening situations. It can assist the emergency services locating vulnerable people. And it is critical to protecting national security against terrorism. Maintaining this essential capability will become more complex in the future in the face of technological change ... it is clear to me that the way we collect communications data needs to change so law enforcement agencies can continue to do their job; to tackle serious crime and gather evidence to fight terrorism and prosecute criminals. Of course, there must be stringent safeguards to control how data can be obtained.' The nature of those safeguards is going to need to be reviewed in line with the developments in the technologies concerned. The security case to be made is that—as in Operations Crevice and Overt—intelligence and security agencies will need access to personal information and have the ability to reveal patterns of interest if they are to protect society from the most serious threats of modern international terrorism and serious crime. Limiting the access of the intelligence and security services to these sources of personal information and the technologies to exploit it, and surrounding their use with excessive regulation, will likely result in greater risk to the public. There is thus a trade-off between personal privacy and security that has to be weighed for each technique, accepting that intrusions into personal privacy can and should be limited to the most serious challenges to security, from terrorism and serious crime and not from the multitude of minor misdemeanours that authority must therefore find less intrusive ways to prevent—and parliament must legislate where necessary to ensure that is the case.

As already noted, to encourage the provision of information to the authorities requires maintaining public confidence in the actions of the state, including in the protection provided for minority communities by the framework of human rights and the quality of justice. The actions of the security authorities therefore must be—and be seen to be—both necessary and proportionate. Modern intelligence access will also often involve intrusive methods of surveillance and investigation. Being able to demonstrate proper legal authorization, stringent safeguards and appropriate oversight of the use of such intrusive intelligence activity becomes even more important for the intelligence community, if the public at large is to be convinced both of the desirability of such intelligence capability and of the necessity of paying heed to its threat assessments. This aspect of security policy deserves more attention that it has so far been given.

5

THE INTELLIGENCE CYCLE

FROM WHENCE OWE YOU THIS STRANGE INTELLIGENCE?

From whence owe you this strange intelligence?
(Macbeth, *Act 1, Scene 3*)

Intelligence as a trade has been gradually becoming a profession over the last 100 years since the British Secret Intelligence Bureau was set up in 1909, from which the present UK intelligence community grew. If we think of *l'histoire a la longue durée* we can explain much of the dramatic change in intelligence work over that period in terms of the transforming impact of the two World Wars, a Cold War and most recently a new age of jihadist terrorism and insurgency. Chapter 4 examined some of the issues for intelligence that arise from responding to the most recent developments.

There is another way of looking at the history of those 100 years that may provide further clues as to how the activities and processes that make up the cycle of secret intelligence should be encouraged to develop, and that is to consider three scientific revolutions that took place within that 100–year period, and to speculate on what might be the next.

The first phase, or first intelligence revolution, was the radio era, just under way in 1909, following the exploitation of Herz's discovery of radio waves, predicted through the application of Clerk Maxwell's equations that unified electricity and magnetism. Let us take the words of the pioneer, Herz, as a warning to us that it is hard to predict how science will impact on life: 'It's of no use whatsoever … this is just an experiment that proves Maestro Maxwell was right—we just have these mysterious electromagnetic waves that we cannot see with the naked eye. But they are there.' But the consequences for the military art, in particular naval warfare, mobile ground forces and the direction of fighter air power were profound. The intelligence world was very quick to cotton on to the power of so-called traffic analysis (the pattern rather than content of communications) along with direction finding as an essential tool of military intelligence, enabling the enemy's order of battle to be reconstructed from examination of call signs and patterns of communication, and allowing military units and warships to be identified even when the messages themselves could not be read. Nor did it did not take long for the intelligence world to adapt the new technology for the purposes of agent communications or for deceiving the adversary using *Funkspiel*, as the Germans called radio deception.

The very success of this new form of offensive intelligence-gathering also stimulated defensive technological developments to provide greater security, notably more secure cryptography and electromechanical devices, such as the German Enigma machine, to encode messages. An immediate response by the intelligence agencies was to find smarter ways to get round the encyphering of messages, whether by recruiting cypher clerks as agents or stealing the code books without the enemy becoming aware of the compromise.

The second revolution was the electronic era, accelerated by the intelligence effort in the Second World War with the development of valve-based computing and such breakthroughs as germanium diodes designed initially for radar. Notably at Bletchley Park, supported by the Post Office engineers at Dollis Hill, the technology was harnessed to the industrialization of intelligence processes, initially in terms of workflows to handle large volumes of intercepted material and then by building machines capable of replacing human brain power in the routine processing of information required for the decryption of encyphered material, the direct ancestor of today's programmable computer. Ways were developed to extract more usable intelligence from the pattern of communication through traffic analysis even when its content remained unreadable. The lineal descendant is the current use of billing data to examine patterns of communication by mobile telephone in order to uncover the structure of terrorist or criminal gangs.

The ramifications of electronics for the military world are too many to list, especially in weapons systems, paralleling their impact in commercial life. By the late 1940s, the Bell labs had invented the transistor starting the next technological tectonic shift, whose effects are still being worked through today. That first quantum revolution brought transistors, micro-miniaturization and electro-optics. Within a decade, primitive electronics were sufficiently miniaturized to allow sophisticated airborne and naval collection of signals intelligence. They transformed the communications between agent and intelligence officer. They enabled new forms of eavesdropping and surveillance. The launch of Sputnik shocked the US, and the ensuing race for intelligence collection from space dominated US intelligence budgets with optical, then electro-optical, radar, SIGINT satellites, stationary, low earth and elliptical orbiters and so on. Space dominated US intelligence spending, a hugely significant fact in intelligence, and intelligence organizational, history. The role of National Technical Means as a stabilizing force in the Cold War was highly significant and brought secret intelligence out of the closet.

The next phase has been called the second quantum revolution, when quantum understanding led to lasers, optical readers, disk storage and micro-miniaturized solid state devices to be designed and computer chips manufactured equivalent to billions of transistors. Still in progress, that revolution has given us the mobile telephone, the laptop computer and the internet, cloud computing and the massive data storage and manipulation behind much modern intelligence analysis and battlefield intelligence fusion. It has brought powerful super-computers, increasingly cheap bulk data storage, massive parallel processing, strong encryption using public key cryptography (a discovery by GCHQ mathematicians), packet switched networks, the internet, video and voice communication using internet protocols and the explosion of wide area connectivity. This phase has seen the technological lead pass from the defence research and development labs to those of the civil sector as the cutting edge became consumer not military electronics. Consumers here, of course, can mean terrorists and criminals as much as honest citizens.

The offence/defence race in intelligence now has a new domain: cyberspace where three quite different contests are under way. The first is technical, how to defend the critical infrastructure and provide information assurance against malicious attacks that could leave the nation vulnerable in time of crisis to a hostile state or open to attack by terrorists. The second is to protect the government networks that carry security and classified information (and those that operate the systems) from penetration from other intelligence services, and, it must be said, the other side of that coin, to develop our own ability to gather intelligence by such means. The third contest is moral, countering the use of internet technologies by extremists to spread hostile ideology, promote radicalization and recruitment, maintain contact within networks and disseminate information about targets, tactics and weapons as has been well developed by the radical takfiri jihadists. The issues thus spill over quickly from the technical to the political, given the intrusive power of these technologies and their transforming effect on political debate and the difficulties of tackling such a transnational problem.

The volumes of information now involved in intelligence work are huge. A whole branch of intelligence work is therefore having to be created to access (not a straightforward matter), monitor and exploit open source material and to present it in a way that provides real-time situational awareness to commanders using virtual reality visualization tools that would have been unimaginable to Montgomery or Patton. That said, we should recall the caveat that John Keegan has so clearly described in his writings on intelligence in war, that in the end the clash of arms is determined by classic factors that Clausewitz would have understood. The battle for Crete in 1941 is perhaps the classic and tragic example that even good intelligence cannot always win battles.

And the next technological revolution, yet to come? I cannot be sure, but let me offer two possibilities that could profoundly affect the intelligence community. One is the next quantum revolution that stems from recent discoveries in basic quantum physics showing the theoretical validity of quantum computing, that would make previously wholly infeasible tasks possible, since the calculations would be being carried out simultaneously in a near-infinite number of parallel universes in which one will have already found the answer. Basic proof of concept has been achieved, but the technical problems of scaling up are formidable so practical application may be a generation or more away. When (if) this ever becomes a practical tool then the implications will include making transparent much of the world's communications and transactions together with near-instantaneous access for the analyst to specified data.

The second example of a technological revolution has already started, in the biological sciences, as genetic engineering becomes ubiquitous. New compounds can easily be synthesized, including cognitive enhancers, which, combined with direct person brain-machine interfaces, open up new possibilities for the analyst. The daily work of an analyst or the J-2 at a military headquarters, literally plugged into their computers and databases, would no doubt consist of walking through virtual reality representations of visually presented information, like some giant computer game.

But those are just guesses. What is certain from history is that the military art, and the way intelligence supports it, will change yet again.

The intelligence cycle

As technology has developed it has both broadened the range of information that can be accessed and speeded up its dissemination, so it has come to play a greater part in improving tactical decision-taking on the part of government policy-makers, diplomats and military commanders and in the pursuit of terrorist networks and countering insurgency. Intelligence practitioners describe their trade in terms of an 'intelligence cycle' of activities.[1] During the Cold War, NATO developed and used a characterization of the organization of intelligence activity that started with the setting of requirements for collection and ended with the dissemination of finished product to the intelligence staffs of the NATO military commanders. Essentially it was a linear process, with a final stage of seeking user comments on the value of the intelligence reporting at the end to curl it round into a cycle of continuous activity (Figure 4).

Such a cycle is generally described as starting with a function of *direction* that sets the requirements and priorities to be given to the intelligence agencies as to what areas of intelligence customers would like to see on their desks or screens. Validation confirms that an intelligence collection or production requirement is sufficiently important to justify the dedication of intelligence resources, does not duplicate an existing requirement, and has not been previously satisfied (and cannot be met by non-intelligence means). The agencies thus authorized then engage in the *collection* of intelligence, to be sent back to the agency headquarters. The *processing* of that intelligence then takes place, including decryption if necessary, translation, and then validation of the source. The intelligence is normally subject to some degree of *analysis* by the collecting agency, for example to identify the names

117

Figure 4: The Classic Intelligence Cycle

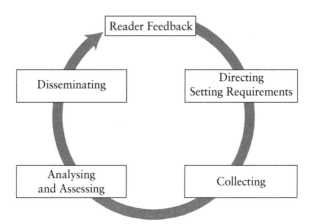

that may be mentioned in an intelligence report and to link to previous reports from the same source. The cycle then moves on to the stage of *all-source assessment* bringing different lines of reporting together and deriving key judgments about the meaning of the intelligence picture thus revealed, and finally ends with the *dissemination* of the finished intelligence product to end-users and some form of user feedback on its value.

The traditional model had different staffs with very different sets of professional skills engaged at each stage in the cycle, with in most cases clear organizational boundaries between collectors and analysts, between individual single-source reports and all-source assessments, and between analysts and customers for the intelligence. For some of the most technical of Cold War intelligence (the acoustic signatures of Soviet submarines, for example, or the analysis of radioactive by-products of a nuclear test) there would typically be a long time gap between the initial requirement, collection and analysis and a finished technical report being in the hands of the relevant military and scientific staffs. Outside the limited area of intelligence and warning indicators, most of the intelligence base of the Cold War was not time-sensitive in a tactical sense.

It is still possible to look on some intelligence activity in terms of a stately progression around the intelligence cycle. But increasingly the reality of what staff in the intelligence community actually do, especially when working on targets such as terrorists, proliferation networks and criminal gangs, seems to be rather different from what the categories associated with the traditional intelligence cycle might suggest. In a post-modern spirit, therefore, rather different terms may be helpful in describing some key components of the cycle so that thinking about the developments to be expected over the next few years is not unconsciously narrowed by the familiarity of the discourse, for example through using words like 'collection' and 'analysis'. Indeed, a description of a future cycle that would best support the UK National Security Strategy is really best thought of as an interactive network rather than a cycle, but more of that below.

Access

A version of such a modern intelligence cycle is given in Figure 5. There is an outer loop that, for the purposes of discussion, we can break into at the function labelled '*Access*'. The term 'access' rather than the more traditional 'collection' was suggested in chapter 2, since it carries the double meaning of 'that which is capable of being reached' and 'that which is approachable in different senses', to cite the *Shorter Oxford English Dictionary*.

   The main point to be stressed here is that, as explained in chapter 2, there is now a much wider range of ways of obtaining information for decision advantage. Intelligence work has become internationalized as

Figure 5: A 'National Security' All-risks Intelligence Cycle

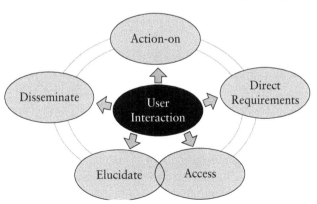

nations have realized the common dangers that threats such as terrorism, proliferation and serious crime pose for the international community. It has become clearer to intelligence collectors that sought-for information may more easily be obtained (or may already have been obtained) by another country with whom it may be possible to set up intelligence relationships. The effort going into maintaining intelligence liaisons has in the last few years greatly increased as a result. The trend is not unproblematic, given the methods still in use in some countries with whom intelligence liaison may be necessary for public safety, a problem that is examined in chapter 10.

The internet provides immediate access to background information of all types of value to the analyst or J-2. Advanced information technology is also providing new means of access to, and analysis of, personal data on individuals of interest from an intelligence perspective. The intelligence requirements of those designing and implementing modern national security measures can now be met therefore by drawing on three types of information: traditional secret sources; open sources; and a third important category, that of personal protected data.

The technologies of recovering intelligence from human or technical sources may have changed over the years (hidden messages on an internet website not microdots hidden under the stamp on the envelope, public key cyphers not one-time pads) but the principles have remained. And to the original HUMINT and SIGINT there is now to be added the vast amounts of information to be accessed from satellite and photo-reconnaissance (IMINT), radar and electronic intelligence (ELINT) and measurement and signature intelligence (MASINT). Essentially, these categories provide the basis for recruitment, skill development and organizational structure for national intelligence communities.

The volumes of information provided by those secret sources are however now dwarfed by the availability of open sources of information (OSINT) now accessible via the internet. To the huge changes happening in the world of OSINT must be added the growth of the third category of information from which intelligence for national security may be derived, one that I labelled in chapter 2 'protected information', or PROTINT, involving personal information about the individual that resides in governmental and private sector data bases. A significant challenge in that respect will be how the intelligence community can access the full range of data (and meta-data) relating to individuals, their movements, activities and associations in a timely, accurate, proportionate and legal way, and one acceptable in a democratic and free society including appropriate oversight and means of independent investigation and redress in cases of alleged abuse of power, an issue that is discussed in chapter 9.

The ability to conduct intelligence work in a hostile environment, behind enemy lines as it were, (the Cold War paradigm) will remain an important part of intelligence work. A significant challenge for HUMINT agencies, as for example discussed by ex–Chief of MI6, Sir Richard Dearlove[2], is however said to be adjusting operations from the small number of very long term recruitment of high value deep penetration agents to the many short term, often casual, sources of the international counter-terrorist paradigm. Much of the information needed, for example, to track terrorist groups, including their financing, resides in open sources, on the internet and in databases within our own societies, where the barriers to entry for the intelligence authorities are of a very different kind and call for access expertise of a different order. The intelligence analyst will often be best placed to steer access in near-real time. It is not hard to see the development of a new function of access or mission management that can access, manipulate and collate the required sets of information using the most effective set of sources.

To these access challenges must be added the difficulties of keeping up with new communications technology such as voice over the internet, packet switched networks, and the general volume of modern communications together with the ubiquity of commercially available hard encryption. The global nature of communications also finally washes away the old distinctions in military circles between tactical and strategic intelligence collection methods or intelligence assets.

The distinction between domestic and overseas intelligence collection is also blurring. In the US the term 'intelligence' is still normally synonymous with 'foreign intelligence' and that is how the role of the Central Intelligence Agency has been framed in legislation. The 1878 'posse comitatus' Act limits the powers of the federal government to use the military for law enforcement or policing to maintain law and order and the major technical intelligence functions run by the Pentagon including signals intelligence and satellite reconnaissance likewise were geared to overseas intelligence. The US domestic space has been the domain of the law enforcement not the intelligence community, and includes notably the FBI and the Drug Enforcement Agency. Post 9/11, the Homeland Security Department has struggled to build a model in which it can receive intelligence from national agencies relevant to its domestic mission (including from satellite surveillance) and can collect and distribute intelligence gained from police and other domestic bodies with which it works through local fusion centres.

For the UK, perhaps because of a longer history of secret intelligence being used to deal with internal threats, the term intelligence is commonly used to cover the internal as well as external security space. The development of the jihadist terrorist threat, the need to connect the dots between domestic and overseas theatres, and to ensure that intelligence in an assessed form is available for those who need to take policy decisions on counterterrorism and protective security has meant that the Security Service is now very much part of a national intelligence requirements, collection and dissemination community, although it retains as described in chapter 4 it special status as a statutory security agency. Cases that arise domestically are likely to have links to extremist circles overseas and such linkages will have to be pursued overseas. Likewise intelligence operations overseas may well directly illuminate emerging domestic threats. The targets themselves of course respect no such distinction. Joint operational pursuit of cases will become more common; and the same pressures will be felt by the UK's intelligence allies and partners.

Elucidation

Moving round the cycle in Figure 5 leads next to the analytic processes that are central to the derivation of meaning from this mass of secret, open and protected information. In Figure 5 this part of the cycle is labelled 'elucidation' since that word helpfully carries the meaning of throwing light upon and explaining that which is in shadow.

'Elucidation' describes the activity of analysis and assessment, throwing light on the underlying meaning behind the information that has been accessed. The description looks ahead to chapter 6 that describes the ways in which intelligence analysts can 'join up the dots' to expose tactical threats such as those from terrorism, serious crime and narcotics. Chapter 6 also examines the trap that evidence will be over-interpreted and other pitfalls for the analyst. The danger is also identified that short term tactical needs will be met at the expense of work on longer-term analysis of future risks and the generation of strategic explanatory hypotheses.

We have to recognize that modern national security strategy places two types of demand on the analytic community to elucidate—cast light on—a complex world. These represent forces pulling the analytic community in two different directions: the recent emphasis on using intelligence for the purpose of immediate action (for counter-terrorism, counter-proliferation, narcotics interdiction etc) pulling in one direction, but also the need to provide strategic situational awareness of longer-term developments of wider security interest, pulling the community in a different direction. In both cases however the task is to generate and test hypotheses in order to provide the best explanation possible consistent with the observed facts and the deepest possible understanding of the individuals, groups and regions concerned, their people, language, customs and mores.

The first shift in emphasis is to intelligence for action-on, as the SIGINTers call it: actionable intelligence that is sufficiently accurate, precise and timely to allow someone to use it for the purposes of public protection, or in pursuit of a tactical military objective. That shift has profound implications for the extent to which the members of the intelligence community must work as a single community, and the deeper relationships with law enforcement and homeland security policy-makers that are required, along with the wider relationships with overseas services. It has implications for a change in relations with the media, for the role of oversight and for the degree of public confidence in the ethics of the intelligence community.

All possible sources of information will be examined in the course of preparing an intelligence assessment. In some cases the secret intelligence content may be small in comparison with diplomatic and attaché reporting, media, academic writing and scientific literature and other open source material. And there will be cases in which the contribution from intelligence allies forms the main justification for issuing the assessment. The UK benefits hugely from the long-standing intelligence relationship with the wartime signals intelligence allies, the US, Canada, Australia and New Zealand. The pressing need for secret intelligence to counter the activities of international terrorist and criminal groups has in addition in recent years brought together in liaison arrangements many previously mutually suspicious if not hostile intelligence agencies from governments that would not naturally have seen themselves as partners in terms of world view, values or mutual interests. The influence of liaison reporting should not be underestimated, although it does raise problems about differences in methods and their acceptability, an aspect discussed in chapter 10.

As already noted, much of this work will rest on open sources of information. Often the assessments concern mysteries relating to how situations may develop rather than the secrets of what already exists—the plans, orders of battle and equipment tables of the classic assessment function (still needed of course, since the potential for inter-state conflict has not disappeared with the end of the Cold War, although its form is likely to be asymmetric and increasingly novel[3]). The demands on the analyst community of such work are very considerable, not least because the local players themselves may not fully understand the dynamics of the situation. It will not just be a question of what analysts 'know' but what they 'understand'. More attention will be needed in future on training analysts to think clearly and to be conscious of the methodologies they are using, and their pitfalls. And proportionately more of the budget will have to be spent on the activities that allow meaning to be derived from accessed intelligence as against the mechanisms of access themselves.

As discussed in chapter 2, the UK already has in the JIC a well-understood mechanism for strategic intelligence assessment and has JTAC for operational terrorist analysis and threat warning. Other subjects, such as counter-proliferation, might benefit from a similar all-source assessment centre, but the small size of the UK analytic community on such topics may make that impracticable. In which case, in support of national security priorities, other virtual analytical centres using advanced secure technology will have to be developed. Analyst spaces are needed, scratchpads, areas of secure cyberspace where work in progress can be posted for peer discussion by a chosen group, techniques now common in academic work in natural history such as species taxonomy. All this calls for the sort of changes that Tom Fingar, as Chairman of the US National Intelligence Council, described[4] under the rubric of 'analytic transformation'.

Analytic cooperation internationally has developed considerably on counter-terrorism since 9/11. Sharing assessments and warning and alerting information is likely to increase in importance in years to come. In considering the implications of sharing, for example for cooperation at a European level, it may be helpful to think of the intelligence community serving three levels of government: these are the classic distinctions between working at the strategic level, at the operational level and at the tactical level, with the distinguishing feature between the levels being the time horizon of the customers receiving the intelligence.

At the strategic level, nations need to share assessments to guide policy-making, for example in the European Council on future protective or border security measures, on collective measures on criminal justice, on informing judgments over trade-offs between civil liberties and security, or trade-offs between data protection and privacy and enabling intelligence access. The UK has been active already in building up the EU Sitcen, for example, so that nations can share their strategic assessments to inform debate in the Council of Ministers and thus help a consensus emerge at a European level. The pressure will grow for more intelligence-based assessments to be shared in this way.

At the operational level, the main international demand is likely to remain for sharing of timely all-source analysis to support operational decision-making, in the manner carried out domestically by JTAC. It is encouraging that a number of countries are creating their own inter-agency mechanisms for operational threat assessment (although naturally with the exact organizational geometry varying from country to country). What matters is that mechanisms develop over the next few years that will help nations act consistently when faced with the same threat, an example being through warnings to travellers in countries affected by terrorism or natural disaster.

At the tactical level, individual lines of intelligence are largely going direct to other intelligence specialists, to defence staffs or to policy customers who are themselves expert and able to interpret the material. Making progress with such information-sharing arrangements with allies and partners to support counter-terrorist operations overseas is a plank of the UK National Security Strategy. But sensitive tactical details of current operations on the ground are only going to be exchanged internationally between the services concerned where there exists prior trust that operations—sources and methods—are not going to be compromised by precipitate unilateral action, or unwise media briefing.[5] It takes time, and shared experiences, to build up such confidence. The UK is fortunate in having agencies with relationships of trust with many sister agencies on a global basis. These relationships are developing and deepening and that trend will need to be encouraged, particularly at a European level. The UK is also likely to face future initiatives from some of its partners for intelligence and security institution building at a European level. At the same time, the importance of maintaining close relations between traditional close allies will not diminish, and may increase under the pressure of national security strategy. The wisest course for the UK is likely therefore to be to make progress at all three levels set out above in ways that recognize the nature of the subject matter, and the need to accommodate different national constitutional and historical experiences, but without diverting energy into creating new freestanding institutions.

Of course what will not change in coming years are the many ways in which elucidation can fail to shed sufficient light, or can cloak the subject in quite misleading colours. The risks of such errors today may be thought to be higher than during the Cold War simply because there is more human judgment to be applied in modern circumstances, and the assessments have inevitably to answer questions that are more of the nature of mysteries than secrets. Analysts have to be trained to become self-aware of these pitfalls, and encouraged to think consciously about the methodologies they are following, a topic discussed in chapter 7.

Dissemination

'Dissemination' describes the policies and processes necessary to get the intelligence into the hands of those who will use it, and sometimes to those who have no idea that they need to know, or indeed might prefer not to know, the assessments being reached by the intelligence community. The term conveys a helpful sense of sowing seeds for later germination. The existence of widespread circulation of both single-source reporting and all-source assessments has given rise in the British system to least three quite different intelligence dissemination processes at work simultaneously in central government.

The first model of intelligence use relies on the existence of expert intelligence customers, for example analysts in the Defence Intelligence Staff and military commands, researchers in the Foreign Office and officers within the intelligence and security community itself who receive streams of individual intelligence reports from an originating agency. Such experts are able to assess the value of an individual report in context, and have the time and experience to relate one report to others in the same series or to information from other sources on the same topic. Such subject experts can contribute to CIG discussion of papers to be submitted to the Joint Intelligence Committee, but by the same token such expert readers of intelligence are often going to find the high-level JIC assessments add little to their existing knowledge. In my observation, reductions in civil service and diplomatic service staff numbers (and the subtle effect of the demotion of the status of the subject expert in favour of the managerially competent) means that there are fewer deep experts than there used to be, throwing an additional load on to analysts in the individual agencies.

The second intelligence distribution model to be found in the UK is aimed at the policy staffs who brief the most senior decision-makers, including ministers and senior military officers. They are, in strict intelligence terms, lay readers: they may be very versed in their range of policy subjects, but are not experts in reading intelligence. Only the most high level single-source intelligence reports will be sent to these individuals, both because they are not likely to have the available data and expertise to place fragmentary reports in the context of earlier reporting, and simply because of the other pressures on their time which will inevitably severely restrict the space in a long day available for reading secret intelligence, which is a task that for security reasons has to be conducted in the office. On the other hand, this group is in practice probably the main audience for the Joint Intelligence Committee all-source assessed product. A strategic appreciation of what is going on, and why, is essential for the formulation of policy advice, and having available up to date all-source assessment is important as the background against which policy options can be put to ministers, senior officials or service commanders, or be incorporated into briefs written for meetings and negotiations.

The third model of intelligence use is the one that is perhaps most idealized by the media and the academic intelligence studies community, and that is the provision of high-level intelligence assessments direct to the Prime Minister and the most senior Cabinet members. It is often assumed in the media that all assessments from the Joint Intelligence Committee are eagerly awaited by ministers and will be keenly studied by such senior readers. Sometimes, when the topicality of the subject merits it, such attention will be given. In practice, most ministers have little time to read the paper they should relating to their responsibilities from advisers, think tanks, academics, overseas governments and international institutions, and outside commentators, let alone secret intelligence assessments. Their focus is inevitably on the short-term management of political business, not the longer-term assessments on subjects that do not demand early decisions. If, on the other hand, the subject is one on which they are already actively engaged, for example through the participation of British forces overseas, then JIC assessments may have little to add to what they will have already been told in their frequent operational meetings and briefings on the subject.

In practice, the ministers most directly involved in national security work will be given a mixed diet by their Private Offices, who will flag up any JIC assessments on subjects of interest, together with a selected few single-source intelligence reports that directly bear on ministerial concerns. An example would be the report on the attitudes of the Soviet leadership that Oleg Gordievsky was able to provide SIS in preparation for Mrs Thatcher's first meeting with President Gorbachev.

The intelligence community also faces the same dilemma as journals such as *The Economist* or *Newsweek*: there is a tension between the editor selecting what topics might be appropriate to the target readership group and delivering that as a printed journal, and investing in a much larger internet site of news and articles from which individual readers may pull what looks to them to be interesting and relevant (perhaps having received an email to alert them to fresh material in areas they have previously registered as being of interest). Intelligence systems based entirely on customer 'pull' do run a real risk that key information will not come to the attention of the policy-maker or the military commander in sufficient time. On the other hand the traditional 'push' or flow of written reports is too limited and slow for many needs, such as that of the military commander who needs annotated maps, pictures, biometrics, video and data of all kinds. A supporting infrastructure of secure broadband communications stretching out into the customers' space becomes essential.

There is implicit in the world of secret intelligence a contest: you will have decision advantage if you obtain the information you need when you need it; your opponent will correspondingly lose ground. It is important to note here that not only does the information have to be acquired but it also has to be available to the decision-maker when it is needed. That last consideration is of course especially important in the counter-terrorism and military settings. In the case of the latter, the doctrine of the OODA[6] (Observe, Orient, Decide and Act) loop describes the need to get inside the decision time of the enemy commander so that intelligence on his moves is available in sufficient time to allow counter-measures before he in turn can detect them and change his plans. This demand for total information awareness has a major effect on investment to support military operations in what has been called 'the revolution in military affairs'. It has to be doubted, however, whether it is really the case that modern intelligence gathering can make the fog of war transparent. Glimpses through the swirling mist would be a better analogy.

Need to know or requirement to provide

One of the first things in an adversarial contest that it is useful to understand is how much the opponent may be presumed to know about how much you actually know about what he knows about you. His objective is of course to maintain sufficient secrecy to prevent such understanding; and vice versa, since the situation is usually symmetrical. If the extent of your intelligence becomes known to the opponent then counter-measures can be taken against the likely sources of the information, or deception plans prepared to sow doubt in the minds of the intelligence assessors about what they think they know. Or, at the most basic level, policies may be adjusted by an opponent confident in the knowledge of what the opponent does not appear to know. Paradoxically, therefore, having access to the considered strategic assessments of a nation (what in UK terms would include the output from the Joint Intelligence Committee) would give an opponent an invaluable insight into the thinking of government at the highest levels—even if the details in the assessments were themselves nothing more sensitive than could be read in the pages of the *Financial Times* or *The Economist* (in practice, of course, frank intelligence assessments are also likely to contain comments about the policies of other nations and their leaders that government would not want to see published). So we should not be surprised that intelligence communities do not just protect their own secrets, and governments guard the details of their military capabilities and the performance of their weapons systems, but nations will guard the overall intelligence assessments that they make of other nations even when much of the information may have come from open sources. Terrorist groups can certainly benefit from knowledge of the methods of the security authorities—which is why the proceeding of criminal trials will be followed avidly by terrorists and their sympathizers for clues as to how their activities, movements and communications came to the notice of the intelligence authorities and were tracked by them. Against that argument must be set the counter-example of cases when it is helpful for the adversary to know what you know, and thus for example dash any hopes he might have harboured of stealing a march on you.

In controlling the dissemination of intelligence, elaborate schemes exist for grading the degree of secrecy that should surround an intelligence report, not just in terms of whether the information is to be kept confidential, or secret or even top secret, but in terms of carefully limiting the number and positions of those who are allowed to know the information. The definition of 'Top Secret', for example, covers information whose unauthorized disclosure could reasonably be expected to cause exceptionally grave damage to national security; for 'Secret' information the threshold is serious damage; and for 'Confidential', simply damage to the national security. When new sources are on trial, or are especially fragile and vulnerable to counter-measures, then the intelligence agencies can rightly be expected to limit the distribution of the resulting reports, often to only named officers with strict instructions that they may not share the information without permission from the originator (what in US parlance is called Originator Controlled or ORCON material). Special codewords may be used on reports to define compartmented intelligence where only those on the list controlled by the agency, and briefed by the agency on its sensitivity, can have access to material in that compartment. Such security can cause real difficulties. As the Butler inquiry concluded[7] in the case of a report from a sensitive new source on trial that was of significance in the drafting of the UK government's published dossier on Iraqi WMD, it was wrong that it was not shown to the key experts in the Defence Intelligence Staff who could have commented on the validity and credibility of the report (which was later withdrawn as unreliable). Butler concluded that arrangements should always be sought to ensure that the need for protection of sources should not prevent the exposure of reports on technical matters to the most expert available analysis.

Today the need is for dissemination to be seen in terms of both circulation outward, including to partners and allies overseas, and downward to law enforcement and other governmental and private sector partners. The latter raises issues around classification, tear-line reporting (where the intelligence report contains a sanitized version of the key points at the end that can be 'torn off' and handed to those who need to know but have no need to be aware of the detail of the reporting) and the creation of 'fusion centres' which are now well discussed in the literature.[8] As the distribution of product becomes increasingly electronic, it is not hard to imagine reports officers annotating their product with Amazon or iTunes style comments: 'readers who found this report of interest might like to click on the boxes below to request the following reports on related subjects...'

In the traditional intelligence cycle, the reports officer or requirements officer of the relevant secret agency would know personally most of the readership in Whitehall of the most sensitive intelligence. Trust would build up that these individuals could receive very sensitive reporting (that is, intelligence which by its content or nature could reveal much about the source or method by which it was obtained), understand its limitations and follow the rules, in particular not mixing that information with less classified material and not passing it on to those known to be security-cleared to receive it. In the world of counter-terrorism, highly sensitive information from delicate sources (either human or technical that might be fragile to counter-measures were the suspects to learn of them) could be used to great effect in protecting the public. A partial solution adopted in the UK is to have, in areas likely to be of greatest concern, collocated Security Service and specially selected police officers able to see sensitive material and judge to whom and how its gist should be conveyed locally. Less sensitive tactically, but nevertheless classified, operational assessments of terrorist capabilities and intention can also in this way be shared with those planning the 'Protect' and 'Prepare' responses, for example in local government and in key parts of the critical infrastructure.

Action-on

At this point it should be noted that a new feature has been added to the traditional cycle as shown in Figure 4, *action-on* intelligence. There is an increasing emphasis in post Cold War intelligence work on dealing with 'action this day' intelligence material, particularly in the areas of proliferation, terrorism, narcotics and serious crime, in contrast to the background intelligence that traditionally informs policy-making or builds up a long-term picure of military capabilities. The media report police raids on suspected terrorist hide-outs, or additional security precautions surrounding a ministerial meeting, or passengers being told they cannot take liquids in hand-luggage, or that an air-to-surface missile from a drone is seen precisely to target a vehicle on the other side of the world: all visible signs of intelligence being acted upon. During the Cold War such use was normally covert, away from public gaze, and there was usually time to apply collective consideration of use including with allies[9]. Now it could not be more visible. The pressure on the intelligence community to allow its product to be used, including in court, can only increase. The requirement to be able to integrate multiple sources of intelligence in real time or near real time to support security operations, whether at home or in far-off theatres, will increase. There will continue to be pressure from government to use intelligence to justify its actions to the public and to bolster support for policies. The risk management judgments between longer-term exploitation and short-term public protection will become harder, as will the trade-offs between maintaining security for the source and allowing action-on. The long-standing rule must be upheld that the providing intelligence agency must have the final say on whether action can be taken and the risks to sources and methods accepted.

There is a necessary caveat to be added to this modern view of the intelligence cycle. Accepting that in national security work 'interaction with the user' will be increasingly at the centre of most intelligence work, care will be needed to preserve a sense of psychological distance between the intelligence analyst and the policy customer when it comes to strategic assessment. There needs to be awareness on the part of both analyst and policy-maker of the dangers of conscious or unconscious politicization of intelligence. This dilemma of how to maintain safe 'interaction with the user' is explored further in chapter 6.

Direction

As Figure 5 shows, the cycle comes back round to *direction*, the capacity needed to manage the cycle, including evaluation of intelligence priorities based on a review of the changing security environment. It is not hard to see what should remain key priority requirements from the point of view of the traditional pol-mil customers. But the broader definition of security means that there will be a broader range of customers for intelligence, covering a wider range of governmental activity, who may benefit from intelligence support. Future threats identified in general terms in the National Security Strategy will have to be turned into specific statements of intelligence priority as part of the normal intelligence requirements process, and regularly reviewed and updated as part of the cycle of intelligence activity. Care will also be needed to ensure that the policies being followed by the components of the intelligence community, and the balance of investment between their capabilities, fits the overall likely needs of the national security strategy and of external pressures ranging from technological advances to public opinion. A start has been made but, as chapter 11 argues, the UK still has some way to go in developing the capacity to direct the intelligence community as a whole.

Spy versus counter-spy: recognizing the race between offence and defence

We can see see in the history of secret intelligence and counter-intelligence an arms race between those on the offence, seeking information, and those on the defence, seeking to prevent access. *Mad* magazine satirized it as 'Spy versus Spy', a cartoon strip featuring two spies, Black and White, dressed in trilby hats and long overcoats, who are constantly in conflict, seeking increasingly sophisticated ways of doing away with the other. Clausewitz based much of his thinking on war on what he saw as the inherent superiority of the defence. For him, for the offence to be successful required more things to go right (and for sufficient genius on the part of the military commander) since the fog and friction of war would be likely to affect the offence more than the defence. In the case of intelligence work, the opposite applies. Having the initiative to decide what information to seek and when and how to try to acquire it gives the offence a natural advantage; intelligence attacks are by definition usually covert and the attention of defensive sentinels is bound to wander and eyelids droop, missing signs of offensive action under way. Only such complacency, and the strong feeling that 'it can't happen to me', can explain such extraordinary security lapses as the major German wartime success in recruiting the valet to the British Ambassador in Ankara, Sir Hughe Knatchbull-Hugessen. This agent, Cicero, photographed secret documents on the ambassador's desk in 1943 and 1944 while his master played the piano at diplomatic soirées. Thankfully, as a result of bitter internal rivalry within the German wartime leadership, his information was not taken as seriously as it deserved, another salutary lesson in assessing the contribution of intelligence to national security.

The historical record shows that there are nevertheless periods when advances in technology—the introduction of security vetting, or frequency hopping radios, or strong encryption—can put the defence in a stronger position, at least until ways round the defence have been devised. We must expect this arms race to continue, and for the advantage to ebb and flow as the offensive intelligence triumph of one nation becomes the defensive security failure of another.

Is it inevitable that the intelligence cycle, seeking and delivering value-adding intelligence, has to be a zero-sum game, with winners and losers? In traditional inter-state competition, the answer was almost always that it was. The uncovering of the Soviet Atom spies and then the Cambridge spy ring with the defection of Burgess and Maclean, the exposure of Kim Philby as a long-term KGB agent, followed by Anthony Blunt and John Cairncross (the 'fifth man'), raised public awareness of the intelligence battle that was going on during the Cold War. The activities of Soviet spy rings seriously harmed British and Western interests and represented a major failure of British and US counter-intelligence, but in Moscow their exploits were celebrated in the KGB museum as an inspiration to future generations of intelligence officers. The museum of the Secret Intelligence Service is likewise a place of respect and learning for young British officers, where the tradecraft of those who recruited and ran such agents as Gordievsky and Mitrokhin can be celebrated. In the depth of the Cold War, both sides were actively seeking to obtain intelligence for the purposes of counter-intelligence by the unmasking of spies within their own ranks through the penetration of the intelligence apparatus of the other side and the poisoning of the wells of the opponent. As graphically described by James Angleton of the CIA, it was a wilderness of mirrors.[10] In *The Spy Who Came in from the Cold* (1963) John le Carré captures the essence of that struggle and the vertigo induced by recognizing one's tradecraft in one's opponent, fighting fire with fire. The fact that there was a mirroring of intelligence activity in this period should not be taken to imply moral equivalence, since it is relevant that the record shows that the advantage lay with the Western intelligence agencies who received offers of support from those who rejected the Soviet system, whilst recruiting in the other direction by the KGB and GRU was a largely a matter of using the levers of blackmail and money, less reliable motivators of human behaviour. Soviet behaviour, with the Molotov–Ribbentrop agreement, the subjection of eastern Europe and the crushing of the Hungarian uprising in 1956, put a virtual end to the ability of the Soviet Union to recruit ideological spies, in the way that they had been able to in the very different political atmosphere of pre-war England.

Today, we would be entitled to question that modern intelligence activity has to be a zero-sum game. Successful UK and US intelligence operations between 1998 and 2003 patiently pieced together the details of Libya's proliferation plans and uncovered the support for them provided by the Pakistani scientist and entrepreneur A. Q. Khan[11]. Libyan intelligence and security services were no doubt actively trying to prevent US and UK agencies from obtaining that secret knowledge, but they failed and the proliferation networks were exposed and disrupted. That information provided, no doubt along with the example of the invasion of Iraq, the key leverage to persuade the Libyan leader, Colonel Ghaddafi, that it was in his interests, given that the information was in the hands of the UK and US, to change his policy. It is hard not to conclude that both Libya and the West have gained from the eventual outcome. The same argument could be mounted over the masterly SIS operation that ran Oleg Gordievsky as Head of KGB Station in London, and that enabled Margaret Thatcher to be more confidently briefed for her initial meetings with Soviet President Gorbachev, a man with whom she famously declared she could do business; a key moment in the history of the end of the Cold War. If the 1940s Soviet atom spies had not succeeded as they did in providing information that allowed faster development of the Soviet thermonuclear weapons, and if the US had held the monopoly of such power during the Korean war, it could be argued that General Macarthur might not have been restrained from using them against China when the conventional battle went for a time against him. But counter-factual history cannot be pressed too far.

As already mentioned, intelligence from satellite reconnaissance was a stabilizing factor in providing confidence to both the US and USSR that their respective 'national technical means', the euphemism for observation by intelligence satellites, would detect arms control cheating. In some circumstances at least we can think of the situation as analogous to the classic 'prisoners' dilemma' in games theory where two suspected accomplices in crime are arrested and kept separate: if one agrees to testify against the other and the other remains silent, the first goes free and the other receives ten years in gaol; if both prisoners remain silent, both can only be charged with a minor offence and receive light sentences; and if each betrays the other, each receives a five-year sentence. If the prisoners cannot communicate, then rationally the best course for each is to confess so both receive five years. If they can communicate—and there is a sufficient level of trust—then they can agree to remain silent and both get off on the minor charge alone. If, however, irrespective of any assumed level of trust each had secret intelligence capabilities sufficient to give confidence that they would know if the other prisoner was going to cheat, then they could both rationally and independently (that is, there is no need to assume cooperation between them) work out that both remaining silent is in their mutual interests, and proceed to keep quiet knowing that the other would not be able to 'break out' into confession without the other knowing and quickly adjusting their own behaviour.

Espionage should also have given the Soviet leadership considerable insight into NATO nuclear war planning and exercising, and thus its genuinely defensive character. But according to Oleg Gordievsky as an agent of the Secret Intelligence Service inside the senior ranks of the KGB, the Soviet leaders Brezhnev and Andropov became convinced in the early 1980s that the US was planning a first-strike attack against the Soviet Union. Agents overseas, including Gordievsky as KGB Chief of Station London, were charged with monitoring for early signs of such preparation for war, including the number of lights burning late in the British Ministry of Defence and the state of supply in the UK Blood Transfusion Service. The NATO exercise Able Archer in 1983 triggered Soviet paranoia that the exercise could be cover for attack preparations and led to some Soviet nuclear and air defence forces being put on alert. Such examples show the importance of understanding underlying assumptions that totalitarian leaderships may harbour, which may well colour the interpretation of intelligence and lead to contrary intelligence being suppressed.

Do we even have to have to have the concept of an adversary in mind when we talk about secret intelligence? The concept of having to beat an opponent who by taking defensive measures is seeking to frustrate the gathering of secret intelligence is present in almost all intelligence work. The use made by policy-makers of secret intelligence once gathered need not nevertheless be confined to adversaries if that term is interpreted as meaning potentially hostile states or organizations. India and Pakistan are both friendly nations with whom the United Kingdom maintains good relations. But in 2002, when for a moment it looked as if those two nuclear armed nations could go to war, the dangers of escalation certainly would have led British and all Western intelligence communities to focus their attention on the crisis and to try to provide their governments with assessments on which diplomatic moves could be based to help defuse the crisis. Measured by the proportion of effort, British secret intelligence is now no longer principally concerned with the activities of potentially hostile nations, but much more concerned with the activities of non-state actors, especially terrorist groups. The UK Security Service in 2008 devoted around 90 per cent of its effort to countering terrorism and providing protective security advice against terrorist threats of all types, and SIS devoted some 2/3 of effort likewise to terrorism related intelligence according to the 2000 Annual Report of the Intelligence and Security Committee.

Direction is both the starting and ending point of the new intelligence cycle, and describes the capability now needed at the centre of government to enable a collection of intelligence agencies and bodies to function as a single intelligence community, one that is more than the sum of its parts. Chapter 11 will describe some of the tasks that should now fall to those who are charged with the direction of the UK intelligence community and suggests some of the directions in which they should be seeking to shift that community. For individual intelligence agencies, direction principally means the set of requirements from customers that launches them on the processes of access and elucidation that, with some luck and a lot of skill, ends up with high value-adding reporting and assessed intelligence that improve government's performance, especially in managing security risks. The next chapter breaks back into the cycle to examine the function of 'elucidation'.

6

ELUCIDATION

YE SHALL KNOW THE TRUTH, AND THE TRUTH SHALL SET YOU FREE

The validation of single-source reporting

Applying great ingenuity, not inconsiderable resource, and at times great personal courage, intelligence agencies will succeed in penetrating their opponent's screen of security and return with secret intelligence. The intelligence may self-evidently tell its own story, but often, however, raw intelligence represents a piece of a jigsaw that may fit one of several mixed-up puzzles, for none of which was there a picture on the lid of the box. The piece itself will need validating to ensure that its shape can be relied upon and that it has not been cast our way to confuse us; then its likely place in one of the puzzles can be estimated. It may be spotted straight away that the piece has two straight edges and thus represents a corner of a puzzle, and such a prized piece will be quickly forwarded to those assembling the overall picture. It may be that it has no obvious meaning, and it will have to be added to the growing pile of pieces yet to be fitted together. Often the same pieces can be assembled into very different pictures, introducing the real danger that intelligence can be cherry-picked to support the policy-makers' desired view of the world. With analytic skill, however, and some luck the pieces can finally be placed alongside all the other related pieces and what was previously hidden, especially that which was deliberately sought to be hidden, becomes visible.

These processes of analysis and assessment are what were described in the previous chapter as 'elucidation'.

The process of elucidation should start the moment raw intelligence arrives in the hands of the desk officer of the relevant intelligence agency. It may be reporting from human agents via a case officer, from the product of technical operations such as eavesdropping, from intercepted communications and telemetry, as photographs and radar images, as reporting from liaison services and in many other forms.

Before the actual content of an intelligence report can be considered, the validity of the reporting chain which has led to its production must be confirmed. For imagery and signals intelligence this is not usually an issue, although even here the danger of deception must be considered. But for human intelligence it is vital that there has been an effective validation process before intelligence is shown to policy customers. The validation of a reporting chain is thus a first step in the provision of secret intelligence to the customer. Suppose a secret report comes from a well-placed agent who has access to circles in which interesting topics are likely to be discussed. The agent may have recruited sub-agents within that circle, and will use them to put together reports for his controlling intelligence officer on topics that he or she will have been briefed would be likely to be of interest to the intelligence agency. The case officer responsible for that source will have to judge whether his reporting chain is robust, and the information is valid. He will have to assess whether the source may have felt under pressure to report a positive finding on the subject, or is seeking to curry favour, perhaps for financial gain or to gain assistance for their family. It may be that the source is being controlled by a hostile intelligence service or is in some way acting as a double agent. The information may have come from a casual contact, or a new source still on trial whose reliability has not been fully tested. Even having endorsed the bona fides of the individual agent, the case officer will need to be satisfied that the information being reported was itself valid and not just palace gossip or material deliberately put in the way of the agent in order to deceive. Such questions become even more pressing when the source is relying on sub-sources not known personally to the case officer, or when the information has been taken from internet chat-sites when the participants may have suspected they were being monitored.

Every kind of intelligence access needs validation. The intercepted conversation between terrorist suspects may have been carried out by the parties knowing that it might be eavesdropped or intercepted. For example, an agreement between suspects to meet at the garage at noon with the spare parts may be a pre-arranged code to mean two hours earlier in the park and with the detonators (an example of the difference between evidence and intelligence). What is shown on the aerial photograph may be a dummy not a real tank, or there may be intention to deceive through the deliberate hiding of activity, for example during the known pass-time of a low earth orbiting satellite. The country concerned may have other motives for deception that might end up being reflected in intelligence, for example a desire by Saddam Hussein to convince Iran that his WMD programmes were still in being.

Such probing of the material is very similar to what would be in the mind of an experienced historian examining a primary or secondary source document, regarding its age, provenance, authorship, audience for which it was written and why. The historian will question whether an account is self-exculpatory and what is known of the other reporting from that source, whether it is the original document or a copy, and if the latter how long after the original it was made, by whom, and where. And there will be a caution about whether an account is based on direct observation and whether it was likely that the author had firsthand experience of what he was writing about, or if reporting the views of others whether they had direct knowledge. Similar lines of historiography apply to the scrutiny of technical intelligence, including intercepted or overheard conversations, and the oldest question of all, *cui bono*, what were the speakers' intentions in having the conversation.

For many high priority subjects such as weapons research and development, especially where novel technologies are involved, a degree of expertise would be necessary to know whether the information being relayed made technical sense, and if it did whether it added anything to what is already known. The case officer must check whether the agent had the necessary expertise to report accurately overheard conversations about, say, chemical or biological warfare programmes. There are also 'reality check' questions, such as whether the content of the reporting makes sense in the light of everything already believed about the subject, or whether it contradicts what is believed to be known. In the case of secret intelligence there is the further complication that the agent may not have been aware of the true identity, occupation and nationality of the case officer with whom he is dealing, a so-called false-flag operation. All such questions apply to the analysis that the analyst in an intelligence agency should apply to a source report at the outset, and certainly may qualify whether and how it should be circulated. The validation process will often have involved consideration of the coherence and consistency of intelligence being provided by an informant, as one of the ways in which that source's reliability can be tested.

Evidently, there will be times when reporting appears to contradict received wisdom. The officers of the intelligence agency are faced at that point with the classic dilemma of setting their cursor between the risks of Type I (sometimes called false positive) and Type II (some times called false negative) errors. If they are too conservative then they will screen out themselves challenging reports as obviously wrong (outliers) when in fact it was received wisdom that needed to be revised (Type I error), and if they are too imaginative then there will be plenty of Type II errors (crying wolf) when ill-founded reports are nevertheless forwarded to customers as contributing fresh insights. Trial and error, informed by feedback from the users, is a guide as to where to set the risk cursor, but it will help if the analyst has a good understanding of what the decision-taker is trying to do.

Degrees of truth

From such single-source analysis it should be possible for the relevant agency to fit the intelligence inside a reporting framework that will describe to the reader the confidence level placed in the source, such as *Status* (is the source new, one that is developing, or established? Does the information come from a liaison service?); *Reporting record* (reliable, or unverified); *Access* (indirect or direct, quoting an individual, or based on a recording of a conversation, or documentary record); *Familiarity with subject matter* (opportunity basis, occasional access or a regular source on this subject). In the UK all intelligence reporting from any of the UK agencies is handled through a special distribution system known as the UK STRAP system, with different levels of sensitivity. In the US, the most sensitive material is graded ORCON, or originator controlled distribution. In both cases, additional codewords will be used to refer to the material, and only those on special distribution lists approved by the originating agency will be authorized to know of the existence of this line of reporting and to see reports selected for them by the agency.

An indication by the issuing agency of suggested importance, from Cat A (influencing decisions) to Cat C ('building block' intelligence), will help readers prioritize their reading of intelligence and help in feedback. It should also be possible for the officer in the agency responsible for issuing the report to have identified how much extra detail, such as references to past reporting from the same source, explanation of technical terms, or identification of names mentioned in the report. (very important for counter-terrorist intelligence) would be likely to be useful to the reader. In the UK system single-source reports are issued direct to customers in MOD and the armed forces or in the civil departments only on condition that any comment accompanying the report confined itself to such largely factual matters and did not spill over into assessment, or incorporate other lines of reporting such as mixing SIGINT and HUMINT. As will be described below, all-source assessment is clearly distinguishable by the reader from source reporting. In that way, the risk is minimized that assessments and reports arriving from different quarters could erroneously be thought to be mutually corroborating when it was the same underlying intelligence in each case.

A common media criticism has been that intelligence agencies, unlike the media themselves, are prepared to run with a story on the basis of a single uncorroborated source. This line of criticism is based on a media myth that, before taking the decision to broadcast or publish an investigative revelation, editors require the journalist concerned to have more than one independent source in order to verify the story, not least to reduce the risk of libel action. Part of the *Washington Post's* Watergate lore is that they had a 'two-source' rule. The myth seems to have originated over Woodward and Bernstein's arguments with Editor Ben Bradlee over information from their covert source, 'Deep Throat' (much later W. Mark Felt, the former FBI second-in-command, owned up). Barry Sussman, the editor who oversaw the *Washington Post* story, described it thus: 'According to this notion, if a Watergate prosecutor or conspirator or US Senator or Senate investigator—or anyone—made an important allegation to us, we had to confirm it with at least one other source before running it. I don't know who concocted this two-source nonsense. I do know that none of the editors above me ever mentioned it, nor did I mention it to the reporters. The two-source rule, usually referred to reverentially, is a smug way of suggesting that *Washington Post* editors were 100 per cent sure of what we were printing. We did, of course, try to confirm and expand on leads, and that often meant going to two, three, four or even more sources. What responsible reporter or editor would want to run some unconfirmed assertion from a shaky source? There was no two-source rule. There was only, as with most news organizations, an attempt to find reliable sources.'[1]

The same mythical rule was, however, used to attack simultaneously the UK intelligence community over their reliance on a single report on Iraqi chemical weapons (the 'ready in 45 minutes' claim) and the BBC for failure to insist on corroboration of BBC reporter Andrew Gilligan's report into the alleged 'sexing up' of the dossier on weapons of mass destruction (Lord Hutton's inquiry finding that that part of the BBC report was unfounded led to the resignation of the Director-General of the BBC). The BBC sensibly concluded that they will continue to use single-source stories but they must be 'of significant public interest and the correct procedures followed. They will undergo greater editorial scrutiny.'[2] Needless to say, that should also be the practice in the US and UK worlds of intelligence when the reporting comes from a source with an established reputation.

Sharing the outcome of validation with analysts and users

For the most part, the customers of intelligence will have to accept the agency validation, for example that the source is regular and reliable or is documentary, or some other descriptor. The customers, on the other hand, do have a responsibility to satisfy themselves that they know enough by way of validating information to be able to know how to use the reporting responsibly, and if in doubt they should raise the issue with the originating agency at the appropriate level. Two examples relating to Iraq, from either side of the Atlantic, will make the point.

The Butler Committee of inquiry into British intelligence on WMD drew attention to the inferential nature of most of the intelligence reporting on which assessments of Iraq's WMD capabilities were based. It was the case that those in the Defence Intelligence Staff, and in the central Assessments Staff drafting papers for the JIC, who were charged with trying to assess the overall intelligence picture were not fully aware of the degree of access and background of the key informants who were being run by SIS, and even more so of their sub-sources and sub-sub-sources, and thus take into account their possible motivations for providing the information. In one instance, a new sub-source to another main source, who provided a significant proportion of human intelligence reporting, turned out to have links to opposition groups of which SIS only became aware later, causing SIS to have to warn readers of the dangers that reporting might have been embellished. In other cases, Butler suggested that one reason why the reporting from a number of agents turned out to be unreliable or questionable may have been the length of the reporting chain, so even where the principal source might have been shown in the past to be reliable on other topics, sub-sources or sub-sub-sources might not have direct access to what they claimed to be reporting on WMD.

On the other side of the Atlantic, at the same time, US Defense HUMINT officials in the Pentagon were receiving from the German Intelligence Agency, the BND, substantial reporting on Iraqi biological warfare programmes from a defector, code-named 'Curveball'. The BND wished to protect their agent and would not allow direct access by US or UK officers to Curveball, and so there were inevitable problems for analysts in validating his reporting and in correctly describing to their policy customers assessments based on it. The rub was that the reporting was exactly what the US policy customers wanted to hear. As a defector being controlled by another service, there must have been the risk that he might have deduced what it was that US and Western intelligence services most wanted to hear and therefore have concluded that by embellishing such material he was materially increasing his chances of a generous resettlement package in the West. The US Defense HUMINT officials took the line that their responsibility was limited to being a conduit for the liaison reporting—if analysts assessed what Curveball was reporting as technically valid then that counted as validation. Curveball's reporting in relation to mobile biological warfare trailers was demonstrated by US experts to be credible in scientific and technical terms; the facilities he described could indeed be built and would be effective. That was valuable knowledge, but it did not mean that the trailers existed. Curveball had been a chemical engineer with some past exposure to the BW programme, and not surprisingly his reporting of recent developments made technical sense. That of itself did not make his story true.

The Senate Select Committee on Intelligence concluded that the US Defence HUMINT view of their limited responsibilities in respect of validation represented a 'serious lapse' in tradecraft. In the view of the Robb–Silberman inquiry, analysts play a crucial role in validating sources by evaluating the credibility of their reporting, corroborating that reporting, and reviewing the body of reporting to ensure that it is consistent with the source's access. But analysts' validation can only extend to whether what a source says is internally consistent, technically plausible, and credible given the source's claimed access. The process of validation also must include efforts by the operational agency to confirm the source's bona fides (i.e. authenticating that the source has the access he claims), to test the source's reliability and motivations, and to ensure that the source is free from hostile control. To be sure, these steps are particularly difficult for a source such as Curveball, to whom the collection agency has no direct access. But, as Robb–Silberman concluded, such lack of access does not preclude the responsible intelligence agency from attempting to assess the credibility of the source. Indeed, it is incumbent upon professional intelligence officers to attempt to do so. Those strictures apply, of course, to SIGINT as well as HUMINT sources.

As a general rule. therefore, where the material is being provided by a foreign liaison service, then additional care will need to be taken to test the overall credibility of the source, in so far as the foreign service concerned is prepared to cooperate in giving any information about their sources and methods. In the case of terrorism intelligence, all that may be passed over with a request that it be checked out may well be telephone numbers, addresses or identification of individuals in photographs with no indication of where and how the information came into the hands of the liaison service. Chapter 9 examines some ethical issues that arise from the risk that thereby an intelligence agency may be implicitly colluding in the mistreatment of suspects by an overseas service.

Judging the likely customer interest in a single-source intelligence report

When raw intelligence is received in the intelligence agency headquarters, a first judgment is made about whether the contents are likely to be of sufficient interest and value to be disseminated as a formal report to the customers of the intelligence agency. In the case of the Secret Intelligence Service, since its earliest days as a separate service their reports have been known as CX Reports from their reference number that is prefaced by the digraph CX. Some early Enigma decrypts in 1940 from Bletchley Park were issued with a CX/FJ number to disguise them (successfully) as human agent reporting. That historical experience holds a lesson for us, since it had the unfortunate consequence that for some military intelligence readers the true importance of the reporting was misunderstood, such was the poor reputation of some early SIS human agent reporting.

The main customers in question are likely to be the 'expert' users elsewhere in the intelligence agency concerned and in the rest of the intelligence community, in the other agencies and the all-source assessment bodies, notably the Assessments Staff supporting the Joint Intelligence Committee (JIC) in the Cabinet Office, the Defence Intelligence Staff supporting defence chiefs, senior officials and commanders and JTAC located in the headquarters of the Security Service. Later in the chapter we look at the all-source assessment process when different streams of reporting as well as open sources of relevant information are examined side by side to derive key intelligence judgments for senior policy-makers, for example in the UK as JIC papers or in the US as National Intelligence Estimates. The single-source intelligence reporting can be regarded as an intermediate input into the production of a 'final product', an all-source report, that will be sent to policy or operational customers. In the UK system, however, it is very important to recognize that on many subjects, particularly in operational and tactical areas, it is the single-source report that is the main output of the intelligence community as far as the expert user is concerned.

In the UK, unlike many other nations, there is a very high level of sharing of relevant single-source intelligence between the relevant sections and cleared individuals of the other intelligence agencies. We can best regard this reporting from one agency to another as an essential input to improve the understanding by each other of their own material. An important and under-recognized part of this process is the building up of systemized information about the subject area, including databases accessible across the community of individuals mentioned in reporting, indexes of aliases known to be used by suspects, lists of companies suspected of facilitating proliferation, narcotics smuggling, telephone numbers contacted by terrorists, frequencies used for telemetry associated with missile tests and so on. The world of secret intelligence relies more heavily on the connections that organized information can provide, and the routine disciplines of the modern archivist, than Hollywood directors would allow. An outside observer would be surprised to see the volume of reporting passing round between components of the secret world of the UK and its close allies.

To manage the reporting from an SIS HUMINT source, along with the oversight provided by the operational line controlling the case officer concerned, what are called 'requirements' officers in a separate line relationship to senior agency management will see the reporting and help to provide a critical eye. It is the requirements officers who are in regular contact with the readers and users of intelligence across government. The 'internal audit' provided by the requirements line is intended to help counteract the natural tendency for intelligence case officers to see all their geese as swans, a natural bias that must be expected from time to time. The requirements officers will have been in direct contact with customers (who would not normally have access to the case officers concerned). They should therefore be able to judge the degree of interest there will be in a report and whether it should be flagged up as likely to be of exceptional importance, in which case an alerting telephone call to the relevant desk officer or Private Office may be made, and accelerated arrangements made for distribution, of interest in terms of policy relevance or merely likely to be useful background. The skill of the requirements officer is to know the likely levels of knowledge and understanding of the customers for his reporting. A trained military intelligence officer in a command headquarters is likely to need far less context to use an intelligence report on detected enemy movements than a busy policy desk officer, with many other non-intelligence related duties, will need to be given to appreciate the import of intelligence bearing on his subject. This is a good example of a knowledge management system that would benefit greatly from the application of the latest information technology.

As noted at the outset of this chapter, some secret reporting requires little analysis. The purloined document or intercepted message may for the intended customer speak for itself. That, however, is not always going to be the case. As we noted in the case of Curveball, just because an agent reports to his case officer information that is technically plausible, or describes scientific or other developments that are technically feasible, does not mean that the report itself should be accepted at face value. Technical credibility is a necessary but not sufficient condition for endorsing a report. In *Our Man in Havana*, Graham Greene satirizes Wormald, his hapless SIS officer inventing intelligence about a new weapons system being built in Cuba with drawings based on a scaled-up version of his vacuum cleaner; pure fantasy—but illustrating the need for care in validations of sources and validation of content.

The analysis of single-source reporting

The British experience is that regular customers for intelligence prefer to know which type of source report they are reading, rather than having a homogenized product constructed from different types of source. This approach is applied particularly strictly in the case of signals intelligence, where the terrorist expert is likely to want to have the exact words as they were spoken, and indeed to know whether the speakers were agitated, appeared to know each other or any other colouration that an experienced transcriber could provide. A rule applied therefore in the British intelligence community is that reporting issued by individual intelligence agencies should inform the reader of the secret intelligence being reported, as closely as possible to the terms in which it was accessed (after translation and explanation of unfamiliar technical terms). There is an evident risk of circularity if the same piece of intelligence is used in different reports, since the incautious reader may conclude that he is being given corroborating evidence, when it is simply the same report in different clothes. This danger is evidently all the greater when reports come in from the liaison sources that may have their origins in a common source, such as a captured document.

The place of all-source intelligence assessment

Pride of place has traditionally gone to assessed intelligence, where all the possible sources of information on the topic, open and secret, have been brought to bear in order to arrive at a judgment of the meaning and significance of intelligence on a topic or development. Such assessments, if done well, have genuine explanatory power. Crucially, they will be forward-looking and often predictive, based on understanding of the past. As the Director of the CIA Center for the Study of Intelligence has warned,[3] there is a real difficulty here if the analyst is to be creative, bold and aggressive in judgment. Such expressions of view need to be clearly labelled as such, and distinguished from the grounded care for cautious analysis that sticks closely to what can be said with high confidence from the intelligence. Both approaches are needed, but they are different. In the past the bold and provocative paper reaching ministers in the UK might have come from an overseas ambassador in a farewell despatch (now, alas, banned for fear of leaks despite Francis Bacon's advice[4] that despatches were *ad historiam pretiosissima supellex*) or from the departmental policy planning or strategy staff given a jester's licence to analyze policy effectiveness even if it means challenging orthodoxy. Although strategy units have proliferated in Whitehall, their work tends to be with the grain of current political thinking, a tendency accentuated by the practice of consulting or even subcontracting contributions to sympathetic think-tanks. Such approaches are entirely understandable in social policy, where there are political differences between political parties and ministers are entitled to expect papers to be written that reflect their political philosophy, but can become very difficult when applied to matters of security, defence and foreign policy. 'Professional judgment' is a form of freedom of expression that must be allowed those writing intelligence-based assessments, including identifying frankly the implications of policies being followed by the government (stopping short, of course, of advancing policy recommendations as to what then should be done).

All-source assessments should therefore be prepared to tackle mysteries as well as shed light on secrets. Thus analysis is more than validation: it implies understanding of context. Assessment is more than analysis; it implies the understanding that comes from having a satisfactory explanation of events. That understanding should enable the evaluation of the likely reactions of adversaries and third parties to policies being followed. An example was given by the ISC, the UK parliamentary oversight committee, of an assessment by the JIC on 10 February 2003 'that al-Qa'ida and associated groups continued to represent by far the greatest terrorist threat to Western interests, and that threat would be heightened by military action against Iraq'. And a subsequent JIC assessment leaked in 2006[5] stated that 'We judge that the conflict in Iraq has exacerbated the threat from international terrorism and will continue to have an impact in the long term ... it has reinforced the determination of terrorists who were already committed to attacking the West and motivated others who were not ... Iraq is likely to be an important motivating factor for some time to come in the radicalization of British Muslims and for those extremists who view attacks against the UK as legitimate.' The risk of pulling punches in such assessments because of worries that they may not be welcome is obvious. In the military sphere Professor R. V. Jones concluded[6] after the Second World War that if intelligence was called upon to assess the effectiveness of operations (for example, through analysis of bomb damage reports), then it would be best to have separation between intelligence and operational functions, to the highest possible level in government organization.

A *hierarchy of intelligence analysis*

We can envisage a hierarchy of intelligence analysis, serving Clausewitz's strategic, operational and tactical levels of warfare.

As described in chapter 2, at the strategic level, intelligence judgments in the UK are reached by the Joint Intelligence Committee (JIC) whose members include not just the heads of the intelligence agencies and the central intelligence machinery, but also the key policy-makers from the Foreign Office, the Ministry of Defence, the Home Office and the Treasury, and with the attendance of senior representatives from other departments if necessary. The presence of the senior policy officials on the JIC does not of course commit their ministers to agree with the judgments thus reached.

A never-ending debate about intelligence assessment at this level is how far the work of a strategic assessment body such as the JIC should be deliberately restricted to topics where there is a substantial intelligence base, and thus avoid issuing reports that make judgments about mysteries and, even more, about complexities (bearing in mind the distinctions explained in chapter 2). There are a number of considerations. The first is who is best placed to reach an authoritative judgment on a mystery that bears on national security. There is no necessity for this to be the JIC, but the advantage is that the committee has well-established procedures for scrutinizing evidence and subjecting judgments to informed peer review within both the intelligence and departmental policy community. This means that judgments are less likely to be biased, consciously or unconsciously, by any strong views that happen to be held by particular senior individuals. One disadvantage is that the intelligence community will suffer reputational damage from being too closely associated with judgments that are much more speculative by nature than would be the case for traditional topics of intelligence assessment. To a large extent, however, that can be avoided by careful drafting to identify where key judgments are based directly on intelligence reporting and where they are just best estimates. Another disadvantage, of a different kind, is that the UK JIC process has evolved to give an authoritative view emerging from not just the intelligence specialists but the expert policy analysts as well. The tradition is that JIC debate continues until consensus is reached.

At the operational level, the main intelligence demand is for timely all-source analysis to support operational decision-making with a level of detail greater than, and more appropriate to, that expert level. Examples of the issues that the policy-makers have to deal with at this level include the allocation of security and intelligence resources to meet conflicting demands, what advice to give travellers overseas, how to respond to the threat to an embassy overseas threatened by terrorists, the implications of high tech weaponry reaching a country of concern, whether a particular export of specialized steels should be permitted, additional protective security measures taken at a big public event, or what passengers should be allowed to be taken onto aeroplanes. In major cases ultimately ministers will decide whether and how to act.

At the tactical level, individual decisions are being made, within the operational policy framework, by the front-line, whether armed forces, police, Security Service, or government department. Lines of intelligence are largely going raw to other intelligence specialists in support of operations on the ground, for example the tactical application of intelligence to guide a counter-terrorist raid, or to follow a drugs shipment, or to intercept a breach of sanctions. This is the part of the iceberg of which the public rarely is conscious, unless things go awry.

Intelligence agencies do not routinely report nil results, that is to say that agents have been tasked on a topic but have come up with nothing, or that no SIGINT relating to a function has been detected. There is a danger therefore that the customer could be misled by such partial indications as are reported by single-source reports into believing he is receiving the whole picture. That is one reason why wider assessments are necessary, especially in examining all potential sources, in addition to single-source reporting that has actually been issued. For example, an individual intelligence report could be read as consistent with the existence of an illegal proliferation programme. But if the hypothesis to be tested is that there is such a programme, then what other indications should we expect to pick up? Are these indications ones that the coverage of the intelligence agencies might be expected to detect, and if so why are these not being reported? Thus, for example, the absence of confirmatory signals intelligence may be a key indicator that should give pause for thought as to whether a single HUMINT report is likely to be reliable. And the converse proposition should be tested: is there intelligence that runs counter to the existence of the programme?

An analyzed intelligence report, placed in its context, with understanding of significance, is likely to be more powerful provided that its timeliness is preserved. However, when Churchill was frustrated by the delays in intelligence assessments reaching him warning of Operation Barbarossa, Hitler's operation to invade Russia, he wrote in his memoirs: 'I had not been content for this form of collective wisdom, and preferred to see the originals myself. I had arranged therefore, as far back as the summer of 1940, for Major Desmond Morton to make a daily selection of titbits, which I always read, thus forming my own opinion, sometimes at much earlier dates.'

The nature of intelligence assessment

It is in the nature of explanatory theories that they are all provisional. Even the firmest of assessments may well need to be qualified or updated, or even discarded, as new information becomes available. As we shall explore in the next chapter, here lies a crucial difference between the world of the intelligence analyst and of the policy-maker. For the former, judgments are only as good as the fit of the explanation, and there is no shame in revision in the light of new evidence (indeed, the reverse; the shame is in failing to update one's theories); for the latter, policy-making is about shaping the world in the image of the desired policy outcome, and contrary evidence is just another obstacle to be overcome by the application of greater resources and will. Having to admit publicly that one's opinion on a matter has changed is very hard for a politician; it has to be second nature for an intelligence analyst. 'When the facts change, I change my mind; what do you do, Sir?' was Keynes' ripost to a critic who accused him of changing his mind on monetary policy during the Great Depression. Delay in admitting that a key judgment should be changed may prove fatal in the intelligence world.

When the facts change, when new evidence is uncovered, we should reassess the degree of confidence we have in a judgment. The answer as to how to reassess our judgment of probability was discovered in the papers of the Reverend Thomas Bayes, a cleric from Tunbridge Wells, after his death in 1761. Bayes' theorem allows us to calculate by how much we should alter the degree of confidence we have in a judgment A (i.e. the probability that A it is true) when we take account of fresh evidence B on the matter. Put precisely, the posterior probability that A is true, given the evidence B, is equal to the prior probability we had estimated for A before the evidence B was available, adjusted by a factor measuring how relatively likely it is that if A really is true we would have found the evidence B. The adjusting factor therefore is a measure of our degree of surprise when the evidence B turns up, were A to be the case. If therefore we were to conclude that if the judgment A is correct then the evidence B would always be present, then B adds nothing and the adjusting factor is unity: our confidence in the proposition A is unchanged. On the other hand, if the judgment A being correct would mean that B is never seen, then if the evidence B turns up then logically we should no longer believe in the proposition A and the factor should be zero. Most cases of course lie between these two extremes. This approach provides the rational way to alter an assessment of judgment A in the light of fresh evidence B.

Let me set down a light-hearted example with some illustrative numbers to show how such problems can be tackled. Prime Minister Tony Blair once observed to me that he knew I had a background in defence because I wore polished black brogues, and the rest of senior Whitehall men either had gone casual or didn't bother to clean their shoes even for meetings in No. 10 Downing Street. So suppose you pick a male senior civil servant at random outside in Whitehall. How likely is it he works in defence? An initial answer could be got by finding out the ratio of the number of civil servants in defence as against the rest of government. So if we invent some numbers on a back of a fag packet, then suppose the starting point is that from open sources (National Statistics) 1 in 20 male senior civil servants works in defence. That is the chance of your random man being from defence, given no other information. But suppose that you notice that his shoes are polished. What do you now conclude about the parent department? How could you use the new evidence, the shined shoes, to alter the estimate in a scientific way?

Bayes' theorem therefore says that the probability of the man being from MOD, given the shined shoes, equals the starting point—the probability that any randomly picked Whitehall senior civil servant is from defence—multiplied by a factor that adjusts for the crucial fact that you have 'intelligence' about the shined shoes fetish of defence civil servants (a habit learnt from the military). That factor is equal to the probability of finding shined shoes on a man known to be from defence divided by the likelihood of shiny shoes amongst senior civil servants generally (e.g. taking account of other sartorially old-fashioned departments like the Foreign Office).

So from open sources (National Statistics), 1 in 20 senior male civil servants works in defence. That is the chance of your random man being from defence, given no other information. But say you know from intelligence that 7 out of 10 senior civil servants in defence wear shined shoes; and suppose that outside the defence community the equivalent figure is only 4 out of 10. So we can calculate the total probability of shined shoes as $(1/20)*(7/10) + (1–1/20)*(4/10) = 0.42$ (i.e. the sum of the shined shoe brigade in MOD and their equivalents elsewhere in Whitehall). With those numbers we can easily calculate the adjusting factor as $(7/10)/.42$ and the required posterior probability that, given the intelligence on shiny shoes, the senior civil servant is actually from defence becomes: $1/20*(7/10)/0.42 = $ approx. $1/12$. So the intelligence on shined shoes enables the analyst reliably to report that the result, the confidence that the man comes from defence, is almost double what we would have thought from chance alone.

Let me take another simplified example. Suppose we learn that Ruritania has tested a long-range rocket. The Ruritanians say it is for civil space purposes. We assess that is very likely true, based on other evidence of an active civil programme known to be at flight testing stage; but you leave a one in five (20 per cent) chance that it might after all be part of a military programme, leaving a 4 in 5 (80 per cent) chance it is a civil programme. We then learn from technical intelligence that the rocket's telemetry was encrypted with a system associated with past military programmes. How do we now reassess the probabilities? What information would an analyst look for to help the assessment?

We check on past data and we might discover that all civil tests also use military cryptography. So the technical information adds nothing, and we keep our estimate at 80 per cent likelihood of it being a civil test. On the other hand, we might discover that no civil tests have ever used cryptography. So we might reasonably reassess the chances of its being civil sharply downwards, or even say they are zero. If, however, the analyst finds 8 out of 10 past tests used military cryptography, and

5 out of 10 tests known to be civil did, then a Bayesian calculation is needed to reassess the probabilities.

If we let A be the hypothesis that the test was civil and we let B be the evidence that the cryptography was military, then the prior estimate for the probability that A is the case was 80 per cent = 4/5. We know that 8 out of 10 past tests used military cryptography, and 6 out of 10 tests known to be civil did. So the adjusting factor is (6/10)/ (8/10) = (3/4). So the new estimate for the confidence in the judgment that the test was civil, given the evidence, is now (4/5)*(3/4) = 3/5 = 60%. We are thus able to reduce our prior estimate that the test was civil from the prior 80 per cent down to the posterior 60 per cent. We are less confident in the judgment but still think it is significantly more likely than not that the Ruritanians are to be believed.

That is a grossly oversimplified example and I would not suggest there are many intelligence problems directly susceptible to that type of formal analysis. But the logic underlying the Bayesian concept is universally present under the surface. To illustrate this point, pause to think about the risk that we might be influenced by the exciting nature of some new piece of intelligence that is in itself highly interesting but on closer examination would not help discriminate between competing hypotheses (e.g. are we looking at a civil or military application). This way of thinking forces to the surface those cases where the intelligence reporting, although in its own terms fascinating and a triumph of tradecraft, nevertheless does not enable the possible hypotheses to be distinguished. This important concept is known in the literature as the *diagnosticity of evidence*.

Part of the evidence base to be brought to bear is an understanding of the context, the political, social, economic, demographic position of the group under study. The situation the analyst is then in is not so different from that of the historian attempting to make sense out of a past that he was not present to observe first hand. As the novelist L. P. Hartley put it, 'The past is another country; they do things differently there.'[7] Or as Donald Rumsfeld is said to have put it: 'I would not say that the future is necessarily less predictable than the past. I think the past was not predictable when it started.'

The analyst too is operating on incomplete information, with only a partial understanding of the culture and sensibilities of the target group in question. The inherent problem is the way that the historian, and the intelligence analyst, has to impose a pattern on complex reality using those features that appear to them to stick up most prominently through the clouds of the past. The interpretation has to be consistent with the known facts. But different evidence can be uncovered that forces a reappraisal of conventional wisdom, and can sometimes overturn it. It is also the case that historians/analysts can come up with radically differing macro-interpretations of the same evidence as a read of, say, R. H. Tawney and Eric Hobsbawm on the impact of the industrial revolution will show.

On dealing with fragmentary and incomplete information

At heart, intelligence analysts are not so very different from the professionals in other walks of life who daily face the problem of seeing through a glass darkly when the information available to them is incomplete or partially hidden: the fragments of fossilized bone to the palaeontologist or the presenting symptoms of the patient to the clinician. Secret intelligence is almost always going to be incomplete. The analyst, like the palaeontologist with gaps in the fossil record and the clinician with the masking of symptoms of underlying disease, has to have a store of theoretical knowledge on which to draw. But no model will exactly fit the present case, and to devise a likely hypothesis or diagnosis is a matter of informed judgment. Part of that process of judgment is working out where evidence should be expected, and whose absence might be significant, and what evidence would be inconsistent with the hypothesis and thus reduce confidence in it and cause it to be modified.

The palaeontologist is used to (literally) fragmentary evidence and to vigorous debate over the place of new finds in the corpus of knowledge. Peer review in the academic world is a discipline that uncovers inconsistencies and sloppy thinking, whilst keeping the wilder hypotheses in their place as interesting, but outside the body of accepted science. As with most modern scientists, palaeontologists today would be likely to adopt a post-positivist approach, accepting that the deep past will never be fully known to us (we were not there) and that our models are therefore provisional, but proceeding systematically to build upon and incorporate the advances in accumulating knowledge made before in order to arrive at better approximations to the truth. New techniques, such as DNA analysis, may cause upsets in conventional wisdom as considerable rethinking of the relationship of species to each other may be required. From time to time there is a revolution in thought, what Thomas Kuhn called a paradigm shift, causing a major reinterpretation of the meaning of the available evidence. An example from the world of intelligence would be the re-evaluation long after the end of the Vietnam war of the essentially nationalistic motives of the North Vietnamese and their historic suspicion of China, rather than the 'domino' theory of international communism prevalent at the time.

The 'Piltdown Man' palaeontology fraud of 1912, when fragments of a skull and jawbone were held to be those of a previously unknown form of early human, also illustrates another danger for the intelligence analyst, that of falling victim to deception. That is a danger that is especially strong, as it was with the Piltdown case, when evidence that is turned up is just what was being sought. The scientific world of the day wanted to find evidence of a 'missing link' between the apes and modern humans (the 'evidence' that it represented was cited by Clarence Darrow in the famous Scopes trial over the teaching of evolution). Despite contrary views over the years from a number of leading experts, the fraud took more than forty years to be uncovered. Professor R. V. Jones, the wartime founder of scientific intelligence, advised intelligence analysts to stick to what he described as Crow's Law after his colleague John Crow who taught at King's College London: 'Do not think what you want to think until you know what you need to know.'

The inductive fallacy, the Achilles heel of analysis

Reference has already been made to the risk that intelligence analysts fall into an inductive fallacy, regarding fresh intelligence that is consistent with a judgment they have reached as strengthening their belief in it. The potential problem is likely to start back at the point at which access to intelligence is planned. For example, we can imagine in 2002 the call going out to the intelligence agencies: 'We need urgently more intelligence on Saddam's WMD programmes' as the top priority requirement. Sources would be tasked accordingly, and unsurprisingly would yield fragments of intelligence that were consistent with the existence of the presumptive WMD programmes. Although there might be no definitive first-hand intelligence reports, the fact that the reporting being received is consistent with the existence of the WMD programmes is liable to be taken as strengthening belief in the actual existence of these WMD programmes. An additional risk might be of course be that agents will deduce what it is that the agency is most anxious to have information on, and since they will not want to report information that does not fit, and thus risk the displeasure of the case officer, they will remain silent rather than report negatively.

Writing about the scientific method,[8] David Deutsch, a leading Oxford theoretical physicist, warned of '… the asymmetry between experimental refutation and experimental confirmation. Whereas an incorrect prediction automatically renders the underlying explanation unsatisfactory, a correct prediction says *nothing at all* about the underlying explanation. Shoddy explanations that yield correct predictions are two a penny, as UFO enthusiasts, conspiracy theorists and pseudo-scientists of every variety should (but never do) bear in mind.' It is very tempting for intelligence analysts to fall into this trap, often described as the 'black swan'. The hypothesis is that all swans are white, based on the large number of UK swans thus reported. To provide additional evidence, wider European observation shows even more cases of white swans. Belief in the hypothesis strengthens. Not until a black swan is seen (in Australia) is the underlying hypothesis shown to be refuted. Or as Nobel prize-winner Paul Dirac said of the ability of Nils Bohr's 'solar system' model to predict the spectra of the simplest atom, hydrogen: 'It is possible to get the right answer for the wrong reasons' after the model had comprehensively failed to produce results for the next element, helium.

A related analytic issue arises from what Professor R. V. Jones called 'Crabtree's bludgeon'[9] as a comment on the principle of Occam's razor: 'No set of mutually inconsistent observations can exist for which some human intellect cannot conceive a coherent explanation, however complicated.' We like to see patterns in the flames in the hearth; we feel satisfied when we have imposed a pattern on disorder. The explanation, even if complicated, can connect the evidence with an apparently plausible ex post narrative, and can feel disconcertingly convincing. In John Buchan's 1924 novel *The Three Hostages*,[10] the hero Richard Hannay has explained to him how a thriller writer can construct an ingenious plot inductively which the reader then enjoys unfolding deductively. Thus Buchan postulates a number of randomly chosen 'mutually inconsistent observations', such as a blind old woman spinning in the West Highlands, a Norwegian summer barn, and an old curiosity shop in East London, and shows how they could be linked together and woven by the author into a plausible tale; the naïve reader then admires the author's skill in how the plot unfolds to include these events. This ability of the human mind to force unconnected observations together connects dangerously with the attitude of the out and out conspiracy theorist seeking to make sense of unpleasant reality by postulating malevolent hidden hands. There are many such examples associated with the 9/11 attacks, such as the assertion that the collapse of the twin towers was due to a controlled explosion. For those who wish to believe such explanations, no amount of contrary evidence will cause them to change their mind since the evidence can always be re-interpreted within the conspiratorial frame of reference in order to fit the theory. Thus the fact that a large number of people, none of whom have come forward, would have had to be in the know for such a theory to hold water can be taken by the paranoid as positive evidence of just how powerful is the reach of the hidden group behind the conspiracy. This is an example of a self-referential state of mind, the most dangerous psychological state for an analyst to fall into. During the Cold War there were at times such attitudes seeking to place the worst possible construction on the evidence on both sides.

A failure of imagination 'to join up the dots' may thus be a highly misleading if not dangerously superficial criticism to level at the analysts. Valid lines of criticism on the other hand would include the adequacy of information filtering and sharing mechanisms across the intelligence community and the lack of satisfactory liaison relationships at that time between the worlds of intelligence and law enforcement.

How to go about solving a problem

Creativity is not something that can be mandated. Faced with a hard problem, and the need to formulate a hypothesis, the analyst needs intuition, knowledge of the subject and knowledge of the analytic arts, including nowadays knowing what the possibilities for additional access to information on the subject might be. In some domains the analyst is directly setting the parameters for intelligence collection. There may be a Eureka moment, the most satisfying experience for the analyst, or it may be a gradual dawning in discussion with colleagues that there is a better hypothesis that might provide a more convincing explanation. In the words of John Le Carré,[11] 'Through the remainder of that same night, unchanged, unshaven, George Smiley remained bowed at the major's table, reading, comparing, annotating, cross-referencing... At this point his mood could best be compared with that of a scientist who senses by instinct that he is on the brink of a discovery, and is waiting any minute that logical connection. Later ... he called it "shoving everything into a test-tube and seeing if it exploded" ... And he had it. No explosive revelation, no flash of light, no cry of "Eureka" ... merely that here before him, in the records he had examined and the notes he had compiled was the corroboration of a theory.'

There are parallels with every branch of intellectual study. The Hungarian mathematician Georg Polya wrote a deep but misleadingly simple book, *How to Solve It*,[12] in which he summarized a heuristic to help those stuck in front of an obstinate problem. His approach involves such devices as using visual representations of the problem, solving simpler versions of the problem first, understanding how the available evidence links to the problem, and so on. For example, his heuristic can be adapted slightly for an intelligence analysis problem.

Suppose we wish to explain the appearance of complex new structures on an industrial site of a nation suspected of having a covert nuclear weapons programme. First we have to understand the problem, so we play around with it and decompose it into its component parts, identifying the unknowns and what is already known about the site and who runs it and pays for it. Imagery might show, for example, that the site is heavily guarded. Has this changed recently? Who is known to visit it? Are there any military related communications associated with the site? The next stage is to externalize the problem by getting it down on paper, perhaps with a diagram or a time-line in order to see the relationship between the parts of the problem. Then the analyst can bring to bear other related knowledge, for example other suspicious signs such as cargoes unloaded from suspect vessels associated with proliferation networks or intelligence from a very recent defector that the site was purely for civil nuclear power. The analyst can then start formulating hypotheses about the possible explanation for these suspect facilities, and list what would need to be known to discriminate between the hypotheses. The analyst might discover, for example, that sites known to be civil are also heavily guarded, so that evidence is consistent with either hypothesis.

The analyst is therefore connecting what he wants to know and what is known already. It may be possible that this problem has been seen before, with examples of such construction elsewhere, albeit in a different form. A related problem in the past may provide a guide. If stuck, the analyst may however be able to solve part of the problem and check whether, if the problem was simplified, or if it were a simpler form of problem, then it might then be solved, and thus guide him to solving the more complex problem.

Often there will be a team working on the problem, when a plan will be needed to attack the problem methodically. A useful check is whether all the available information has been used, and whether there is critical missing information that intelligence might be able to access and use to check the result. At the end of the process, if each step in the argument seems sound, then solution should be expressible in terms of the best and simplest explanation consistent with the facts. The very final step is to document the process so that others can see whether the approach can be used to help with their problems.

A systematic method for comparing different explanations and preventing the analyst becoming fixated on one most likely solution has been developed by Richards J. Heuer,[13] an ex–CIA analyst, and is known as the ACH model, for Analysis of Competing Hypotheses. The idea is simple enough, which is to use the power of discrimination of the intelligence and other evidence available to weigh up the strength of case for the different possible hypotheses (including the null hypothesis) for what is going on of interest to the analyst.

Heuer cites Benjamin Franklin in Paris, in a letter of 1772 to Joseph Priestley, the discoverer of oxygen, as setting down the basic approach

'... divide half a sheet of paper by a line into two columns; writing over the one Pro and over the other Con ... put down over the different heads short hints of the different motives ... for or against the measure. When I have thus got them all together in one view, I endeavour to estimate their relative weights; and where I find two, one on each side, that seem equal I strike them out. Thus proceeding I find where the balance lies ... and come to a determination accordingly.'

The very act of brainstorming the possible hypotheses is likely to trigger critical examination of the evidence. In the case of Saddam Hussein's WMD programmes in 2002, for example, the method would force examination of the null hypothesis that the programmes had been halted, and the evidence that would have been expected to have been found (such as SIGINT) if there really were active WMD development and production programmes. The Heuer method recommends the analyst works with a decision matrix, showing how far, for each hypothess, the available evidence is consistent or inconsistent, and the weight, in terms of type of evidence, credibility and relevance, of each category of evidence. The example just discussed might be set out in a matrix as shown in Figure 6 below.

Figure 6: A Hypothetical ACH Matrix (after: Heuer, 2008)

	Source type Credibility Relevance	Hypothesis 1 Nuclear weapons associated site	Hypothesis 2 Civil use site
Evidence 1 Past regime behaviour continues	An assumption Medium High	consistent	inconsistent
Evidence 2 Lack of full cooperation with UN inspectors	An inference High High	consistent	inconsistent
Evidence 3 Heavy security around site	Imagery High Medium	consistent	consistent
Evidence 4 Senior defector	Humint High Medium	inconsistent	consistent
Evidence 5 Sigint, Imagery (lack of)	Sigint, Imagery High High	inconsistent	consistent

What the matrix highlights is that it is premature to reach a judgment that the site is part of a military nuclear weapons programme, since that hypothesis rests largely on an assumption, an inference and intelligence from imagery that might be consistent with either hypothesis. Evidence consistent with the alternative hypothesis includes intelligence, but from a new source still being evaluated, and the negative evidence of an absence of military associated communications that might have been expected. Life is messy and typically the evidence, as in this example, is not clear-cut.

This brief example illustrates that the analyst needs to have a very close relationship with those responsible for accessing intelligence information and to have a sound understanding of what may be possible. In some cases the analyst may be able to set directly the collection parameters by specifying the information that should be sought (such as, in the example above, requesting further overhead photography or air sampling above the suspect site).

Ye shall know the truth, and the truth shall set you free

These words are engraved on marble at the entrance to CIA headquarters at Langley, Virginia. The assumption is that we will know the truth when we see it. But there are different ways of 'knowing' available to the analyst.

The first category is *Authority*. The analyst is typically a member of a group or section, with a head who is in turn part of a bureaucratic structure. Much of the debate in the literature is couched in terms of the analyst/policy-maker relationship, forgetting that the analyst is not an individual researcher but part of a disciplined government hierarchy. There comes a point at which the debates will have to stop and a senior analyst has to lay down what is the authoritative answer to be given to the customers. The Butler Inquiry into WMD intelligence criticized the higher management of the UK Defence Intelligence Staff for accepting wording of a draft JIC assessment that went further than their specialist analysts might have felt comfortable with.

At some point however the arguments must stop, and a judgment be reached, which is the job of the senior managers inside the intelligence community. Their role is often underestimated by academics seeking to model the analyst/policy-maker relationship. An intelligence agency or all-source analytical body is not a university comprised of scholars each with academic freedom to publish their views. The corrective mechanism in the academic world is open peer criticism. Academics may, and some do, publish strange and controversial theories. In so doing they know that their peers will be quick to point out flaws and engage in (sometimes acerbic) debate in the journals. The single-source product from an intelligence agency, and even more so the all-source assessment, are documents that carry the reputation of the organization that issued them. In the case of the UK JIC or the US NIE these are the national estimates for which the intelligence heads must take responsibility. There is therefore the ever-present danger of bias being enforced by management upon an analytic product that does not conform to the 'agency' or house view. Matters of editorial choice, style and clarity are normally enforced to provide consistency for the reader, as would be the case in any journal or newspaper. But this could shade into pressure to soften views, even before the drafting begins, that are known in advance to be antithetical to important elements of the senior leadership.

A mechanism for expressing analytic dissent is therefore advisable as a safeguard against dictatorial tendencies on the part of senior management. In the case, for example, of the US Defence Intelligence Agency guidance to staff lays down that 'intellectual honesty and analytic rigor require processes that enable the analyst to present ideas and concepts that run counter to the prevailing wisdom or challenge the consensus. The preferred method for incorporating an analytic alternative is through the standard process of coordination ... In those rare instances where analysts build a strong case, but cannot achieve consensus support for their analysis, an alternative judgement is justified ... but due to bureaucratic realities, the demands of time-sensitive tasking, or the unwillingness to accept contrary opinions, sound alternative judgments may be lost to the customer. Analysts ... whose judgments have been rebuffed can produce an Alternative Judgment (AJ) to inform the senior leadership. Analysts who produce an AJ do so secure in the knowledge that they have improved the prevailing analysis ... An AJ may not be used to circumvent normal coordination. The AJ must explain succinctly the prevailing judgment and the alternative, without prejudice to the former. The analyst must display trust in the senior leadership, both to give due consideration and to protect the analyst's best interests ... whilst avoiding the emotional ... the analyst forwards it through the immediate superior to the Group [senior intelligence officer] who reviews it for accuracy and decides to put to the Senior Analytic Board or rejects it (with reasons) copy to the Directorate Research Director.'

A second category of 'knowing' is *Received Opinion*. Not every point can be researched and argued out afresh. There is a base of presumed knowledge and opinion on which fresh assessments are built. The danger is that of 'layering', that the inherent uncertainties that surrounded previous estimates are incorporated unwittingly into the fresh assessment. Readers of the final new assessment may well not be aware of the pyramid of doubt on which the judgments have been built, and they need to be reminded. That is another lesson from the problems encountered with intelligence on Iraqi WMD.

A third category is *Induction*. The danger of inferring a pattern from data and predicting that future observations will conform to that pattern has already been referred to. For most of the time, as with the weather, forecasting that tomorrow will be like yesterday, but more so with the current trend extrapolated, will enhance your reputation for prediction. But you will, on a small but significant number of occasions, be wrong, and when you are wrong you may be spectacularly wrong. Intelligence agencies will say truthfully to their customers that 'there is no evidence', for example that there is no evidence of any terrorist group with a serious WMD capability intending to attack the UK. But absence of evidence is not evidence of absence. Should the evidence appear, then the intelligence judgment will change instantly, as the equivalent of the black swan is observed. So great care is needed by users of intelligence in correctly interpreting whether they are being told 'there is no intelligence that ...' or rather 'we do not at present assess the risk as significant that ...', a topic to which we return in the next chapter.

A fourth category is *Deduction*. 'All men are mortal; Socrates is a man; therefore Socrates is mortal' is an example of deductive logic. All erector launchers are associated with missiles; we observe an erector-launcher in Cuba; missiles are being introduced into Cuba. No new information is generated since the conclusion is contained in the premises, although the presentation of the information itself may stimulate further thoughts. Deduction has therefore only limited use for the intelligence analyst. The inverse form of the syllogism has however some interest for the counter-intelligence officer: if A implies B, then not-B implies not-A. So if Venona decrypts tell us that Soviet agent code-named Homer was handing over intelligence to his handler in New York on a specific date in 1946, and we find that a possible suspect, the First Secretary at the British Embassy, was in California on that day, then he cannot be agent Homer. In fact, such logical chains were used on the Venona material to track down Donald Maclean, Counsellor at the Embassy, and expose him as agent Homer. He was however tipped off, probably by Kim Philby, also a Soviet agent in the Embassy, and he and Guy Burgess fled to Moscow in 1951. We should note, however, that the more usual situation in intelligence could be described by 'fuzzy logic', a topic we touch on in the next chapter. So not-B *probably* implies not-A, because the categories cannot be precisely defined.

Finally, we come to modern *Scientific Method*—the most effective methodology for intelligence analysis. We start with curiosity, an essential attribute for the intelligence analyst. We accept that there is no universal set of procedures that will guarantee results, so ingenuity is another key attribute. We recognize that posing acute questions about what is not known or not understood forms an agenda for inquiry, and that can drive the collection of new evidence from intelligence sources. The analysts examine the available evidence with an open mind, but bringing to bear all the sum of previous knowledge of the subject, and as a result formulate a provisional explanation of what has been reported. The implications of that explanation are then deduced and turned into further questions to be tested on fresh evidence. The analysts refine or reframe their hypotheses, where possible as alternatives, and examine the intelligence base especially to see if there is evidence that would enable one hypotheses to be preferred over another, including the absence of evidence that might have reasonably been expected to be present. At the same time the assumptions made in formulating each of the alternative hypotheses are made explicit, along with the reasons for believing them to be reasonable. The final stage, when a most likely explanatory hypothesis has been identified, is to try to define the range of applicability of the explanation.

An important aspect of scientific method is replicability. The same experimental set-up should, in the hands of different scientists, generate comparable results. The equivalent for intelligence analysis is the audit trail of intelligence reporting that led to the judgments made. Thus, for each conclusion reached in a paper by the UK Joint Intelligence Committee it will be possible to identify the individual intelligence reports, whether HUMINT, SIGINT or other reporting, that led to that judgment. The Butler Inquiry into intelligence on WMD was thus able to track back a crucial hardening of judgment to a single report. Thus, the JIC concluded on 15 March 2002

'We judge that Iraq could produce significant quantities of BW agents within days of a decision to do so. There is no intelligence on any BW agent production facilities, but one source indicates that Iraq may have developed mobile production facilities. A liaison source reports that the transportable production programme began in 1995....'

But six months later, on 24 September 2002, the JIC had hardened their conclusion in the publicly released 'dossier' that

'We know from intelligence that Iraq has continued to produce biological warfare agents ... UNSCOM established that Iraq considered the use of mobile biological agent production facilities. In the past two years evidence from defectors has indicated the existence of such facilities. Recent intelligence confirms that Iraqi military have developed mobile facilities ...'

The difference between these assessments in relation to biological weapons, Butler explains, rests on a single report from 'a reliable and established source reporting a new sub-source who did not subsequently provide any further reporting'. That intelligence was later described as 'open to serious doubt'. At the time, however, the JIC described this report as 'confirming' intelligence on Iraqi mobile BW production facilities that was being received from a liaison service (believed to be the reporting from Curveball, the Iraqi defector being managed by the German BND). The Curveball intelligence was also later withdrawn as 'seriously flawed'.

A key step identified above was for the analyst to use evidence as discriminating between alternative hypotheses. That example shows how important it is, as the Butler Inquiry emphasized, for the intelligence community to be explicit about the assumptions being made, the depth of the intelligence base on which reliance is being placed, and when hypotheses have been changed to highlight why that is justified

I describe this phenomenon of making implicit assumptions about human behaviour explicit as the problem of 'Bertrand Russell's chickens', after an example he used in his philosophy lectures to illustrate the nature of truth and which I adapt for the purpose. Imagine a chicken farmer in which the chickens conduct an espionage operation on the farm. They discover that he is ordering large quantities of chicken food. The Joint Intelligence Committee of chickens meets. What do they conclude? Is it that the farmer has finally recognized that they deserve more food; or that they are being fattened up for the kill? It is the same secret intelligence but two diametrically opposed interpretations depending upon implicit assumptions that might be made about farmer motivations.

We might extend the metaphor further and speculate on which interpretation the chicken JIC is likely to adopt. Much will depend on how they frame the issue in terms of their view of the farmer's motivations. The risk is that they will unconsciously mirror their own attitudes into those of the famer. Thus if the experience of the chickens has been of a happy barnyard where they have never known hardship, then their past experience may lead them to be unable to conceive of the economics of farming as seen by the farmer. On the other hand, a chicken farm regularly raided by the fox may well be all too ready to attribute the worst of motives to the farmer.

The only advice to be given to intelligence analysts in those circumstances is to try to frame the risks and benefits as they are likely to be seen by the adversary (which may very well be different from those of the analysts and their policy customers). The analyst should ask what benefits and costs would different courses of action bring the adversary, and what does he risk if he does nothing (including 'face')? Nations may be prepared to run significant risks if faced with the certainty of losses to vital interests. Opportunity to make gains and threat of losses are rarely perceived as symmetric, as a matter of national as well as personal psychology. NATO was not willing to take risks during the Cold War, even for the potential prize of a free Hungary in 1956 or a free Czechoslovakia in 1968. NATO would have been prepared to run very considerable risks to keep West Berlin free and to defend its flanks in north Norway or in Turkey. These perceptions were understood in the Kremlin. The Soviet leadership showed consistently that they were not prepared to risk military adventures to gain territory that could lead to armed confrontation with the US. As the US National Intelligence Estimate correctly put it, 'The USSR would almost certainly never … hazard its own safety for the sake of Cuba' (S-NIE 80–62). The basis of Khrushchev's miscalculation over Cuba in 1962 was probably that he thought he could get MRBM missiles installed and operational (and gain considerable strategic advantage) before the US detected them, and once faced with a fait accompli the US would not risk war to reverse the situation. In that, at least, he was probably right had Soviet operations remained undetected. The US intelligence community had failed to read Krushchev's calculation correctly and so did not provide forewarning that might have allowed the US to forestall the missile deployment. In his assessment of US reconnaissance capabilities Krushchev was however proved wrong, and the US reaction was as he must have known it would be, and he was forced to back down.

The example also illustrates the importance of analytic integrity going where the evidence leads. Cognitive biases have been much examined in the literature since they distort the objectivity that is the goal of analysis. There are important lessons from study of past failures. But the lessons are as much for the policy community as for the analysts. We reserve therefore an examination of biases until the next chapter when we look at the interactions between policy-makers and secret intelligence.

7

ANALYSTS AND POLICY-MAKERS

IDEALISTS AND REALISTS

The sources of failure

The opening years of the twenty-first century have seen two powerful and contradictory criticisms levelled at the US and UK intelligence communities. The cry has gone up that intelligence analysts lack imagination. They 'failed to connect up the dots' that could have provided warning of terrorist attacks. US intelligence is thus held by critics to have failed to prevent the 9/11 attacks in New York and Washington, and most recently failed to link the fragments of intelligence that might have prevented the attempt to bring down an airliner near Detroit on Christmas Day 2009. British intelligence is also seen to have failed to follow up leads that might have led to those who went on to conduct the 7/7 attacks on London transport. At the same time, and in the same hot media breath, the fiercest criticism has been levelled at both US and UK intelligence communities for having over-much imagination. Their over-imaginative interpretation of sparse and fallible intelligence on Iraqi weapons of mass destruction led to the misleading presentation to the UN Security Council by Colin Powell, the US Secretary of State, and the infamous 'dossier' of JIC conclusions presented by Prime Minister Blair to the UK parliament. The Commission on the Intelligence Capabilities of the United States Regarding Weapons of Mass Destruction concluded that 'the intelligence community was dead wrong in almost all its pre-war judgments about Iraq's WMD'. We therefore have criticisms of different kinds: of passivity and timidity in the exercise of intelligence judgment on the one hand (failure to join up the 9/11 dots) and of aggressive analytic judgment (exaggeration of Saddam's WMD capabilities) on the other. These are not necessarily mutually exclusive criticisms. They do not cancel each other out, but may instead be indicating the limits of reasonable expectation at either end of the scale of confidence in analytic prediction. A cynic, and I am not one, might say that intelligence reporting is liable to let you down just when you most need it, at either end of the spectrum from tactical warning of imminent danger to strategic appreciation of long-term risk. That would, as we shall see, be to attribute too much importance to analytic failure and not enough to the complex interactions between analysts and policy-makers, the subject of this chapter. The reason things often appear to go wrong when crisis looms is because the quality of the relationships involved between leaders and advisers, measured in terms of trust and mutual understanding, and at times the personality of the decision-maker, is not enough to cope with the emotional pressures of the moment.

In his pioneering work[1] *On the Psychology of Military Incompetence*, the psychologist and ex–soldier Dr Norman Dixon related costly military blunders to the social psychology of military organization and to the personalities of the military commanders concerned. His work has considerable wider relevance when we look at how it is that intelligence reporting and assessment comes to be misunderstood or ignored. We need to explore the social psychology of the analytic community and the unconscious influences that may cause the analysts to fail to ask the right questions or to pull punches in their reporting, and the psychodynamics around the decision-makers, whether civil or military, and whether these are conducive to rationality.

Some alleged failures of intelligence therefore may be put down simply to straightforwardly inadequate analysis or faulty assessment, but for the most part those are the minority. There is a complex set of relationships and processes that link access to secret intelligence to a decision (or absence of a decision) by a military commander or by a policy-maker. When questionable decisions arise over the use of intelligence, and they do inevitably, then we can analyze them in terms of the problems that can occur at a combination of some or all of the following different levels:

• An inability by the analysts to be able to access sufficient information that bears on the issue to allow them to reach sound judgments;

incomplete and fragmentary intelligence collection is of course the norm in relation to secret intelligence, a topic that was considered in the previous chapter in terms of the continuing 'arms race' between offence and defence in intelligence work.

• Errors by the intelligence analysts in interpreting correctly the reliability or the meaning of the intelligence that was obtained, including processing it in a sufficiently timely fashion; how analysts address their task of relating judgments to evidence, of distinguishing between evidence and belief, is the topic that was the subject of the last chapter. This part of the intelligence cycle I described in chapter 5 as *elucidation*, the shedding of light on hidden aspects of reality.

• Difficulties in communication between the analytic and user communities, leading the former (consciously or unconsciously) to be overly influenced by the expectations of the latter, and leading the latter to fail to appreciate the proper significance attributed to the assessment by the former and thus failing to take seriously enough the analysts' assessment; examining the pathologies in the analyst/policy-maker relationship is the main topic for this chapter, in particular looking at what happens when intelligence judgments run counter to (or are taken as reinforcing) strongly held policy views.

• Policy failure on the part of the decision-makers, again an inevitable occurrence from time to time. In particular without strategic notice of threatening developments (or of long-term opportunities) governments are flying blind. Without strategic notice it is unlikely that sufficient intelligence will be available and unlikely that policy customers will be that interested in what there is. There are many possible reasons why surprises occur. Political leaders, military commanders and policy-makers may resist early warning signs of trouble ahead, thus we are constantly surprised by technological, economic and social developments. Such absence of strategic notice is usually due to systems failure between those charged with strategy formulation, horizon scanning and strategic intelligence assessment. This problem is the subject of chapter 8.

Looked at in that light, the criticisms of intelligence performance over 9/11 and Iraqi WMD with which this chapter opened can more convincingly be re-interpreted as co-incident problems at several of these levels, leading to major 'perfect storm' failure. We should also keep in mind the inherent difficulties of prediction, discussed in the next chapter. Reforms may not bring as much improvement as reformers hope, since there is an irreducible level of uncertainty about intelligence work.[2] Post mortem inquiries often reveal poor information handling processes, but it does not follow that these were responsible for the intelligence failures.

The intelligence base on the AQ network before 9/11 fell far short of what it is now, but nevertheless was sufficient to make bin Laden a very high priority target both for the US and her close allies including the UK, although not to the same extent elsewhere in Europe; wider international liaison was under-developed and indeed required the impetus of 9/11 to overcome natural obstacles to closer cooperation with such a wide and varied range of nations. In his memoir[3] of the events of 9/11, the US DCI at the time, George Tenet, provides a dramatic account of the intelligence received only months before 9/11 and his insistence to the National Security Adviser, Condoleezza Rice, that 'There will be a significant terrorist attack in the coming weeks or months' and that 'This country needs to go on a war footing now'. It was duly noted by the system, but no Presidential directives followed until after 9/11 when President Bush authorized CIA-led intervention in Afghanistan. The veteran Washington journalist Bob Woodward has taken Tenet to task for working through Rice and not raising hell directly with the President. The impression Tenet leaves in his memoirs is that was because that was simply not the way that things were done in the Bush White House. The then Head of the CIA's Counter-Terrorism Center, Michael Scheuer, in his own *Washington Post* review of Tenet's memoirs, is also sharply critical of Tenet's refusal to push the White House to authorize attacks on bin Laden before 9/11 when he felt CIA had acquired possible pre-emptive intelligence that could have indicated his whereabouts. Tenet has played down Scheuer's recommendations as those of 'an analyst not trained in conducting paramilitary operations' and of an analyst who, on Scheuer's own admission, did 'not care about collateral casualties in such situations'.[4]

As the Pentagon Inspector-General later concluded, the US Intelligence Community had been unable to satisfy the US military for the precise, actionable intelligence that would have been needed by the military leadership. Tenet describes how events tragically intervened on 9/11 and after that it was running to catch up all the way, weaving around the domestic politics of blame whilst trying to retain the space to focus on defeating the real enemy that had penetrated the gates. Chapter 8 considers the wider organizational implications for intelligence communities of the lessons of 9/11 and Iraq in terms of the need to provide government with strategic notice, operational alerting and warning and tactical pre-emptive intelligence of terrorist activity.

The subsequent operations in Afghanistan of course generated many intelligence leads. Although some of the methods used by the US on those captured were not accepted as legitimate by the UK, the intervention in Afghanistan did provide valuable intelligence that, in the words of the UK parliamentary oversight committee 'saved lives'. As the various 9/11 inquiries have established, the administration did have 'strategic warning' of impending danger from AQ, although this was reasonably assessed in the first instance to be more likely to arise against US interests overseas since that had been the earlier pattern. There were however fragments of intelligence that were never brought together to help form a pre-attack jigsaw, largely because the intelligence agencies did not themselves form a coherent counter-terrorist intelligence community and because the relationships between them and the law enforcement users (immigration and customs border security, police at federal, state and local levels etc.) in the US were deficient in relation to the likely level of threat.

We can see therefore that the interactions between the members of the intelligence community and with the customers for their product lie at the heart of the inability of the intelligence community to give forewarning of the 9/11 attacks. If we turn to the pre-war intelligence on Iraqi WMD a similar picture of overlapping problems at each level emerges, including the nature of the strategic decision itself. Arguments will continue over how far the subsequent decision by President Bush to invade Iraq, and the decision by Prime Minister Blair to support him to the hilt, were directly linked to the intelligence assessments they saw. Indeed, had the US and UK intelligence analysts concluded (it would have been correctly it now appears) that Saddam Hussein had against expectations ordered a halt to his WMD programmes, would the US political leadership have concluded anything other than that was a tactical ploy to outflank the UN and get sanctions lifted so that the programmes could restart? An email provided to the Robb–Silberman Senate Commission[5] revealed that the Deputy Director of the CIA responsible for intelligence assessment commented to one of his analysts who had concerns over a particular source, Curveball (see chapter 6)

'Greetings. Come on over (or I'll come over there) and we can hash this out. As I said last night, let's keep in mind the fact that this war's going to happen regardless of what Curve Ball said or didn't say, and that the Powers That Be probably aren't terribly interested in whether Curve Ball knows what he's talking about. However, in the interest of Truth, we owe somebody a sentence of two of warning, if you honestly have reservations.'

In describing the intent of his email, the Deputy Chief told the Senate Committee staff that he had the sense that war was inevitable from reading the newspaper and that he had not had any interactions with government officials in the CIA or with any policy-makers that led him to this conclusion

'I was reading the same newspapers you were. It was inevitable, it seemed to me at the time, and to most of us, that war was coming. I was not privy to any particular information indicating war plans or anything. My level was too low for that. ... My source of information was the *Washington Post*.'

In the same spirit, as revealed in a leaked No. 10 record of discussion with the Prime Minister,[6] Richard Dearlove, the then Chief of SIS, reported back to the Prime Minister after a visit to Washington that military action was now seen as inevitable. Bush wanted to remove Saddam, through military action, justified by the conjunction of terrorism and WMD. Dearlove is reported to have warned the Prime Minister that in Washington 'the intelligence and facts were being fixed around the policy'.

There was therefore an inadequate intelligence base, particularly in HUMINT. There was therefore too much reliance on inferential extrapolation of the evidence provided by the arms inspectors immediately after the first Gulf War. The fact that these arms inspectors had shown at the time that Saddam Hussein's illegal programmes were more advanced than the intelligence assessments had judged had been a shock, and unconsciously analysts would have wanted not to be caught out that way again. The Iraqi practice of deception at all levels was well known and confirmed by Saddam Hussein himself in his interrogation after his capture in 2003. The onset of preparations for war led to huge urgent pressure for more intelligence and that caused quality control problems, as discussed in chapter 6.

The issue of politicization of intelligence has been much debated in the light of the Iraq experience. Accusations of direct interference in intelligence judgments from the political level in the US administration were examined by the Robb–Silberman Congressional Commission who concluded that there was

'no evidence of politicization of the ... assessments concerning Iraq's reported WMD programs ... and no evidence of politicization even under the broader definition used by the CIA's Ombudsman for Politicization, which includes any unprofessional manipulation of information and judgments ... to please what those officers perceive to be policy-makers' preferences'.

The Commission did however go on to say 'there is no doubt that analysts operated in an environment shaped by intense policy-maker interest.'

The position in the UK is similar. The accusations related less to direct interference by government and more to fears of unconscious influence deriving from an undue desire to please and impress government with the ability to provide agent intelligence when it is most needed. What was in question therefore was the professional health of the relationships between intelligence officers, analysts and policy-makers. This wider definition of politicization[7] would be when intelligence is being illegitimately influenced by the intelligence community's knowledge of the answers that the policy-makers want to hear. Under that definition, politicization can occur even without any active knowledge or pressure from the political class. In Lord Hutton's report on his inquiry into the death of the weapons scientist Dr David Kelly in 2003, he commented[8] on the charge levelled at the JIC that it had 'sexed up' the intelligence on Iraqi WMD: 'However I consider that the possibility cannot be completely ruled out that the desire of the Prime Minister to have a dossier which, whilst consistent with the available intelligence, was as strong as possible in relation to the threat posed by Saddam Hussein's WMD, may have subconsciously influenced Mr Scarlett [the chair of the JIC at the time] and the other members of the JIC to make the wording of the dossier somewhat stronger than it would have been if it had been contained in a normal JIC assessment.' 'Although this possibility cannot be completely ruled out', Lord Hutton went on, 'I am satisfied that Mr Scarlett, the other members of the JIC, and the members of the assessment staff engaged in the drafting of the dossier were concerned to ensure that the contents of the dossier were consistent with the intelligence available to the JIC.' In writing that passage, Lord Hutton may have been unconsciously reflecting an earlier judgment about unconscious influences in the criminal justice system reached by another distinguished judge, Sir William Macpherson:[9] 'We are not talking about the individuals within the service who may be unconscious as to the nature of what they are doing but it is the net effect of what they do'—a quote from a police inspector cited by the Macpherson Inquiry into the death of the black teenager Stephen Lawrence in support of the concept of 'institutional racism'. Even, there-fore, where individuals are themselves free of conscious bias, the effect of the institutional context is to produce outcomes that are highly undesirable.

There can be little doubt that in both the US and the UK the intelli-gence/policy relationship was put under huge strain by the intervention in Iraq. Although for the UK the Butler Inquiry found no evidence of deliberate distortion or culpable negligence, or of JIC assessments being pulled in any particular direction to meet the concerns of policy officials, the Inquiry concluded that the public presentation 'went to (although not beyond) the outer limits of the intelligence available' and essential caveats about the nature of the intelligence were lost. Evi-dence to the most recent UK Inquiry into the Iraq war chaired by Sir John Chilcot has confirmed that that serious problems with an inade-quate intelligence base on Iraq were made worse both by faults in analysis and by the cultural tensions between the analytic community and ministers when it came to public presentation of the position[10]. The resulting description of Saddam's WMD capabilities was then amplified hugely in public debate by media headlines that misrepre-sented the position but which the government's spin doctors had no interest in restraining. The words of Humbert Wolfe may have been in their minds: 'You cannot hope to bribe or twist, thank God! the British journalist. But, seeing what the man will do unbribed, there's no occa-sion to.'

Idealists and realists

What then should be the optimum relationship between analyst and policy-maker, and between the intelligence community as a whole and their customers? The question has been much argued over in the aca-demic intelligence studies community. There are two broad schools of thought, whose 'patrons' are identified in the literature as Sherman Kent, the 'father of US intelligence analysis', and Robert Gates, now US Defense Secretary but before that US Director of Central Intelli-gence for President Bush senior.

The 'Sherman Kent' or 'idealist' approach is modelled on profes-sional objectivity. Thus, for example, the medical, statistical or military professions would be expected to give objective advice to government based on a set of professional ethics that put objectivity and freedom from outside pressure as cardinal virtues. A clear dividing wall could therefore be drawn round the professional advisers separating them from the political arena in which the users of such advice circulate. Intelligence is collected on potential threats identified by the intelligence community itself, and its assessments are then to be tossed over the wall, in the hope that they will be picked up and acted upon. This 'push' model is an idealization, and perhaps for that reason much beloved by academics: 'the only hope for improving the quality and reliability of the intelligence community ... lies in distancing it from the political arena'.[11] It is the case, as emphasized in the UK government's official guide to central intelligence[12] that JIC assessments are intelligence-based (although they may contain relevant information from other sources) and they are clearly stated not to be policy documents. This 'professional' approach[13] fits lay expectations of how strategic intelligence assessment should be handled. As Michael Goodman, UK Official Historian of the JIC, has noted:[14] 'Things have changed from the time before WW2 when the British Foreign Office could object to the formation of the JIC on the grounds that it, the Foreign Office, was the only authority for assessing foreign countries.' Thus there was outrage in some quarters, especially academe, when it was revealed that the chair of the JIC had attended a meeting called by Alastair Campbell, the strategic communications director of Prime Minister Blair, to discuss the preparation for publication of the infamous 'dossier' on Iraqi WMD. This was, it was alleged, surely evidence of politicization of the intelligence process. As one academic had earlier noted,[15] 'policy-makers quickly learn that intelligence can be used in the same way that a drunk uses a lamp post—for support rather than illumination'. The Butler Inquiry in fact found no evidence of politicization of the intelligence content of the UK 'dossier', although the public presentation of the material was heavily (and with hindsight, rightly) criticized.

The 'Robert Gates' or 'realist' approach starts from the other end of the process, seeing the intelligence community as essential partners in the day-to-day business of government, providing added value through improving the quality of decision-making. Intelligence is in that view a service industry. How is the intelligence community to know where it can add value, or by when its National Intelligence Estimates and JIC assessments would need to be available, if it does not have a close relationship with the policy-makers really to understand their objectives and everyday needs? This is what we might call a 'realist' approach. Intelligence is thus seen to have a vital role to play in the formulation of policy, and in the maintenance of a supportive public opinion. Policy-makers accordingly need to 'pull' intelligence by suggesting to the agencies what targets to concentrate on, what are the timelines for key decisions and where the greatest value-added from secret intelligence would be in order that intelligence serve the policy-makers' requirements. Without such context, the intelligence product risks being irrelevant or too late to be of value.

When examining the actions of a foreign government or its armed forces, the intelligence analysts need to be highly aware of the political context within that country, on which the policy-makers may well have much to contribute. The UK JIC, in which intelligence professionals and key policy officials co-produce the assessments, should be seen as the result of a long (from 1936) evolutionary process to bring two opposing forces into balance: the need for recognized independence of thought and expression in intelligence assessments and the value of having senior policy contribution to their construction. In an often-quoted remark, Sir Percy Cradock, a distinguished chair of the JIC, described the position thus: 'The best arrangement is intelligence and policy in separate but adjoining rooms, with communicating doors and thin partition walls, as in cheap hotels.'[16]

As we have seen in the previous chapter, intelligence assessment is by its nature provisional given the inherent ambiguities in the incomplete evidence base. And those ambiguities enable policy-makers to justify taking a different view from intelligence analysts. In the words of Michael Handel, 'Ambiguity legitimizes different interpretations, allowing politically motivated parties to select the one they prefer. The absence of clarity may also strengthen the tendency of some statesmen to become their own intelligence officers.' We accept nevertheless that professional advice should stand on its own, and should be independent and objective; but equally, however, in a democracy, we accept that those responsible for decisions have the right to ignore it and to be held publicly accountable for the results. So at the strategic assessment end of the scale, public perception of significant psychological distance between the analytic and the policy communities would seem to be wise.

An important part of making an assessment lies in understanding what the adversaries' motives may be, and what they might seek to gain by different courses of action, and what they would most fear to lose. Such an appreciation of the context of adversary decision-making is an exercise in political not intelligence analysis, yet it is fundamental to the intelligence process. The policy community, including ambassadors abroad, have much to contribute. So the rules of engagement for inter-communication between intelligence and policy need to be well set out. In the case of the UK JIC, the policy-makers are members of the committee alongside the intelligence professionals, an arrangement with other significant advantages (as explained in chapter 8). It was therefore prudent for the Butler Inquiry after the Iraq war to emphasize that the Chairman of the JIC had to continue to be someone 'demonstrably beyond influence, and thus probably in his last post'.[17]

The closer we get to the tactical level of operations the more necessary it becomes to have a model in which analyst and user work very closely together, as explained in the modern version of the intelligence cycle presented in chapter 5. It is clear for example in relation to signals intelligence that, in Maureen Baginski's words (as the Director of SIGINT of the US National Security Agency), the new doctrine is to be 'hunters rather than gatherers'.[18] The model of active access is that of a detective acquiring evidence (including recruiting new sources and placing suspects under surveillance) whilst at the same time developing the case as an integrated analytic process. We should also expect to see analysts working alongside policy-makers, for example in the areas of counter-proliferation and counter-terrorism. In the UK JTAC there are policy civil servants from government departments, including the Home Office, Foreign Office and Transport, working alongside intelligence analysts, and the result undoubtedly is to the benefit of all, as departmental understanding of the value of intelligence increases and analytic understanding grows of the uses to which JTAC assessments and warning can in practice be put in order to improve public security. Yet, precisely because often judgments at the operational and tactical levels will trigger publicly visible action, whether by security and law enforcement domestically or diplomatic and military means overseas, they have to be seen to be the outcome of a professional analytic process. There would be dangers in the analyst becoming embedded within the policy community[19] if that were to become the sole analytic resource. There needs to be the ability to stand back from the immediate policy preoccupations if the analytic function is to be carried out fully. What is needed therefore is not just product, but process. There needs to be process that brings the analysts and their products into dialogue with the policy-makers to test the strength of propositions and establish the priorities. In the UK, at the highest level, this is the function of the JIC and its Current Intelligence Groups.

Setting requirements: marketing versus sales models

In both 'idealist' and 'realist' models, there has to be some process of direction of the intelligence community towards priority targets. It is also necessary then to establish which agencies and what techniques are likely best to be able to deliver against those requirements. Government has the responsibility to safeguard the public and protect national interests, and given the power of intelligence to improve decision-taking it would be a dereliction for government not to steer the intelligence community with a set of its priorities. Government also has to have a care to value for public money and thus to help ensure that scarce intelligence resource is deployed where it can make most difference. Prudent government would however recognize another truth, and that is that it is in human nature not to want to admit policy upset and to resist being told unwelcome news. Thus wise government will ensure that its intelligence community understands that it has an obligation to direct on its own authority sufficient of its resource to be able to give government adequate warning of trouble brewing, especially where government would not otherwise see it coming in time. The UK JIC has this warning and alerting function (discussed in the next chapter) built into its terms of reference.

The position of the domestic UK Security Service has in the past been rather different from that of the externally focused SIS and GCHQ. As a security agency, it has been accustomed to being largely the customer for its own intelligence, and to regard itself as self-tasking rather than part of a national intelligence requirements process. The development of the international terrorist threat, the need to connect all the available evidence, and to ensure that intelligence in an assessed form is available for those who need to take policy decisions on counter-terrorism and protective security has meant that the Security Service is now more part of a national intelligence collection and dissemination community than during the Cold War. The highest priority targets for the Security Service will feature with the same priority in the overall national intelligence requirements. But its legal status preserves its independence if necessary to choose itself to direct resources at countering emergent threats.

For those in charge of the intelligence community there are hard choices to be made in meeting requirements as to whether it is better to sweat the assets and maximize short-term pay-off in order to satisfy present customers, or to divert resources to invest in long-term capability leaving some current targets uncovered. For both technical operations (such as the cost of supercomputers and satellites) and human agent running (the cost of opening up new stations overseas, investing in language training etc.) it takes significant time and expense to develop new capability. Short-run marginal costs of switching priorities within the current capabilities may however be low. Once we get below the headline priorities of supporting military operations, countering terrorism and proliferation, it should not be expected that there will be a direct and simple relationship between the government's detailed list of current priorities and the pattern of expenditure by the agencies.

That same consideration means that putting costs of production on intelligence reports is highly problematic. There is no simple way for meaningful cost/performance data to be obtained. And there is no simple correlation at any one time between what agencies spend and the list of priority targets. A high priority target may be extremely expensive to meet in full (and could absorb the whole budget) since it would involve setting up a new line of access, whereas a lower priority may be easily met by reprogramming a search parameter within a given line of intelligence. Thus it is inherent in the intelligence world that a product is being provided free to customers who have no concept of the opportunity cost of their demands. This problem can be minimized by having a requirements setting process that involves regular agency/customer dialogue, and that allows the agencies to know which parts of their reporting are especially valued and allows them to feed back views to customers on the difficulty and expense of meeting hard requirements. The UK system uses a form of points rationing so that policy customers have to allocate their 'points' to the subjects they most care about getting intelligence on (often but not always, however, the same as the subjects they most care about).

There is therefore no substitute for close liaison between those in the agencies who influence the overall allocation of effort to targets and their military and policy customers. Such close working is not of itself 'politicization'. As already noted, the fact that in the UK system most of this contact will be between agency staff and senior military officers and permanent civilian officials who are apolitical helps keep these relationships professional. There is however a line that should not be crossed, comparable to that between commercial marketing and sales. The former has been defined in *The Management Dictionary*[20] as a management process through which goods and services move from concept to the customer. As a philosophy, it is based on thinking about the business in terms of customer needs and their satisfaction. Marketing differs from selling because (in the words of Harvard Business School's emeritus professor of marketing, Theodore C. Levitt) 'Selling concerns itself with the tricks and techniques of getting people to exchange their cash for your product. It is not concerned with the values that the exchange is all about. And it does not, as marketing invariably does, view the entire business process as consisting of a tightly integrated effort to discover, create, arouse, and satisfy customer needs.'[21]

The risk of a sales approach is that the intelligence will come to be presented in such a way as to make it more convincing to anyone less expert than the analyst. Professor R. V. Jones confesses[22] to coming close on two occasions during the Second World War to putting the intelligence case more strongly than the evidence justified, when his service chiefs looked like making what to him were serious errors of judgment. Advocacy is however no part of an intelligence officer's brief. In Prime Ministerial meetings it is to be expected, if there is—as there usually is—a good rapport between ministers and intelligence chiefs, that at a crucial point the former will ask the latter, well, what do you think we should do next? A key UK public service virtue is impartiality, serving political masters regardless. Integrity is another, so that the recipient of advice knows that it is being given honestly, and has not been spun to achieve a particular outcome. A school solution would be for a reply along the lines, 'Well, Prime Minister, if we were to do this, then I would expect the adversary to respond in the following way; and if we were to do that, then the response would be likely to be... But the decision is up to you.' In real life, senior ministers will want to know the views of their trusted key advisers on the risks associated with their choice of policy option, and thus on the wisdom of the option itself. What is really important is that at that point to make clear that they have departed from the intelligence brief and are giving a policy view. To avoid that potential conflict, since I had significant policy responsibilities at that time for counter-terrorism strategy when I was Intelligence and Security Coordinator in the Cabinet Office, I did not chair the JIC and there was thus a separate channel from the

Chairman of the JIC for intelligence reaching the Prime Minister. It would be safer not to have in the same person the responsibility for delivering the threat warning and for giving advice on the best policies to respond to the threat.

So 'marketing', but not sales, should be seen as a valid function for an intelligence agency. In practice, all three UK agencies go to some lengths to carry it out by making customers aware of their capabilities (backgrounders on successful operations, personal briefings, awaydays etc.) as well as discovering from customers what their short- and long-term objectives are. Intelligence agencies can also reasonably seek to 'create' a need for their product, in the way in which Apple 'created' a market for the iPod, a device that would not have occurred to the bulk of consumers to ask for but which is now regarded by them as indispensable. The policy staff and military users of intelligence are most unlikely to be able to assess what it may be possible to know through developments in secret intelligence techniques, and how their activities might be transformed if new forms of intelligence were available. 'Sales' on the other hand is across the line: customers have to be able to trust the agencies not to hype their products, nor to use 'trade-craft' on customers (for HUMINTers in particular, their professional stock in trade is the ability to establish relationships of confidence). It is also important that agencies do not see themselves as competing with each other for the attention of customers or manipulating the distribution of intelligence reporting to further some office politics of their customers. In the end it is all Her Majesty the Queen's information, available for her government to use.

Readers, users, customers, or consumers: push and pull

Recalling the intelligence cycle described in chapter 5, after the processes of 'access' and 'elucidation' have taken place, somehow the resulting knowledge must be put to use in what we have called 'action-on'. It must therefore be available to users in a timely and reliable fashion. For some users, located elsewhere in the intelligence community, the intelligence is an intermediate output that can be used in the production either of further intelligence of greater end value (for example when a HUMINT operation succeeds in recruiting a cypher clerk) or as a contribution to an all-source assessment. For most customers (departmental policy-makers, military commanders, law-enforcers etc.), the intelligence is already a final output that can be used directly to improve the quality of their decisions. In all cases, the context needs to be set in the report so that the import of the intelligence can readily be grasped by the user. That last point is vital. It is not enough for the raw intelligence to be written up and the report 'thrown over the wall' separating analyst and decision-taker, for the latter to read if the inclination takes him.

How should the recipients of secret intelligence therefore best be described? The official Cabinet Office guide to the UK's central intelligence machinery[23] refers to 'readers' of secret intelligence, a traditional term. It conjures up the 'Sherman Kent' vision of the separation between analyst and policy-maker. The Butler Inquiry report similarly refers to 'recipients' but also to 'users', implying a more active role. The Cabinet Office guide also refers briefly to 'customer departments' for secret intelligence, and 'customer' is a term with which the intelligence community has had to become comfortable after the Cold War as it moved from a world in which there was one dominant set of users of intelligence on the Soviet Union and the Warsaw Pact to the multiplicity of customers for intelligence on terrorism and instability, proliferation and serious crime. The 'customer centric' doctrine borrowed from the commercial world has the great merit of emphasizing the need to delight the customer with prompt service (delight being of course an ironical term when the news is bad), and to provide material that adds value, as well as being prepared to listen carefully to customer feedback. 'Customer' also carries a connotation of personalized service, taking account of specific needs, and that is certainly what is needed for example in terms of the service required by a field commander in a military theatre such as Afghanistan.

A possible danger in the commercial analogy is that it implies that 'the customer is king' and thus that the provider of intelligence is supplying what the customer wants—which in terms of content runs the risk of perceptions of politicization through delighting the 'customers' by telling them what they want to hear, not what they need to hear. Old hands in the intelligence world have thus been suspicious of talk of customers. The answer in the UK has been to place 'intelligence brokers'[24] alongside the customers. GCHQ, for example, headquartered in the west of England, maintains a team in London acting as client account managers, and both SIS and GCHQ would today often be asked to sit in (even if in the back row) on Whitehall planning meetings so as to have an up-to-date feel for priorities and the management of current events. Clearly the 'intelligence brokers' need to be really conversant with the potential of their agency to deliver value-adding support, and to be sufficiently in touch with one another not to be irritating the customer with rivalrous calls for attention. One of the developments that may come is to see such roles as a community one on behalf of all the agencies, a point considered in the final chapter.

The term 'consumer', even more than customer, implies a financial transaction with a supplier, buying a product or service for personal use. Charging consumers for intelligence is a subject that Finance Ministries like to examine every few years on the (superficially reasonable) grounds that a free-at-point-of-consumption service will always generate an excess demand beyond the point of economic efficiency which a market-based solution would have established. But different lines of intelligence do not compete, they contribute to the whole (often in unexpected ways not always evident at the time), and costs of production of individual reports do not necessarily correlate to the potential value of the line of reporting. Such charging for intelligence proposals has always foundered on the problems associated with the necessary large expenditure to keep a capability in being for when it is really needed (for example in cryptography, photo-reconnaissance or in maintaining a human intelligence network in a particular country) and the low short-run marginal cost of an additional report once the capability is in being.

A related issue is that of achieving the best balance of 'push' of material to users of intelligence, as selected by experienced analysts, assuming that they know well enough the needs of their customers, and of 'pull' from customers deciding for themselves what intelligence they need from the system, as allowed by modern secure communications systems and databases. This is the same dilemma that owners of journals such as *The Economist* face. Is it better to have the editor select what might be appropriate to the average reader and deliver that as a journal, or to invest in a much larger internet site of news and articles from which readers may pull what looks to be interesting and relevant, having been sent an email to alert them to the latest webpages? As the continued existence, in an internet age, of newspapers such as *The Economist* and the *Financial Times* demonstrates, busy people with highly responsible jobs value a diet of news and comment pre-selected by experts who push at them items worthy of attention.

There is also clear value for staff to be able to pull detailed information onto their desks just when they need it, and hence the value to be obtained commercially from 'paid-for content', and subscription services to website databases.

Commercial practice to get the best of both modes continues to develop. Systems based entirely on customers selecting their own material do run a real risk that key information will not come to the attention of the policy-maker or the military commander in sufficient time. On the other hand the traditional flow of written reports is not a complete answer to the needs of the busy policy customer or the intelligence officer supporting a military command who may need at short notice to access a range of material drawn from databases that are continually being kept up to date by the intelligence community—but which are themselves far too large to be circulated as individual reports before the nature of the specific need for information arises.

Thus a model of intelligence distribution is needed that takes account both of traditional producer 'push' of relevant intelligence to users, whether the user had put in a request for or was expecting that specific information or not, and modern user 'pull' of intelligence from producers when and where desired. The intelligence staff of a field commander must, for example, be able very quickly to access the information needed to support operations, ranging from geographical and weather data, enemy order of battle and equipment parameters, to high resolution all-weather radar imagery or network analysis of an insurgent group and their communications. A model for 'pull' is the modern IT-enabled public library holding some material immediately available but able to access online knowledge from around the world using advanced user-friendly search programmes. A parallel for 'push' is the commercial accountancy senior partner providing tailored updates to his clients on tax developments around the world, advising on due diligence on the prospects for mergers and acquisitions and forecasting the financial outlook, all to enable the clients to maximize their returns.

Elements of both models are needed, and come together when modern technology enables secure communities of analysts and users to share common areas of cyberspace, a goal to which the US and UK intelligence communities and their client base are slowly moving. We should of course recognize here that secret intelligence today no longer consists of just a written report following the debrief of an agent or the text of an intercepted message. Today it could be video or still photo-graphs, scientific data, radar images, data streams or in the form of annotated maps and diagrams. Broadband connectivity is therefore an essential part of running an effective national intelligence community. Such a system has to have a very high degree of information assurance, both to guarantee security from interception but also confidence that data received is the same as data transmitted. The UK has some con-siderable way to go before it has the networked connectivity at the appropriate level of security for sharing information and supporting analytic communities of interest working on common problems, span-ning intelligence and customer communities. We return to this issue in chapter 12.

The view from the top: Prime Ministers and Presidents

Important intelligence reports will go directly from the collecting agency to the relevant set of customers, including political leaders. The personal style of Presidents and Prime Ministers, and the circumstances in which they find themselves, will dictate how much secret intelligence goes into the in-tray or overnight box. The Prime Minister most inter-ested in reading intelligence (and with good reason) was Winston Churchill. But the practice of Prime Ministers acting as their own intel-ligence analyst has fallen out of fashion since then (and modern leaders rarely have the service experience that Churchill brought to his pre-miership). Even Churchill was liable to jump to unjustified conclusions on the basis of his own reading of the intelligence.

After the German attack on Russia in 1940, which it took the JIC some time to assess, Churchill famously remarked in his memoirs[25] that 'I had not been content for this form of collective wisdom, and preferred to see the originals myself ... thus forming my own opinions, sometimes at much earlier dates'. On 5 August 1940 he instructed his chief military assistant Major General Ismay (later Lord Ismay, first Secretary General of NATO) that 'I do not wish such reports are received to be sifted and digested by the various intelligence authori-ties. For the present Major Morton [Churchill's personal Intelligence Adviser in 10 Downing Street] will inspect them for me and submit what he considers of major importance. He is to be shown everything, and submit authentic documents to me in their original form.' That well-known story has a curious twist, however, since it is now believed[26] that Desmond Morton had access on Churchill's behalf to human source reporting and to diplomatic decrypts but not to the key 'Ultra' material from Bletchley Park's exploitation of the German Enigma machine. The story is informative for those who study the power that secret intelligence can bestow: how to acquire it, how to use it and how it can be lost.

Any newly arriving Prime Minister, and often senior Cabinet Ministers as well, sweep in with them a set of aides, advisers, paymasters, cronies and the odd adventurer, bound together by a shared personal loyalty to the boss. The early days are confused, the official machine appears too all-knowing and silky, and leaders need a few gritty people around them whose loyalty to them is proven and who are not part of the system. Churchill certainly had his 'horsemen of the apocalypse' as they were known at the time, among them Desmond Morton: well-born, a distinguished military record in WWI, director of operations for SIS between the wars, a friend and confidant of Churchill, with a full address book thanks to his Secret Service work that was unrivalled in offering access to some unusual and useful contacts.

But government is different from opposition. There are many clamouring for the leader's ear and court rivalries increase. The diary fills with official business, and there is less time for the old gang. For government is about perspiration as well as inspiration, policies as well as politics. Industrialized war needs organization and process, such as the War Cabinet machinery that Bridges, Alanbrooke, Ismay and Jacob created and operated.

Some in the court used their influence as a springboard to high-office themselves: Beaverbrook, for example, in Aircraft Production; or Brendan Bracken as Minister of Information. Some succeeded in carving out territory as part of the official payroll: 'the Prof' F. A. Lindeman (later Lord Cherwell), for example, creating the positions of what effectively later became those of Government Chief Statistician and Chief Scientist. Some adapted and learned to co-exist with the official system; and some found themselves being moved into circles further and further away from the heat and light of the centre of power.

Was it simply that Morton had not quite grasped the essence of becoming a grand vizier to Churchill's Pasha? Which is to give the appearance of greater influence than you have with those who wield power, and to be utterly unscrupulous in implying to fellow-courtiers and to the world around the court that not only will falling in with your schemes bring long-term benefit but if thwarted a word in the ear will swiftly bring loss of reputation and downfall. The implied influence rapidly then becomes real, as you are seen to get your way. The result is certainly to inspire deference if not respect. Morton seems to have allowed the then 'C', the Head of SIS, Sir Stuart Menzies, to cut him off at the knees by not bringing him into the circle of those who read the key Ultra material, the product of Bletchley Park's Enigma successes. Morton handled the decrypts of diplomatic telegrams from GC&CS, the forerunner of today's GCHQ, and must have known that Bletchley Park was generating vital intelligence. But the buff boxes containing the crucial Enigma decrypts were, it appears and contrary to popular legend, delivered unopened through Morton to Churchill, and Churchill had the only key in No. 10. Since those boxes contained the intelligence crown jewels, there was no way that Morton could actually be the PM's intelligence adviser in the proper sense of the term. No wonder his access declined. And 'C' would have known that, in thus sidelining Morton, he could take his place as the primary interlocutor for Churchill on intelligence and much else besides; which he duly did.

If all knowledge is power, secret knowledge is turbo-charged power. It is in the nature of secret intelligence that it can be used to ensure access to policy-makers and build influence and prestige for the collecting agency. The risks in terms of over-promising to buy favour and then under-delivering, as seems to have been the case with Iraq WMD intelligence, become all the greater if secrecy is being used to reinforce personal relationships and ensure face-time with the leader. As a US insider has commented,[27] where the institutional link between the CIA and the President did not become properly established, it was usually because the DCI attempted to handle the relationship single-handedly. The heads of British agencies are appointed today as laid down in legislation by the Foreign Secretary (SIS and GCHQ) and the Home Secretary (Security Service), in each case with the consent of the Prime Minister, following a conventional selection process. An incoming Prime Minister would be expected to adjust (and vice versa) to his senior official team and not to make fresh appointments. The US system is of course entirely different. Although some Presidents have wanted continuity, it is striking that of the five DCIs who were fired/resigned since the post was created after the Second World War, none was appointed by the President whose confidence he later lost. The psychological and political commitment a US President makes to the intelligence director he has appointed is obviously critical to sustaining their relationship.

These questions have been endlessly debated over the years between the policy and intelligence communities of most nations, especially the US and the UK, both inside government and in the academic journals. The debate is not merely of academic interest, as a recent example will illustrate. After 9/11, the CIA looked for but could find no substantive evidence of a link between Saddam Hussein and Al-Qa'ida. That intelligence finding was not accepted by the policy-makers in the Pentagon, who set up their own intelligence assessment capability and, controversially, reached a different conclusion that was then briefed to the US Defense Secretary and to the Vice-President. In chapter 18 of his memoirs, DCI George Tenet recounts his conflict with US Under-Secretary of Defense for Policy, Doug Feith, over these alternative intelligence assessments on the Iraq and Al-Qa'ida relationship, which included some conclusions that were inconsistent with the consensus of the intelligence community. That exercise was described in a subsequent inquiry[28] by the Pentagon's own Inspector-General in these terms: 'The Office of the USDP [Under Secretary for Defence Policy] developed, produced, and then disseminated alternative intelligence assessments on the Iraq and AQ relationship, which included some conclusions that were inconsistent with the consensus of the Intelligence Community, to senior decision-makers... As a result, the Office of the USDP did not provide "the most accurate analysis of intelligence" to senior decision-makers ... we believe that the actions were inappropriate because a policy office was producing intelligence products and was not conveying clearly to senior decision-makers the variance with the consensus of the Intelligence Community.' Tenet[29] called this 'Feith-based analysis' and Feith, in response, in his own review of Tenet's book, describes it as aiming low—to settle scores. All those interested in diagnosing pathologies in the relationship between intelligence analysts and policy customers should read up on this cautionary tale. As Tenet concludes, 'Policy-makers have a right to their own opinions but not to their own set of facts.' Such is the importance of secret intelligence for the implementation of national security strategy in the modern age that we must expect the policy/intelligence relationship to remain controversial.

In the US the fact that the President is also Commander in Chief in peace as in war has always provided a different dynamic from the UK, involving the President in daily intelligence briefings at a level of operational detail on current events that would be unthinkable for any modern British Prime Minister. Harry Truman entered the White House in 1945 without any knowledge of secret intelligence, and at his initiative since 1952 each Presidential candidate has also been offered a PDB (Presidential Daily Briefing) style of briefing service by CIA briefers.[30] Successive DCIs have groused about the distraction of the PDB that starts each day before dawn, and that involves the President and his key national security and intelligence advisers in operational, not to say tactical, detail when it could reasonably be argued that it is strategic awareness and direction on which the Oval Office should focus. It has been estimated that over 60 per cent of items in the PDB do not appear anywhere in the media, even in unclassified form. But no DCI (and now DNI) could have contemplated giving up daily face-time with the President, a level of access that even the most senior Cabinet members would long for in vain.

Writing for policy-makers

Whether Prime Ministers, Presidents and senior government figures should really try to be their own intelligence analysts, as Churchill at times was, to the frustration of his staff, is another matter. Senior policy customers, like the general public, are in general not good at understanding risk and relative probabilities, important skills in assessing intelligence. On being briefed on a possible terrorist threat, the temptation is to issue a Churchillian order for 'action this day', causing the system to lose perspective and impose costly security clamp-downs and encouraging the intelligence community to chase quick results rather than playing cases long to allow for development. After 9/11 the CIA used a 'threat matrix' to flag up new threats that could (and sometimes did) cause problems on both sides of the Atlantic: 'We recognized that the matrix was a blunt instrument. You could drive yourself crazy believing all or even half of what was in it.'[31] We consider this issue in chapter 8 when we look at some of the inherent difficulties of prediction.

In looking at the dynamics of such interactions between the analytic and policy communities, we should bear in mind that different personality types are likely to be involved.[32] As a generality, policy-makers are driven by a sense of public duty and want to change the world for the better, through possessing and using power. That in the UK context will be particularly true of those in party politics, but will also apply to many diplomats, civil servants and senior military officers. Those who reach key positions tend to be confident in their judgments, and are not prone to nervous introspection. Analysts are recruited more in an academic or professional mould and will tend to distrust formal power structures that they would regard as 'playing politics'. They are likely to be more comfortable with the concept of debate and criticism—especially giving it—than taking instructions. They are likely to have questioning personalities.

Ministers will have spent most of their time in office building support for programmes of action that they wish to carry out in achieving their mandate. They may well be open to impartial advice about the best way of achieving their objectives, particularly at the level of detailed delivery. But they are likely to be highly resistant to advice that appears to be at variance with their belief system in what works. That of course is precisely the situation that the intelligence analyst may find when putting forward a view of the world that does not fit the ministerial preconception. Officials, on the other hand, in the British system at least, are used to working for politicians of different parties, and this effect is likely to be less noticeable. But both groups, once their minds are made up, are likely to resist taking on board information that appears to undermine the basis on which their decisions were taken. This problem of cognitive dissonance is well documented[33] in military circles too.

When events do burst upon a government, ministers want to know quickly what the trouble is about, and what is likely to happen next, and to be given a sense of how quickly a response may be needed. The national intelligence assessment machinery needs to be capable of responding to this need, and to provide regular and frequent updating. Someone needs to pull the available information together impartially, and that person should be someone who does not have an institutional agenda in relation to what might be done. For that reason, in the British system, the responsibility rests with the Chief of the Cabinet Office Asssessments Staff to issue on his or her own authority urgent updates on developing issues.

Intelligence analysts, as a generality, are used to looking at other people's systems, their economies, armies and secret services as they find them. They are enjoined to avoid commenting on policy, and therefore on the actions of their own government. Policy-makers on the other hand are used to trying to shape the world as they would like it to be, and are resistant to being told of evidence that runs counter to that belief. The analytic mind, in order to reach judgments, imposes patterns of behaviour—the explanation of tensions between reformers and conservatives in government x, the hidden hand of the military leadership being shown in country y—and this inevitably over-simplifies the chaos of reality. They may have that in common with the senior ministers reading their assessments whose political world view also requires that they look at the world through simplifying spectacles. In the UK system it is likely to be the senior officials who are more tolerant of continuing ambiguity and contradiction.

It is important, therefore, for the leaders of the intelligence community to be at ease within the policy community, and to understand how things get done within it, yet retain their independence of judgment. In the UK the way the JIC works naturally brings these worlds together on a weekly basis. For the US this is more of a problem, given that senior figures in both communities are appointed as part of the political process. It is also important to ensure that, as far as is consistent with the integrity of the analytic product, the presentation to customers is tailored to the working pattern and prior knowledge of that customer group. A long paper, as many of the US National Intelligence Estimates are, academic in its objectivity with full apparatus of footnotes, references and alternative views, is unlikely to be read by the senior customer. Such papers have the great value in that they are considered, with every word weighed, and can thus form a background corpus of knowledge invaluable to the expert briefer. But the decision-taker needs something different. Henry Kissinger for example, as National Security Adviser, was reported[34] as having told DCI Helms: 'You know the most useful document you fellows turn out is that Weekly Summary that you put together. That's much more valuable than the daily stuff. That I can sit down on a Saturday morning and read and bring myself up to date and I think it is a good publication.'

A frequent failing of undergraduates writing an extended essay is to approach the topic by 'writing down everything you know' then adding a summary at the beginning. That too is a temptation for intelligence analysts writing for a non-expert audience. A better approach is that laid down by the Cabinet Office for those writing minutes of

Cabinet meetings. Start by writing down what was decided ('Summing up, the Prime Minister said that the Cabinet had agreed that...') then briefly set out the arguments that led to those judgments, including major points that were considered but not accepted. Points made that may have been interesting in themselves but did not materially contribute to the conclusions should be omitted. 'Key judgments' were introduced some years ago into JIC papers on the same logic, to direct the drafters away from description of the issue towards analysis of its meaning, and to focus attention on answering the questions behind the commissioning of the paper. Even key judgments can, however, end up so condensed that they become statements of the obvious. No policymaker needs really to be told that 'If widespread street rioting continues in country x then the hold of the government on power will be challenged.' What they want to know is the judgment of the intelligence community on which circumstances might make the challenge successful. In the policy world the normal way to get attention of ministers is to write a short punchy minute, in much less formal language than would be used in a JIC assessment. Behind such alerting minutes should, however, lie more formal assessments—otherwise the minister may regard the submission as just another point of view. Summarized digests of intelligence have their uses too—a few moments to scan them and then it is possible to call up a single report that looks particularly relevant. But too often such summaries become the bottom item in the in-tray, and once several pile up then the risk of something important being missed increases.

Potentialities, possibilities and probabilities

As described in earlier chapters, a strategic intelligence assessment is a justified set of judgments about the course of events, informed by having reached the best possible explanation of the underlying motives and circumstances of the individuals and organizations being observed, informed by a real understanding of their past behaviour. It cannot represent more than the best explanation of the situation consistent with what is known at that moment, and may need revision as new intelligence comes to notice. The duty of government on receipt of such an assessment is to evaluate the implications for national interests in the light of these intelligence judgments and other information available. It is in the nature of the intelligence business that most of the attention is given to the risk management of potential threats and hazards rather than the opportunities that intelligence may indicate could be exploited. Insufficient attention is given in the literature to the value added by intelligence on how to capitalize on a situation.

As in any exercise in risk management, the implications as evaluated by government will depend as discussed in chapter 2 upon the combined effect of three different kinds of factors: likelihood, vulnerability and impact (and likelihood, exploitability and pay-off in case of opportunities identified). Intelligence can illuminate all three factors, but principally likelihood. It does not follow of course that government should only act when the intelligence judgments say that a future event seems highly likely to arise. As described in chapter 3, governments have, as a matter of course, to take action on the basis of low probability but high impact future threats. The UK government rightly spent a significant amount of public money in stockpiling smallpox vaccine against the very low probability that the disease could become a terrorist weapon, knowing the huge loss of life that would be likely should that occur. In that case therefore it was judged worth the significant opportunity cost in terms of other public benefits foregone in order to take the risk off the table. Where, as in the case of a military response, the impact is not just monetary but has to be measured in terms of lives likely to be lost, then the overall risk assessment has to be that much more persuasive.

Intelligence analysts have long made the distinction between capabilities and intentions when assessing the likelihood of aggressive steps being taken by a potential adversary (whether for example military action, the nationalization of assets, state-sponsored terrorism or WMD development). Capabilities take time to build up and can be monitored objectively and are thus in the nature of secrets to be uncovered; intentions can change overnight and are in the nature of mysteries to be divined. The distinction between capabilities and intentions is an example of a much more general proposition of interest to the intelligence analyst, and that is the difference between potentialities and probabilities. How realistic, for example, would the threat have been that the secret service of Saddam Hussein would respond to invasion in 2003 by mounting terrorist attacks in the UK? The question would have been broken down into first of all the 'potential' for such attacks when the judgment might have been 'possible but limited in scale', based on intelligence analysis of his European agent network, number of expatriate Iraqis who could have been strong-armed into facilitating an attack, and so on. Given that assessment of potential capability, the second question would have been: how likely was it that Saddam's regime would seek to launch such attacks if Iraq were attacked? The assessment would be of a different kind, based on analysis of what Saddam's motivations and incentives and disincentives might be, and again the answer could have been expressed in terms of likelihood, perhaps 'very unlikely'.

In both types of analysis, what is really being expressed is a 'degree of belief' in the hypotheses regarding capability and intention respectively. In the absence of perfect knowledge, the assessment of capabilities will have a range of possible error associated with it that must be provided to the reader. The policy reaction would be very different in the example above if the capability judgment were hedged about by considerable uncertainty due to little intelligence being available on Iraqi networks, compared with the reaction if there was a high degree of confidence. That uncertainty is different, however, from that associated with the judgment of intentions. Both are often expressed in probabilistic terms, as 'it is a realistic possibility that…' or 'it is probable that…' and so on, but one refers to the degree of belief in the potentiality and the other in the intention. The former conveys assessed likelihood or probability of an event; and the latter the level of confidence ascribed to the judgment. It is therefore very important that the reader of an assessment is able to separate them in his or her mind and then to bring them together to comprehend the overall nature of the risk. The US National Intelligence Estimates use the following scale. In expressing the overall degree of confidence, *High confidence* generally indicates that the judgments are based on high-quality information, and/or that the nature of the issue makes it possible to render a solid judgment. A 'high confidence' judgment is not a fact or a certainty, however, and such judgments still carry a risk of being wrong. *Moderate confidence* generally means that the information is credibly sourced and plausible but not of sufficient quality or corroborated sufficiently to warrant a higher level of confidence. *Low confidence* generally means that the information's credibility and/or plausibility is questionable, or that the information is too fragmented or poorly corroborated to make solid analytic inferences, or that we have significant concerns or problems with the sources.

Another, completely different, example illustrates the complexities that can arise in arriving at key judgments. Suppose the tasking on the intelligence community was the apparently straightforward one of providing a key judgment of the likelihood that Japan would develop a nuclear weapons capability should confidence in the US nuclear umbrella wane for any reason over the next decade. The first part of the argument, on potentiality, would examine the current state of Japanese technology, availability of skills and nuclear materials etc. The second part would be an analysis of the international context, Japanese public opinion, the attitude of likely government leadership and so on. Both parts of the argument are valid questions to be answered in the intelligence domain. It will be noted, however, that the assessment of intentions in that hypothetical situation would probably depend crucially on judgments about possible Chinese and US reactions they might threaten to take that might discourage such an intention, and what would be Japanese responses to them. So a key judgment will end up as highly conditional. Not only is the judgment conditional on the stated assumption that these are hypothetical circumstances in which there is a perception that confidence in the US nuclear umbrella might wane (in ways that the assessment would need to spell out), but the judgment is conditional on hypothesized reactions, including by the UK's major ally. Such complexities are the rule rather than the exception in the intelligence world.

A remarkable example of such conditionality in an intelligence warning to government was the key judgment of the JIC at the time of the ill-fated Suez operation in 1956, when certainly the Chairman, Sir Patrick Dean, although not most members of the JIC, knew of the prior collusion between France, Israel and the UK to provoke the conditions for intervention and were almost certainly aware when they wrote this that the condition spelt out in the beginning of the judgment could not be met:

• 'Should Western military action be insufficient to ensure early and decisive victory, the international consequences both in the Arab States and elsewhere might give rise to extreme embarrassment and cannot be foreseen.'[35]

For another real example, take the following judgments from a declassified US National Intelligence Estimate of 1990 on the situation in the former Yugoslavia:

- 'Yugoslavia will cease to function as a federal state within one year and will probably break up within two. Economic reform will not stave off the break-up.
- Serbia will block Slovene and Croat attempts to form an all Yugoslav confederation.
- There will be a protracted armed uprising by the Albanians in Kosovo. A full-scale, inter-republic war is unlikely but serious inter-communal violence will accompany the break-up and will continue thereafter. The violence will be intractable and bitter.
- There is little that the US and its European allies can do to preserve Yugoslav unity. Yugoslavs will see such efforts as contradictory to advocacy of democracy and self-determination ... the Germans will pay lip-service to the idea of Yugoslav integrity, whilst quietly accepting the dissolution of the Yugoslav state.'[36]

What these examples illustrate is what in a military context is called a 'net assessment'. That is, an assessment is made of the relative capabilities of two military forces, not just the absolute capability of the adversary. Without capability we need not normally fear intention (at least for now, although future capability has of course to be the subject of careful assessment). But capabilities are not of themselves indicators of hostile intent. In assessing intentions, the danger of implicit assumptions about the hostile nature of the adversary is that they quickly lead to a paranoid state in which all developments are read as hostile. Thus the 'domino' theory that gripped Washington when the French withdrew from Indo-China and left a power vacuum. Another example might be the 1960s US assumption that South America was at risk of succumbing to Soviet-backed international communism. After the Cold War, and released from such deep ideological assumptions, the analysis of future intentions of foreign states becomes a much more sophisticated matter. How intelligence is interpreted and used depends crucially on the world views both of the analyst and of the reader of the assessment, which will not necessarily be the same. Indeed, the same intelligence may bear very different interpretations.

Fuzzy logic but plain speaking

In logic, but not alas in politics, it is simply not necessary for governments to have to pretend to certainty when they act. It would be perfectly justifiable to say that from intelligence a possible serious source of threat has been identified and that although intelligence can never be certain the nature of the potential threat were it to occur is so serious that it justifies pre-emptive consideration now. The elements of that case would then no doubt be subject to critical public examination, especially if action involving military force might be involved. But in politics, it is so tempting to elide the certainty of the need for action based on overall risk with the degree of certainty of the evidence of likelihood. It is difficult to over-estimate the importance of clarity about probability in conveying intelligence to customers, especially to decision-takers. Governments must not mistake possible for probable and probable for certain. Somehow, the language of the report or assessment must convey a proper sense of the strength of commitment to the key judgments of an assessment or the main conclusions of a single-source report.

Intelligence analysts have therefore to be brought up to shun vague terms, of the type that slip out when we are not sure but do not want to admit it, such as 'more or less', or 'apparently', or that standby 'on the one hand/on the other hand'. The Butler Inquiry found that there was an unjustified mystique amongst the writers of intelligence assessments that fine distinctions such as that between 'intelligence indicates' and 'intelligence shows' would convey meaning to the readers, but in truth such word-smithing passes them by. Words that concentrate meaning in terms of quantifiers (most, several or few) or probabilities (likely, certain) need to be handled with care. Terms such as *probably, likely, very likely*, or *almost certainly* are held to indicate a greater than even chance. The terms *unlikely* and *remote* indicate a less then even chance that an event will occur; they do not imply that an event will not occur. Terms such as *might* or *may* reflect situations in which we are unable to assess the likelihood, generally because relevant information is unavailable, sketchy, or fragmented. Terms such as *we cannot dismiss, we cannot rule out*, or *we cannot discount* reflect an unlikely, improbable, or remote event whose consequences are such that it warrants mentioning. The formal association of probability with these terms has been laid down by the UK Defence Intelligence Staff in 'The Uncertainty Yardstick'. In the case of urgent short-term assessments, of course, analysts will have to assign a probability to their judgments knowing that these may have to be revised, and the readers will need to be warned accordingly.

The Uncertainty Yardstick

Qualitative Statement	Associated Probability Range
Remote/Highly Unlikely	< 10%
Improbable/Unlikely	15–20%
Realistic Possibility	25–50%
Probable/Likely	55–70%
Highly/Very Probable/Likely	75–85%
Almost Certain	>90%

Source: UK MOD 2009

The intentional gaps between the levels are said to be to encourage analysts to be clear about what their assessments mean. Given the inherent uncertainty in the intelligence analysis business, this is meant to preclude a debate about whether something is at the lower end of one grade or the upper end of the one below it.

This commendable attempt to introduce more consistency into intelligence analysis should not however lead us to ignore the inherent 'fuzziness' around words as descriptors of categories. 'Enemy strength' conjures up an image of the order of battle and manning levels of regular units. But in counter-insurgency warfare, who counts as an 'enemy'? In Vietnam in 1967, the CIA argued for higher numbers of Communist strength since they believed that all irregulars should be included as relevant to judgments about progress with the campaign. The US Military Assistance Command in Vietnam (MACV) wanted lower numbers of enemy so as not to alarm public opinion, and so they included just North Vietnamese regulars. Bob Komer in charge of the pacification programme also argued that there must not be any counting of irregulars since so doing would produce a politically unacceptable total over 400,000. What the MACV ended up doing was compounding the problem by scoring all irregulars in their body count of kills, but comparing to their overall total of regulars only, thus giving a false view of the extent to which operations were resulting in attrition to enemy numbers. Another well-known example is the differing impressions given if the growth in size of the navy of a potential adversary is counted in numbers of ships or in tonnage. Categories in intelligence work are rarely categoric. The 'law of excluded middle' is not a good guide: a weapons system may not be either defensive or offensive but a bit of both. The intersection of the set of defensive weapons and its complement non-defensive weapons is not empty.

There are some unambiguous facts uncovered in intelligence work. But most of the evidence base suffers from fuzziness in two ways: it will help in forming sound judgments in assessments to be able to distinguish when we are dealing 'uncertainty' due to inevitable lack of precision in the intelligence reports we have—our measurements of reality—and that due to 'fuzziness' because of the definitions of reality we are using. There are, as we have just been discussing, degrees of belief in the evidence; and the evidential categories themselves may not be straightforward with clean edges. It is therefore dangerous for an intelligence analyst to apply Sherlock Holmes' dictum, 'When you have eliminated the impossible, whatever remains, however improbable, must be the truth', since the fuzzy nature of so much of the evidence means that elimination is never complete.

As noted in chapter 2, much of modern intelligence work is now focused on the tactical, especially in relation to counter-terrorism, counter-narcotics and counter-proliferation. A written report of an intercepted conversation is useful—but much more useful if the linguist and transcriber of the conversation is sitting in the same room as the analyst doing the reporting and can describe the tone of voice, the emotional register and the degree of agitation of the speaker, all of which may well be indications that would be very relevant to assessing the threat significance of the conversation. If the analyst is simply working on a pile of written transcripts, or more likely nowadays scrolling down the transcript on a screen, then key meaning may be lost.

Words also can change their meaning over time. A classic study[37] was that of Simpson in 1944 who asked 355 high school and college students to place terms like 'often' on a scale between 1 and 100. This study was repeated in 1968 by Hakel. There was no significant change in the median meaning given to terms such as 'very often' (88 times out of a 100 in 1944 and 87 out of 100 in 1968) and 'frequently' (73 and 72 respectively). But for 'now and then' the ranking went from 20 in 1944 to 34 in 1968, and for 'occasionally' from 20 to 28. Would politicians interpret 'hardly ever' in the same way as intelligence analysts, I wonder?

The human race does not seem to have found an instinctive feel for probability to be an evolutionary advantage. The Poisson distribution expresses the probability of a number of events occurring in a fixed period of time if these events occur with a known average rate and independently of the time since the last event. Asked to divide up a line with randomly allocated marks, most people will space out their ticks more than a true random distribution. Random events cluster more than intuition would indicate, so analysts can fall into the trap of over-interpreting the coincidence of independent reports arriving one after another. And likewise policy-makers can easily be misled into thinking that having had two different problems to grapple with in short order they can expect to be spared for the next few weeks! Combining probabilities also provides scope for misunderstanding. The probability of throwing two sixes in independent consecutive rolls of a dice is 1/6 *1/6 = 1/36, but the events have to be independent and in intelligence work they often are not, so on the first six being thrown the analyst should examine the hypothesis that the dice has been fixed. Or the equivalent of the first roll of the dice was reported in a JIC paper long ago, and the fresh assessment has neglected to take account of it, a phenomenon known as the sub-additivity effect where the tendency is to judge the probability of the whole to be less than the probabilities of the parts. Both UK Butler and the US Senate committee inquiry spoke of a 'layering' effect, whereby assessments were based on previous judgments without carrying forward the uncertainties. Much of the reason why each new bit of information that could be read as showing that Saddam had WMD was interpreted in this way was because of the underlying belief that Saddam really wanted to get a WMD capability.

In the next chapter we consider the dangers of being caught by surprise when biases creep into assessments, not least what is known as choice-supportive bias, the tendency to remember one's past judgments as better than they actually were. It is useful to distinguish between cognitive biases (psychologically-based distortions) and motivated biases (distortion in information-processing driven by world view, ideology or political preference).[38] Among cognitive biases some that have been recognized are:

- The Von Restorff effect—the tendency for an item that 'stands out like a sore thumb' to be more likely to be remembered than other items.
- Contrast effect—the enhancement or diminishment of the weight of a piece of evidence when compared with recently observed contrasting information.
- Focusing effect—prediction bias occurring when people place too much importance on one aspect of an event.

- Anchoring—the tendency to rely too heavily, or 'anchor,' on one trait or piece of information when making decisions.
- The halo effect—if one aspect is bad (or good), a tendency to interpret all aspects as bad (or good).
- The observer-expectancy effect—when an analyst expects a given result and therefore unconsciously misinterprets data in order to find it.

Consensus amongst analysts and intelligence agencies should clearly not be striven for at all costs. As mentioned in chapter 2, a criticism heard of the British JIC system is that in the search for consensus in key judgments, areas of disagreement are skirted round and the policy-readers are left unaware of where fault lines may exist between different interpretations of the evidence. The US National Intelligence Estimates, on the other hand, provide for the expressing of alternative views and opposing interpretations. This has the great merit of providing more information upon which the policy expert with time to spare can chew, but the disadvantage is that for highly charged subjects it allows cherry-picking of the interpretation that best suits the policy of the day. The argument for the British approach would be that such are the cultural norms of the process that the search for consensus engages the participants in deeper argument of the relative merits of their case than if they knew in advance that they could take a stand on a departmental position and insist on its inclusion. The debate leading to an assessment needs to be open, the JIC needs to be made aware by the Chief of the Assessments Staff of lower level disagreements so that consensus is not reached at too low a level, and no one viewpoint must be allowed to dominate.

Provided then that agreement can be arrived at without splitting differences and producing the lowest common denominator, consensus-seeking is not of itself dangerous. The role of the Chair of the JIC is for that reason key to the integrity of the assessment process. The presence of senior policy officials on the JIC is also some safeguard that those in the major departments briefing ministers will be aware of where the arguments between different interests were on any given subject. In my experience on the JIC under a number of different chairs the system delivers what it should, and the recent changes to use key judgments rather than summary conclusions and to give the reader a feel for the depth of the intelligence base underlying the paper are additional improvements on a basically sound system. Outside the formality of JIC assessments, however, it has to be recognized that senior intelligence and policy officials and senior officers will be engaged in meetings with the Prime Minister and key ministers and what is said round the table or from the sofa by a forceful interlocutor may carry considerable weight in shading ministerial interpretation of an assessment from 'glass half full' to 'glass half empty' or vice versa.

Conformity is not always a bad thing: the fact that several conscientious and intelligent people believe something is a valid reason for us to take it seriously. Also, much has been made of the dangers to objective intelligence assessment of *group think* defined as 'A mode of thinking that people engage in when they are deeply involved in a cohesive in-group, when the members' strivings for unanimity override their motivation to realistically appraise alternative courses of action'.[39] Thus in the context of intelligence on Iraqi WMD, the Butler Inquiry drew attention to the danger of group think as the development of a prevailing wisdom. In such cases there may be confirmation and disconfirmation biases at work, the tendency to search for or interpret information in a way that confirms one's preconceptions, and the tendency to extend critical scrutiny to information which contradicts the prior beliefs of the group and accept uncritically information that is congruent with their prior beliefs. Butler also pointed to the opposite danger, that when problems are many and diverse, on any one of them the number of experts can be dangerously small, and individual even idiosyncratic views may pass unchallenged, or there may be a *déformation professionelle*, a tendency to look at things according to the conventions of one's own specialization or profession, forgetting any broader point of view. Psychologists recognize a well-known 'bandwagon' effect—the tendency to believe things because many other people do. A related tendency to be guarded against is 'herding', where rational behaviour by individual analysts can lead to an irrational conclusion. Imagine an individual looking for somewhere to dine in a foreign city. He finds a street with many restaurants. All are empty except one, which has a couple dining. He rationalizes that they must have had some reason for choosing that establishment and decides to eat there. A little later another stranger comes by and notices three people eating in the restaurant. He makes the same calculation and also dines there. And so on, each additional diner reinforcing the herding effect until a consensus is reached.

There are therefore many cognitive biases, conscious and unconscious, that can affect analytic objectivity. The psychodynamics of the relationships between analyst and policy-maker also require attention, as we discuss later in the next chapter. There is for example the obvious danger that the analyst will tend to stress the negative since the penalties for crying wolf are less (there are always many reasons to be found as to why a prediction failed to materialize) than penalties for failure to predict an important strategic event (it happened and you did not warn us).

An under-researched aspect of the topic is the recognition that in practice there are three parties to the relationship: the policy-maker, the analyst, and the management structure above the analyst. The motivations of management may well impact on the way that assessments are presented to policy-makers, for reasons that are not irrational or ignoble but which will, if not recognized, tend to bias the judgments presented.

A particular difficulty is when belief systems become self-referential and closed. Thus if it is taken as an assumption that Saddam is trying to conceal his WMD by deceiving the inspectors, then absence of findings by the inspectors is liable to be taken as positive evidence confirming the hypothesis that he is even more cunning than was previously thought in concealing his illegal programmes. If the analysis is conducted only in those terms, then there is no way to break out of this loop. Instead, the analyst must continually examine the alternative hypotheses and hope to recognize that the evidence being seen is consistent with another explanation, based on Saddam's known reluctance to cooperate with any form of international inspection, his paranoia etc. Another factor is over-steering to compensate for past lessons, as was seen with the lessons drawn from the under-estimations of Iraqi WMD programmes after the first Gulf War.

With so many ways of falling into error, it is remarkable that there are intelligence successes and occasions when assessments make a difference in improving the quality of decisions taken. But there are indeed such positive results. The continued funding of this expensive set of capabilities in support of good government depends upon it. In the next chapter we return to analysis of surprise, and counter-surprise, but for now let us accept the conclusion of the Butler Inquiry, that the UK community did at least put up an impressive performance in its work on assessing proliferation in North Korea, Libya and Iran, resting on 'close collaboration between all involved, in agencies and departments, to build the jigsaw, with teams able to have access to available intelligence and to make the most of each clue. It also depends upon continuity of shared purpose amongst collectors and analysts, and between the intelligence and policy communities in gathering, assessing and using intelligence.'

8

INTELLIGENCE FAILURES

ON NOT BEING SURPRISED BY SURPRISE

The three watchful faces of Prudentia: observing past, present and future

We saw in the fourteenth century Sienese vision that good government is flanked by the figure of Prudence. In Renaissance iconography, Prudentia is shown as having three faces illustrating the arts of *memoria* (past), *intelligentia* (present) and *providentia* (future).

Prudentia thus symbolizes what the Greeks called phronesis: practical wisdom, the application of good judgment to human conduct consisting, according to Edgar Wind,[1] in a sound practical instinct for the course of events, an almost indefinable hunch that anticipates the future by remembering the past and thus judges the present correctly, as good a description as we could have of what wise rulers might hope to gain from their intelligence advisers. As we saw in chapter 1, national security strategies today rely more than ever on anticipation as a key feature in assuring public safety.

Governments hate surprises. They hate it when they have to perform U-turns and ditch cherished policies in the face of unexpected events. They hate it even more when headlines shriek 'government caught napping'. Intelligence agencies too hate being blamed, in what are invariably called intelligence failures, for the inevitable uncertainties of the world. The public assumption is that British intelligence should have known, and the public should have been warned, before events such as

SECURING THE STATE

a terrorist attack or the emergence of an unexpected threat to British interests somewhere in the world. Even in circumstances (such as the operation of markets) when tactical warning would have been impossible to achieve, an inability to spot trouble approaching is regarded as a strategic failure of government. The proposition is nevertheless sound that in general it is better to know the bad news earlier, when there are likely to be more policy options open, and when avoiding or mitigating action can be taken at lower cost. Governments have therefore equipped themselves with complex systems for horizon scanning, forecasting and prediction in order to minimize the risk of being caught by surprise. The CIA itself was founded in 1949 as a central US intelligence assessment capability with the Presidential intention that there should be 'no more Pearl Harbors'. The UK JIC has as a central part of its purpose the provision to government of warning of approaching threats. This chapter looks at what lies behind intelligence-based prediction and at what governments can at least do to prepare themselves, if they cannot eliminate surprise, in order not to be surprised by surprise itself and to adjust their resilience and other planning accordingly.

What is surprise?

No subject has been more studied in the theory of intelligence than the effects of surprise on military tactics, especially of surprise attack, and the motivations behind surprise.[2] If we return to Niccolo Machiavelli in 1520, we find him advising his Florentine Prince that 'Surprise is the most essential factor of victory ... nothing makes a leader greater than the capacity to guess the designs of the enemy ... to recognize, to grasp the situation and take advantage of it as it arises ... new and sudden things catch armies by surprise.'[3] Clausewitz states 'that Surprise very frequently has ended a war with a single stroke'. And Basil Liddell Hart, mindful of the carnage that the immobility of trench warfare brought in the First World War, advised future British commanders that the secret lies in surprise, the surprise of thought, leadership, and time; it lies in the surprise of attack and the execution of manoeuvres. Military surprise involves boldness, catching the adversary unawares and thus at a disadvantage, and additionally placing their commanders in the confused psychological state of having been surprised, a state that then can lead to serious failures in their response, compounding their problems. Today we have to examine another form of surprise,

210

that caused when there is an unexpected crisis that affects the fabric of everyday life, in particular that inflicted on society by the terrorist for whom surprise is both a tactical device and a strategic weapon.

For the security policy-makers it is the overall risk represented by the shock of possible unexpected events that has to be uppermost in their minds. Risk is the product of likelihood,[4] vulnerability and impact should the event occur. Investment in security will in most cases consist of a balance between, on the one hand, measures to reduce high risk due to a combination of low probability (which it may well be hard to influence through policy) coupled with high levels of vulnerability and potential impact and, on the other hand, measures to reduce the high risk from events that may be much more likely but of lesser vulnerability and impact. The former reduces the risk by minimizing the damage caused by low probability but high impact events (the worst the enemy can do to you) and the latter reduces the risk by maximizing the minimum level of assurance against higher probability but lower impact events (the best general level of security that can be offered to the public). We described these approaches in chapter 3 as the 'mini–max' and 'maxi–min' risk strategies respectively and noted that a mix of both is sensible in trying to use limited resources to best effect for public security. The resilience planner in particular must not only think about surprise in terms of the unexpected occurrence itself but be aware of the unexpected vulnerabilities and the unexpected depth or breadth of impact when disruptive events happen.

What the policy-maker traditionally wants above all from the intelligence analyst, meteorologist, seismologist, political scientist or futurologist is the estimate of likelihood. Taking a leaf from Charles Perrow's study of living with high-risk technology[5] we can categorize the likelihood of unwelcome surprises as coming in three forms. There are those surprises that can best be described as *unique*, infrequent Acts of God, that cannot be affected by policy measures, and whose individual occurrence is inherently hard to estimate. Then there are those *discrete* events whose frequency of occurrence can be rationally influenced by policy measures, such as the risk of terrorist hijack of an aircraft at Heathrow airport with a predicted occurrence that can, at least broadly, be estimated and presented in an alert state. Further security measures to reduce the likelihood can be taken if it is judged cost-effective to reduce the overall risk. And there are those *normal* events that are the inevitable consequence of living with highly complex interactive systems. Perrow in his analysis of the Three Mile Island nuclear disaster labels these 'normal accidents'. In the complex field of warfare, as Clausewitz recognized, with military operations there is always the fog and friction of war and unfolding events cannot be understood and their consequences controlled as planned. There will be surprises. Similarly, in complex (that is in virtually all) security and intelligence operations there will be unexpected interactions. As resilience planners know, and as was discussed in chapter 3, nasty surprises can come from the unexpected interaction of elements of the critical national infrastructure when there is a disruptive event causing cascading failure, or from impacts in surprising directions, perhaps arising from a crisis lasting longer than expected. As we shall see, it is important for policymakers, including those responsible for authorizing military, security and intelligence operations, not to confuse these categories. The inevitable post-mortems after a major disruptive event usually lead to demands that 'this must never be allowed to happen again'. The result is often stable-door-closing measures that, if the problem is a 'normal accident' not a 'discrete' one, may well just add more complexity and thus paradoxically increase the risk of future 'normal' accidents.

Leaving to one side rare 'unique' events, we can readily imagine that some disruptive events emerge from long gestating but often hidden processes, suddenly to erupt when the process reaches a tipping point. There are crises that flash up like a tropical storm, apparently out of a blue sky, but for which actually a skilled meteorologist given access to the appropriate data might well have been able to give some warning. The question for good government is how far forecasting and prediction can be relied upon. It is reasonable to expect the intelligence and strategic planners and horizon scanners in their different, but sometimes related, domains of interest to be organized to provide early warning, but of what kind? At the same time, a glance backwards shows that history provides many examples of discontinuities that were not anticipated, low probability but high impact events, that set life on a different course, as seen most notably in the responses to the 2008 global financial crash. The business school parable of boiling frogs comes to mind, creatures that if thrown into hot water will leap out immediately but if in water that is slowly heated will be unable to register the danger until it is too late. Slow gestating crises are hard to detect since analysts will become acclimatized and such intelligence as may be produced is hard to accept since it would involve those concerned in being prepared to admit that things will change (and that present policies will prove to be inadequate or flawed) before the evident need for change is upon them. A good example would be the failure of US analysts in the summer and autumn of 1962 as intelligence gradually built up of Soviet activity in Cuba, presence of Soviet personnel and of unexplained freighter movements to Cuba to re-assess their fundamental estimate that the Soviet leadership would not risk placing offensive missiles in Cuba.

The lessons of military surprise

We start by looking at traditional military surprise, and seeing how far the concepts involved can be applied to the broader field of national security, especially counter-terrorism.

Surprise may come upon the sleeping city, literally as well as figuratively, because the watchtowers of the city walls are complacently empty or the guards distracted, allowing the enemy to creep up on the defence unawares, as the Japanese carrier force did before Pearl Harbor. Or it may be that the defence is taken in by active deception, as in Operation Fortitude that provided tactical surprise for the Normandy landings (an invasion that could not be counted a strategic surprise; what could have been less unexpected than that there would be a second front opened in 1944?). Or surprise comes because the defence was led astray by self-deception when, despite warnings, the commander persists in misreading the enemy's intentions, as in the case of the siege of Troy despite Laocoön's warning to fear Greeks bearing gifts; or as Stalin underestimated Hitler in 1941 despite numerous intelligence reports of an impending attack on Russia. Or it comes because the defence failed to spot that the enemy had an unexpected technological advantage, as the Confederate side demonstrated at the first battle of Bull Run concentrating superior forces by moving troops by railroad, the first such exercise of such mobility in war. Or it comes because the offence decided on tactics that were unexpected or had been rejected as unfeasible by the defence, as when in their 1940 offensive German gliders landed right on top of the key Belgian fort of Eben-Emael, previously thought to have been impregnable. For reasons such as these, military surprise provides tactical advantage through superior numbers, method of attack, capabilities, technology, terrain or timing, and is made all the easier if the defenders have adopted a Maginot line mentality.

It should count as a *strategic* surprise in military affairs if the intelligence community is unable to give any warning at all of trouble brewing, and a *tactical* surprise if despite such warning the time, place or nature of the attack still comes as a surprise. The classic position was stated by Clausewitz in favour of tactical surprise, although he discounted the value of attempting to generate strategic surprise given the limitations in time and space taken to mobilize the numbers involved, transport them and generate the logistic capability to mount a strategic offensive. He could not have been expected to anticipate the industrialization of war with the railway and later air and amphibious transport. It was however the nuclear age with the Cold War confrontation that made the potential for strategic surprise an everyday reality for defence planners. Fears grew on both sides of losing strategic advantage through the other side gaining a first-strike capability, and the risks of strategic instability in a crisis of action and reaction. The KGB agent Oleg Gordievsky reported to SIS on Operation RYAN, a KGB operation to detect signs of the US preparing for a First Strike on the Soviet Union. He was instructed by Moscow Central to count the number of lights burning at night in the British Ministry of Defence, and to establish a source within the British blood transfusion system since stockpiling would be an early indicator of mobilization. 'National technical means', space-based intelligence sensors, acquired huge significance in the latter stages of the Cold War as the only means of verifying that arms control agreements were being kept and that the risk of 'strategic break-out' was kept acceptably low. Today, the fear of strategic surprise is a different one. Should neo-jihadist terrorists come to acquire means of significant mass disruption through radiological, chemical or biological means, or worse a proliferating state pass nuclear weapons to such groups, then the strategic significance for the West—and for any sense of security in living in cities of the West—would be immense.

The Falklands conflict provides an interesting example where not only was there strategic notice of the potential for conflict, but the JIC did give strategic warning of trouble as the negotiations between the UK and the Argentines failed to make progress—but alas this pointed in the early spring of 1982 to the possibility of conflict in the autumn, and that in turn produced a sense of false security in the spring. It appears that the Argentine junta brought forward their plans, thinking that the UK was intent upon sending a nuclear submarine to the South

Atlantic (the submarine movement that Argentine intelligence reported was in fact, another irony, leaving for an intelligence gathering mission in northern waters). British intelligence analysts did not pick up on this Argentine interpretation at the time and had no inkling that the Argentine invasion was imminent. Tactical surprise in the sense of inability of the UK to respond militarily in time was therefore complete, although the signals intelligence warning did at least provide just sufficient time for Prime Minister Thatcher to prepare her public response. The tables were turned a few months later when the British forces were able to land unopposed at San Carlos, having deceived the Argentine commander into expecting a later landing at a different place.

It is especially important that the intelligence analysts correctly read the motivations of a potential adversary in relation to the likely political goals of that regime. Is it posturing, or a natural concomitant of economic growth, or a prelude to an attempt at coercion or blackmail or even a developing military threat? For the British government, the regular presence of senior policy-makers from the Foreign Office, Defence, Home Office and Treasury alongside professionals from the intelligence community at JIC meetings is one way of trying to provide the different perspectives needed to bring policy context and intelligence reporting together to generate strategic notice. In the first Gulf War, for example, warning of Saddam's invasion of Kuwait was inadequate because the intelligence community did not have the correct situational awareness of why Saddam Hussein was behaving the way he was in making financial demands of Kuwait, and of the likely reaction of the ruler of Kuwait to his demands. It is also necessary in such cases to read the likely perception of the leader concerned to countermeasures that might be taken, and thus the analyst must also have a good grasp of the policies being followed by other major players, in that case the United States.

The distinction between assessing capabilities and intentions becomes blurred at this point. Capabilities should, in principle, be easier to estimate since they involve facts that can be uncovered (although an important part of available military capability rests on non-material factors such as morale and training that are harder to gauge than counting formations and major equipments). Intentions are notoriously difficult for an intelligence service to provide firm evidence for. The views of those close to the leader, even if they can be accessed from outside, may simply reveal internal arguments within the ruling circles. This applies regardless of the nature of the regime. Open source information may be as valuable as secret sources in proving context within which to assess intentions. Past behaviour is a guide, although not always a wholly reliable one. There may be memoirs and writings by those in power that reveal a leader's intentions (the historian Hugh Trevor-Roper was one of the few in wartime British Intelligence to have read and understood the implications of Hitler's *Mein Kampf*).

Simply assessing relative military capabilities between two opposing parties may also not be a good guide: the inferior side may nevertheless decide upon aggression, perhaps judging that the effect of surprise will outweigh inferior numbers (as the Japanese at Pearl Harbor), or even as a deliberate act knowing that the initiation of conflict will break a diplomatic stalemate and create a new status quo (as with Egypt in the Yom Kippur War or Argentinia over the Falkland Islands) or start a process leading to political victory (as in Indochina) or perhaps act aggressively simply through miscalculation of what can be got away with (as Khrushchev did in trying to install nuclear missiles in Cuba). For the terrorist, of course, it is always '*du faible, au fort*'.

It may also be misleading to rely too far on the structure of military forces as a guide to long-term intentions, such as the building of 'offensive' capabilities represented by amphibious forces or missile defences. Understanding context is everything. To take a current example, the (undoubted) Chinese nuclear force build-up could be taken as a guide to long-term aggressive intentions to dominate the region militarily, neutralize US carrier based forces and thus allow the re-integration of Taiwan by force. Alternatively, the observed programmes, nuclear missile firing submarines, long-range road mobile missiles, anti–satellite capability etc. could best be explained by fears of current US regional military superiority based on the vulnerability of Chinese systems to US pre-emption in a time of crisis through possession of conventional precision strike weapons. It is an understanding of political context that will guide the analyst. It must be hoped that warnings to the policy-makers will always include the caveat that whatever the intelligence judgment may be, capabilities take time to build up but intentions can change overnight. Another example would be Cold War interpretation of Soviet military doctrine and the scenarios of training exercises as indicators of political intent. It is hard to distinguish between the military strategy that a government might have to follow were war to come and the policy of the political leadership in relation to the desirability of future conflict. Thus the Red Army had, building on its harrowing experience during the Second World War, a very aggressive military strategy in the event of war with the capitalist West, including massive armoured offensives, widespread use of tactical nuclear weapons, and use of Special Forces (SF) to paralyse NATO rear areas. For many analysts this was read as the signs of an aggressive intent on the part of the Soviet Union to provide itself with the means to over-run western Europe. For the Soviet leadership, on the other hand, it now appears as if the policies they followed consistently were designed to avoid open war. That argument came to a head in the 1976 'Team A/ Team B' dispute within the US government over Soviet strategic capabilities and intentions. The President's Foreign Intelligence Advisory Board (PFIAB) commissioned a 'Team B' assessment to set against that of the official 'Team A' who had produced the National Intelligence Assessment, with Team B deliberately chosen from scholars and experts known to have more hawkish views about Soviet intentions and led by Harvard Professor Richard Pipes. Predictably Team B produced an alternative, more pessimistic assessment judging that the Soviet Union sought military superiority not a strategic balance. As Michael Betts, a leading analyst of surprise, has commented,[6] part of the problem was confusion about the level of analysis at issue. Pipes and Team B were judging strategic intent should war come; Team A was judging political strategy. Pipes justified Team B's inclusion of judgments on objectives as well as capabilities thus: 'it is not possible completely to divorce an assessment of capabilities from the judgment of intention: the significance of a person's purchasing a knife is different if he is a professional chef or the leader of a street gang, although the technical 'capability' which the knife provides is the same in each case'.[7]

The 1962 Cuban missile crisis also provides lessons for strategic warning. The US intelligence community assessed in early autumn of 1962 that despite reports that the USSR was seeking to install nuclear armed missiles in Cuba, it was highly unlikely that the Soviet regime would adopt such a high-risk policy. In that case they were proved wrong in their conclusion, not because their analysis of Soviet political strategy of avoiding direct conflict was wrong, or because the Soviet leader fundamentally misjudged how unacceptable the presence of the missiles would be for the US, but because Khruschev miscalculated his chances of getting the missiles operational in Cuba without being detected and challenged. When the US responded firmly but also demonstrated the wish not to let matters get out of hand, the Soviet leadership was able to back down. In that case, it is worth noting, the JIC in London also correctly read the minds of the Kremlin leadership in terms of how they would manage the crisis: 'We have considered the possibility of large-scale action against Berlin but suggest that this is unlikely... Indeed, central to Russian thinking in deciding upon their reply will be their fear of doing anything that might escalate into general war. Their overriding concern therefore is likely to be to limit their reply to the least dangerous place... Their aim indeed would be to conduct an exact tit-for-tat and no more... It seems unlikely that the Russians will use nuclear weapons in reply to such a US attack as may be envisaged.' Analysts work for the most part, as do most economists, with the assumption of 'economic man' capable of making rational choices based on self-interest. But what is rational for a trained Western professional intelligence analyst may be very different from that of a non-democratic leader with a very different world view. And leaders do miscalculate or misunderstand their opponents.

But military surprise is usually only temporary. The advantage of surprise comes because the normal rules of war have been suspended in the adversary's favour so that locally he can have superiority in numbers, equipment, timing or terrain. It is therefore a tactic that favours the weaker side. The weaker side may even be lured by the possibility of surprise into aggression. But as the conflict progresses the natural correlation of forces reasserts itself, and the stronger side will prevail. Sides that mount surprises, even devastating ones like the Japanese attack of Pearl Harbor, usually end up losing the ensuing war. Despite the advantages of surprise in catching the Soviet Army relatively unprepared in 1941, the Germans eventually were ground down by Soviet weight and tenacity of effort.

Government may be surprised by developments in all threat domains. The UK National Security Strategy[8] identifies as of special concern in the early twenty-first century the domains of hostile and destructive capabilities, including nuclear proliferation as well as physical domains, including especially in maritime and space, technology, especially cyberspace, and even in public information and ideology. A surprise may thus be triggered by unexpected developments in a political situation overseas; it may be new technology breakthroughs, or the uncovering of weapons programmes including proliferation of WMD, such as the proliferation activities of the A. Q. Khan network. Surprises may be at the level of the state, or may be caused by non-state actors. We may be faced with hostile ideologies, covert action, political manoeuvring against our interests (for example at the United Nations); economic or cyber action; as well as emerging military threats to our allies and partners.

Terrorism, surprise and shock

The necessity to be ready not to be surprised by surprise thus extends well beyond the world of surprise attack. Having strategic notice of potential future developments can provide an alert government with the possibility of materially reducing risks to the public, for example through the preparation of contingency plans and policies and through careful preparation of public opinion. There is, however, an important distinction between the 'most likely' set of outcomes and the residual risk, including the 'worst case'. For some purposes the latter is needed (for example in the run-up to the Gulf War having the worst case intelligence assessment of Saddam's BW and CW capability in order to provide for the inoculation and protection of troops). But government cannot be run on the basis of all the worst cases that can happen to society, any more than individuals can run their lives on the assumption that they are schlimazels, those to whom the worst will always happen.

As we saw in the previous chapter there is a complex chain of events involved in the provision of early warning. There has to be evidence available that is capable of being interpreted as a warning sign. The existence of such evidence, for example enemy troop movements, has to be accessed by intelligence means (which the adversary is of course at pains to try to frustrate). Analysts have to place the right interpretation on those fragments of intelligence against the background of noise, fog of war and deception, and to communicate the intelligence assessment in a sufficiently timely way to busy decision-makers. Finally, the latter have not only to comprehend the import of the intelligence warning but to be prepared to take action upon it—and even then the action may come too late to prevent the surprise from occurring. Given the number of things that all have to go right in this chain it is surprising that there are not more surprises.

Terrorism itself implies surprise. Without tactical surprises the terrorist or insurgent group would quickly fall to the stronger forces of state intelligence and security. Without strategic surprise terrorism would fail in its purpose to shock and thus disturb normality and by so doing convey a powerful communications signal. Governments and even populations become deadened to repeated attacks of the same type. In terrorism, the weaker side engages in an asymmetric conflict in the hope of being able to choose the time, place, method and target of attack so that the security forces will always be caught unawares. Terrorists become adept at mounting secondary attacks to catch security forces off guard, such as leaving a second explosive device to detonate as the security forces and 'blue light' services arrive to deal with a first attack. There are even cases of tertiary attacks, directed at the hospitals that can be expected to receive casualties, to try to kill the VIPs who will be bound to visit the survivors. Even more than in conventional warfare, the defence must rely on intelligence to pre-empt offensive attacks and to reduce the level of violence so as to deny the attackers the disruption they seek and thus remove their potential leverage over the government to achieve their campaign aims.

Since most terrorist acts are themselves acts of communication (to intimidate the population, to influence governments, to rally supporters and to gather recruits) the more that the shock of the act can be muted the better for the society being attacked. Even if tactical warning is not always possible, which is the case even with the most effective of police and intelligence authorities, strategic and operational warning can help condition media attitudes and strengthen public fortitude, a very necessary condition for the defeat of terrorism.

Acquiring foreknowledge to counter surprise

It will help manage the impact of surprise if government is already alerted to possible danger, even in general terms. With such strategic notice, the search for operational and tactical warning information can be cued and decision-makers sensitized to the possibility of surprise. The analytical community that is assessing information on the potential danger can be strengthened, and having some strategic warning may make it less likely that intelligence analysts or policy-makers will fall victim to the biases and pitfalls that were discussed in the last chapter. Some form of alert or counter-surprise system can be introduced, such as the US DEFCON alert states developed during the Cold War and the NATO counter-surprise equivalents. The equivalent today is the colour-coded Terrorist Alert states issued by the US Department of Homeland Security, and the UK counter-terrorism alert states issued by JTAC, discussed later in the chapter.

In the case of terrorism, there may well be indicators that are associated with an increased likelihood of an attack. Examples might include movements of known terrorists, evidence of transfer of funds to a cell or network, members and associates 'going dark', chatter on the radical internet websites and so on, but none of these would be definitive and each would have to be interpreted in context. The big difference with the military warning systems of the Cold War is that today's alert states are intended to be made public. That is consistent with the need, as was discussed in chapter 3, to involve individuals, communities and the private sector in taking more responsibility for their security. As we discuss later in chapter 9, putting intelligence-based information into the public domain is not without its risks. There is also a tendency in an increasingly litigious age to add warnings, however vacuous, so that after the event the risk of comeback can be reduced. Advice on individual countries on the Foreign Office website, for example, when not linked to specific information that will genuinely help the traveller, can easily become banal.

Living with surprise

To improve the chances of not being caught by surprise, there are nevertheless a number of steps that a prudent government can take. We look at each of these steps in turn.

The first step is for government to put itself into a position where it has a reasonable chance of having the necessary foreknowledge of trouble ahead. There is what I term *strategic notice*, where government is being put on notice that there are developments of which it needs to be aware. These changes could be, as was discussed in chapter 1, in the fields of technology (such as the development of nanotechnology or quantum computing), in diplomacy (such as the development of potential new alliances or groupings of nations), in nature (such as the effects of global warming on scarce resources) or in other aspects of security (such as the possible development of violent ideologies). Government also needs strategic notice of demographic changes, and prospective shifts in public attitude. Strategic notice in the form simply of a list of conceivable future possibilities is however of only limited use (in the same way as corporate risk registers that are simply a catalogue of all the disasters that might befall are only building-blocks for a sensible risk management process). What is required at this level of thinking about security is understanding of the phenomena in question, and their roots and causes, expressed in ways that will help the policy staffs develop options for government. One of the most important benefits of good strategic notice is in enhancing the ability of government to commission longer-term scientific and other research to illuminate the phenomena, which it should do systematically as a cross-government exercise.

At a more practical level, we can identify a second type of foreknowledge that I term *operational warning* in which government is made aware of the nature of specific threats and opportunities (in practice more of the former, alas, than the latter) with some sense of timeline to enable urgency to be calibrated. Typically, in the case of threats, operational warning does not provide government with sufficient detailed evidence to neutralize the possible threat itself, for example by the arrest of a terrorist group.

When more specific intelligence arrives, or the situation becomes clearer in some other way, then *operational alerting* can be issued that will trigger precautionary deployments or contingency planning, or even allow the putting into effect of previous contingency plans commissioned on the basis of operational warning. A simple example from the field of terrorism would be the identification of a new type of attack mode following terrorist attacks overseas (for example the Mumbai attacks of 2008) leading to operational alerts being issued to the operators of the critical national infrastructure, triggering adjustments to programmes of protection and hardening for key facilities, in advance of any specific intelligence of an identified group actually planning such an attack.

The final category of foreknowledge is what I term *tactical warning* specific enough to allow the security authorities to counter an actual threat. This is ultimately the most valuable intelligence to have, but also the hardest to obtain. We may think of the guard dog that barks or the alarm rocket that goes up when the perimeter wire is crossed. Life is never quite so simple, however, and warnings can be ambiguous. Even unambiguous tactical warning can be rejected if it conflicts with strongly held contrary beliefs. The psychology of both analyst and decision-taker and the level of trust between them are key, and this is a phenomenon we examine later in the chapter.

Warning fatigue and handling residual risk

Warning fatigue will dull senses. Intelligence agencies that 'cry wolf' too often will be discredited. Governments may however come paradoxically to rely too much on intelligence agencies that have regularly delivered the goods, and the shock of surprise when something slips under their radar will be all the greater. The only sound advice to give is to educate government, the media and the public to come to see tactical warning as an exercise in risk management. There is no guarantee that any warning system will always pick up the signs, and therefore there is no absolute level of safety that can be offered to the public. Active intelligence effort, however, will shift the odds in favour of the defender, where every little bit of advantage helps.

The rational approach is to plan on the basis of the best achievable expected outcome. A caveat is however required. Even where there is high confidence in the predicted course of events, there will be *residual risk*. There will in particular be some low probability but high impact events that could destroy the basis of the plan. In counter-terrorism planning, for example, as discussed in chapter 4, we could discover ideologically driven terrorists of a millenarian outlook equipped with effective means of mass destruction, up to and including a viable nuclear device. That combination of hazard has not yet arisen, and may never. At present it would be regarded as a low probability but extremely high impact risk. But if it occurs then it would mark a rupture with the past, and the entry into a new and harsh future in which living in cities, the defining characteristic of our civilization, would become problematic.

The attacks on 9/11 2001 demonstrated, as did those in Mumbai in 2008, a combination of planning skill, suicidal determination and complete disregard for the taking of human life. Had Al-Qa'ida planners had access to WMD, it is hard to believe that they would not have hesitated to use such means, causing even larger loss of life and devastation, in order to give history a decisive nudge. Such an event would change international and domestic politics, in directions hard to predict, but the public clamour for security can only be imagined, whatever the cost in terms of individual rights or resources expended. There are therefore some possible residual risk events that may be unlikely but have consequences that require nevertheless pre-emptive policy responses. Consideration of such high impact scenarios emphasizes the importance of government having sufficient strategic and operational

notice to be able to work out sensible policies in the face of such a
danger but before it materializes, at which point the danger is that
rationality will go out of the window.

An example of how using foreknowledge might help generate security

To illustrate this model of foreknowledge, let us take a (so far, thankfully) hypothetical case, that of the developing threat of the misuse of
synthetic biology, to see how a well-performing intelligence community
might operate at each of these levels.

The story might start outside the intelligence and security community altogether, perhaps triggered by a government scientist attending
a science policy discussion at the Royal Society in London on the latest
scientific research findings on synthetic biology and advances in gene-
splicing techniques and flagging up the subject within government. As
part of its work in predicting strategic trends, we can imagine that the
JIC would pick up on the possibility of long-term security risks being
associated with this new technology, and decide on its own initiative
(or at the request of a department such as the Home Office) to write
an assessment, identifying possible vectors of threat to British and
allied interests at home and overseas, such as terrorist use or interest
by international criminal gangs in developing new illegal recreational
drugs. A JIC paper receives widespread senior ministerial and official
circulation, and in that way such a JIC paper would thus provide government with *strategic notice* of an emerging threat, well before it has
shown itself in reality. We can imagine that further long-term research,
or advice from an external scientific panel, might be commissioned as
a result, and that any evidence of terrorist or criminal interest in such
technology might feature on the next JIC statement of intelligence
requirements.

To continue the hypothetical example, it might well be that knowing
of this interest in the subject the Secret Intelligence Service and GCHQ
would allocate extra effort, and brief their existing assets, and might
uncover active terrorist interest in such technology, for example through
discovering relevant academic papers being accessed on the internet by
an individual with a terrorist trace. We can also easily imagine information being passed from a liaison service to SIS of the arrest in an overseas country of a terrorist planner who is discovered to have appropriate

experience, such as a doctorate in biochemistry. Such intelligence reporting would count as *operational warning*.

Given those operational warning signs having been reported, more intensive investigations would be triggered into the subject, notes would be compared with intelligence allies, and with luck more intelligence would turn up. At an operational level of detail, we might expect a report from the Joint Terrorism Analysis Centre, JTAC, that would critically assess the feasibility of certain techniques to make pathogens and the comparative likelihood that a cell in the UK could be planning the use of such means to cause disruption, rather than more traditional means of attack. An *operational alert* would be sounded if such investigations showed that there was indeed strong evidence for interest in the subject, and that might trigger JTAC to raise the formal UK alert state and for their police contacts to brief forces across the country.

Finally, *tactical warning* would come if there was specific intelligence, for example resulting from a Security Service and police surveillance operation relating to an identified group in the UK, or a group overseas planning to attack British or allied interests, ideally with sufficient detail to enable effective, and safe, counter-measures to be taken and the risk averted.

Reducing the risk of bias

As already noted in the previous chapter, both analysts and policy-makers are at risk of falling victim to some of the many possible biases that were described, such as group think, herding or the bandwagon effect and as a result warning signs may thereby be missed. The trained mind is to be encouraged since it is able quickly to assess evidence, recognize the possibility of bias and know the shortcuts that can safely be taken with assessing evidence on the topic in question. But experts can end up more resistant than lay readers to accepting evidence that appears to overturn conventional expert wisdom. And with highly specialized topics, and in organizations with significant division of labour, the dogmatic expert will have the upper hand and it may be hard for an analytic body, such as a current intelligence group, to challenge such definitive views.

The traditional intelligence model is incremental.[9] It focuses on patiently tracking developments step by step, for example by comparison over time of series of reconnaissance images. The typical intelligence briefing of senior policy-makers, whether by government analysts or the many private sector firms that now produce a service for commercial clients, tends to be of 'overnight developments' or updates since the last brief. That model is sound in terms of applying linear thinking to gradual changes that can be observed, for example as a potential opponent builds up their forces and for generating predictions for as long as the underlying reality remains stable.[10] But induction becomes unreliable as soon as major shifts in circumstances loom. It may be induction in time, extrapolating for example from correlation of past observed evidence of activity at a nuclear test site followed by a nuclear test to a likely future test, or induction from the particular to the general, such as the observation of different patterns of submarine deployment leading to a conclusion that a new class has been accepted into service.

It is in general therefore not sensible for governments to base contingency planning wholly on predictions coming from extrapolating present trends. For most of the time, it is likely that better than average results will be obtained—until the discontinuities appear and the trend changes. That appears to have been the case with the financial analysts before the crash of 2008, basing their risk models of new derivative products on data that only reflected the good years and expecting a normal distribution of price movements, when in reality the distributions were 'fat tailed'. When that sort of assumption is built into the model, predictions are likely to be seriously, even spectacularly, wrong when the unexpected happens. Behind this paradox is the truth that unless there is a satisfactory explanation of the underlying phenomena and relationships then forecasts will be badly out when, as inevitably happens, the run of good luck changes.

In chapter 6, the 'black swan' problem of over-reliance on inductive thinking was identified. This can be an obstacle in trying to gauge the intentions behind military deployments, such as the manoeuvres of the Warsaw Pact on the borders of Czechoslovakia in 1968, of the Egyptian army on the Suez Canal in 1973, or of Saddam Hussein on the borders of Kuwait in 1990. The adversary may have been detected engaging in such manoeuvres before and each time it turned out to be an exercise, so the problem for the analyst is to answer the question: why is this time any different? In another context, all the jihadist recruiting and financing activity originally seen in the UK was (correctly) ascribed to support for theatres of conflict overseas and not directed against the

UK. The factual statement 'there is no evidence of a jihadist domestic threat against the UK itself' can quickly be elided into the judgment 'there is no current domestic threat from jihadists', which may have been literally true (as a description of all-white swans) but masks the real possibility that we were about to be surprised (by seeing our first black swan). As the astronomer Carl Sagan (and later Donald Rumsfeld) said: 'Absence of evidence is not evidence of absence.'

Spotting the discontinuities before they occur is much the hardest part of forecasting. It is important that governments do not have exaggerated expectations that surprise can be anticipated. The late Sir Michael Quinlan formulated a law of deterrence to explain this phenomenon in relation to his own field of expertise, nuclear weapons. What we forecast, he said, we prepare for. What we prepare for, we deter. So what we actually experience by way of events is, alas, what we have not prepared for, and will catch us by surprise.

When we look at how the policy-maker reacts on receiving the intelligence warning or alerting intelligence, other factors may come into play. If the warning is real then the cost of reacting to it through mobilization or widespread protective security measures may be very high indeed. Who wants to be responsible for ordering the cancellation of the Cup Final because of a terrorist alert? Such decisions are usually best left to the independent judgment of operational police officers and not elevated for political decision. Reasons for putting off the decision can always be found by those who unconsciously fear the decision. Meetings drag on and have to be rescheduled, more information can be requested or further analysis commissioned (the so-called Information Bias). A phenomenon often seen in crisis management when first news of an impending problem arrives is a general reluctance to accept that normal life will have to be put on hold whilst everyone focuses on the emergency. 'This can't be happening, really' at a subconscious level can lead to a 'business as usual' reaction from ministers and officials not steeped in operational management. Yet police did once have to close Aintree racecourse for the Grand National as a result of information received. Having strategic notice of the issue helps everyone prepare themselves mentally for the rethinking that may become necessary if the feared development appears to have arrived.

In cases where the warning information appears to undermine a decision already made, particularly if only just made after great agonizing, the phenomenon of cognitive dissonance may surface and paralyse the capacity of the decision-maker to reconsider when fresh evidence arrives. There are several psychological mechanisms that can kick in subconsciously to allow the policy-makers in that situation to reassure themselves that the data is not to be believed.[11] There is confirmation bias, the natural tendency to pay more attention to news that appears to confirm your views, and to impose stricter tests upon information that challenges them. It will always be possible to challenge the track record of the source or that of the intelligence agency concerned, and to point to past warnings that did not turn out to be valid. There are, as mentioned earlier, plenty of excuses for prevarication, perhaps conceding some limited steps but asking for more information or more time for analysis before deciding on major moves. It may be that a command decision had set in train major deployments or consequences and a counter-order could simply, as the military saying has it, create disorder and make matters worse. A decisive and strong commander who accepts he has cast the die and, right or wrong, that is the score may be better able to provide necessary leadership than a commander who is seen by the staff as too ready to change his opinion and lacking grit. Such thoughts will go through the decision-maker's mind, and can readily be used to justify delay on receipt of bad news. Policy-makers are very good at providing rationalizations to argue away awkward evidence, since they are well used to selecting evidence to argue a positive case for some new policy. This can, as the example of the Yom Kippur War described below shows, lead to dangerously dogmatic assumptions about the motivations and behaviours of the adversary. It may be that the weaknesses of the adversary will be highlighted to show the risks he would be running by aggression, and thus how unlikely it would be that a surprise attack will come. Michael Handel's paradox of surprise then comes into play: 'The greater the risk, the less likely it seems to be, and the less risky it actually becomes. Thus, the greater the risk, the smaller it becomes.'[12]

And all of that is without taking account of the possibility of deception.

The record of the JIC in helping successive British governments anticipate trouble is mixed. In the late 1970s the JIC commissioned Doug Nicoll, a seasoned GCHQ intelligence veteran, to examine the JIC's own performance in warning government about foreign acts of aggression.[13] Nicoll examined seven detailed case-studies: the Soviet invasion of Czechoslovakia (1968); the Egyptian/Syrian invasion of

Israel (1972–3); the Chinese attack on Vietnam (1978–9); the Soviet invasion of Afghanistan (1979); the Iraqi attack on Iran (1979–80); the Soviet attack on Iran (1980); and Soviet intervention in Poland (1980–81). By one of those awful coincidences of history the JIC approved his final report listing the pitfalls into which analysts had fallen and concluded that it was alert to the lessons learned; only a month later, the JIC itself was the victim of the surprise of the Argentine invasion of the Falklands. The Franks Committee, set up to investigate what had gone wrong, asked Nicoll to submit a further analysis.[14] What Nicoll found was that the JIC had 'found it difficult to believe that the potential aggressor would indeed find the use of force politically acceptable'. Dictators are hard for democrats to fathom. By looking at the intelligence estimates with the benefit of hindsight Nicoll discovered that 'there has been a tendency to assume that factors which would weigh heavily in the United Kingdom would be equally serious constraints on countries ruled by one-party governments and heavily under the influence of a single leader'. This is now a well-known epistemological trap, known in the jargon as mirror-imaging: the misperception that the enemy will behave as you would yourself in his place. This effect may in some circumstances be exaggerated if the analytical intelligence staff are themselves monocultural in political outlook: during the Cold War the intelligence world, for obvious reasons, recruited from those it regarded as sound on the dangers of left-wing thinking. Related to mirror-imaging was another fallacy to which, as Nicoll observed, the JIC often succumbed, identified as 'perseveration', or sticking to a line of thought once begun even in the face of contrary evidence, a problem that was to resurface in 2002 with its intelligence assessment of Saddam's WMD programmes.

To highlight just how difficult a task have the intelligence agencies when faced with trying to decide whether military moves are a prelude to surprise attack, Nicoll emphasized that for an aggressor 'the essential point to note is that while planning, preparation and training may last for up to a year from the initial order to the armed forces to prepare, the period of readying, mobilization and deployment of forces may be quite short'. In this context, by analyzing in detail several case-studies of Soviet aggression, the judgment was reached that there was 'a 21–30 day Soviet system of reaching full combat readiness'. The important policy conclusion inferred from this and the detailed examination of the case-studies was that 'wars very rarely happen by chance'.

Finally, Nicoll speculated on whether it would lead to a better service for government to have JIC papers written as forecasts based on the evidence, or whether they should be cast as reports that provided the evidence itself with additional comments. To Nicoll this latter method was better suited to the requirements of ministers and the Chiefs of Staff. Subsequently the JIC has evolved an intermediate position of laying out an explanatory assessment in the body of the paper as to what it thinks is going on, including appropriate citation, caveats and limitations on the intelligence evidence itself, but prefaced with a set of key judgments that are, as far as is possible within the boundary of the evidence, predictive in scope.

Setting thresholds for response: indicators, warning and alert states

As already noted, a further step that can be taken by a prudent government is to decide in advance on an alert or counter-surprise system such as the US Defense readiness condition or DEFCON, introduced in early Cold War days (in peacetime, DEFCON 5 provided the lowest level of alert, rising in stages to DEFCON 2, the level of alert to which the Strategic Air Command was raised during the 1962 Cuban missile crisis and DEFCON 1, the expectation of actual imminent attack, a state that has never been declared). NATO had a comparable alert system during the Cold War (one that now has the less provocative title of the NATO Precautionary System). The key NATO Military Committee document[15] of 1957 implementing NATO's strategic concept provided the rationale:

'The Soviet Union is unlikely to resort to war so long as she can achieve her ends by other means. Nevertheless, with her growing armory of nuclear weapons and her formidable land, sea and air forces, she might turn to planned aggression to realize her aims if she misconstrued NATO intentions, if she believed that the forces of NATO were unprepared or incapable of effective retaliation, or if she believed that she alone had developed a scientific breakthrough which would reduce our retaliatory capability to an acceptable level. In this regard, the Soviets have the advantage of initiative and surprise. This results from their monolithic political system, which, in contrast to the political systems of the West, gives them the power of immediate decision.'

In the case of counter-terrorism, alert systems exist in most Western countries linked to precautionary or response measures by government, thus reducing the time likely to be taken arguing about what to do on the day and enabling a consistent response to be given. Examples would include the number of guards on duty at a facility, the arrangements for searching visitors and their vehicles, closing car parks near buildings and so on. When JTAC was set up it was given the responsibility for setting UK counter-terrorism threat levels ranging from low, an attack is unlikely, to substantial, an attack is a strong possibility, up to critical, an attack is expected imminently. Similarly, JTAC provides to the Foreign Office for overseas countries and territories a set of counter-terrorism warning states, ranging from a low threat from terrorism when there is no or limited known terrorist activity up to a high threat from terrorism when a high level of known terrorist activity is observed. Similarly the US Department of Homeland Security makes public a system of advisories, with the comparable threat alert range of low, guarded, elevated, high and severe.

Given the existence of a set of alert states, it is logical for governments to try to select a number of key indicators of potentially hostile activity that can act as warning geese whose cackle will awaken the guards. Such an Indicators and Warning (I&W) system agreed in advance with the policy-makers or military command thus represents a threshold of evidence that would trigger a higher state of alert. NATO operated an Intelligence Warning System (NIWS) to decision-makers of any developing threat, risk or concern that could impact on the security interests of the alliance at the earliest possible stages of a developing crisis. NATO defines a warning problem as a clear and concise statement of a potential or existing threat, risk or concern to national or NATO interests. A critical indicator is then an event or condition that may cause an analyst to change his warning assessment on the overall outcome of the situation. It is believed that the Soviet Union had an equivalent system, and as noted earlier the KGB and GRU both tasked their networks to report on any preparatory signs amongst the NATO allies. The Ministry of Defence had 'an effective 24–hour watch for the study of Soviet indicators' that could marry operational information such as communications patterns monitored by GCHQ and movements of Soviet forces with the longer-term analysis of the international situation monitored by the JIC. In modern times, open source information has become more important, such as from the BBC Monitoring Service and other media reporting of developments.

The problem with an I&W approach has always been the difficulty of choosing the right indicators of warning. This is another example of

Type I/Type II error choice. Too many tightly prescribed indicators underpinning an alert, and the risk increases that the state of alert will be declared too late. Too few and too loose the indicators, and false alarms must be expected. The ideal set of indicators should be unambiguous in terms of what they reveal about the readiness of the forces of the potential adversary and provide the equivalent of a volume control. Danger should not be able to creep up without triggering the indicator, which has therefore to be a necessary condition of alert. There should be certainty, or at least a very high probability, that the indicators will be observable and not masked by other effects, and providing some balance against the possibility of a rogue indicator. Finally, it should be possible to keep open observation on the indicator without this becoming known, and thus avoid the risk of deliberate manipulation of indicators by an adversary in order to deceive or confuse. It will clearly help[16] if military planners and the intelligence community have worked together to establish what are the likely warning indicators of hostile intent, and thus enabled the intelligence community to build up a background picture of what normality looks like, differences between what is currently being detected and what would be expected on the basis of past experience, and the frequency with which individual indicators in the past have blinked amber or red.

Nicoll, in his report to the JIC (see above), examined the capacity of the JIC, meeting weekly, to fulfil the task of watchdog for government through a system of 'special intelligence watches' coordinated usually with the US when a situation developed, linked to regular (could be two or three times a day) mini–CIGs to agree 'sitreps' for Whitehall and military commands that issue without JIC agreement. But for both Irish and most recently jihadist terrorism the volume of operational reporting would be impossible to manage in the small central assessment staff, and special means had to be created with a separate Assessment Group, Northern Ireland for the former and JTAC for the latter.

All the above steps leading to advance warning have to take place within the decision loop of the defender; but there are many cases where warnings arrived too late for action to be taken effectively to blunt the attack. The Falklands case is a good example, given the transit time for reinforcements to the garrison to arrive, even had a few days' warning of the invasion been obtained. One of the first acts of the British government after recapture of the islands was therefore to construct a long enough runway to take large jet troop transports and air defence aircraft.

The example of the Yom Kippur War

One of the first major crises I can recall during my time in the Ministry of Defence was when I was junior Private Secretary to the Secretary of State in 1973. On 6 October 1973 Egyptian and Syrian forces launched a surprise attack on Israel across the Sinai and Golan Heights catching Israeli forces unprepared. On 25 October, just before the war ended, escalation threatened as US forces went on Defense Condition (DEF-CON) 3 alert status, as possible intervention by the Soviet Union was feared. Anxious morning briefings at the outset of the crisis by the MOD Director-General for Intelligence, Vice-Admiral Sir Louis Le Bailly, explained that intelligence showed preparations consistent with an Egyptian intention to attack Israel. Egyptian forces were mobilized and engaged on what Cairo described as more exercises, following those held in May and August that year. Was their intention to attack or was this more brinkmanship? The same questions were being asked in Washington and Moscow, and even more urgently in Tel Aviv.

The problems encountered in Tel Aviv illustrate perfectly the prob-lems of providing tactical warning, and of the difficulties that arise when strategy is based on the assumption that adequate tactical warn-ing will be available; that is, on having about 48 hours' notice prior to an Arab attack: if war was imminent, Israel would launch a pre-emp-tive strike as the best means of defence. As it was, although the Israeli air force was placed on alert and would have been able to carry out a disabling first strike, PM Golda Meir advised by Defence Minister Moshe Dayan feared being blamed by the US for starting a war with-out certain cause (she was probably right since after the war the then US Secretary of State Henry Kissinger confirmed Meir's assessment by stating that if Israel had launched a pre-emptive strike, Israel would not have received 'so much as a nail'). The Israeli Defence Forces' Directorate of Military Intelligence (Aman) advised up to the last minute and beyond that Egypt and Syria were bluffing. They based their assessments about the likelihood of war on key assumptions. It was assumed correctly that Syria would not go to war with Israel unless Egypt went to war as well. It was also assumed (on the basis of good HUMINT) that Egypt intended eventually to regain the Sinai. But crucially it was assessed that Egypt would not go to war until they were supplied with, and trained on, new Soviet fighters and surface-to-surface missiles. That had not yet happened, so Aman felt justified in asserting that Egypt's own assessment of the balance of forces with Israel had not changed and therefore predicted an Egyptian attack as not imminent. This assumption about Egypt's strategic plans (known as 'the concept') strongly prejudiced the intelligence department's thinking and led it to dismiss other indicators and warnings (I&W). Unknown to Israeli intelligence, Egypt had in fact considerably strengthened her air defences with anti–aircraft guns and surface-to-air missiles.

Egyptian deception fed the Israeli Amon misconception with false information on maintenance problems and a lack of personnel and spare parts to operate the most advanced equipment. Two days before the attack Egypt publicly demobilized some of the reservists it had called up the previous month, adding to the deception. Israeli intelligence nevertheless detected relevant SIGINT and large troop movements towards the canal, and movements of Syrian troops towards the border and other I&W signs such as the evacuation of Soviet personnel from Cairo and Damascus. Nevertheless Aman's Director of Military Intelligence and his principal analyst dismissed evidence from the HUMINT and SIGINT agencies and stuck dogmatically to their view that Syria would not attack without Egypt, and Egypt would not attack until the weaponry they wanted arrived. Finally the head of Mossad, Zvi Zamir, personally went to Europe to meet with his most valued agent at midnight on October 5/6 to be told that a joint Syrian–Egyptian attack was imminent. Just hours before the attack began, orders went out for a partial call-up of the Israeli reserves (which proved to be easier than usual, as almost all of the troops were at synagogue or at home for Yom Kippur).

In that intelligence disaster we can see many of the common elements of failure identified by Nicoll in respect of the JIC: assumptions overruling evidence; mirror imaging (the Israelis would never have started a war they knew in advance they were not equipped to win); group think and the dominance by an expert; the wish to avoid the decision (mobilizing in response to the two earlier exercises that year had cost the Israeli army some $10 million each time). There may also perhaps have been arrogance leading to under-estimation of the enemy, recalling the Six Day War that had been conducted by the Israelis with classic use of surprise, mobility and speed when Israeli fighter-bombers, striking without warning, destroyed some 400 Arab aircraft. Israeli military intelligence did not appear to be able to conceive of the Arab nations being able to achieve the same effect.

Even if warning evidence is believed by analysts, ministers and generals have to be convinced by it. It is not easy to frame key judgments for ministers. How such a judgment is framed, and crucially what the intelligence chiefs say to senior ministers about it, whether the glass is presented as half-empty or half-full, is influenced by the general attitude of the intelligence community, and crucially by the perceptions of the national interests at stake. We would expect an intelligence officer from a country fearing attack to flag up the situation in stronger terms than, say, a British analyst observing from the sidelines. To arrive at the appropriate key judgment, additional information to the latest intelligence reporting is needed, and this is generally the case for any alerting system.

We need to know the level of 'background radiation' and have a sense of what normality looks like. We need to have a sense of how indicators have altered over time: is the situation worsening, and worsening rapidly? We need to have a sense of policy threshold, for example what would trigger mobilization, and of the political context, and whether there are significant anniversaries or diplomatic or other deadlines approaching. Finally, we also need to understand the extent to which the intelligence collected reflects the adversary's response to his perception of moves that have been made by one's own side, or may be contemplated. The interaction between 'blue' and 'red' moves is not always easy to separate out. NATO's Able Archer exercise in November 1983 was an annual event to test nuclear weapons release procedures and communications. Like all such exercises it was monitored by the Soviet High Command. But in that year it had been preceded by US 'psy-ops' and by harsh rhetoric from President Reagan on the Soviet 'evil empire' and on the Strategic Defense Initiative, all of which fanned fears in the ageing Soviet leadership that the US was seeking strategic superiority. Misinterpreted evidence led Marshal Ogarkov to raise the alert status of the land-based Soviet missile component and secretly to redeploy himself and his staff to his wartime bunker. These moves were not detected by US or Allied intelligence at the time. Oleg Gordievsky, the KGB resident in London, received an urgent telegram from Moscow claiming in turn that the US had put their forces 'on alert' when, as Gordon Barrass who later debriefed Gordievsky reported,[17] the US was actually tightening security after the major terrorist attack in Beirut. Significantly, one of the possible explanations given by Moscow Central that Gordievsky and the other Soviet residencies around the world were asked to check out was whether this alert was part of a nuclear countdown to a first strike. In the case of Able Archer the risk of nuclear war by accident was still remote, but even so it is a salutary lesson on counter-surprise that there could be such mutual misunderstanding.

The coastline of the future

How does anyone begin to predict what will happen in the future? We can imagine drifting on a small boat scanning the horizon, peering ahead trying to fathom out the distant coastline of the future. Looking backwards we have our knowledge of where we have come from to guide us. Looking forwards there are an infinity of possible landing places on the shore of the future—and the more closely we try to enumerate those possibilities the more complicated they become. There is a simple analogy here with the old question, how long is the British coastline? The answer depends on the size of your measuring ruler. The finer the scale of the measuring instrument, the larger the answer becomes as every bend and curve is measured. The best model of a coastline is that of a fractal, where the coastline is neither one-dimensional nor two-dimensional (although it encloses space, it has dimension somewhere between one and two). So it is with the complex web of events that make up the transition from the past into the future. The finer the detail that the intelligence analyst tries to bring to bear, the more interrelationships are discovered that have to be taken into account. The old military expression 'big hands, small map' comes to mind. The only way to is to approximate, to try to identify the safer harbours and larger archipelagos that stick out from the coastline, the existence of which mariners seeking to navigate safely the coastline of the future should certainly be warned.

It may therefore be possible for the experienced analyst to discern the principal characteristics of possible futures, or in Braudel's memorable phrase, the wisps of history. We can imagine a number of possible promontories ahead, each with its own cultures and ecologies. Some we would count as hostile to our preferred way of life, for example dominated by criminal and terrorist gangs; others are benign, with good government and civic harmony. As we sail (or rather are blown) towards the future we cannot predict exactly which currents or winds will arise to affect us, and thus where we will make landfall.

It helps, however, to have a sense of what may lie ahead, positive and negative, and how we can influence our passage through time to make it more likely we will end up captured by the winds that lead us to more favourable future shores, and to know the directions away from which we should sail. Some of the futures thus identified will be ones we should be comfortable in contemplating; others will have characteristics that we strongly want to avoid, such as the development and spread of widespread knowledge of how weapons of mass destruction can be made by terrorists. We can see them as 'strange attractors' in the jargon of chaos theory. The fractal nature of reality means that it is not possible for the analyst to plot an exact course from here to the future to establish into which orbit we will be pulled, and thus in which future we will end up. Identifying possible futures, and their characteristics, if done sensibly can nevertheless help policy-makers to devise strategies which make it less rather than more likely that the future landfall will be at the least desirable spot.

Another advantage in presenting policy-makers with careful horizon scanning is in reducing the sense of surprise that would otherwise occur when events appeared to be leading towards a particular unwelcome future. To use the example given earlier, a government that has been sensitized, for example, to certain aspects of the spread of knowledge about synthetic biology—the ability to manipulate gene sequences so as to create new organisms by splicing DNA from different organisms—is likely to be able to understand and respond to alerting signals from the intelligence community should signs be detected that groups are intending to misuse such technology. Of course, what governments really want is what they have asked the JIC to provide in terms of specific early warning of direct threats, but that should not blind us to the importance of having strategic notice of possible developments in the external world.

The benefits of hindsight: intelligence gaps and intelligence failures

We might describe an intelligence failure as a case where it would be reasonable to have expected that an operational alert or tactical warning should have issued when it did not. An intelligence gap on the other hand is the term we should use to refer to an absence of intelligence input on a topic. *The Economist* at the end of 2008 published[18] an apologia for failing to forecast some of the most striking events of 2008: 'We also failed to foresee Russia's invasion of Georgia (though our Moscow correspondent swears it was in his first draft). We said the OPEC cartel would aim to keep oil prices in the lofty range of $60–80 a barrel (the price peaked at $147 in July). We thought that Romano Prodi would probably see out the year as Prime Minister of Italy (his government collapsed and Silvio Berlusconi triumphed in an election); that Canada would pull its troops out of Afghanistan's Kandahar province (it didn't); that Ken Livingstone would be re-elected as mayor of London (he was defeated by his Conservative rival, Boris Johnson). Oh, and we expected that by now Hillary Clinton would be heading for the White House.' The article went on to explain that the record was not quite as bad as that, since many of the predictions were cunningly nuanced or hedged in a way that would be familiar to readers of any government intelligence assessment. Yes, Mrs Clinton was predicted by *The Economist* to become US President, but that feature also warned that it is a golden rule of American politics that every election season brings at least one big surprise. In the previous chapter we looked at the use and misuse of such drafting devices for blunting the risks to the analyst associated with sticking one's neck out when forecasting.

The Economist to its credit did ask rhetorically in its article why then, with such a dismal record in the previous year, including missing the scale of the once-in-a-lifetime global financial crisis, would anyone bother to read their current batch of predictions? And their answer was in part the reasonable one (and a thought that would also be shared by intelligence analysts) that the newspaper would also have provided many forecasts that were spot on and would have been of great value to their readers. The newspaper had better luck (their term) for example in predicting slumping US house prices and the battle to resist recession through government spending, interest-rate cuts and surging exports, the fall in the Shanghai stock exchange and the storm facing London and the British economy at a time when the UK government was still issuing bright forecasts, as well as a string of correct political predictions concerning international elections. The overall track record of government intelligence-based predictions of international affairs would similarly show a mixed picture, but with the value of correct predictions outweighing the (sometimes very embarrassing) misfires. Where intelligence has been acted upon, and policy-makers have altered course, the true comparison is not with the situation before and that observed now, but between the situation then and what it would be now if the intelligence had not been provided. Such counter-factual judgments are notoriously difficult to make, and critics of intelligence performance often fail to try to make them.

But beyond the predictions, there is a deeper argument to be considered, one that the writers on *The Economist* also deployed in their defence. The argument is that, oddly enough, getting predictions right or wrong is not all that matters. The point is also to capture a broad range of issues and events that will shape the coming years, to give a sense of the global agenda, to which decision-makers ought to be paying more attention. This important phenomenon is what I have described in this chapter as the spreading of 'strategic notice'. With strategic notice, government is more alert to signs that would otherwise be read as noise in the system, and intelligence agencies are more likely to be attentive to material that may bear on the problem.

When we come to look back in any particular case at how well the intelligence community has carried out its key task of elucidation, we are by definition in a position of advantage since we have the knowledge that hindsight brings. We know, or think we know, what really turned out to be the case and can compare that with what the intelligence reports told us before the event. That provides of course an overall sense of the credibility of the assessment. We can then go on to examine what was done with the assessment and thus get a feel for whether it made a successful difference, for example to the way that a military commander deployed his forces to avoid concentrations of enemy armour. It may be that the value was not in a single report, but in a stream of reporting, such as the build-up of intelligence on the German V-weapons. It may only be that the intelligence enabled more confident rather than different judgments to be reached, such as in the selection of the Normandy landing sites, but still added value. Or it may be that even good intelligence failed to make a difference, as in the failed defence of Crete in 1941, or may positively mislead, as in 1942 when intelligence reports that the *Tirpitz* and other capital ships had sailed to intercept the arctic convoy *PQ17* contributed to the tragic decision to scatter the convoy.

When examining the performance of the analysts as part of the overall intelligence system, however, judging their effectiveness requires us to stand in their shoes. We should judge them only equipped with the intelligence they had at the time of the assessment, and the information and background knowledge they could in practice have been expected to have had. We can then try to form a judgment as to whether, by using the best techniques available, it would have been reasonable to expect them to have done better by way of elucidation, of shedding light on to the unknown.

The media are nevertheless likely to brand every shortcoming as an 'intelligence failure', and in a general sense of the word that is right if the system failed to deliver the value-adding intelligence. But 'failure' carries the connotation of culpability, i.e. that those involved can reasonably be blamed for not doing better. Intelligence failures in the wider sense will regrettably occur from time to time, such is the nature of the fragmented access and the imperfections of analytic process, resting as they do on fallible human behaviour. In most cases it would be more accurate to refer to there being an 'intelligence gap' to describe such cases, but intelligence gaps and flawed judgments by policymakers go with the territory and are certainly inevitable. There is no such thing as gap-free intelligence or reliable knowledge of the future, and government can be given no guarantee (and in turn must not mislead the public into believing) that intelligence is going to be anything other than fragmentary, incomplete and sometimes wrong. As we noted earlier, there is a parallel between the world of intelligence and that of complex engineering and social systems, in which 'normal accidents' have to be expected due to the coincidence of events which, taken simply, would be regarded as unexceptionable occurrences.

Let us suppose in a hypothetical example that it is 08.00 in the morning of an ordinary day. Alice, an intelligence analyst, is cycling to work (supporting her organization's green credentials) when she has a puncture. Her partner had borrowed her repair kit and not put it back so she has to push the bike back home. She then waits for the bus, which is very late because of industrial disruption. She finally arrives at work at 11.00, just in time for the weekly meeting which then runs over time. It is 12.30 by the time she is back at her desk. Her PC is down for an hour to allow new software she ordered to be installed and explained to her. She decides to forego lunch to catch up and at 14.00 she tackles her in-box.

She is intrigued by the transcript of a flowery message from an unknown male in Ruritania to another unknown male in the UK, a message with an innocuous content but ending by saying a prayer for the 'final meeting'. She knows Bob in the Joint Terrorism Analysis Centre (JTAC) perhaps because they were on a joint training course together, and that he has been interested for some time in the existence of a possible terrorist group with Ruritanian connections, so she decides the message is worth forwarding directly to him, which she does electronically at 15.00.

It is 15.00 and Bob in JTAC is briefing a visiting foreign dignitary. It is 16.00 before he gets back to his PC. He finds a dozen high priority emails and works through them. It is 17.00 when he reads the message from Alice. Being an experienced analyst he recalls a report that a group of UK extremists did last year have contact with a preacher from Ruritania, but investigation at the time revealed no terrorism-related activity. By 18.00 he has dug out the past reports, and discovers that the CIA has recently reported the preacher as having AQ links. It is possible from internal evidence in the style of the message that the author could be this preacher. He consults his boss, who alerts the Security Service branch concerned and they agree the reference to 'final meeting' could be significant. The wheels are set in motion with police officers detailed to visit known haunts of the key figures in the group. At 20.00 an officer calls at a past meeting place of the group, a local gym. A trusted contact tells him they were there but have just left. The group have gone dark. The attack happens next day.

It is hard to fault Alice. Dedicated to duty, having struggled in to work and given up her lunch break; sensitive to her subject, she spotted a message that many analysts would have passed over. Similarly, could you fault Bob, whose background knowledge and acumen enabled him to trigger action on the intelligence without delay? Had events worked out slightly differently, the terrorist attack might have been frustrated. As it is, the inevitable fingers will be pointed. Following Perrow,[19] the causes of failure might be:

- Human error (Alice forgetting the cycle repair kit, not telephoning Bob in JTAC to warn him)
- IT/mechanical problems (Alice's PC was down for an hour)
- The environment (an industrial dispute affecting the buses, and having an unexpected VIP in JTAC)
- Design of the system (the timing of the weekly meeting, not having someone else to see all material first thing when Alice was late)
- Procedures used (weekly meetings, unnecessary priority flagging of some emails, where we might note that these procedures are actually

safety systems introduced into offices to make communication failures less likely)
* All of these or none of these

Readers may wish to try their hand, and come to their own conclusion, both about what would be a reasonable analysis of the causes of failure, and indeed what the popular newspapers and the lawyers acting for those affected by the terrorist attack would make of it. It is a cliché of chaos theory that the flapping of a butterfly's wing can trigger a tropical storm. But we do not blame the butterfly for the resulting damage.

The only practical conclusion that might be drawn from such examination is to expect that some you will win, some you will lose. A greater degree of buffering can sometimes help accommodate the inevitable knock-on effects of the normal accidents of everyday life in complex close-coupled systems, but it should be noted that safety measures, such as having a daily meeting to keep everyone on the same page or rigorously prioritizing incoming messages (often the response to previous inquiries into other failures), can themselves contribute to the likelihood of further breakdown. The more complicated the safety systems, the more likely they are to add destructive complexity. In addition, an attitude of mind borne of past castigation that mistakes are not allowable will lead to a degree of caution in assessment that itself is likely to be counter-productive. In the example above, the intelligence 'failure' is known about only because a bright analyst, working in a single-source agency, spotted a clue and acted on it. Had she been more cautious in her judgment and simply consigned the message (along with most others) to the out tray then there would have been no obvious abortive police action for the subsequent public inquiry into the terrorist attack to focus on, and the intelligence community would have been spared much criticism. Professor Adams of University College London has described the persistent effect of risk-averse conditioning—criticism hurts more than praise soothes—as 'bottom loop bias' to the individual's risk thermostat.[20] The message has to be that, in most lines of work, if there are no 'mistakes' then perhaps the staff are not trying hard enough to innovate and push the boundaries of what is possible.

Analysts and intelligence managers need to understand the conditions in which genuine failure becomes more likely, all along the spectrum from negligence to irrational belief in faulty judgments, and what can be done to reduce the likelihood of falling into avoidable error and to describe accurately the degree of belief that should be associated with an estimate. Policy-makers in turn need to understand how intelligence analysts go about their tasks. They need to know how best to weigh up what they are being told by their intelligence community, what questions they should always ask about what they are being told (as described in chapter 6), and to be sufficiently self-aware to know when they may be unconsciously influencing what the intelligence community is prepared to tell them. They need too to understand the analytic processes in order to be able to convey accurately yet safely to the public when appropriate the warnings that intelligence analysis can provide, and to establish a more realistic public perception of the limitations of all attempts to forecast what the future will bring.

Uncovering secrets and mysteries as ways of reducing surprise

In chapter 2 we touched briefly on the basic distinction in the world of intelligence between secrets and mysteries. The distinction is important for understanding the nature of surprise.

Secrets are sets of facts that are capable of being known provided that the intelligence apparatus is sufficiently sensitive to detect the information, and to avoid being misled or deceived by the opponent. The order of battle of a foreign army and the characteristics of its weapons systems, or the location of a cache of terrorist weapons and explosives, are all secrets that an intelligence service would set itself to uncover. Considerable uncertainty may nevertheless surround the assessment of intelligence about such secrets, since information about them may be fragmentary and incomplete. Considerable skill and experience will be needed to fit the jigsaw puzzle together. The major Cold War debates about Soviet bomber strength, and later Soviet strategic missile numbers, provide good examples of the difficulties of providing government with reliable, unbiased estimates of the secrets that the opponent is either desperate to prevent becoming known, or to falsify. The USSR for example sought to deceive the United States into believing that ballistic missile production was more advanced than in fact it was (a line that the US military were predisposed to swallow)—as Khrushchev boasted, turning them out like sausages.

Secrets thus uncovered can be surprising, for example learning that a potential opponent's capabilities are very much larger than was previously thought. An example was the discovery during the latter stages of the Cold War that Soviet developments in tank armour would defeat the proposed armament that was being fitted to the new British main battle tank, and a rapid up-gunning had to be introduced into the procurement process. Another example, from the Falklands conflict, was the discovery that the Port Stanley airfield after its capture by the Argentines was capable of taking much greater traffic than initial British intelligence estimates had assumed, because additional hard-standing had been added in previous years as part of Britain's overseas development programme, but not recorded by the defence intelligence staffs. The estimate for the UK Chiefs of Staff committee was based therefore on out-of-date information. That was an example where the problem arose not out of the failure to acquire a secret, but the failure to manage successfully open-source information relevant to the military task, a problem that is likely to recur more often in the future as open-source information grows in importance. In chapter 7 we considered methodologies that may be applied, and the pitfalls into which the analyst may fall, in trying to penetrate such secrets.

In this chapter, however, we are principally concerned with the second of Professor R. V. Jones's categories of intelligence challenges, that of mysteries. Aristotle famously asked in chapter 9 of *De Interpretatione* what truth might be ascribed to the statement 'There will be a sea battle tomorrow'. His tentative conclusion, much debated in the Middle Ages, appears to have been that it is neither true nor untrue, but is indeterminate. Many centuries later, Erwin Schrödinger posed the quantum mystery of the cat shut in a closed box with a phial of poison to be activated by a random quantum event of radioactive decay. Without opening the lid, do we judge the cat to be dead or alive or in a quantum state where these dead-and-alive states are superimposed? Mysteries in intelligence concern intentions of the opponent that have not yet turned into decisions, such as predicting the likely choice of target by a terrorist group before they themselves have decided, or they concern the internal stability of countries of interest and the evolution of international relationships, such as whether a dictator is likely to consider armed aggression against a neighbouring state. In such cases the answers are not to be found ready-made in intercepted dispatches, or even from well-placed HUMINT agents. The dictator may still change his mind at the last moment about whether to invade his neighbour, or whether to launch a crack-down on dissidents. Terrorists may decide (as a British terrorist gang did) to take a break from their plotting of an imminent attack to attend a friend's wedding overseas. Predicting the course of mysteries, therefore, by definition, involves more than access to good sources of intelligence and takes us into the heart of the intelligence assessment process.

A further useful distinction[21] in seeking to avoid surprise is to recognize the difficulties for the intelligence analyst that arise when the likely outcome of the mystery being examined depends crucially on the actions of one's own government or allies. This is a point discussed in more detail in the last chapter when we looked at the relationship between the intelligence analyst and the policy customer. Here we just need to recognize that there can be cases when the quality of the intelligence warning depends as much on the analysts' ability to understand the actions of their own government than that of the potential opponent. As we saw earlier in this chapter, the apparent failure to predict the timing of the Argentine invasion of the Falkland Islands in 1982 can be interpreted in that way.[22] Additionally, as any intelligence analyst will know, it can at times be harder to predict what one's own government will do, or indeed understand the policies being followed, than to know the enemy.

The main question being addressed in this chapter is what it is reasonable for a government to expect by way of forewarning from its intelligence community. The JIC is explicitly charged with responsibility to monitor and give early warning of the development of direct or indirect foreign threats to British interests, whether political, military or economic, and to keep under review threats to security at home and overseas. For the most part, such assessment will draw on secret intelligence—but the judgments of the JIC about the future in such areas will inevitably be of the nature of mysteries and complexities, rather than the more straightforward assessment of secrets uncovered. There are some circumstances that should trigger extra care from analysts. One of these is if there has been deadlock in diplomatic or other negotiations that might lead to the perception that force, or the threat of force, might break the stalemate. The example of the Yom Kippur War has already been cited. Another warning sign may be if there are perceptions of a capability gap opening or a window of opportunity closing. The following quote[23] from a 1936 UK assessment based on secret intelligence from a well-placed German diplomat is a good example of such reasoning. Note the dynamic: we are responding; the adversary's window of opportunity is closing; the danger of surprise is rising.

'Apparently the reason which was supposed to have led Herr Hitler and his advisers to come to this decision was that they felt the rearmament of the democratic powers was proceeding at such a pace that Germany's relative strength would inevitably decline. This was therefore the moment to strike ... by reason of the report quoted above, and of a number of others which show which way the wind was blowing, it is unfortunately no longer possible to assume that there is no likelihood of Germany "coming West" in 1939.'

As another example, let us consider the case of the 2008 global financial crash in terms of a model of foreknowledge. It could be argued that there was indeed strategic notice available, with awareness at the most senior levels of the fragility of the international financial system and of the specific dependence of the UK economy on the financial sector. The financial sector had long been recognized as a strategic component of the UK's critical national infrastructure. There was certainly an appreciation in the UK government of the importance of being able to rely on the financial plumbing working even in conditions of significant disruption. Beyond such need for business continuity and contingency planning, there does also seem to have been strategic appreciation, well before the crisis broke, on the part of some investors and international institutions of the vulnerability of the financial system to the then levels of mortgage lending and household indebtedness, as well as Warren Buffett's advice to 'beware of geeks bearing formulas'.[24] Reference to UK reliance on continued financial stability can be found in the UK National Security Strategy of July 2008:[25] 'The first set of challenges and vulnerabilities is economic ... business and consumers increasingly benefit from global supply chains, and from our status as a global hub for business and travel. Our success in exploiting those opportunities contributes to high levels of employment and standards of living, and to international influence. But it relies on a relatively benign international environment, and requires us to consider our vulnerability to risks to open markets and global financial stability, and potentially to physical threats to global supply chains.' The National Security Strategy also states: 'Stronger international financial institutions, particularly the International Monetary Fund and World Bank, are essential to deal with the changes brought by globalization, and to sustain a framework for global economic stability, growth and open markets, which is one of the most important drivers of security and stability. We will work within these institutions to adapt their governance structures to the new global economic realities, to provide surveillance to prevent world economic crises, and to enable fast economic recovery and growth after conflict.'

Having such a general strategic appreciation of dependency on continuing good financial fortune in the of the markets is, however, very different from having an operational, quantified understanding of the risks to mechanisms that might lead to system break-down. In the case of the financial risks to the UK, there was not sufficient belief among policy-makers in specific potential dangers to justify inclusion of financial instability or liquidity problems in the national risk matrix, and such concerns as there may have been do not seem to have been operationalized into risk mitigation programmes. In part it may have been because the issue fell between the cracks between HM Treasury, the Bank of England and the FSA. In part it may have been also because that charmed circle did not connect itself sufficiently to the central nervous system of government contingency planning. We could see this as an example of cognitive dissonance: a reluctance to reconcile such strategic warning signs as there were with deeply held beliefs in the benefits of letting the system of financial oversight alone and unconscious fear for what might follow taking responsibility for attempts at intervention. Tactical warning of the impending crash would not have been a reasonable expectation, given the nature of the market. What seems to be the case is that there was no operational alerting to trigger intensive contingency planning.

Linking the intelligence model to the policy world

In the provision of strategic notice it is unlikely that there will be specific secret intelligence on most of the subjects of potential interest. There will be exceptions to that rule of course, for example in interpreting the build-up of foreign military forces and of long-term measures to secure energy and raw materials. But for the most part the sources of information will be open source. What is needed in forecasting is the capacity of the analyst to visualize a set of circumstances, causes and consequences that have not (yet) occurred in reality (and if wisely anticipated, may never occur). What is being asked of the analyst is to generate in the mind of the policy-maker the equivalent of a virtual reality model of a possible future to which the policy-maker needs to respond. Normally the warning function will be concerned with threatening futures, but even perhaps on a few occasions a set of opportunities.

Effective horizon scanning needs strong high-level political support, since its very value lies in the presentation of uncomfortable pictures. There is no necessity, and there may be disadvantages, in government trying to corral all open-source analysis or horizon scanning within a single organization. This is a field of activity in which multiple competing hypotheses may offer more enlightenment. But the need to provide high-level support, and to have assurance that the results are not being biased by political preferences, would suggest that the activity should be overseen and its objectivity protected in professional terms by the national intelligence leadership.

Significant developments can arise quickly, for example following a change of regime, the unexpected modification of equipment or the introduction of a new method of terorrist attack, and these are the kind of surprises that the national security community is traditionally most concerned to avoid. Surprise can also be exploited: the British introduction during the Falklands conflict of air-to-air refuelling in tanker aircraft to support long-range reconnaissance, and even long-range attack, is an example. Although the military effect of a few bombs landing on Port Stanley runway may have been slight, the added complications for the Argentine commander of realizing that contrary to all expectation there was a vulnerability to air attack long before the task force was within reach must have been a complicating factor in his planning. As we have noted earlier, surprises can also be of the slow-burn kind that creep up on government unrecognized until the last moment, such as those of the implications of generational changes as new types of tactics or equipment are introduced. Bagehot[26] expressed the dilemma of planning in an age of change in 1867: 'The naval art and the military art are both in a state of transition; the last discovery of today is out of date, and superseded by an antagonistic discovery tomorrow ... in their foolish constructive mania the Admiralty have been building when they ought to have been waiting; they have heaped a curious museum of exploded inventions; but they have given us nothing serviceable.'

Practical ways of reducing surprise

Various devices have been advanced in the intelligence literature, and tried in practice, as ways of reducing the chances that analytic bias will lead to failure and surprise. Asking meta-questions during the analytic process to get participants to raise their consciousness beyond the immediate debate and to think about the processes they are engaged in is a commonplace of group analytic work. There may be value in going beyond this to appoint a 'devil's advocate' team with licence to argue the opposite hypothesis, or to establish a 'challenge' team inside the analytic community (there is one such supporting the work of the JIC) to examine the methodologies in use and to engage drafters in testing dialogue. 'Red teams' are another device, where analysts are asked to play in role the part of the adversary using only the information that is assumed to be available to the adversary. Such role-playing of dictators or violent ideologues is, however, hard for analysts brought up in rational discourse to adopt. Yet another method that has been used is 'team A/team B' where an alternative group of analysts known to have a different outlook on events is asked to carry out parallel analysis to 'team A', but as earlier noted that method is open to abuse if there is bias in the choice of team members. The most obvious safeguard is the simplest: self-awareness of the issues, stimulated by training and good management.

Peer review is fundamental to the scientific method, as noted in chapter 6, and the ability amongst close intelligence allies to share analysis separately undertaken is of great value. With a small analytic community in the UK, there is, however, little scope for having competing national teams working on a topic. There will always be intelligence gaps. And it is in the nature of intelligence work that results—whether from the recruitment of a well-placed agent, or a cryptological breakthrough—cannot be guaranteed in advance. Legitimate criticism may well be justified if insufficient resources have been provided, or if the agencies have failed to take reasonable steps to cover likely requirements.

Good government should set a very high standard for the provision of strategic notice. That is not to call for government to put itself in the hands of soothsayers. Only in exceptional cases will it be possible for government to be given reliable predictions about future events. But the identification of possible futures allows rational assessment of when it may be sensible to take precautionary actions, including research, development and intelligence gathering. Providing for public security is an exercise in risk management not risk elimination. It is in the nature of things that not everything can be predicted. There will be surprises, and the trick is not to be surprised by surprise.

'…The textbooks agree, of course, that we should only believe reliable intelligence, and should never cease to be suspicious, but what is the use of such feeble maxims? They belong to that wisdom which for want of anything better scribblers of systems and compendia resort to when they run out of ideas.'[27]

(*Clausewitz, On War*)

9

IN MEDIAS RES

SECURITY AND INFOTAINMENT

Peering through Hollywood's lenses

Governments need public support and understanding for their security policies. There is therefore a very strong case to be made for government to reveal sufficient of the real nature (and value in terms of public security) of its security and intelligence world to enable the media and the public to retain a sense of perspective. The secret world does however contain both unusual people and fascinating activity that has high 'infotainment' value, and that makes even a limited exposure to public gaze a difficult matter to control. Prurient curiosity still sells newspapers in large numbers and, as every sub-editor knows, the word 'secret' acts as an accelerant on a breaking story. As a former chairman of the JIC, Roderick Braithwaite, has quipped[1]

'Intelligence is a subject that ought to be intrinsically uninteresting. The subject of intelligence attracts attention out of proportion to its real importance. My theory is that this is because secrets are like sex. Most of us think that others get more than we do. Some of us cannot have enough of either. Both encourage fantasy. Both send the press into a feeding frenzy. All this distorts sensible discussion.'

In considering public views of intelligence and security we are dealing with a magical reality, a psychological construct, not direct portrayals of the real world. But it is one that sells cinema tickets and newspapers. It is hard for journalists to write about this subject, how-

251

ever serious and well informed they are, without these harmonies being evoked in the reader or viewer. And sub-editors and editors of course play on this, since the economics of journalism are harsh, competition is fierce, and people have a living to make. We have therefore the fantasy world of James Bond or Jack Bauer, the guy who is on our side and will do whatever it takes to keep us safe, freed from the normal conventions of society. Another iconic image is of the actor Alec Guinness as George Smiley, all the time conscious that there will be no public thanks, no military bands and no parades to mark another successful security operation, toiling in the shadows to keep us safe like Tolkein's Rangers of Middle Earth so that the hobbits can sleep carefree in their hobbit-holes at night.

Not only did the fascination with the idea of hidden guardians of the state have a powerful public resonance, it became during the Cold War an unconscious self-image for many within the secret world who felt they were manning the watchtowers of freedom (to cite the US government tribute[2] to those who served during the Cold War) whilst the city slept and dreamt. Such attitudes within a security establishment have their dangers, not least if officers come to see themselves as a group separate from society, able through their secret knowledge to have insights denied to the public, and feeling they have a purity of motive that sets them above the political process with its equivocations and compromises. In military and security circles 'political' can all too easily become a term of abuse. *Spycatcher*, the memoirs of the ex–Security Service officer Peter Wright, convey clearly that he was convinced that since the enemy had in his mind penetrated high into the citadel, the ends, catching these communist spies and exposing subversion, justified any means. This paranoid state of mind was most clearly shown in his assertion that he had been one of a group of thirty MI5 officers who had plotted to get rid of Harold Wilson as Prime Minister because they suspected him of being a Soviet agent, or at least of being excessively sympathetic to the Soviet Union (Wilson had been secretly accused of being run by the KGB by Soviet defector Anatoly Golitsyn). Wright later withdrew his allegation, and admitted in the course of a Panorama interview that what the book said about the so-called plot was not true. The authorized history of the Security Service[3] has, we must hope, now finally demolished Wright's fantasy.

Secrecy and intelligence: the smile on the face of the Cheshire cat

The British public seems at times all too ready to believe the worst of its intelligence institutions when revelations hit the headlines following failed operations, court cases, or when disaffected employees vent their grievances in public. This reinforces the case for public education in the realities of modern intelligence gathering and in the essential part that it plays in helping provide public security—but the dilemma of how much to reveal remains: an intelligence organization that cannot keep its genuine secrets secret will not survive long; the recruitment of agents requires absolute trust by the individuals that their identities will be protected at all costs, and cryptographic successes are often very vulnerable to counter-measures.

Secrecy has to be an essential attribute of intelligence and security agencies, but in times past that would have been said of much of government itself. To quote Harold Laski writing of the need for radical change at the start of the Second World War:

'The theory of the Civil Service is that it does not make mistakes; it is, of course, like other human institutions capable of monumental blunders. But one of its main ardours, to which immense energy is devoted, is the conceal-ment of those blunders from the public view, and especially from the view of Parliament… Now I cannot myself believe that it is not dangerous for men who assist in the making of vital decisions to devote any part of their energy to building this twilight world. It makes them anxious to have as little as pos-sible seen in its stark clarity; it persuades them to postpone the consideration of anything which may arouse acute controversy; and it tends to make them shrink from those positive innovations which so easily put a bureaucracy on the defensive.'[4]

Sixty-five years after that quote, the Freedom of Information Act 2000 finally became law and opened up much of British government to a greater degree of openness—but understandably the intelligence agencies were given an absolute exemption in recognition of the fragil-ity of their sources and methods to exposure. So the suspicion can quickly arise that secrecy in the intelligence community is being used to cover inefficiency, or worse, incompetence, and as a shield against modern practice.

There is a history of such suspicions. An early casualty of intelli-gence secrecy, to his own great surprise, was the author Sir Compton

Mackenzie when he was prosecuted under the Official Secrets Act in 1932 for daring to publish a memoir of his time in the fledgling Secret Intelligence Service, drawing on his experience of running agents across the eastern Mediterranean during the First World War. His offence was deemed the greater since he revealed a number of bungles and fiascos. His revenge at being, as he saw it, scapegoated by the secret establishment to discourage others was the satirical lampooning of the public-school types who then ran British intelligence in his comic novel *Water on the Brain*.[5] As he later wrote in 1939 (in terms that subsequent generations could have echoed)

'that the tendency of our democratic rulers moves steadily towards repression, and the Official Secrets Act is a convenient weapon for tyranny ... there is no clearer sign of the decay of statesmanship in this country than the eagerness of second-rate politicians to preserve the secrecy of their own place-hunting and time-serving'.[6]

In the face of a torrent of fictional accounts and revelations, the real world of secret intelligence confronts a dilemma. Intelligence and security agencies cannot escape back into the shadows, nor adopt a Cheshire Cat position of trying to appear when convenient and disappear when not, leaving only the grin behind. To be effective, and even to begin to match up to the public expectations of what secret intelligence can deliver by way of public security, the work of the intelligence community must remain shrouded in secrecy, particularly regarding its sources and methods. For past generations that was not much of a dilemma, merely a set of tricky practical problems of how to keep secrets. However, the old view of secret intelligence as a small, unacknowledged, well hidden and highly specialized extra-legal function of the state at its highest level of national power is no longer tenable. This poses a paradox. We now need to have acknowledged, democratically accountable, independently overseen government intelligence agencies whilst at the same time expecting their intelligence officers' agencies to penetrate to the heart of the threats we now face and to engage in effective secret action to disrupt those behind the threats.

The lure of covert action

Much policy succeeds because at least initially the moves are not visible to the public. Initial feelers between the British government and Sinn Fein (the political wing of the Provisional IRA) took place whilst the terrorist campaign continued. Intelligence agencies can likewise provide back channels to persuade a country like Libya to renounce its WMD programmes, or can mount covert operations such as a 'sting' against terrorist groups seeking to buy surface-to-air missiles. If there is one constant in the world of covert action, however, it is the law of unintended consequences when governments try to follow in the dark policies that they cannot admit to pursuing in the light. As we noted in chapter 2, like launching surprise attacks, nations can be tempted into covert action because it appears to be an easy win, and so it may be in the short term as temporary advantage is pressed home. Once the surprise is over, the laws of war and diplomacy reassert themselves and the long-run outcome may not be favourable. This is especially the case where intelligence agencies finance, arm and train proxies to achieve ends that government cannot use its own forces to achieve. Covert policies usually get exposed eventually and can be highly controversial, generating scandals such as the US Iran-Contra affair. The paradox is Wagnerian. As with Wotan's attempts to bypass the treaties engraved on his spear-point, attempts to try to achieve surreptitiously by the use of controlled proxies ends that are not publicly admissible or lawful can end in Wagnerian disaster. If the proxies are fully controlled, then the links back to the initiating government are more likely to lead to eventual repudiation (as Wotan had to withdraw his protection from Sigmund's magic sword). In the US Bay of Pigs episode, the Cuban covert invasion force had to be left to its fate. On the other hand, having armed the proxies (as Siegfried the free hero was able to reforge the shattered sword) they are liable to assert their free will, and once their immediate aim is achieved they may turn and bite the hand that armed them. Cuba under Castro, Iraq under Saddam during the war with Iran, the fight in Afghanistan against the Russians, have all created unforeseen consequences.

Problems can arise when the nature of the sensitivity of a security story is not obvious to the media, or the journalist concerned has only got hold of part of it. Over the years, the UK has evolved a much misunderstood voluntary mechanism, the 'DA Notice' system, bringing together senior print and broadcast news editors with senior government officials in the belief that there is a state of affairs that both media and government wish to arrive at, whereby a free press takes its own decisions, within the law, as to what to publish, but does so in the light of up-to-date advice from those who ought to know in order to prevent unintentional damage to national security.[7] Any recommended advice to the media on such issues must of course be capable of being followed in the world of the new media as well as the old. The internet with everyone as a blogger, and with cameras ubiquitous on mobile telephones, everyone becomes their own news correspondent, which carries significant risks for the viability of traditional journalism with accompanying opinion increasingly crowding out factual reporting.

The intelligence community needs to keep pace with the changes taking place in the studios and editorial offices in which the media confront government. The 24/7 media age has brought the rolling news broadcast, which profoundly shifts the grammar of news reporting. Availability of multiple windows, graphics and stock footage (including visual clichés of the intelligence world such as the modern MI6 HQ) govern the editorial and production decisions over the story dominating newsroom and production decision-making. I have already alluded to the commercial pressures on both print and broadcast media, with increasingly fragmented and segmented audiences and channels. Highly portable recording and transmission equipment is now standard for the media with on-location live-feeds. These developments carry obvious real risks for compromise of security operations. Screening of amateur footage of the police raid in Forest Gate helped reinforce the impression of an excessively heavy-handed operation (an impression the police may have mistakenly fostered from the outset by briefing the media on the scale of the operation, over-estimating perhaps the precision of the intelligence behind the raid). Whereas in the military sphere 'embedding' of journalists with deployed forces has led, for the most part, to sensitizing a generation of war correspondents to the realities of combat and its dangers, no such opportunity is obvious for the front-line work of the secret agencies. The level of general knowledge of operational sensitivities in domestic security remains low.

Putting secret intelligence into the public domain

There is a difference between British and US thinking in how far it is useful to share with legislators and the public more generally the key judgments that government has reached as a result of the deliberations of its intelligence community. It has been the practice in the US for some of the assessments, what are termed National Intelligence Estimates (NIE), on major issues of policy concern to be published in a redacted and unclassified form. The example of Iranian nuclear ambitions was given in chapter 8. The impact of that US NIE being published at a time when the political rhetoric was being cranked up certainly caused controversy and risked drawing the intelligence community into what was a policy debate. British readers on the other hand should not expect to see equivalent JIC conclusions on current subjects being published. There is a notable UK exception, and that was the publication in 2004 of very substantial extracts from the relevant UK JIC assessments on Iraq as part of the inquiry chaired by Lord Butler into intelligence on weapons of mass destruction. That inquiry following a major intelligence failure will no doubt be seen as a precedent for other inquiries into events where it is important to know what intelligence was being reported to decision-takers.

Iraq posed a particular communications problem in 2002/2003 because the government had to convince the public and parliament that there was justification for pre-emptive military intervention. Prime Minister Blair, with his key advisers, had convinced themselves that supporting the United States in this venture was in the national interest. The Prime Minister himself believed in the wider justification for the action as it was seen in Washington. In cases of direct self-defence, under article 51 of the UN Charter, there are facts that can be put before the public, and there is a clear choice of whether to support government action to use military force if necessary to reverse aggression. In cases of pre-emptive self-defence, using military force to create conditions that mean the direct threat will not arise, then government has a much harder task in justifying its proposal, and will have to present a case based on intelligence assessment. In any real situation, that case is likely to be complex and nuanced. Putting to one side the important questions of international legal authority and legitimacy that will also have to be demonstrated, the government in justifying military action knows this will result in loss of life, including of British military personnel. This is what military intervention means against a nation that it must be assumed will resist. Here we reach the root of the difficulty identified by Lord Butler. British ministers wishing to use military force are unlikely to want to do so on the basis of 'possibly' or even 'probably' as qualifiers. Ministers will have to demonstrate that they are certain in their minds, beyond reasonable doubt, that the potential costs of inaction outweigh not only the costs (of all kinds) of intervention, but the possible risks that might flow subsequently from that intervention. Ministers will have doubters to persuade. Advocacy of their position is part of proper political debate. Advocacy on the other hand has no part in the intelligence process.

In any specific case, the inherently uncertain nature of secret intelligence needs to be explained with any warnings on the limitations of intelligence spelt out for a lay audience, and clear and effective dividing lines between assessment and advocacy need to be maintained. The Butler Inquiry concluded sensibly that it is preferable for government to take responsibility for justifying its own conclusions in its own words (albeit cleared for accuracy by the intelligence authorities) and not fall back on exploiting the 'branding' of the name and authority of the intelligence authorities such as the Joint Intelligence Committee.

What, however, the Butler Committee and its witnesses clearly saw as a wholly exceptional event—the problem of how to publish an unclassified JIC intelligence 'assessment' on Iraq—becomes an everyday dilemma in the case of the justification for counter-terrorist action. As chapter 1 illustrated, CT intelligence is being thrust into an unaccustomed and uncomfortable public role front of house rather than backstage.

The golden rule is not to wait until crisis hits before trying to communicate with the public. There is a progression of circumstances in which government may feel it necessary to draw on at least the headlines of intelligence derived from secret sources in their interactions with the media: helping to maintain a knowledgeable and supportive public opinion, informing and alerting public services and private sector organizations to potential future threats against which they should plan, and finally, in emergency, warning the public of impending danger and advising on what to do to minimize the risk. When times are quiet, government should be seeking to sustain a supportive public opinion and a proper understanding of the role of the intelligence community and its constituent parts (and importantly what it is not) and to understand how the work of that community is regulated and overseen, both through statute law and as a matter of practice. Threats need to be explained in ways and at times that distance the dialogue from the pressures of the introduction of legislation or the need to justify some new security measure.

There is an inherent paradox in talking in that way about security threats today: the risk to any individual of being in the wrong place at the wrong time and caught up in a terrorist or other catastrophic incident, for example when travelling on the London Underground, is extremely low—so low that the only rational advice from government is for people to continue to go about their normal business. But from society's point of view it would only take a small number of attacks to create considerable disturbance, and loss of confidence, with potentially significant economic damage. So whilst the public should be warned to be 'alert not alarmed', the public also needs to recognize that it is rational for the government to take such threats extremely seriously. The risk is that by even mentioning the need to plan for, say, decontamination services capable of dealing with a 'dirty bomb', the government is read by the more excitable sections of parliament and the media as predicting such catastrophe rather than making it less likely. When the British government in 2002 invested £32 million in smallpox vaccine, the BBC rightly reported that 'Millions of doses of the smallpox vaccine are to be stockpiled by the government to prepare for mass vaccination in the event of a bio-terrorist attack.' The Department of Health was quoted as saying that 'while there was no evidence of a specific threat, it was carrying out intensive planning', but the *Daily Mail* still managed the headline: 'New smallpox terror alert'. The UK emergency services and health services and the operators, mostly in the private sector, of the key critical national infrastructure do need authoritative planning assumptions about what to prepare for. Similar considerations must apply to the way that government describes its exercises and training, and the challenge is to do that without raising public anxiety.

10

ETHICAL ISSUES

THE GOOD OF THE CITY AND THE CITY OF THE GOOD

The justification for secret means

What is the justification for a modern government maintaining intelligence and security agencies? We saw one answer in chapter 2 in terms of the contribution that intelligence makes to a better quality of decision-making. Secret intelligence is, as we have seen, especially valuable in helping the management of risks to national security, thus helping government discharge its first responsibility to the public. If we take the example of counter-terrorism, which we considered in chapter 4, then the priority requirement placed on the intelligence community is to deliver intelligence support, both through investment in national means and in partnership with friendly services, so as to allow:

- Protection of the public directly by providing the leads that allow disruption of terrorist networks and thus prevent criminal acts before they occur.
- Lowering of the level of violence, gaining time for longer-term measures addressing the roots of the current problems to take effect.
- Provision of the leads for criminal investigations that will lead to prosecutions, thus reassuring the public, reducing the threat and upholding the rule of law; and additionally
- Understanding of the nature and future development of the threat, helping the government to plan ahead and police and security authorities to operate in ways that reassure the communities in which the terrorists seek support, not to alienate them.

261

The delivery of secret intelligence cannot ever be guaranteed in advance. Its production involves overcoming constant friction in the system. When accurate pre-emptive secret intelligence is available, however, its use has the huge benefit of enabling the security authorities to act selectively to remove the trouble-makers from the community without the need for 'the bludgeon of state power'[1] to be deployed (mass arrests and house-to-house searches, detention without trial, coercive interrogation and so on) thus helping to maintain community confidence. The ability to take pre-emptive action in the interests of public security depends crucially on obtaining advance notice of terrorist preparations, and on having the quality of trust between security authorities that enables secret intelligence to be used effectively. In the UK the evidence to date from disruptions and convictions in court is that both conditions are being met to a high degree, and certainly ahead of most comparable nations.

The Theseus Syndrome

Nevertheless, one of the themes of this book has been that security work is an exercise in risk management. There is no certainty that pre-emptive intelligence will be obtained on any specific terrorist plot, and given the fragmentary nature of intelligence there is no guarantee that the puzzle will be pieced together in time and acted upon. We must expect false alarms from time to time. Not every prosecution will succeed in convincing a jury (although the fact that there has been no conviction does not mean that no crime was committed for which someone should be held to account).

The public mood will swing from critical concern to sceptical complacency and back again, as cases come to court and convictions are obtained, or as the public is inconvenienced by security measures whose justification they find hard to understand. Over the last few years transatlantic flights have been cancelled for fear they have been targeted for attack; traffic jams have built up whilst roads are dug up to install barriers outside public buildings to deter vehicle bombs; armoured vehicles surrounded Heathrow airport in response to intelligence suggesting a possible surface-to-air missile attack; and large numbers of armed police stormed a house in a residential area of London looking for a chemical explosive device. The common factor behind these (real) UK examples of counter-terrorist action is that they were based on secret intelligence reporting that may or may not have been accurate, but was in each case sufficiently well sourced that it could not be ignored. The intelligence forced the security authorities to act, to act quickly, and to act publicly. From the public point of view (and often even for the intelligence agencies themselves), it is hard to know whether such steps have prevented a specific terrorist threat, forced changes in terrorist targeting and disrupted terrorist preparations; or whether it was over-reaction and heavy-handedness by security authorities, in what I would call the Theseus syndrome: 'in the night, imagining some fear, how easy is a bush suppos'd a bear' (Duke Theseus in *A Midsummer Night's Dream*).

In the area of security the public has to take a lot from government on trust, and trust is a quality in their relationship that is often lacking in both directions. The temptation in government and police media briefings to exaggerate the threat is always present, especially to justify actions that have not led to visible results. It is hardly surprising that such incidents are usually followed by media stories questioning the quality of the intelligence behind the warnings, with commentators claiming that the threat is being talked up for political motives.

A certain amount of scepticism about the claims of government is healthy in a democracy. Not everything should be taken on trust. For relations between nations, 'trust, but verify' is a prudent policy, as Ronald Reagan famously kept repeating to Mikhail Gorbachev during arms control negotiations. For much of domestic government, trust can be rebuilt (at a price in terms of reinforcing the image of elected representatives as unable to see public as against partisan interest) by citing professional expertise in support of policy decisions. The tele-visual role of the Chief Medical Officer of the Department of Health in relation to swine flu is a good example. A doctor in a white coat with stethoscope is more credible with the public than a Cabinet Minister, as regular opinion polls confirm. JTAC, as described in chapter 2, has a 'professional' status in deciding upon threat states, but for security reasons shelters behind ministers so has no equivalent publicly visible face. In the last few years the Director-General of the Security Service has been encouraged periodically to speak publicly about the threat (an unthinkable step a decade ago), and so far has retained credibility with the media, although the timing of each such statement has been scrutinized hard to see if there is a hidden agenda of government behind it.

Oversight

Another device increasingly used by government is to 'export' oversight and supervision through arms-length bodies with strong lay representation, for example in the cases of banking, safety of medicines, misuse of drugs, farm animal welfare and food safety, and such bodies often have open meetings that the public can attend. For the secret activities of government, that would self-evidently create problems. Where there is domestic legislation governing intrusive investigative practices, then members of the judiciary can be appointed to provide independent verification of compliance with the law. For building confidence in the wider activities of the secret world, the route that most democratic nations have gone down is to have proxy trust. That is, to have a group of specially chosen members of the national legislature who can be authorized to be given in strict confidence the access that has to be denied to the public and media. These overseers can then provide their verdict on whether all is as it should be, without being required to provide detailed evidence, or whether there are any legitimate grounds for concern. The public can thus take on trust from them what they would not accept from government itself.

The Intelligence Services Act of 1994 established the Intelligence and Security Committee (ISC) of parliamentarians to monitor the work of all three UK intelligence and security agencies. Thus, for the first time, members of both Houses of Parliament were to be involved in the scrutiny of the expenditure, administration and policy of the secret agencies. The ISC has demonstrated since 1994 that it can investigate even very sensitive matters requiring access to top secret information without compromising its security. The recommendations of the ISC are almost always immediately accepted by the government. Building on this track record, by agreement with the government, its remit has expanded in practice beyond the original legislation to cover not only the agencies but also the entire UK intelligence community, including the work of the JIC and its staff. The ISC investigations, such as those into intelligence relevant to the 2002 Bali terrorist bombing and into the London bombings of July 2005, now extend beyond matters of agency administration. This has been welcomed by the agencies as providing a group of senior parliamentarians who could vouch for the integrity of their work and, where necessary, recommend improvements without risking uncontrolled exposure to a wider audience.

The effectiveness of the oversight of the UK intelligence community by the ISC has been questioned[2] including highlighting the drawback that it is a statutory committee with members appointed by the Prime Minister who has the final say (for security reasons) about which parts of its reports can be published. It can be fairly argued that the committee's work would have greater external credibility if it enjoyed the privileges of a Select Committee of Parliament (as do most counterpart organizations in other countries) to write its own rules of procedure and have the power to 'send for people and papers'. Those optics have to be balanced against the major advantage it has over UK Select Committees in that official witnesses before the ISC give evidence on their own behalf; those in front of Select Committees do so on behalf of their minister,[3] leading inevitably to more cautious evidence from officials under an obligation to try to protect their ministers, and a party political edge being put on questioning from some committee members. The system of oversight depends crucially on the existence of trust in the integrity of the scrutineers and robustness and independence from government of the scrutiny. Further development of the UK oversight system is likely, but there may be a choice to be made in revising the arrangements between greater public credibility in terms of perception and greater effectiveness in reality. One change that would make a difference would be always to appoint as the chair of the Committee a prominent politician from an opposition party (as happens with the Public Accounts Committee of the House of Commons). Another would be to have a panel of experienced retired officers from the agencies who could be called on by the ISC to support their own investigator and act as 'Inspectors General' in pursuing specific inquiries and recommending changes in internal procedure following an ISC investigation, and subsequently providing the ISC with assurance that recommendations had been followed up satisfactorily.

The level of public understanding of what collecting secret intelligence involves

As one British Ambassador was to write in 1785 to the Secretary of State in London about his involvement with secret agents, 'I abhor this dirty work, but when one is employed to sweep chimneys, one must black one's fingers.' A serious challenge to public confidence in government is the questioning that has followed recent events over the morality of methods that were alleged to have been used by the police and intelligence agencies to obtain intelligence[4] and to pursue prosecutions. In a statement attacking the security authorities read out by their law-yer[5] after the trial, the defendants in the 2007 trial of the Operation Crevice bomb plotters declared that

'This was a prosecution driven by the security services, able to hide behind a cloak of secrecy, and eager to obtain ever greater resources and power to encroach on individual rights. There was no limit to the money, resources and underhand strategies that were used to secure convictions in this case. This case was brought in an atmosphere of hostility against Muslims, at home, and abroad. One stoked by this government throughout the course of this case. This prosecution involved extensive intrusion upon personal lives, not only ours, but our families and friends. Coached witnesses were brought forward. Forced confessions were gained through illegal detention, and torture abroad. Threats and intimidation was used to hamper the truth. All with the trial judge seemingly intent to assist the prosecution almost every step of the way. These were just some of the means used in the desperate effort to convict.'

In this case, the trenchant comments of the trial judge about their murderous intent were well reported. The later conviction of three of the Overt defendants for the more serious charge of conspiracy to detonate explosive devices on airplanes and the life sentences for con-spiracy to murder involving liquid bombs handed out (including one of forty-one years in prison for the ringleader) will also have reassured majority opinion as to the justice of the convictions and the abhorrent nature of the crime. Nevertheless, there is a ready minority audience for believing the worst about the authorities.

A skim of the blogosphere and radical websites shows how far con-spiracy theories swirl around terrorist plots and trials, as they do around the actual attacks in London on 7/7, and as they still do over 9/11. A Channel 4 News survey[6] of 500 British Muslims, carried out by GFK NOP, found that nearly a quarter did not believe the four men identified as the 7/7 London bombers were responsible for the attacks; and a similar number said the government or the security services were involved. Nearly six in ten of those polled believed the government had not told the whole truth about the 7/7 bombings—and more than half said the intelligence services had made up evidence to convict terrorist suspects. The evidence brought out at the Opera-tion Overt trial of the airline plotters, including video surveillance footage of the suspects and their pre-prepared suicide videos, may have shaken some of this denial of reality, but conspiracy theories continue and controversies continue to be sparked off by police actions, for example the arrests of suspects who are then later released without charge. Accusations of collusion in torture by intelligence agencies overseas, and in facilitating US extraordinary rendition operations, have made the headlines and top stories in the news bulletins, and have been amplified in websites and blogs. Measured responses from those with access to the facts, including the parliamentary oversight committee, the Intelligence and Security Committee (ISC), have received far less coverage.

The questions impose themselves therefore of whether the minority communities from whom the terrorists might hope to seek support can be persuaded of the real nature of the threat (for example that the terrorists attack Muslims and non-Muslims indiscriminately) and of the proportionality of the security response. Reassurance is needed that their community is not being stigmatized or discriminated against domestically, at the same time as vigorous and effective intelligence-led action is taken to uncover the existing terrorists hiding within the community. This need for reassurance extends to being able to demonstrate to the general public that the methods being used by our allies and partners in the wider fight against terrorism overseas are in keeping with the underlying values of a democratic state ruled by law.

Human rights are a public good, as is security. The balance to be struck by wise government is not between security and rights, as if to argue that by suspending human rights security could be assured. The balance has to be within the framework of rights, recognizing that the fundamental right to life, with the legitimate expectation of being protected by the state from threats to oneself and one's family, is an important right that in some circumstances must be given more weight than other rights, such as the right to privacy of personal and family life. This is a choice that society is able to make when there is a serious terrorist threat, as was discussed in chapter 4. In those circumstances, checks and balances of good government should come into play to provide confidence that the balance is a genuine one and that red lines are not being crossed. Remaining within the framework of rights is important, however, not least as a constant reminder that there are rights, such as the right not to suffer torture, which cannot be derogated.

Just intelligence

Since the defining characteristic of secret intelligence is that others are actively trying to stop it being acquired, it follows that exceptional and unusual means will be needed to overcome these obstacles. This immediately raises ethical dilemmas. Secret intelligence will not be obtained by sticking to the morality that one might hope would govern everyday life: obtaining secret intelligence is the equivalent of invading privacy, listening at keyholes, steaming open family mail, subverting friends from their duty, consorting with low life and so on. The British learned generations ago the value of national information superiority, and especially when its conventional power no longer held sway. British governments accepted that obtaining it involves when necessary a degree of what in everyday life would be called cheating. Using insider information in a stock market is a criminal offence; using insider information in a diplomatic negotiation with a proliferator over an illegal programme is a national asset.

The current focus on use of secret intelligence for public protection puts activities by the secret world under an unwelcome spotlight and increases the importance of retaining public confidence, as well as making it essential that the staff also are comfortable with the ethical framework within which they are operating. The government too needs to have confidence in its own intelligence community and its adherence to agreed standards of behaviour and propriety.

Moral hazards can be expected to arise in disruption operations, including 'sting' operations that verge on entrapment and incitement to commit criminal offences. The intelligence objectives might be to see who falls into the net, including for example terrorists not previously identified, or to bleed off resources from the terrorists in return for dud armaments. In criminal cases, the objective is to collect evidence for prosecution that will be admissible in court. These approaches can coincide, but sometimes not. It may be necessary to hold out the prospect of personal gain, or threats of consequences for failure to cooperate or exposure of personal weaknesses, in order to secure cooperation in intelligence work. The Cold War provided many examples of brave agents offering their services to British intelligence in rejection of the Soviet totalitarian system; contemporary circumstances of terrorist and criminal networks are not so clear-cut. Recruiting informers (CHIS: covert human intelligence sources) and running 'participating' agents within a terrorist or criminal organization may provide life-saving information, but for their own safety the individual will have to continue as a member of a prohibited organization and to be conscious of criminal activities. Such agents, even where they provide valuable intelligence, are not likely to be fully under control of their handler, which will compound the problem.

Maintaining intelligence liaisons with countries less scrupulous about the methods they use is likely to bring the moral dilemma of receiving and making use of intelligence from possibly tainted sources, as does passing intelligence to other nations for action when that might result in their responding in ways not allowed to one's own forces. Allegations of collusion in supplying questions to liaison services who may use coercive means will follow. Collateral damage involving innocent third parties may well result inadvertently from intelligence-based operations, for example the US operations to target terrorist suspects overseas using missiles fired from drones.

Surveillance, both audio and visual, and interception of communications constitute intrusions into the personal life of individuals and families, as does access to personal protected data about individuals, such as their biometrics, immigration status, finances, habits and movements held on government and private sector databases, as well as maintaining files on suspect individuals and their associates that come to the notice of the security authorities. Use of intelligence material under special evidential rules to allow it to be used to secure control orders or immigration decisions whilst preserving its secrecy, for example by the use of special advocates appointed by the court, is likely to lead to individuals not being able to know the full basis of the charge against them. Only the most serious national security threat is likely to justify such departure from the principles of natural justice.

The list of sensitive areas where intelligence work may involve moral hazard is a long one. One controversial area that is not on the above list for the UK intelligence community is assassination. The UK intelligence community does not carry out extra-judicial targeted killing (and successive governments have made clear that any such request for authority would be rejected). It should be noted that other nations do not have such a declaratory policy, and a few nations admit to this practice as state policy (the Israeli Supreme Court examined their practice in 2006,[7] and concluded that in the last resort it might be necessary if other methods were impracticable but that the burden of proof would be weighty).

Distinguishing good from bad government

We have here the ancient problem faced by well-meaning rulers down the ages. How is the good of the city to be reconciled with being the city of the good? Machiavelli's advice to the ruler in those circumstances was to present a virtuous face to the public whilst doing in secret whatever was necessary for the survival of the state (or, rather, in his day of its ruler). As we shall see, changing public attitudes and the development of an active media have made such advice highly problematic today. We have a contemporary example in the way that the Bush administration followed the Machiavellian line of keeping from the public the aggressive measures taken to safeguard the citizens from terrorism. The Commander in Chief of a government of consent, to use a phrase popularized by Philip Bobbitt,[8] felt entitled secretly to authorize targeted killings, extraordinary rendition, extreme methods of coercive interrogation and secret domestic internet interception. In each case these steps in 'the war on terror' were not fully disclosed to the public at the time, but certainly the Bush administration could with justification claim that immediately after 9/11 taking the fight to the terrorists in those ways would have had majority public and congressional support.

Not everyone would have gone as far as the ex–Director of the CIA Counter-Terrorism Center, Michael Scheuer, in his evidence to Congress on the subjects of rendition: 'I would not, however, be surprised if their treatment was not up to US standards. This is a matter of no concern as the Rendition Program's goal was to protect America, and the rendered fighters delivered to Middle Eastern governments are now either dead or in places from which they cannot harm America. Mission accomplished, as the saying goes.'[9] The DCI of the day, George Tenet, recognized in his memoirs that after 9/11 the adminstration had asked for the gloves to come off: 'As for the treatment of detainees, the senior leadership at CIA understood clearly that the capture, detention, and interrogation of senior Al-Qa'ida members was new ground—morally and legally.' Tenet concludes: 'Our role as intelligence professionals is to inform policy-makers of both the hazards and the value of such programs. We should say what we think but the final decision belongs to the political leadership of the country.' In the case of the US government the decision was, for example, to authorize coercive interrogation methods. The British government on the other hand took a different decision, to uphold their longstanding ban on such practices.

Scheuer also told Congress that:

'If mistakes were made, I can only say that that is tough, but war is a tough and confusing business and a well-supported chance to take action and protect Americans should always trump other considerations, especially pedantic worries about whether or not the intelligence data is airtight... To destroy the Rendition Program because of a mistake or two or more would be to sacrifice the protection of Americans to venal and prize-hungry reporters like Ms Priest, grandstanding politicians like those mentioned above and sanctimonious Europeans who take every bit of American protection offered them while publicly damning and seeking jail time for those who risk their lives to provide that protection. If the Rendition Program is halted, we will truly be able to say, by paraphrasing the late John Wayne, that war is tough, and it is a lot tougher if you are deliberately stupid.'

It may be unpalatable to some but it needs to be recognized that the 'American protection' offered in the form of Al-Qa'ida terrorists captured and killed (for example through cross-border attacks from unmanned drones in the Afghanistan/Pakistan border regions) has seriously degraded AQ as a terrorist organization. The intelligence passed to the UK over the last few years by the US and other partners has enabled plots to be uncovered and lives to be saved. To refuse to have intelligence relationships would be to place the UK public in greater jeopardy. So even the commendable policy being followed by the UK government in respect of the actions of its own officers including trying to avoid collusions in such practices, does not allow an easy cost-free moral stance to be taken over benefiting from the actions of others. Responsible governments that care for the security of their citizens will remain impaled on this dilemma.

If, as I believe, states do need to have secret agencies able to reach out and take actions in the dark that they cannot be seen taking in the light, then there need to be some red lines of conduct drawn that are not to be crossed, and executive power needs to have checks and balances brought into play to prevent abuse of secret power.

We can use as an example the way that the Obama administration in 2009 took a different policy course to its predecessor, in balancing these considerations of public good in a new way, most notably by repudiating the previous policy on the interpretation of what constitutes inhumane and degrading treatment, upholding US commitment to the universal ban on torture and adopting a 'hearts and minds' counter-insurgency strategy[10] giving priority to the protection of the Afghan people from the Taliban. The administration has however continued with a robust policy of attacking AQ leadership in the tribal areas, whilst defending intelligence gathering, including domestic surveillance, as being essential for American security and consistent with American values and the US Constitution.

In part those changes of policy reflect a different set of political values. We can see from the experience of the previous US administration that trying to pursue under a cloak of invisibility measures that are incompatible with publicly espoused national values, measures that when exposed government is reluctant to justify publicly and are thus politically unsustainable, is ultimately incompatible with an active democracy and a free press. Even the covert world of statecraft nowadays has to have regard to what government is prepared to defend as ethically proper behaviour.

The changes that the Obama adminstration has brought also reflect a more strategic view of the longer-term impact of short-term security actions, a perspective that is key to success in counter-terrorism and counter-insurgency (and are strongly reflected in the strategy being followed by the new US Commander in Afghanistan, General McChrystal). Given the passage of time since 9/11, it was possible to gauge the cumulative adverse impact of the US 'war on terror' on Muslim communities and international opinion more generally, and the loss of US 'soft power' overseas, and thus the extent to which this approach had become self-defeating since it played into AQ's own long-term strategy to diminish US global influence and authority.

To take another example touched on earlier, the British government has had to reconcile the demands of providing intelligence for public protection with public expectations of desirable standards of conduct over the maintenance of intelligence liaisons with states that have very different standards of conduct from those of the UK in tracking down and dealing with terrorist suspects. The UK has incorporated human rights protection into the fabric of domestic law through the Human Rights Act 1998 and has always been clear that it will not condone, let alone allow the practice of, torture. The memory is still strong of the dire consequences of the brief use in 1971 by the British army in Northern Ireland of coercive interrogation methods, found by the European Court of Human Rights to have amounted to inhuman and degrading treatment[11] and subsequently banned by Prime Minister Heath from use by any British personnel for all time. The fall-out from that episode polarized attitudes in Northern Ireland and overseas for many years. By no means all countries affected by terrorism provide equivalent protection for their citizens, nor do their intelligence and security agencies have standards of conduct towards suspects comparable to those of the UK. The UK's principal ally, the United States, authorized under the Bush administration rendition and interrogation practices by its intelligence community that were outlawed for members of UK agencies and service personnel. As the Parliamentary Intelligence and Security (ISC) oversight committee recognized,[12] the UK agencies were slow to detect the emerging pattern of US extraordinary renditions and slow to apply greater caution in their dealings over cases of mutual interest. The injunction to apply greater caution, however correct, does not however eliminate the dilemma for intelligence agencies seeking pre-emptive intelligence.

Terrorism is an international problem, and sharing intelligence on terrorists, their networks and their modus operandi was recognized after 9/11 by the United Nations Security Council[13] as an imperative for nations 'to assist each other to the maximum extent possible, in the prevention, investigation, prosecution and punishment of acts of terrorism, wherever they occur'. It should be added that the UN itself now needs intelligence to support its own operations, both for the force protection and effectiveness of peacekeeping missions and to enable UN inspectors to do their job. Such intelligence can only come from national means of member states, especially the permanent members of the UN Security Council, since the UN possesses no capability of its own. For all these reasons, intelligence and police services have therefore since 9/11 been steadily deepening and expanding their range of international contacts. In the case of the United States, the key partner in the NATO operation in Afghanistan in which UK forces are so heavily engaged, intelligence exchange between US and UK continues at a high level, as it does with the other long-standing partners, Canada, Australia and New Zealand. Such intelligence exchanges typically take place on condition that a strict 'third party' rule (sometimes referred to as the control principle) is applied: any intelligence passed may not be shared with another country without the originator's permission nor used in criminal proceedings or made public. The third party rule (and thus the essential flow of intelligence) is however under constant pressure from the conflicting needs to issue warnings to the public or to ensure justice is done in terrorist cases. The Court of Appeal in London examined this control principle following a challenge by the Foreign Secretary to disclosure by a lower court of paragraphs from a US intelligence report, a matter that in the words of the Lord Chief Justice required the Court 'to address fundamental questions about the relationship between the executive and the judiciary in the context of national security in an age of terrorism and the interests of open justice in a democratic society.' The conclusion of the Lord Chief Justice[14] is worth quoting in full, not least because it reinforces the longstanding view of the Courts that it is for the executive not the judiciary to say what is in the interests of national and public security:

'43. The effective combating of international terrorism involves mutual co-operation and intelligence sharing. There is no obligation on the intelligence services of any country to share intelligence with those of any other country. The relationships cannot be considered in contractual or commercial terms. The process is entirely voluntary. The arrangements are not permanent, and they are not set in stone. Either country can end the relationship, or alter it, and certainly review it at any time, for good reason, or for none. Although in the modern world national safety is almost inevitably linked with the defeat of terrorism and international crime whenever and wherever they may arise, the first responsibility of any intelligence service is the safety of the country it serves.

44. At the risk of repetition, in general terms, it is integral to intelligence sharing arrangements that intelligence material provided by one country to another remains confidential to the country which provides it and that it will never be disclosed, directly or indirectly, by the receiving country, without the permission of the provider of the information. This understanding is rigidly applied to the relationship between the UK and USA. However although confidentiality is essential to the working arrangements between allied intelligence services, the description of it as a "control principle" suggests an element of constitutionality which is lacking. In this jurisdiction the control principle is not a principle of law: it is an apt and no doubt convenient description of the understanding on which intelligence is shared confidentially between the USA services and those in this country, and indeed between both countries and any other allies. If for any reason the court is required to address the question whether the control principle, as understood by the intelligence services, should be disapplied, the decision depends on well understood PII principles. As the executive, not the judiciary, is responsible for national security and public protection and safety from terrorist activity, the judiciary defers to it on these issues, unless it is acting unlawfully, or in the context of litigation, the court concludes that the claim by the executive for public interest immunity is not justified. Self evidently that is not a decision to be taken lightly.'

Another very important relationship for the UK in tackling terrorism is the newer but very important link to Pakistani intelligence, security and police agencies. The UK has received actionable intelligence from Pakistani and other liaison services that has helped prevent attacks in the UK and thus saved British lives, but at the same time there has been legitimate doubt about the detention and interrogation practices of these nations. Criticism has been levelled at the UK intelligence community on the grounds that passing back information from UK investigations on a suspect of interest held in custody in Pakistan, or providing questions to be asked of such a suspect, amounted to collusion in ill-treatment even though UK abhorrence of such practices had been previously made clear.

Typically, an overseas service will want to offer their UK liaison agencies information that relates to terrorist threats that have links back to the UK, in the expectation that the UK will reciprocate. Such information exchanges are the main rationale for intelligence liaisons. Most of the major terrorist plots, and most of the actual attacks, which have been uncovered in the UK certainly have links overseas, often to individuals in Pakistan. The information provided to the UK may be as little as an address or a telephone number with a request that it be checked out, or a warning that a British embassy or consulate, company or tourist destination in the overseas country is known to be the subject of a terrorist plot. Or it may be an offer to allow follow-up questions to be put to a suspect being held who has admitted to plotting against UK interests. Such exchanges are central, as the UN Security Council recognized, to the prevention of terrorism. In return, liaison services will expect information from UK agencies that will assist their own investigations, for example whether a suspect had associations with terrorists in custody in the UK.

As with the 'ticking bomb' scenarios used in ethics classes to illuminate the nature of human agency, the 'blood on the report' media headline is not how in practice the problem presents itself. Intelligence agencies guard their sources, and typically it will simply not be apparent whether a piece of information has come from a human agent, from a technical operation, a combination of these or from the interrogation of a suspect—and in the last case it will normally not be apparent on the face of the information whether it has been extracted through a voluntary confession, by some form of plea bargain or covert deal with the suspect (something the agency concerned will be most anxious to conceal if the individual has agreed to work as a double agent for the authorities) or by coercive interrogation. Questions to the liaison service on that last point will simply not be answered (or if answered, not answered truthfully).

Such considerations make it essential that procedures and safeguards already in place, for example to report cases of suspected ill-treatment of suspects, are strictly enforced to reduce the risk that UK intelligence officers will find themselves caught up in appearing to condone ill-treatment or torture by countries overseas. It must continue to be made clear to all British officials who may become involved in liaison work that they must in good faith ensure, both generally and in individual cases, that there are no misunderstandings on the part of the country concerned that the UK in any way expects its requests for information to be met through mistreatment of detainees or suspects. Such messages should be reinforced by the continuing work that UK security and justice officials and military staffs are conducting with liaison partners to raise standards and professionalism in these areas. It is already the case that such liaison support is making a positive difference.

The real risk remains that in the eyes of defence lawyers, the media, and thus the public, the very existence of a liaison relationship with such a country will be seen as collusive. The only way to avoid that risk would be not to have external diplomatic or intelligence links with nations known to have, or suspected of having, lower standards for detention and interrogation than in the UK. However, that is simply not an option that would be diplomatically feasible or could be responsibly regarded as being in the public interest in relation to counter-terrorism. Intelligence exchanges are, as the ISC recognized, critical to UK security. It is the case that information from such exchanges has disrupted attacks planned against the UK and has thus saved lives. There was no sure way of knowing at the time whether information received came from torture, or whether sources were otherwise tainted, and there is no sure way of knowing now. The furore after the deaths of British tourists in the terrorist bombing in Bali in 2002 showed that the public does expect its intelligence services to provide forestalling intelligence of such attacks, however hard that may be. It is, I believe, a fundamental duty of those charged with the protection of the public to pay heed to information that may directly bear on public safety. The protecting state must make its own standards of conduct clear and its officials must abide by them and promote those standards; but it cannot shun the rest of the world if it wishes to manage, as the public would wish it to, the risks to its citizens at home and when abroad. As the Lord Chief Justice has said[15] 'Co-operation between the intelligence services of friendly nations is a critical element in the battle against the terrorist and without mutual inter-dependence based on trust, the risks would be almost irremediably heightened.'

Intelligence and security as a regrettable necessity

For brief periods, Britain has succumbed to feelings that there is something inherently underhand about the methods of security and intelligence work and that they are incompatible with following ethical domestic and foreign policies. In 1844 an Italian exile in London, Mazzini, complained that his letters were being opened and that 'the spy system of foreign states' had been introduced which was 'repugnant to every principle of the British constitution and subversive of the public confidence which was so essential to a commercial country'. According to the historian of British secrecy David Vincent,[16] 'Mazzini rehearsed the widespread complaints about the betrayal of "official trust" and "British honour" and about the widening gulf between public and private morality'. In the fierce parliamentary debates over the Mazzini affair the Home Secretary of the day attempted to deploy the 'neither confirm nor deny' argument, a communications policy still used by the UK government today when allegations are made about operational intelligence matters. This meant that when over-excited parliamentarians started to allege that the correspondence of Members of Parliament themselves was being opened, the Home Secretary was not in a position to deny it. In the subsequent moral panic, over-righteous parliamentary committees of inquiry then forced the abolition both of the Secret Office and of the Decyphering Branch which had been serving British interests since it opened in 1653, along with the pensioning off with secret service money of Francis Willes whose family had held the position of Chief Decypherer since 1703. Even Mr Punch protested that 'my letters—and the thousands I receive!—had all of them been defiled by the eyes of a spy; that all my most domestic secrets had been rumpled and tousled and pinched here and pinched there—searched by an English Minister as shuddering modesty is searched by a French custom-house' (the comparison with a suitably Napoleonic image was no doubt chosen to reinforce the fear of the vulnerability of the individual faced with the power of government).

The threats that modern national security strategies seek to address are largely about common dangers from the obvious evils of terrorism, proliferation, narcotics, and instability and ungoverned spaces rather than stemming from traditional inter-state conflict. Intelligence and security capability therefore fits a model of much wider international cooperation, rather than the traditional secrecy of the maximization of national advantage through intelligence one-upmanship. Even the United Nations has come to recognize that peacekeeping missions and international counter-proliferation efforts need intelligence support, in other words secret information gathered by one member state on another.[17] International cooperation to deal with common threats has led to representatives of secret intelligence services, security services and security police services being exchanged across many nations with their existence disclosed to their host governments. Networks of cooperation and liaison now exist with a very wide range of countries (not without themselves giving rise to difficulties in avoiding collusive behaviour, as was noted above).

We may safely make the assumption that all developed countries maintain intelligence services and some form of security intelligence apparatus. Mostly, the inverse of the golden rule then applies, accepting that others will try to do unto you what you insist on doing unto them. That does not stop show trials, or even in some nations summary execution, when spies are caught. Diplomatic and public protest to the country thought to be responsible is the norm. But such kabuki theatre masks the pervasive reality of security and intelligence work. *Realpolitik* governs the swaps of spies such as in 1964 when the Soviet agent Lonsdale was exchanged for the British SIS agent Greville Wynne who had helped run the important SIS agent Oleg Penkovsky. As an ex–CIA lawyer has written: 'The core of espionage is treachery and deceit. The core of international law is decency and common humanity. This alone suggests espionage and international law cannot be reconciled in a complete synthesis. Perhaps we should leave it at that.'[18] A former General Counsel of the CIA has written that 'espionage is neither clearly condoned nor condemned under international law'. The rules and the ethics are situational. Countries are much less tolerant when espionage is committed against them than when they are committing it against friends and foes. Whether espionage is legal or illegal under international law, they are realistic about the fact that countries, for reasons of self-defence and for their own interests, are going to commit espionage in other countries.[19]

The absence of an international legal framework

In traditional military terms, collecting intelligence directly on the enemy is a valid activity for members of the armed forces. The old-fashioned name for such a person was a scout (older readers may remember the Scout Car, a US small fast-wheeled armoured vehicle widely deployed during WWII and thereafter). Provided that a scout stayed in uniform or was sufficiently designated as a combatant, then the Hague Regulations of 1907, the Geneva Conventions, the Protocol Additional to the Geneva Conventions all applied, and even if found behind enemy lines he would be dealt with as a prisoner of war. A spy, on the other hand, who conceals his (or her) identity and does not wear a military uniform is not entitled to protection as a prisoner of war. In today's battle-space there can, however, sometimes be no clear front line, and even the Hague Regulations' concept of a 'zone of operations' is moot. In the case of civilians or attachés who have diplomatic status in the country concerned, then they will be entitled to claim diplomatic immunity if allegations are made that they are engaging in activity incompatible with their diplomatic status, acting for example as intelligence case officers. Expulsion is the likely outcome since espionage activity is universally regarded as a criminal offence, whatever the status of the individual. Those without diplomatic immunity ('illegals' in the jargon) if caught are liable to prosecution and punishment (capital punishment in some jurisdictions). In practice, during the Cold War both sides recognized the realities of espionage, and exchanges of captured intelligence officers took place.

Since espionage activity is likely to flout the laws of the country concerned, those planning such operations could in the eyes of British law run the risk in some circumstances of being parties to a criminal conspiracy in the UK. In 'the old days' that would have been a consideration of little or no importance because all the activity was both secret and deniable. With the avowal of the UK intelligence agencies in the 1980s this position had to change, and the relevant legislation, the Intelligence Services Act 1994 Section 7, provides for the Secretary of State to authorize actions outside the British Islands by SIS which then, under the act, removes any liability under UK civil or criminal law. This device of legislating to make lawful what would otherwise be unlawful and thus ensure that at all times UK intelligence officers act within UK law does not of course have any effect whatever on the illegality of the actions under the local law of the theatre of operations.

That might seem hypocritical as a process, but no international agreement to prohibit or regulate intelligence activity on the lines of the Vienna Conventions under which diplomatic activity is conducted is ever likely to be possible due to the difficulty of providing a common definition of what constitutes espionage. For some regimes, even the penetrating questioning of a reporter, or the publication of scientific findings of an academic, would be treasonable. So we are unlikely to find help in the quest for an ethical framework for intelligence gathering in attempts to create an internationally agreed regime.[20]

There seems, however, to be a growing acceptance that, in the face of non-state threats from terrorism, proliferation and organized crime, intelligence is a stabilizing force and it is helpful and not threatening to have members of intelligence services declared to host governments and work within embassies with diplomatic immunity. 'National technical means' such as observation by satellite can be seen to have played a stabilizing role during the Cold War, and even the United Nations has accepted that it cannot mandate peacekeeping missions in dangerous circumstances without its force having the capacity for intelligence in self-protection and pursuit of its mission. It is hard to see how international law could prohibit photography from space, given its peaceful and commercial uses, nor the gathering of information by journalists or scholars within a country whose rulers may object to such information about their country being known. International law can be said therefore neither to prohibit nor to authorize intelligence gathering.

Such considerations quickly lead to the conclusion that, on the one hand, nations will take steps including domestic legislation to protect their secrets, and in some cases the sanctions for an intelligence agent if caught may be severe; whilst, on the other hand, nations will take steps to acquire secret intelligence for themselves. Staff in the intelligence agencies therefore need to know that although what they are planning may very well violate provisions in the law of an overseas state, for example in relation to paying agents or using false identities, they are not breaking UK law. As earlier noted, the British approach to this conundrum has been to legislate nationally to make legal here what would be illegal in the country in which operations are being conducted overseas. The staff of the agencies can therefore be assured that they are not contravening UK law and thus rendering themselves liable, even in theory, for prosecution for acts conducted in the UK such as the planning of operations overseas.

A distinctive British experience: the importance of ethos

The experience of working within a legislative framework has helped the UK intelligence agencies build up a powerful ethos of being law abiding, with strict control over operational activity up their chain of command and political authorization of sensitive activities that might have diplomatic repercussions with overseas governments. Any general international legal framework to prohibit intelligence gathering and make it justiciable in an International Court is however doomed to failure. What has nevertheless developed (as it did to regulate the use of force by nations) is the doctrine of *jus cogens*, or peremptory norms, according to which certain types of conduct are regarded as generally prohibited regardless of any domestic law, including piracy, slavery, kidnapping and torture. We can expect increasing legal pressure for limitations on state behaviour in the secret world in the light of developing international thinking on human rights.

The UK national security strategy rests on the ability of government to be able to understand the different threat domains (see chapter 1) and to have the pre-emptive intelligence to be able to anticipate threats and where necessary intervene to prevent or mitigate them. This is a tall order in a world that is inherently unpredictable, as we have discussed in previous chapters. In his speech in Chicago[21] before 9/11 and before the Iraq invasion, Prime Minister Blair argued that the most pressing foreign policy problem we face is to identify the circumstances in which we should get actively involved in other people's conflicts. He gave a number of conditions that would have to be satisfied before intervention was justified, and the first of these was the duty to be sure of our case. This puts a huge burden on the capacity of government, and its national security and intelligence machine. Throughout this book there are however examples of how the evolution of a distinctively British approach to secret intelligence work has enabled far more significant results to be obtained than Britain's overall national standing might have led one to expect. The risk is of over-confidence, of fostering an over-reliance on the advantages that secret intelligence might bring or an illusion that short cuts existed by using covert means rather than traditional diplomacy. Some of the dangers associated with justifying policies on the basis of secret intelligence have been well demonstrated in the case of Iraq.

Secrecy in the Cold War intelligence world was in tune with the prevailing attitude that the public did not need to know, certainly had no right to know, and was better off not knowing what was being done to protect it by the secret parts of the state. Nuclear deterrence depended crucially on potential opponents not learning the details of military preparations, other than knowing that they existed, they were obviously thorough, and they were well tested. Soviet attempts to obtain sensitive information on the vulnerabilities of the UK posture had to be thwarted through the work of the Security Service and through counter-intelligence operations to recruit agents in a position to know what the Soviet military and intelligence establishments were attempting to do. It was a logical consequence that the British public also had to be kept in the dark about what was being done in its name.

By the later stages of the Cold War, however, much was beginning to change in the British secret world. The comfortable acceptance of secrecy had been punctuated by scandals, not least the long-running story of the pre-war Cambridge spies. The function of GCHQ had been acknowledged in the 1982 trial of the spy Geoffrey Prime. By the 1980s the structure of the UK intelligence community was increasingly visible to the public. The Franks Committee of Inquiry into intelligence failures before the Argentine invasion of the Falkland Islands lifted the lid on the working of the JIC. The banning of trades unions at GCHQ in 1984 by Prime Minister Thatcher led to unparalleled publicity about SIGINT. A different set of circumstances was also affecting the ability of that secretive organization to shelter itself from public knowledge, because the commercialization of cryptography with public key systems (ironically, originally a GCHQ discovery) on which modern commerce depends led to the rapid development of an academic literature and, indeed, university departments of cryptography.

Already by the outbreak of the First World War the secret world had shifted from the concept of 'secret agency' as personal activity, as Conrad would have interpreted it, to secret agency as organization, with hierarchies and institutional learning about sources and methods, a move I have summarized[22] as moving from 'On Her Majesty's Secret Service' to 'In Her Majesty's Secret Service'. Government organized itself into 'departments' each with permanent staff and a ministerial master and a headquarters building. It did not subsequently help that the Secret Intelligence Service was known across Whitehall during the Cold War by the name of its supposedly secret headquarters, Century House, a run-down anonymous office block in south London. It was becoming rather absurd by the 1980s to maintain that these large organizations did not exist.

The changing climate of legally enforceable human rights was, however, perhaps the single greatest factor triggering a new approach in the later stages of the Cold War to public avowal of what previously had been regarded as a state secret. A 1978 police case (Malone[23]) gave rise to a European Court of Human Rights judgment severely restricting the ability of the then unacknowledged Security Service (and others) to conduct interception operations infringing the private lives of suspects in the absence of a statutory code. A concurring Opinion[PEQ1] on the case stated in terms we would recognize today that 'the mission of the Council of Europe and its organs is to prevent the establishment of systems and methods that would allow "Big Brother" to become master of the citizen's private life' and 'the continuing temptation facing public authorities to "see into" the life of the citizen'. The outcome was the first UK legislation regulating the interception of communications. Also in the 1980s, the case of *Hewitt, Harman* v. *United Kingdom* brought Security Service practice up against Article 8 of the European Convention on Human Rights, the right to respect for private and family life, home, and correspondence. As David Bickford, Legal Adviser to the Security Service at the time, expressed it, 'The only international forum in which this question has been decided is the European Court of Human Rights.'[24] In a series of cases in the 1980s the court did indeed work out a doctrine in which on the one hand the reality was recognized that 'states may establish secret agencies to protect the interests of their economic well-being and national security' and within reason 'states can determine for themselves what those interests are' whilst on the other hand 'states, however, must legislate to declare the existence of their secret agencies and to explain their functions and powers, concerning the obtaining and dissemination of information'. Moreover, 'the powers of any secret agency may only be exercised in proportion to the threat, and there must be independent effective oversight of the agencies and the exercise of their powers'.[25] Effectively, the court was putting an end to the traditional British prerogative of secrecy around its Security Service.

According to a former Director-General (DG) of the UK Security Service,[26] we owe the decision to legislate to the influence of diplomat and former Intelligence Coordinator Sir Anthony Duff, who was by then recalled from retirement to become DG of the Security Service. In 1987—largely because of his own personal standing with Mrs Thatcher following his support during the crisis over Rhodesia and then the

Falklands War—he was able to secure her acceptance of the need for legislation for the Security Service. This became the Security Service Act 1989 that legislated the Service into existence, established a Tribunal supported by a Commissioner and able to investigate complaints from the public as well as review the issue to the Service regarding warrants for entry on or interference with property. The precedent of the Security Service Act 1989 was later extended through the Intelligence Services Act 1994 to place the SIS and GCHQ on a comparable statutory basis.

Another innovation was the Interception of Communication Act 1985 that regulated telephone interception, later replaced by the wider Regulation of Investigative Powers Act 2000[27] covering all intrusive surveillance and information gathering by the UK intelligence agencies, the police, and other governmental departments involved in surveillance work. This act laid down the level of authority required for different classes of intrusion, such as the acquisition of communications data (e.g. billing data), intrusive surveillance, use of covert human intelligence (HUMINT) sources (e.g. agents, informants and undercover officers), interception of communications, and access to encrypted data. For each of these powers, the act ensures that the law clearly covers the purposes for which they may be used, which authorities can use the powers, who should authorize each use of the power (with the most intrusive having to be warranted *ex ante* by a Secretary of State, typically the Home Secretary for operations in Great Britain), and the use that can be made of the material gained. The act provides additionally for *ex post* independent judicial oversight by commissioners (i.e. senior judges) and a means of redress for individuals.

It is difficult to overstate the overall impact in recent years of this body of legislation on the ethos of the UK agencies in creating a disciplined culture within the agencies, while enabling them to carry out a full range of intelligence gathering operations for authorized purposes. In the view of a former DG of the Security Service, Sir Stephen Lander:

'It has been wholly beneficial (though that is not to say that scrutiny by MPs has always been entirely comfortable or that the need for additional due process has not been costly). We moved from a position that was based on the rather dubious assumption that if something was not expressly illegal then it was okay. We now had the assurance of statute law as opposed to the insecurity of the royal prerogative, under which much agency activity hitherto notionally took place. That change played a key part in the 1990s and beyond in making the agencies more self-confident and thus more effective'.

It is now in practice as well as in law impossible to envisage reversing this trend and for the secret agencies to retreat back into the shadows.[28]

A comparable US position was clearly expressed by the then director of the CIA in evidence to Congress. General Hayden[29] said: 'We can't break the law... You just can't go to that place... I actually said fairly publicly to our workforce that, as director, I have to be certain that that which I'm asking a CIA officer to do is consistent with the Constitution, the laws and the international treaty obligations of the United States... If I can't say that, I can't ask an officer to do it.' Such an approach is not entirely unproblematic. The pressure is then on government to legislate to make lawful that which would otherwise be unlawful. And so we saw President Bush use his powers as Commander in Chief of the 'war on terror' to authorize such extreme measures as extraordinary rendition, coercive interrogation, determinations that named individuals if they cannot be captured may be killed, and the detention of suspects outside the United States, as well as authorizing the interception of internet and other communications within the United States outside the constraints of having to submit a warrant to the FISA Court.

Underlying dilemmas of counter-terrorism

I have argued that intelligence gathering is now a recognized, avowed activity of government. But there is a need to balance secret actions for the good of the city with upholding the reputation of being the city of the good. There has to be a level of public acceptance of the activity and how it is conducted—and more importantly, perhaps, public acceptance that there is regulatory mechanism that can prevent excesses and abuses, and processes for a rapid independent way of putting things right when they go wrong.

As I have argued in promoting the concept of 'the Protecting State',[30] there are parallels with the arguments that have arisen through the centuries over the circumstances in which war itself would be justified and over how far the inherent violence of war should itself be tempered by ethical considerations. Intelligence activities, as with any principal–agent relationship, carry moral hazard. In the case of intelligence work the problem can become acute where the 'agent' (no pun intended) to get results has incentives to behave in ways that the public interest 'principal' would not be comfortable justifying and which then subsequently places the 'agent' at risk, whether from physical attack or legal action. The first and most important thing is to ensure that members of the intelligence community continue, as part of their everyday professional life, to follow a set of ethical norms set firmly within the framework of human rights.

Given the inevitability of moral hazard, the national intelligence machine should only be engaged for the most significant of purposes, most notably for national security, and individual intelligence operations should be properly authorized and governed by clear principles such as those of necessity and proportionality.

Those charged with the direction of the intelligence community, and with its oversight, would be well advised to have such norms in mind, through a set of guidelines such as the following which I drew up after my retirement with the help of many still serving in senior positions within the British intelligence community:

- There must be sufficient sustainable cause. The deployment of the security and intelligence apparatus of the state, with its attendant moral hazards, must be justified by the scale of potential harm to national interests that is to be prevented. Passing this test is not just about grasping immediate advantage, but is about ensuring that the development and deployment of such intelligence capability is consistent with national strategic objectives including preserving the fundamentals of a free society. Primary legislation should set down limits on what the intelligence machine can be used for, and remove fears that the power of modern intelligence methods will become ubiquitous and thus seriously erode individual liberty.

- There must be integrity of motive: Are the advantages sought justifiable in terms of the public good from collection all the way to presentation to the top of government? Are the motives of all concerned what they appear and is there integrity throughout the intelligence process, especially guarding against any perception of politicization of collection, analysis or reporting? The most important ethical principle for the intelligence analyst is to tell it like it is, without fear or favour.

- The methods to be used on any occasion must be proportionate to the seriousness of the harm to be prevented, within the framework of human rights. Only the minimum intrusion necessary into the private affairs of others should be authorized.

- There must be right authority: is there a proper authorizing process at a sufficiently senior level with accountability within a chain of command and appropriate oversight? Only lawful orders count: and for example no instruction that flouts the UN Convention on Torture can lawfully be given. For highly intrusive operations by intelligence agencies in the UK this involves *ex ante* approval by a Secretary of State of the most intrusive operations such as domestic wire-tapping, and *ex post* judicial oversight of the exercise of this authority, with recourse to an independent judicial tribunal if abuse is suspected by an individual.

- There must be reasonable prospect of success: are the risks acceptable of unintended consequences, such as collateral damage when intelligence is used to target military operations, or the risks of political or diplomatic fall-out if operations are exposed, including applying the golden rule 'do unto others as you would be done by'?

- The recourse to secret intelligence access must be a last resort in meeting the need for information if there are other, more open, ways of obtaining the information from less sensitive or open sources.

Let me conclude this chapter with two additional practical rules of thumb that can be readily applied by those who have to authorize the collection of the secret intelligence, and by policy-makers and law enforcers who may wish to use secret intelligence safely. The first was well stated by Admiral Stansfield Turner when US DCI:

'There is one overall test of the ethics of human intelligence activities. That is whether those approving them feel they could defend their decisions before the public if their actions became public.'[31]

The second is well summed up by the advice given to the hobbits in Tolkein's *Lord of the Rings* to the effect that 'shortcuts make for long delays'. In other words that before following the tactical imperatives as they might be seen from the front line there needs to be adequate consideration of the cumulative strategic implications and whether the tactical move in fact may make harder achievement of the strategic aim. Following these two rules of thumb will normally ensure that the intelligence community is conducting operations that are likely to be politically sustainable.

11

INTELLIGENCE DESIGN

BUILDING INTELLIGENCE COMMUNITIES

The need for change

The US 9/11 investigations identified four principal failures in the intelligence community that should point the way to where future reform is needed: in imagination, in policy, in capabilities and in management. In my view these developmental needs are linked to two fundamental changes affecting the environment in which the intelligence community has to adapt to survive: the adoption by governments in the face of terrorism and other risks of a modern citizen-centred approach to national security strategy, and the new ways of working that are sweeping through the 'knowledge industries'. These changes apply in my view as much to the US intelligence and security community as to that of the UK. What is more, there is a danger that trying to rectify separately each of the perceived failings of the past within the present organizational culture will make matters worse, not better. What is needed is first to recognize the impact of changes in the nature of the task (as it spans domestic and overseas theatres) and in the technological possibilities available (and their ethical implications); then to understand how the concept of an intelligence community arose and how far on both sides of the Atlantic it is now a working reality between the intelligence agencies rather than a politically convenient label on an empty box; then to examine how the boundaries of that community might in future be extended, or at least made selectively porous, to other partners in national security and opened outwards to be able to access the innovation, knowledge and experience needed in modern conditions. It will be important in the process to identify the real barriers to reform, the conditions that led to great past successes and why some past attempts may have faltered.

The requirements of national security strategy

In chapter 1, I examined modern national security strategies and concluded that the shift to a citizen-centric view meant being firm in applying risk management to the design of security policies. The nature of the threats and hazards we will face means that governments will have to be prepared to take anticipatory action, sometimes intervening to prevent the threat arising, sometimes investing in resilience to mitigate its effect should it occur, as seen in chapter 3. So governments seeking to drive security measures and guide security policy will have to look increasingly to their intelligence communities, as we saw in chapter 2, for forewarning of what might be to come.

The close interactions between collector and analyst, and between analyst and user, have become a feature of the modern intelligence cycle. I argued in chapter 5 that to respond to the threats of terrorism, proliferation and serious crime it is better to think in terms of how access is gained, under appropriate safeguards, to the widest range of secret, open and personal data sources. I also argued in chapter 6 for a fresh look at the validation, analysis and assessment processes of intelligence drawn from all these sources in terms of how well they elucidate meaning. The key idea here is the application of modern scientific method in order to test hypotheses and arrive at the best explanation of what is going on consistent with the available facts. Without explanation of what lies behind the information that has been accessed, intelligence judgments risk being biased by implicit, untested assumptions and predictions risk becoming over-reliant on inductive thinking. I sounded a note of caution, however, that a suitable psychic distance should be preserved between analysts arriving at strategic intelligence judgments and their policy customers. Chapter 7 then examined the related problem for governments of the residual risk left by even the most confident of intelligence predictions, and how the chances of being surprised by unexpected turns of events can be reduced through strategic warning, although they cannot be eliminated.

We have seen that governments are going to become even more reliant on the strategic warning, operational alerting and tactical actions of their intelligence communities. Failure of intelligence, as we saw in chapter 8, is very expensive, potentially in lives as well as cost. Intelligence agencies have therefore to become high-reliability organizations working in high-risk environments. As has happened in other organizations subject to the same pressures, authority will have to be delegated more than in the past, stovepiped structures dismantled, and groups drawn from across the community empowered to agree together on future mission planning and new initiatives. The tradition in that world of hierarchical direction, focused on the top of each agency, will have to adjust. The wisdom and experience of those who are close to the front line will have to count as much as position in the headquarters hierarchy. Such developments have become the norm in modern service-based organizations with the helpful side-effect of increasing a strong sense of participation and thus co-ownership in the enterprise.

There are already controversial ethical and political issues arising from the use of secret intelligence for public security, as we saw in chapter 10. The intelligence and security agencies are going to need greater public understanding of what their work involves in terms of access to information and the preservation of essential secrecy about intelligence sources and methods. On the other hand, the intelligence community needs to gain public acceptance of a code of conduct governing such work, including having independent oversight and right of investigation and redress if it is suspected that government powers have been abused. We return to this in the final chapter of this book.

The requirements of being a modern 'knowledge industry'

In chapter 5 we saw the way that successive waves of technology, from radio to the second quantum revolution, have shaped the kind of intelligence that could be made available to military commanders and to support decision-makers. The intelligence community found itself at the end of the Cold War with essentially an industrial production model of intelligence in which linear processes governed both collection and analysis. We can see how there has been since then an acceleration in technological innovation, speeding up the time taken to develop cutting edge science into useful applications. As we saw, the leading edge is now in the civil not the government sector. Commercial information technology in mobile communications, data storage and the internet is now posing a major challenge to intelligence organizations.

Government departments too are struggling to keep up with developments such as web-based services and social networking (as are some traditional companies), given their hierarchical structures and ways of decision-taking that are now hopelessly slow. The Apple iPhone introduced in the UK in 2008 had only a year later over 65,000 separate applications available (for which a new word has already entered the lexicon, an app) built and marketed by independent developers using the open systems aspects of the Apple technology. Cloud computing already means that any start-up company in the knowledge business can buy instant access to massive computing capability and experienced personnel without the need for prior investment in fixed or human capital. Large government departments, with their risk-aversion and bureaucratic procedures, unless they change further may become the dinosaurs of the age. Centralized policy-making has not kept pace with the need to connect with the evidence and experience that is potentially accessible from front-line professionals and those they work with.[1] There is an eerie resonance with the saying of Robert Fludd, the Elizabethan astrologer and magus, that a wheel is much more easily turned from its circumference than from its hub.[2]

Huge quantities of information are now capable of being accessed for intelligence purposes, and from which sense and meaning can now be derived using new data mining and management tools. The intelligence and security agencies will no longer be characterized as institutions that manage stocks of information, as in MI5's archive of files or the accumulated technical intelligence of defence intelligence about foreign weapons systems, and will see themselves as managers of fused flows of relevant information to users where timeliness is essential. Pre-programmed data mining engines can now roam over the relevant data sets and the open internet picking up the references relevant to the search inquiry and reassembling the material in a format of choice. To the user it may look like accessing a massive database; in fact it is information machine accessed and assembled when needed, digested and collated to help the analyst. There will need to be more transparency of analytical work to staff in many different parts of the organization so that they can contribute to the task where they have relevant experience or expertise even if no longer working directly on the subject, thus giving a greater chance that weak signals will be picked up and interpreted correctly.

There are operational implications too. 'Citizen reporters' provide real-time pictures from disasters and battlefields faster than any official channel can convey information. It is the world of Skype, Wikipedia, Twitter, Facebook and YouTube, and their successors that are already being taken up by an increasingly IT-literate generation. Intelligence agencies are not exempt from these pressures. The best of them recognize the need for radical change, but can find it hard to cut through security restrictions and the bureaucratic protections that are designed to safeguard public money and ensure due consultation and coordination across the organization and the community. The point here is not that adequate security safeguards and managerial oversight are not needed—they may be needed more than ever in order to sustain public confidence—but attempting to provide them with traditional processes is bound to slow things down. Traditional organizations will always be significantly slower than organizations where experience and knowledge count for more than position in the hierarchy and ones that have web-enabled transparency to allow flexible, 'liquid' ways of drawing in expertise from across the organization. Here the UK intelligence community may be potentially better placed than much of government, given its 'can-do' culture and its operational nimbleness in taking advantage of opportunities with a very short distance between front line and those developing new capability. The UK community also has a history from its wartime experience, as we have seen in chapter 2, of using new ideas and talent from outside to great effect, traits needed more than ever today. On the other hand, the intelligence community is going to be held back in emulating those triumphs by the culture of secrecy, unless ways are found of reconciling the necessary concealment of sources and methods with the responsibility to share results with all those involved in supporting national security strategy.

Four broad conclusions emerge from all this for the future development of the intelligence community. First, that intelligence for action is now the dominant model, fusing different sources to provide timely decision support, in close to real time, whether for military commanders, police officers or government negotiators. In that model, neat organizational and cultural distinctions between users, analysts and collectors become blurred, and rightly. Secondly, that there is an important place still for strategic analysis that provides explanation of what of importance is happening in the world, and leans forward to provide predictive judgments, but such work needs to follow a different pattern, preserving a psychic distance between analyst and policy-maker. Thirdly, an open horizon-scanning process is needed to generate strategic warning of significant international developments and major shifts in thinking or technology, both to sensitize the intelligence community to look for leading indicators of such developments and to prompt government into thinking about anticipatory R&D or investment in aspects of resilience against such outcomes. Fourthly, the recognition that the intelligence community is a knowledge industry, and that in the outside world such activity is being transformed rapidly by such phenomena as new generation search engines, social networking, cloud computing, high-speed processing and cheap data storage.

We turn now to look at what these four conclusions might mean for the development of the intelligence community and its relationship with the outside world, in order to provide the desired improvements in imagination, in policy, in capabilities and in management. In the final chapter we can then complete the picture by sketching in the relationship needed between the intelligence community, government and public so that national security can be maintained.

Openings and barriers to change

My contact with the world of secret intelligence has included seven years as a member of the UK's Joint Intelligence Committee as a senior defence policy-maker, as head of an intelligence agency (GCHQ) and as Intelligence and Security Coordinator. That experience of policy/intelligence interactions has left me with the impression that the UK has an advantage over the US through being able to bring senior policy-makers and intelligence professionals together in the Joint Intelligence Committee to arrive at agreed strategic judgments. I suspect that this arrangement is only possible because the UK policy-makers concerned are senior civil servants and diplomats who are politically impartial, and not therefore as subject to the pressures of loyalty to the government line as political appointees, however experienced, are liable to feel. The controversy over the presentation of the intelligence assessment in the run-up to the campaign in Iraq tested the impartiality of the UK system severely, and certainly damaged its public credibility. The subsequent Butler Inquiry did however conclude that the JIC assessment system itself is fundamentally sound and is capable of producing excellent intelligence judgments, although in the case of Iraqi

WMD the presentation of the judgments in the public dossier went to (although not beyond) the outer limits of the intelligence available.

The intelligence community has now to support a security effort, at home and overseas, in which there are greater demands to push intelligence judgments further out laterally into other organizations and deeper down to those on the front line. This is an information technology driven culture, where transparency within circles of trust becomes the norm, and where the organization is actively seeking access to the outer world. In the case of secret intelligence, however, the work has very unusual and stressful characteristics deriving from its very nature where success, and the sources and methods by which it is acquired, must be concealed from outside gaze. In a working environment where reticence if not outright concealment is second nature, lifetime vows of secrecy accentuate a sense in the security and intelligence world of being a band apart. Inevitably there will be a risk that new ideas are not picked up quickly enough, and there will be a natural preference for new developments to be managed from the inside using people already within the circle of secrecy. There are signs that the agencies are reaching out more to the academic community and are bringing in specialist consultancy support to help with new technology. But the changes in attitude have to permeate the whole organization.

The intelligence community has in the past taken its overall emotional hue from the HUMINT side of the business. Even analysts are inducted in ways that reinforce this culture of secret duty. In that world, levels of trust in those inside the charmed circle have to be high—and expectations in that respect of those outside, whether politicians, bureaucrats or police officers, can be correspondingly low. Those on the inside who do not respect what would be termed the ethos of the profession are in for a hard time. This is a psychodynamic phenomenon we would expect to see in the intelligence officer, as we do in other professions with comparable requirements for codes of mutual trust, from the armed services to the fire or medical services. Such groups erect social defences and tend to be resistant to any change that is perceived (however wrongly) to risk diluting the essence of the shared ethos essential for psychic survival in such an environment. Those leading change are going to need strong support to carry the day.

As with other high-risk professions, the nature of the intelligence subject matter can also create high levels of stress, especially due to the internal dissonance between objectives in tension, such as the need to retain a sense of self-regard and personal morality whilst behaving in a task-driven way to get results, for example in manipulating the motivations of a potential informer. For some the tension becomes too great and if the expectations the organization has of conduct in such situations have not been sufficiently internalized by the individual then the next step may well be newspaper headlines. Communities and organizations, as well as individuals, can exhibit collective stress, and when they do their rational principal-agent economic relations become swamped by the dynamics of emotions and feelings. That tension will evidently be greater in years to come if there is sustained downward pressure on resources and cost-cutting is elevated above true national value for money.

In such an environment the rationale for change has to be compelling, be seen to be practical and to be achievable at a stretch—and the changes must also be seen to be consistent with the ethos and mission of the organization. For both US and UK intelligence communities that means showing how the adaptations necessary to the future tasks and technology are not breaks with past traditions, but on the contrary just the next stage in a journey that has produced results in the past and will do so in the future. In that narrative the concept of a national 'intelligence community', adding to but not replacing the separate identities of the collection and assessment agencies, should play a central part. An important enabler will be the rise of a generation of young officers, comfortable with the technology and schooled in the new national security world. It is all the more important that the leadership of the intelligence community recognizes that this is where future success will come from and drives hard for more joint training and development of officers from across the community. Joint staff training in the armed services has proved its worth on both sides of the Atlantic as preparation for command, and in the UK has been brought together in a single Defence Academy, prompting the question of when we will see a UK Intelligence Academy.

The state of development of national intelligence communities

From the outset of the modern US intelligence effort, we can see the recognition that there had to be a sense of community amongst all those working closely with secret intelligence. If there were to be no more Pearl Harbors, which was the overriding priority of Presidents Truman and Eisenhower, then the United States had to equip itself in the post-war era with what their advisers had experienced during the war as the British model, not least in joint all-source intelligence assessment and in joint operational work (such as the 'double-cross' system behind the major intelligence and deception effort for the Normandy landings for which Eisenhower had been Supreme Allied Commander). Avoiding unwelcome surprises was the main justification for the creation at that time of the post of Director of Central Intelligence (DCI) as both principal adviser to the President for intelligence matters related to the national security and head of the new Central Intelligence Agency (CIA). That innovation paralleled the creation of a unified US military command system and a single Department of Defense.

The term 'intelligence community' seems to have made its earliest documented appearance[3] in the minutes of a 1952 meeting of the US Intelligence Advisory Committee and was then picked up in amendments to the 1947 National Security Act. The DCI became by law the head of the United States intelligence community (a position now passed to the DNI). Unsurprisingly, successive DCIs focused during the Cold War on the (substantial) task of running the CIA and had only limited impact on the development of the wider community. The DCI had been given direct control over the CIA and its budget but not over the other components of intelligence capability (such as NSA and the subsequent satellite programmes) that were funded by the Pentagon.

Yet despite the legislative mandating of the single intelligence community concept we know that the reality of US inter-agency cooperation was very different. The recently released (although redacted) multi–volume NSA history of Cold War SIGINT[4] reveals the intense rivalry in the 1950s between NSA and CIA (which ran its own covert SIGINT programmes) and later with the National Reconnaissance Office over control of the first SIGINT satellites and with the Pentagon over single-service SIGINT collection programmes. One example is the allegation that the then Director of the National Security Agency, General Ralph Canine, was deliberately kept in the dark by CIA of their plans to dig the Berlin tunnel (1954–6) to tap into landline communications of the Soviet army headquarters in the Soviet-occupied zone of Berlin. It is even alleged that he was left to find out about the operation from the *New York Times* after the tunnel was discovered in April 1956. The CIA on the other hand enlisted the support of the British

SIS in the covert digging and the actual cable taps—and SIS lacking the technical capabilities had no reservations about working with NSA's UK sister organization, GCHQ, whose Director would certainly have known of the operation![5] Despite careful attention from senior management in the CIA and NSA over the years, problems have continued in the US HUMINT/SIGINT relationship to this day, and were for example specifically highlighted by the CIA Inspector-General[6] in relation to counter-terrorism cooperation before 9/11. The collection components of the US intelligence community were highly successful in their own terms, but each wanted to be self-sufficient. As far as a sense of community was concerned, the agencies were working in a loveless relationship from the outset,[7] and that indeed may explain why the legislators knew that it would be necessary to spell the matter out in the National Security Act. Subsequent Presidents such as Richard Nixon may have wanted stronger central intelligence leadership, but were yet unwilling (or congressionally unable) to grant the necessary authority over budgets because of DoD resistance.

There was in the UK on the other hand a natural reluctance after the war to centralize, in part having seen the military disasters that had befallen Germany with its centralized OKW high command.[8] In the UK, the separate service departments, each with their own Secretary of State in the Cabinet, survived well into the post-war period, with only the addition of a small coordinating Ministry of Defence to take the place of the central machinery that Churchill had used with the Chiefs of Staff to run the war effort. In the aftermath of the 1956 Suez debacle, there was a shake-up of defence under Duncan Sandys with the aim[9] 'to provide well-equipped forces sufficient to carry out these duties, while making no greater demands than are absolutely necessary upon manpower, money and other national resources…. Experience has shown that the rapid progress of scientific development and fluctuations in the international situation make it difficult to foresee future military requirements with any certainty, and that consequently a good deal of flexibility must be maintained. Nevertheless, an attempt must be made to establish a broad framework within which long-term planning can proceed.' This then provided the spur for transferring responsibility for the JIC that had developed during the war as a sub-committee of the Chiefs of Staff Committee to the Cabinet Office with the JIC being given the status of a Cabinet Committee. In terms of unified defence organization, it was not until 1963 that two of

Churchill's chief wartime military advisers, Lt.-Gen. Sir Ian Jacob and General Lord 'Pug' Ismay, reported on central defence organization. Finally in 1964 the Mountbatten–Thorneycroft reforms led to a single MOD being created with a joint defence intelligence staff, bringing the single-service directors of intelligence together.

Close operational cooperation between the UK intelligence agencies continued drawing directly on the successes of the Second World War, as Professor Christopher Andrew's authorized history[10] of MI5 reveals. But there was only a very light coordination from the centre. In the UK therefore the preferred term was Central Intelligence Machinery, the title of the first published official Cabinet Office overview in 1993 of British intelligence organization. That title reflected acceptance of the need for a machinery of coordination but implicit in the term was emphasis on the operational independence of the intelligence agencies that was recognized in law when it came to the 1994 legislation. The term 'intelligence community' first seems to have been used publicly in the UK only in 2006 to describe the key responsibility to the Prime Minister of my successor as Permanent Secretary in the Cabinet Office for ensuring that 'the intelligence community has a clear strategy and system for prioritizing collection and analytical effort and that the resources provided for the intelligence agencies are used appropriately and as cost-effectively as possible'.

There is therefore a paradox in comparing the US and UK experience. In the US public acknowledgment of the concept of an 'intelligence community' was enshrined in law from the earliest days, but the reality was of demarcation disputes and budget arguments. In the UK the use of the intelligence community term was resisted until very recently, whilst the reality was the opposite. The experience in the US may have been of constant turf wars between the components of the intelligence community; in the UK, in part because of self-confidence in their individual status, there were no qualms about mounting joint or mutually supporting operations: an example perhaps of the thought behind poet Robert Frost's line: 'Good fences make good neighbours'.

In part, too, the British experience of community cooperation throughout the Cold War, and afterwards, stemmed from the fact that the leadership of the UK agencies met weekly in the JIC. It was natural in that forum to recognize that impressive results, and thus resources, often came from combining the different intelligence trades and that the impetus to such cooperation would quickly turn to competition if the contribution of each partner in a line of reporting was not somehow evident to the senior customers. The leaders of the agencies still have periodic away-days with the Chiefs of Staff and with diplomats and Whitehall policy-makers to review the state of intelligence capabilities on the issues of the day, and to illustrate for them how various forms of human and technical intelligence come together in numerous operations of great ingenuity and value. This easy ability of the UK intelligence agencies to work together to combine the tradecraft of HUMINT and SIGINT or to run cases that span domestic and overseas operations, for example, was always the envy of the US seniors, and in a complex way has been part of the continuing glue that kept the transatlantic intelligence relationship together.

The issue of trust: circles of cooperation

Some of the main lines of development in the intelligence world are clear, and we can see efforts being made by many nations to adapt their agencies and security forces to confront international terrorism and crime. There is evidently no 'right' organizational model for intelligence and law enforcement that will fit all nations with their different traditions and legal systems. But there may be general characteristics emerging that are common and that we might expect to find in a well-regulated and effective security and intelligence community. At their heart are concentric circles of trust.

In an inner protected circle we would expect to find, if things are working well, a community of trust between the intelligence and security agencies, whether set up to deal with internal security or to provide external human intelligence and SIGINT services. Whatever national organizational geometry, there would be no legal or cultural barriers to cooperation in this circle and the agencies would work together to make the best collective use of their capabilities. To borrow a phrase from Senator Pat Roberts, Chair of the US Senate Intelligence Committee, the watchword would be intelligence sharing rather than compartmented intelligence access (as the old saying has it, the only use for watertight compartments is when the ship is sinking). There would be the trust necessary to make joint operations commonplace, spanning where necessary domestic and overseas; and you would see young officers training together, and taking part in cross-postings, really understanding what their colleagues from other disciplines might be able to bring to the party.

Backed by appropriate legislation, and under appropriate safeguards as discussed in chapter 10, the public would trust the intelligence community within that inner circle to use the most modern and effective techniques for acquiring and analysing the mass of communication, travel, border and other data needed to deal with terrorism and organized crime. There would be effective arrangement for parliamentary and judicial oversight, whose form would obviously depend upon national constitutions, but sufficient to provide public confidence that the use of these intrusive powers and the ability to share such information with overseas partners was properly regulated and proportionate and there were effective mechanisms for redress if abuse of power was suspected.

Widening to the next circle, we would see that secret intelligence community working hand in glove with the relevant police services, through fusion centres or co-location of officers at a local level drawing on the latter's knowledge of the communities they serve. We would find secure arrangements for sharing operational detail within a circle of trust between those selected and vetted to work with the intelligence authorities on these sensitive operations. It would be for the police to use their independent authority to enforce the law in terrorist and serious crime cases, drawing on their close relationship with the community they serve, but targeted carefully by the secret work of the intelligence community using their most advanced methods. In this way the power of modern intelligence is harnessed for public protection, but without raising again in Europe the spectre of secret policemen with their own legal authorities and the misuse of state power to collect personal information

And in a third circle of trust, the intelligence and police communities would participate in government processes and structures that enable them to share information and cooperate closely with the key staffs in military commands and Defence Ministry, in the Foreign Ministry, and in Home Office/Interior, Transport, Health, Environment and all those civil departments of government engaged in 'homeland security' to provide the support for policy-making and overseas operations and assistance programmes, and to guide investment in improving national resilience. At the outer limits of this circle we would see links to those in local government and local agencies working on issues such as counter-radicalization, crime and building community resilience.

Finally, we would find that these circles had strong connections running outside government, reaching out to the private sector that now owns or manages most of the critical national infrastructure that keeps modern life going and that provides much of the technological edge that can keep the security authorities one step ahead of the adversary. Strategic assessments can be shared to guide the formation of collective security strategy and international agreements, and to guide research and development through industry arrangements such as the UK resilience and security suppliers' network, RISC. Timely operational warnings and terrorist assessments can be shared for public protection through the JTAC model, and not least the tactical pursuit of terrorist networks improved through bilateral relationships between the secret intelligence services of like-minded nations working together on specific operations and campaigns. These circles of trust should form the secure national base on which sound international arrangements can be developed.

The case for stronger leadership, not just coordination of the community

In the US after the 9/11 Congress called the stewardship of the DCI into question, not just in terms of agency performance but also in relation to the inherent limitations of his role in relation to the leadership of the community. The concept of having an overall Director of National Intelligence (DNI) was revived in the ensuing congressional and public debate. Eventually, as directed under the Intelligence Reform and Terrorism Prevention Act of 2004 (IRTPA), the office of the DNI was established specifically 'to manage the Intelligence Community' although Congress in the end held back from giving the DNI the full authority to match the job specification.[11] The office of the DNI now describes itself as 'a unified enterprise of innovative intelligence professionals whose common purpose is defending American lives and interests, and advancing American values', drawing strength from US democratic institutions, diversity, and intellectual and technological prowess. The DNI himself serves as the head of the Intelligence Community (IC) and is charged with the specific responsibility of leading the Intelligence Community and transforming it into a unified, collaborative and coordinated enterprise. He is the principal adviser to the President and the National Security Council for intelligence matters related to national security, as well as coordinating requirements and priorities for collection, analysis, production and dissemination of national intelligence. Extensive machinery has been established to connect the components of the community together and this should provide the DNI with the opportunity to improve the coordination of community management. Under the present budgetary construct, however, it will be hard pounding all the way.

In the UK, the Joint Intelligence Committee had emerged from the war as the governing body of the loose coalition of UK intelligence capabilities, as well as the strategic assessment authority. The JIC was for example tasked with planning the post-war future, including new relationships with the wartime allies. In the late 1960s, the JIC's capacity to manage community issues was strengthened through the appointment of a senior coordinator (Sir Dick White was the first holder of the post, having exceptionally been both Director-General of the Security Service and Chief of SIS, followed by Sir Leonard ('Joe') Hooper, an ex–Director of GCHQ), advising in particular how best to organize intelligence as the security situation in Northern Ireland deteriorated in the 1970s. The post of coordinator was subsequently downgraded in later years but revived in 2002 with my appointment as Security and Intelligence Coordinator, providing an essential capability to tackle difficult cross-organizational intelligence issues, including requirements and priorities for the limited investment expenditure available.

Further steps were taken[12] in 2009 to strengthen the capacity of the central Cabinet Office staff to manage major policy issues affecting the intelligence community. These issues include future legislation, technological advances, law and ethics, including legal casework, international information sharing, and the impact of parliamentary and wider public scrutiny of the work of the intelligence agencies. Reflecting on these latest UK arrangements, I observe that a major change has thereby been made in the responsibilities of the JIC, reducing its historic role in collective oversight of the intelligence community and transferring this to a Director-General Secretariat post in the Cabinet Office. The JIC, under its Permanent Secretary-level chair, is therefore in future confined to its intelligence assessment and warning role. There is once again no longer a Permanent Secretary-level Coordinator, and the crucial budgetary responsibility for the secret agencies has reverted to the Cabinet Secretary. Although the UK had therefore for a brief period (in a very rough parallel with the US DNI) a Coordinator of national intelligence responsible both for the overall health of the community and the quality of its assessed product, it has now launched out in a new direction.

The additional staff effort being made available to strenghen central direction on intelligence policy issues must be welcomed. The absence of visible leadership of the community and of downplaying the historic collective authority of the JIC may however prove a misstep. The change narrative for the UK intelligence community now has to cover the response to the emerging demands of twenty-first century national security strategy, including the expected persistence of the serious threat from international terrorism, the need to have the pre-emptive intelligence to anticipate future threats with both overt and covert capabilities, the recognition of the blurring of old distinctions between the need to know about the domestic as against the external space, new technological opportunities, and the ending of any distinction between tactical and strategic intelligence collection. All these factors seem to tilt the balance of advantage towards final acceptance of the need to have more visible and stronger central community leadership and the collective means through the JIC to exercise it.

Further pressures for fundamental intelligence reform

As we have seen, the surprise of the 9/11 attacks revived the original Pearl Harbor arguments for stronger central intelligence direction, swiftly followed by the US inquiries into intelligence failures over Iraqi WMD with recommendations pointing in the direction of the intelligence community having a single visible head with sufficient seniority and authority to be able to set the strategic direction and priorities and ensure that resources are aligned accordingly. The appointment of the US DNI fits that logic as a sensible next step.

The rationale for my own appointment in 2002 as a Permanent Secretary in the Cabinet Office, but adding security to intelligence coordination duties, had much more to do with the need to put more effort into the UK's overall policy response to homeland security and resilience, and the impossibility of the Cabinet Secretary having sufficient time to deal with the subject properly, than any UK government desire to have a stronger central intelligence centre per se. But the beneficial effect of up-gunning the intelligence coordinating function again, and giving the Coordinator the important Accounting Officer responsibility direct to parliament for the budget for the three secret agencies, was to push the development of the UK intelligence community in the context of the new UK counter-terrorism strategy, to obtain significant increases in intelligence funding, and to facilitate community-wide changes such as the creation of the Joint Terrorism Analysis Centre (JTAC). This was later noted approvingly in the Butler Report of the Committee of Inquiry into intelligence on weapons of mass destruction following the intelligence failures over Iraq. Butler did identify weakness in one aspect of community performance regarding the development of analytical capability. The appointment of a Professional Head of the Intelligence Community followed, together with expanding the use of the UK academic intelligence studies community[13] to train young analysts from across the community precisely to foster the growth of a virtual analytic community crossing the boundaries of the agencies, MOD, Cabinet Office and Foreign Office.

We might ask whether the intelligence community with those changes is now in a final form. Purpose should come before function, no organizational arrangements are forever, and as the nature of the task changes, for example as thinking about national security strategy evolves, so most probably should organizational form. In the case of a national intelligence effort, it has to be recognized that organization is never going to be simple since, as Professor R. V. Jones remarked many years ago, input is by source and output is by subject.[14] In the case of intelligence, the output may be all source intelligence but the inputs include people of very different skills and character for the different branches of intelligence: technical in the case of signals intelligence, rule-based team players for domestic intelligence, and entrepreneurial soloists for foreign human intelligence, and so on. So somewhere there has to be a universal joint. Nations have differed in where it is located. Some have almost all of their intelligence activities under the wing of national defence, some split with diplomatic or interior ministries, or with national police services. But below the most senior leadership levels the basic organizational structures based on classic type of source remain similar. Collection of intelligence is a highly specialized set of public service activities that involves maintaining functional organizations able to recruit, train and motivate very different and unique kinds of people, whilst being able at the same time to ensure the output of balanced sets of capabilities and sufficient analytical effort to satisfy at the one extreme the intelligence needs of the deployed Commander and at the other the State Department area desk officer in Foggy Bottom. The case for continuing to specialize by source is a strong one.

Defence provides some precedents for tackling complex organizational problems with these characteristics of output form and input function. Both the United States (notably in 1947 and 1949, and then in 1958 and 1985) and the UK (in 1946, 1957, 1964 and 1982) have had to redesign and then progressively refine their central organization for defence to tackle the dilemma of reconciling the existence of separate armed services, each adapted to their sea, littoral, land or air environment, with the joint nature of planning and investment in, and ultimately the generation of, military power. The solution was to have unity of political responsibility for defence, supported by joint commands and joint staffs, to pull together the work of the armed services and manage their rivalries whilst accepting their continued existence as major national institutions.

At one level the parallel with the intelligence world is illuminating. The advantages of retaining the separate ethos and traditions of each service/agency could be made compatible with stronger mechanisms for joint planning and the combination of effort into joint operations and joint analysis when the need arises. There would no doubt be efficiency savings to be gained from sharing back office services, as well as new operational opportunities to be promoted, in having a much more integrated organization for planning intelligence access, although generally speaking the larger the organization the slower will be its responses to changes in its environment. There is however at least one important difference from the defence analogy.

The UK (and US) defence reforms unified political responsibility for the armed forces under a single Cabinet member, the Defence (Defense) Secretary. Can we see that happening one day for the intelligence community, for example under a single minister for National Security and Intelligence sitting in the Cabinet? When the post of Secretary of State for Defence was created on 1 April 1964, the single-service Secretaries of State (First Lord of the Admiralty, Secretary of State for War and Secretary of State for Air) were downgraded to Minister of State and lost their seats in the Cabinet. It is hard to see in the UK how a Minister of National Security and Intelligence, responsible for example for authorizing both domestic and overseas intelligence operations, could coexist comfortably as an equal in Cabinet with the Home Secretary, Foreign Secretary and Defence Secretary given the significant equities that each of them have in the security and intelligence world. In addition to these political considerations, my hunch too is that the British political class would not welcome the extraordinary influence that would inevitably be exercised by the head of a combined single British intelligence agency (covering domestic and overseas HUMINT as well as SIGINT). Future further development in the British community is likely to be more easily pursued by stronger leadership within the framework of the present agency construct rather than by merging two or more of the existing agencies.

12

A FRESCO FOR THE FUTURE

Assembling the picture

In the first chapter of this book I expressed my belief that a modern approach to national security has to be designed from the outset to respond to the major risks as they may affect the citizen, rather than just the institutions of the state. I identified three significant and related shifts as being necessary to thinking clearly about security strategy in that way. The first shift is to an all-risks approach, covering both major man-made threats and serious natural hazards, based on the principles of risk management. The second is for governments to try to anticipate these risks, since increasingly in modern society it will be too late to wait until the enemy is at the gate or inside the city before taking action to prevent, protect and prepare. As we saw in the previous chapter, that shift places a great responsibility on those who are to provide strategic notice of emerging risks and those who have to decide whether and how to act upon such warning. The third shift is to the promotion of a more resilient society, placing new demands on government to work with communities and with industry and commerce. Clearly, these would be important elements in a twenty-first century version of Lorenzetti's fresco.

One defining characteristic of good government is the way that in practice it goes about generating public security and spreading a sense of confidence and normality. Some of the ways of achieving this end should be familiar and include having the necessary intelligence and understanding to steer a course between competing dangers; seeing the rule of law and the independence of justice as essential to civil harmony; and retaining a strong sense of values that infuses all the activities of government, covert as well as open. A distinguishing feature in that respect lies in the public being given confidence in the government's ability to manage the risks. Debate on these topics in the UK in recent years has however tended to fragment. There is a danger of the public not seeing the whole picture and ending up debating individual issues such as privacy in isolation from the security context, and that increases the risk that individual issues become footballs in party political games.

On the other hand, we can begin also to identify features that are likely to be associated with bad government, including excessive secrecy, and lack of promotion of civic harmony allowing internal conflicts to develop, justice being subordinated to security, insecurity leading to failure to invest, and lack of preparation to protect the public with vulnerabilities in critical infrastructure left unattended. A common feature of many of the items on such a list is that they are liable to arise from government not having reacted early enough through not having—or not paying sufficient heed to—the necessary strategic notice of trouble brewing.

Harnessing all the talent

At times of great national danger, daring and innovation are forced upon government, along with an influx of fresh talent drafted in, drawn from the best brains of the universities, the law or commerce. In between times, the temptation to stick to routine is evident. Long conflicts, such as that against jihadist terrorism, demand just as much fresh thinking as sudden struggles for national survival. One aspect of innovation is the bringing together of talent from different services and backgrounds to collaborate to develop new ways of combating the adversary. We have seen this in the joint staff training provided to the armed services by the Defence Academy, and the pay-off in terms of joint capability deployable under a Permanent Joint Headquarters. The joint concept is now extended in UK military doctrine to the 'comprehensive approach' to overseas interventions bringing to bear all the instruments of influence, civil as well as military.

As with the armed services, there is a strong case for each intelligence service recruiting and growing its own experienced cadre of officers. But once the sapling is rooted, then training should start to span the wider intelligence and security community. As noted in the previous chapter, the UK has no joint intelligence staff college. Similarly, promotion to the highest ranks in the armed services is now dependent on having had the right kind of joint command or staff experience. That is not yet the case in the intelligence world, although some individual cross-posting is now taking place between the agencies. Service in the Joint Terrorism Analysis Centre will, we must hope, train for the future more young officers naturally attuned to the work of their sister services.

The role of the private sector in supporting intelligence and security activity also needs careful examination in the light of recent experience. In the provision of physical security the use of private sector (usually ex–military) personnel is now commonplace in areas of threat overseas, especially relieving pressure on regular forces in guarding civil personnel or static installations. It is hard to see how operations could be conducted without them. As we have seen in Iraq, great care is needed, however, to establish the 'rules of engagement' by which such para-military operations are run and how they relate to the chain of command and to the flow of intelligence for force protection.

There are now well-established private sector companies that can pull together a current affairs assessment; and many government departments, intelligence agencies and assessment centres themselves subscribe to such digests. It is easier to pay someone else to do the collation and searching of the open sources. I once sat in on the morning briefing of a private sector 'intelligence' company in the city of London, with analysts (of many different nationalities and speaking many languages) sharing their latest developments both in terms of geographical regional and functional topics. Unlike such a briefing inside an intelligence agency, the focus was less on the information which each area had uncovered and more on the substance of the development itself and what that might mean immediately for their commercial clients—leading directly to alerting telephone calls or emails. There are however tasks, particularly involving domestic surveillance, that for public trust need to be undertaken by those motivated by public sector values not shareholder interest. Where the powers of the state to coerce or to intrude upon personal privacy are concerned, the guiding principle should be that these are always in the hands of those bound by public service values, even if supported by commercial contractors conducting specialist functions such as forensic science and managing complex ICT systems.

Learning from history

A lesson from most conflicts is that after the effort is over, in the words of Matthew Arnold:[1] 'uphung the spear, unbent the bow'. People forget what had to be done to survive and 'it must never happen again' elides into 'it can never happen again'. But it can and it does. Security and intelligence capabilities can take a long time to build up, but they are very quickly run down, as was the case when the so-called 'peace dividend' was taken in reductions in defence and intelligence spending at the end of the Cold War. In defence, the temptation is often to criticize previous generations for clinging to outmoded concepts and ways of warfare and then to argue for adapting to the circumstances of the last conflict, forgetting that history shows how seldom it repeats itself even as tragedy. In intelligence, as in defence, there is a good case for maintaining widespread coverage, at least at a minimal level, so as to retain a footprint, whether in maintaining HUMINT contacts or in the technical area continuing to work on the communications of lower priority targets—which can suddenly surge in importance, as history shows.

A lesson from George Tenet's time as US DCI, as he describes it in his memoirs, is the extreme difficulty in national crisis to be both the detached, objective adviser on what the intelligence says (and, as importantly, does not say) and to be a key player in the President's decision-making policy circle. It is difficult to be a non-partisan player in the highly political Washington system—another lesson for the UK as it struggles and so far fails to find a bipartisan consensus on counterterrorism and wider security strategy. After Tenet's resignation in July 2004, the US introduced the post of National Intelligence Director with a separate Director for CIA. The UK had after 2002 taken steps towards having a single head of the intelligence community, as recounted in chapter 11, including crucially budgetary responsibility, but this has not been taken forward, no doubt due to the centrifugal force of pressure from individual agencies guarding their independence. The UK has, at the time of writing (2010), not yet taken the logical (and, according to the Butler Committee, necessary) step of focussing intelligence community leadership through the chair of the JIC for both the quality of the assessments and the health of the community, keeping that separate from the central policy role of coordinating advice to the government on what to do in response to foreign policy, defence and security challenges.

There are lessons to be learned too from the problems over Iraq WMD. The clearest account so far available of what fundamentally went wrong with the British intelligence on Iraq (as against the justification of the war itself) is still to be found in the spare prose of the UK Butler Committee of Inquiry. Both US and UK communities have admitted mistakes in the pre-war intelligence on Iraqi WMD, in particular as they affected the misleading US National Intelligence Estimate and the crucial presentation by Secretary of State Powell to the UN Security Council and the UK JIC papers of late 2002 and the 'dossier' of intelligence presented by the Prime Minister to parliament. As George Tenet has described the debacle on the US side: 'One by one, the various pillars of the speech, particularly on Iraq's biological and chemical weapons programmes, began to buckle.' This episode had its counterpart in the UK with the September 2002 dossier, where key underpinning reports were later one by one qualified or withdrawn. The fact that there have been so many pointing fingers within as well as outside the intelligence community is testimony to the rawness of the wound that the Iraq WMD episode has made in the reputation of the US and UK intelligence communities. That inquiry also criticized the informality and circumscribed character of the UK government's procedures, thus reducing the scope for collective political judgment. Tenet echoes this complaint from the US end in that there never was 'a serious consideration of the implications of a US invasion' and 'in many cases, we were not aware of what our own government was trying to do. The one thing we were certain of was that our warnings were falling on deaf ears.' For Tenet this included warnings of implications for spread of AQ-inspired jihadist terrorism, Sunni–Shia conflict and the risk of destabilizing the region. This was sofa government, US-style. Tenet writes, 'One of the great mysteries to me is exactly when the war in Iraq became inevitable.' The same question is still being asked on the British side of the Atlantic. We now know that, as Tenet concludes in his memoirs, 'The United States did not go to war in Iraq solely because of WMD. In my view, I doubt it was even the principal cause. Yet it was the public face put on it' because, in the words of Deputy Defense Secretary Paul Wolfowitz, it was 'the one issue everyone could agree on'.[2] Tony Blair much later said[3] he would have invaded Iraq even without evidence of weapons of mass destruction and would have found a way to justify the war to parliament and the public. Had the WMD intelligence been better in terms of depth of coverage and quality of analysis much embarrassment would have been saved, but this author at least doubts that the decision to intervene would have been different.

Another lesson from history is the transferability of criminal and terrorist methods and techniques. Networks facilitate learning. They do not need central hierarchies to direct them. Networks can be self-repairing and can learn faster how to adapt to different environments than top-down models. They are, in short, harder to detect and harder to unravel. So we must expect our future opponents, in whatever sphere, to have absorbed such lessons. Methods that seem to be effective, particularly in catching the attention of the global public (not the same of course as being ultimately successful in the achievement of the terrorist objectives) will be copied. Tactics evolve: terrorists can read our military doctrine and study military technology too. We have seen shaped-charge anti–vehicle bombs, road tankers used as weapons, multiple-vehicle raids first to destroy the defences and then to get through to the target, improved counter-surveillance techniques, covert internet communications and so on. These developments will not be lost on others. The lesson for the security authorities is that technological and tactical nimbleness will be needed in keeping ahead of the adversary, as Professor R. V. Jones and his colleagues did so successfully in wartime scientific intelligence.

And we should not forget the lesson that there is a fashion in shrouds. Recall that it was during the Iran/Iraq war that we saw a significant development in terrorism with the taking of Western hostages in Lebanon, and suicide bombings against the French and US peacekeeping forces in Beirut and against Israeli targets. These Shia tactics were adopted by Hezbollah, in the tradition of their greatest martyr, and then by Hamas in the second intifada. Although Sunni Islam strongly prohibits suicide, martyrdom in the course of jihad became part of the extremist AQ teaching; and as we know all too well from the suicide bombings in London, such teaching continues.

Less easy to deduce from the historical record is where the next big ideological challenge will come from. Bin Laden and Zawahiri are in a long line—over hundreds of years—of those who have promised moral salvation in the next world in return for sacrifice in this. It will not be long however before the impact of climate change, rising temperatures, droughts and failing crops, and population migrations begin seriously to have their impact. There is therefore a deep structural developmental crisis looming going much wider than just the Arab world in finding good governance capable of protecting populations. Seen in that longer-term light, the AQ programme is an evolutionary blind alley that will not satisfy those needs. The roots of the terrorist campaign against us will finally wither away only when the Muslim world comes to realize that truth.

The last French terrorism White Paper[4] included this warning

'Global Islamist-inspired terrorism … seeks to occupy the political space created by the collapse of communist revolutionary or third world ideologies. It occupies the anti–imperialist space that no one else fills any longer. By doing so it seeks to place itself in the continuity of anti–colonialist wars. In the rejectionist wars against the West and the fight against the great economic powers, we cannot exclude that it will one day seek a rapprochement with the most radical of the anti–globalization movements.'

We will need to be alert to spot and pre-empt imitation by narco-terrorists, eco-terrorists, modern-day pirates, warlords, or feral gangs fighting for turf in the mega-cities. Conflict in these conditions, war amongst the people, in Lt.-Gen. Rupert Smith's phrase, is going to keep evolving. Our investment in the armed forces and their equipment must keep ahead of, not lag behind, such developments.

National security and intelligence models

There is a great deal more to modern good government than the management of risks to public security. Yet, as recognized by Lorenzetti in his fourteenth century fresco, security is still a key to everything else. It is still appropriate to imagine the figure of securitas hovering over the peaceful countryside and prosperous city. Nor is it easy for governments to create the conditions, both nationally and internationally, to maintain strong security, not least to promote the trust amongst security partners essential for an effective intelligence effort. Let us examine this requirement in terms of the UK.

In modelling a modern security and intelligence community we can draw on the distinction already made in chapter 2 in describing how intelligence serves three levels of government: these are the classic distinctions between working at the strategic level (including what Churchill called grand strategy), at the operational level and at the tactical level, with the main distinguishing feature between the levels being the time horizon of the customers receiving the intelligence.

At the strategic level

At the strategic level, the centre of national government must be organized to provide strategic direction, mobilize resource across the whole of government, and manage the international implications of events, including any major disruptive challenges. In turn, such a national centre needs to be able to work confidently and securely with opposite numbers in other capitals. All that needs to be thought through in advance, in relation to the full range of possible hazards and threats, and not just the traditional national defence threats. There needs to be unity of purpose between the very many organizations involved. This can only come from strong political leadership, with the Prime Minister visibly centrally engaged, including by chairing the key Cabinet National Security Committee that brings the most senior ministers concerned together with their professional advisers. Exercising detailed accountability to parliament and managing public communications needs much of the time of a very senior Cabinet minister, in the UK the Home Secretary, supported by an official team drawn from across government. The task of officials is to formulate high-level policies for ministers to protect national interests, for example from the future evolution of terrorist movements, cyber-threats, countries at risk of instability or the possibility of conflicts over global trends in energy supplies or water resources, all issues where the horizon is years or decades ahead. An all-party consensus on national security strategy should be sought, enlisting the support of cross-party bodies such as the Intelligence and Security Committee of Parliamentarians.

No single government department can cover from within its own resources the expertise on the totality of what has to be done. The deep knowledge (in transport security, in nuclear security, and in public health for example) resides in many different organizations that will have to act as 'lead departments' for different aspects of the 'campaign plans' underpinning the strategy. This reinforces the need for strong inter-departmental coordination.

For the Ministry of Defence, the direction of travel is already clear, for example in the ability to follow 'the comprehensive approach', with central mechanisms to bring overseas development, civil govern-ance, legal, diplomatic support together with the contribution that military capabilities can bring. The defence community can also con-tinue to provide specialist support for homeland security, for example in explosive ordnance disposal, and chemical, radiological and biologi-cal defence, under the doctrine of aid to the civil power and with the ability to deploy such support overseas. But in the UK at least defence thinking needs to be taken further in such areas as the security of bor-ders, sea and air space, the capacity to provide response to major dis-location, in providing the means to establish situational awareness and emergency communications connecting seamlessly with neighbouring nations that may be affected, and through providing the framework of permanent joint command in the home theatre of operations. Likewise for the Foreign Office and International Development department, there is an increased need to work across boundaries, and to give even greater attention to building multilateral arrangements to help create international consensus, as well as the basic day-to-day diplomacy and consular work in support of security strategy. I would add too that, given the nature of the international risks ahead, development agencies and financial institutions must participate fully in the formulation and execution of modern national security strategy.

For the 'homeland security' functions, we have new organizational drivers: key aspects of national security are once again major domestic preoccupations that should not just be seen as a sub-set of what would otherwise have come under police and criminal justice arrangements. Add the immigration, intelligence, law enforcement and security com-munities and you now have significant parts of government with major overseas liaison roles working for the most part out of diplomatic mis-sions but with their own direct links back to their parent agencies or departments. Overlapping global networks are thus being developed that demand new levels of coordination within the strategic level cam-paigns suggested above.

Providing strategic intelligence support at this level should be the task of the Joint Intelligence Committee, supported by expert Current Intelligence Groups, in which senior policy-makers and intelligence chiefs can arrive at joint key judgments on the evolution of issues where there are important national interests in security, defence and foreign affairs.

At the operational level

At the operational level, the main intelligence demand is for timely all-source analysis to support operational decision-taking. Examples of the issues that the policy-makers have to deal with at this level include the allocation of security resources to meet conflicting demands, what advice to give travellers overseas, or how to respond to heightened threat levels to missions and companies overseas threatened by terrorists, or the implications of high-tech weaponry reaching a country of concern, or whether a particular export of specialized steels should be permitted, or what passengers should be allowed to take onto aeroplanes. In major cases ultimately ministers will decide whether and how to act.

Many of the broad classes of risk referred to earlier are of uncertain nature and require early, targeted responses when they start to emerge. The first requirement at the operational level is therefore specific risk identification at expert level through appropriate intelligence analysis, leading to methodical risk assessments. Arrangements are then needed to share the resulting risk assessments, internationally as well as domestically, developing the networks of experts and policy-makers subject by subject. As an example, in the important area of counter-terrorism, more and more nations are creating special coordinating centres: in the UK the Joint Terrorism Analysis Centre, as described in chapter 2; in the USA the Terrorist Threat Integration Center later replaced by the National Counterterrorism Center (NCTC); in Australia the National Threat Assessment Centre; in Canada the Integrated Threat Assessment Centre; in New Zealand the Combined Threat Assessment Group (CTAG); in Spain the Centro Nacional de Coordinacion Antiterrorista; in France, L'unité de coordination de la lutte antiterroriste (UCLAT).

Not only can relevant terrorist threat assessment be passed quickly between such centres, the developing bilateral relationships between them improve the mutual understanding of the underlying thinking behind national approaches to counter-terrorism and thus support strategic alignment as well as providing greater confidence for tactical engagement. Shared assessments can in particular lead to the development of common or aligned planning assumptions on which specific measures to build resilience can be based. In many areas of risk, individual nations can be only as resilient as their neighbours. The development of the EU Situation Centre under the European Council to share national assessments is a positive recent development to that end.

At the operational level in terms of resilience what is needed for the future is a systematic mapping of critical infrastructure identifying its international dimensions (in terms both of the import and the export of causative events), and the systematic development of the cross-border, regional and global understandings, and, where appropriate, regulation to provide greater assurance and predictability to national resilience assessment.

Finally, we might note that future national security, as at key moments in the past, is going to have to draw on the national talent for innovation in applying science and technology to resilience. And that has organizational consequences for international cooperation in this area, a good example of which is the US/UK bilateral Homeland Security Contact Group,[5] which provides an umbrella for the transatlantic sharing of experience and technology in both directions.

At the tactical level

It is at the tactical level, particularly with military operations, that secret intelligence pays its way. At the tactical level, individual decisions are being made, within the operational policy framework, by the front line, whether armed forces, police, Security Service, or government department. Lines of intelligence are largely going raw to other intelligence specialists in support of operations on the ground, for example the tactical application of intelligence to guide a counter-terrorist raid, or to follow a drugs shipment, or to intercept a breach of sanctions. This is the part of the iceberg of which the public rarely is conscious. But it is much the most significant.

Bilateral tactical intelligence relationships on counter-terrorism are well developed not only with traditional intelligence allies and European partners. The wider international security dimensions are, however, likely to be less well established. International neighbours and partners need to be aware of how each other's national systems will operate in a crisis, and thus know when, how and where to plug in and connect their own emergency management arrangements down to casualty notification and handling schemes for foreign nationals caught up in domestic incidents and for own nationals affected by events overseas, in each case respecting the different religious and cultural issues that may arise. All this needs to be rehearsed and practised, including at EU/NATO level with secure and reliable communications channels.[6]

National security has therefore become a much more complicated business than during the Cold War. We can look on this as a shift from a largely producer-dominated analysis (that is, the outlook of the military and security authorities) to a client-centred one (that is, what is needed to protect the travelling public, daily life in cities, national interests overseas and so on). When working in NATO in the 1980s at the height of the debates over long-range and medium-range theatre nuclear forces, short-range battlefield systems etc. I used to remark that for the unfortunate on whom any one of these carefully distinguished classes of nuclear weapon were to fall, the effect would be felt as 'strategic'. All crises are, in the end, local for someone in their impact.

The 'big picture' implications

Governments need to take a long view, and see beyond today's terrorism; the strategic aim should continue to be the defence of normality to allow people to make the most of their lives, freely and with confidence; investment in national security needs to be rethought in terms of what everyday protection government can reasonably offer the citizen; and thus work to reduce vulnerability to the threat can go alongside work to reduce the threat itself. To that end, government should be looking for ways to increase the physical and psychological resilience of our own society to disruptive challenges; and to support a healthy sense of local community based on a shared sense of place regardless of origin.

A British approach to the nature of conflict in the future must involve the capacity to conduct multilateral military interventions overseas as part of wider international strategies to manage the risks from failing states, and deny havens to terrorists. Weapons and military doctrine must be suited to the nature of the conflicts we will face outside the conventionally defined battlefield. We must accept that such work by the armed forces takes place almost entirely under the public gaze. Pre-emptive all-source intelligence will become even more important; this requires closer cooperation between domestic and overseas services, and between intelligence and policing communities. The measures of success will be not the number of secrets collected or even the truth of the analysis it generates, but the value added, in terms of timeliness, efficiency and accuracy with which it supports national decision-making.

Modern security involves governments in taking steps that involve moral hazard. It will help if there is greater recognition that intelligence and security work can both contribute to public welfare and follow a set of ethical norms set firmly within the framework of human rights. National security requires public confidence in the intelligence community and its methods. Intelligence practices that run counter to our traditions will prove counter-productive.

We should be prepared for the surprise of the unexpected as the methods of terrorism develop and are imitated, and as new ideological challenges develop over the years ahead. If we understand the processes of modernity and the strains they inevitably induce, and the place of science and faith, then we will be better placed to craft policies that maintain a sense of proportion and historical perspective, recalling the values we seek to defend. We should remember the law of unintended consequences; and when contemplating covert actions recall the lesson that the hand that feeds today may be bitten tomorrow. In communicating with the public, a separation should be made between the outcomes that would be disliked, and that government should work to overcome, from the outcomes that would be unacceptable, and therefore are ones that the nation should be prepared to take up arms to prevent.

None of this can be done by one nation alone. Change on an international scale does however take a long time, particularly if a new international consensus has to be built. We cannot any longer rest on the words of that old Victorian, the Duke of Cambridge, whose statue stands outside the Old War Office in London: 'There is a time for everything, and the time for change is when you can no longer help it.' But in building international consensus for joint actions against the range of threats and impersonal hazards we may face we do not have the time to wait for such realization of inevitability of global interdependences to dawn unaided, nor should we wait for fresh disaster to strike before acting. So to accelerate the process we need to work with allies and partners overseas at the strategic level to show that the necessary changes fit a narrative that explains convincingly where and how hazards and threats are to be expected and international cooperation is most needed.

One clear conclusion is that in the future we shall need to put more national effort into ensuring we have the necessary intelligence collation, analysis, assessment and research capacity, broadly defined. That will mean proportionally more intelligence resources should be devoted to these functions, and that more attention should be given to careers, pay and organization in these areas than we have in the immediate past. A common thread is the issue of cognitive bias on the part of those who write and those who read the assessments. We cannot drive this out. We have to learn to accept that they are there and make them explicit.

It is now commonplace to see the top teams of public bodies and private sector corporations using risk matrices to help discharge their responsibilities of protecting their enterprises. Three types of risk deserve such treatment: those whose incidence is outside their control, but for which contingency planning is needed such as freak weather; the risks inherent in the nature of the business, such as communications failures or industrial accidents; and—especially—the self-imposed risks to business continuity involved in embarking on new ventures such as major technology and information innovation. It is the job of the analytic community to reach the best predictive judgments on these risks they can consistent with the evidence. The policy customers for their assessments must be clear about the confidence level attached to such judgments, and the adequacy of the base of intelligence on which they may rest. That will provide the policy-makers with a feel for the residual risk they are being implicitly invited to accept if they go along with the intelligence judgments. That in turn should prompt consideration of how far to try to hedge against such residual risk both in public statements, in commissioning additional work into the ways in which the risks can be mitigated, and in cuing the intelligence community to watch out for any signs that conditions are changing so as to invalidate the key judgments on which policy is being based.

Generalizing that observation, we should see a primary duty of government, local as well as central, as being to work with the other sectors of the economy and with allies and partners overseas to secure the safety of the public by mitigating all three categories of risk. Delivering this objective requires (a) taking anticipatory action to influence directly the sources of major risks facing society, and at the same time (b) to take steps to reduce society's vulnerability to the types of disruptive phenomena that we may face. Such anticipatory action will have international consequences that must be managed, and may also crucially require international understandings and arrangements to be in place in advance of a challenge arising, if the response is to be fully effective.

It is in the judicious combination of these responses, reducing the risks and reducing societal vulnerability to the risks, that we will find future 'national security'. The expression 'building the protecting state' is one that I have coined for this task.[7] The international dimensions arise naturally from this way of framing the issue, since the potential global hazards and threats that really should command our attention are not going to be susceptible to simple solutions, least of all purely domestic remedies. Tackling most of these risks involves international cooperation and action, as does reducing some of the key vulnerabilities in society (for example, in relation to cyberspace).

Towards a grand understanding

This book opened with a fresco, a vision of good government in Siena in the fourteenth century. Linked figures seem to dance across the wall: wisdom illuminates the independent exercise of justice, upon which civil harmony and civic responsibility rest, which mediated through the representatives of the citizens leads to wise government that in conditions of security can deliver the common good through armed peace, prudence, fortitude, the rule of law and the other virtues. In this book I have tried to explore these same universal themes for our times and in our terms, stressing the importance of public understanding through honest communication, and security through pre-emptive intelligence, anticipatory actions, and national and community resilience. I have tried too to highlight what is so very different today in the technology we can use to uncover our adversaries, and that they can use to harm us. Technology is accelerating the pace of events and I have drawn the conclusion that a significant premium must be placed on having timely warning of trouble, despite all the difficulties the book has explored in elucidating the real meaning of intelligence and thus explaining the world around us.

I have also tried to highlight the increasing importance of maintaining public confidence in the government's understanding of the delicate balance between liberty, freedom, privacy and security and the rule of law. As secret intelligence is increasingly seen by the public to be the hidden force driving security measures, so it becomes more necessary for 'the Secret State' to be seen to have given way to 'the Protecting State'. Civil harmony and civic responsibility are as important to us as they ever were, and our communities need to have the reassurance that the security and intelligence authorities working to protect them are doing so in ways that protect their rights and uphold the fundamental values of our society.

What all this adds up to is the need for a 'grand understanding' to emerge between political parties and public based on confidence that the government of the day will be working in good faith and to its utmost to maintain security as a state of normality in which individuals can get on with making the most of their lives as they choose, in freedom and without fear. We can express such an understanding in the form of a series of propositions representing a balance of the competing principles and interests involved.

All concerned, government, its agencies, and the public, have to accept that maintaining security today remains the primary duty of government and will have the necessary call on resources. It follows that upholding the values of a democratic, civilized society is itself a strategic national objective, including upholding the rule of law and working within the framework of human rights, including the fundamental right to life and the absolute prohibition of torture.

Modernity brings with it huge benefits but also increasing fragility in the systems on which everyday life depends: the public should be invited to accept that there is no absolute security and chasing after it does more harm than good. Providing security is an exercise in risk management.

Pre-emptive secret intelligence is an essential key to reducing the risk from terrorism. There will always be 'normal accidents' and intelligence failures, but overall the work of the intelligence and security services shift the odds in the public's favour, sometimes very significantly. If the secrets of terrorists and criminal gangs are to be uncovered, therefore, there will be inevitable intrusions into their privacy and that of their associates. These intrusive methods are powerful and they get results. So public trust that this machine is only to be used for public protection against major dangers will continue to be essential.

To that end, intelligence gathering must include surveillance and accessing protected personal data (PROTINT). Such work must be governed by the principle of minimum necessary intrusion on privacy. Intelligence should be managed within an ethical framework, for which I have suggested (chapter 10) six headings:

1. There must be sufficient sustainable cause

2. There must be integrity of motive
3. The methods to be used must be proportionate, and include the absolute prohibition on torture
4. There must be right authority exercised within the framework of human rights
5. There must be reasonable prospect of success
6. Recourse to secret intelligence sources should be a last resort

The security and intelligence community has to accept in turn that ethics matter: there are 'red lines' that must not be crossed. So some opportunities will have to be passed over and the principles of proportionality, necessity and due authority will have to be followed. The work of the intelligence agencies has to be overseen in parliamentary and judicial terms in accordance with statute.

The aim of those pursuing terrorists has to be to protect the public. Suspects will be prosecuted within the criminal law. Intelligence liaisons will be maintained in the interests of public safety and intelligence received that is capable of helping in that task will be received and acted upon but UK intelligence, police and military personnel will never solicit information that they have reason to believe may be obtained through torture.

The processes by which the intelligence community is managed, staffed and conducts its business will be made sufficiently transparent to build confidence in the integrity of all involved. The public must nevertheless accept that there is no general 'right to know' about intelligence sources and methods, but the public has a right to oversight of the work of intelligence agencies by cleared parliamentary representatives on the public's behalf, and should expect judicial oversight of the exercise of statutory authorities for intrusive investigation, with the right of investigation and redress in cases of abuse of these powers.

Envoi

I have described public security as a shared state of mind, a state of confidence that the major risks are sufficiently under control and can be managed so that people can go about their normal life, freely and with confidence. Life is full of surprises, sometimes unwelcome. Some level of insecurity has to be accepted day to day and lived with. There are also going to be times when due to the overwhelming pressure of events public security in general cannot be assured. Working to keep those risks to a minimum is a primary duty of government, part of the implicit contract between people and their government. Fulfilling that duty is thus integral to good government. Failure to try hard enough to do so is a likely indicator of poor government. But security comes at a price. There is an opportunity cost in terms of resources not available for other public goods such as education or culture. The threat of terrorism imposes restrictions on individual liberty, as the gates to Downing Street mutely remind us. And there is a price in terms of personal privacy to allow the authorities to generate the pre-emptive intelligence on which much of the effort to maintain public security rests. That price buys the security under whose wings the benefits of good government can be reaped.

NOTES

INTRODUCTION

1. Niccolo Machiavelli, *The Prince* (translated by George Bull), London: Penguin Classics, 1961, p. 92.

1. SECURITAS: THE PUBLIC VALUE OF SECURITY

1. Peter Hennessy, *The Secret State*, London: Allen Lane, The Penguin Press, 2002.
2. Cited in Peter Hennessy, *Cabinets and the Bomb*, London: OUP for the British Academy, 2002, p. 107.
3. Institute of Public Policy Research, *Shared Responsibilities: A National Security Strategy for the UK* (the final report of the IPPR Commission on National Security in the 21st century), London: IPPR, 2009.
4. To read the full analysis that underpins these observations see IPPR, *Shared Responsibilities*, June 2009.
5. HM Government, *Security for the Next Generation*, London: Cabinet Office, June 2009.
6. Juvenal, *Satires* X, drawing on the commentary by the Rev. M. Madan, London: 1769.
7. HM Government, *The National Security Strategy of the United Kingdom*, London, Cabinet Office, 2009.

2. SAPIENTIA: THE PUBLIC VALUE OF INTELLIGENCE

1. Intelligence judgments on the Chinese ballistic missile programme are given in US Air Force, *Ballistic and Cruise Missile Threat*, NASIC-1031–0985, 9 April 2009.
2. Lord Butler (chair), *Review of Intelligence on Weapons of Mass Destruction*, London: HMSO HC 898, 14 July 2004, p. 159.

3. Michael Warner, 'Wanted: A Definition of "Intelligence"', *Studies in Intelligence*, 46, 3 (2002), pp. 15–23.
4. Central Intelligence Agency, 'Intellipedia marks its second anniversary', CIA Langley, Press Release, 20 Mar 2008.
5. See http://www.rand.org/ise/projects/terrorismdatabase/ accessed 21 Sept 2009.
6. Examples include the University of Maryland, supported by the US Homeland Security Department, http://www.start.umd.edu/gtd/ accessed 20 Sept 2009.
7. http://www.iiss.org/publications/armed-conflict-database/ accessed 20 Sept 2009.
8. An article by Ibrahim al-Marashi entitled 'Iraq's Security and Intelligence Network: A Guide and Analysis', *The Middle East Review of International Affairs*, Vol. VI, No. 2, June 2002.
9. For an example, see the suite of products produced by UNYSIS http://www.unisys.pt/industries/financial/insurance/operational__risk__management.htm accessed 2 Dec 2009.
10. Lord Butler (chair), *Review of Intelligence on Weapons of Mass Destruction.*
11. W D Howells, 'Intelligence in Crises' in Gregory R. Copley (ed.), *Defense 83*' (Washington DC: D and F Conferences Inc., 1983), p. 351.
12. Sherman Kent, *Estimates and Influence*, CIA: Studies in Intelligence, Summer 1968.
13. Amy Zegart, *Flawed by Design: The Evolution of the CIA, JCS, and NSC*, Stanford: Stanford University Press, 1999.
14. Reproduced in *R* v. *Home Secretary*, ex p Hosenball [1977] 3 All ER 452 in the judgment of Lord Denning, Master of the Rolls.
15. Machiavelli, *The Prince*, p. 46.

3. FORTITUDIO: THE PUBLIC VALUE OF RESILIENCE

1. UK Civil Contingencies Act 2004, Part 1 (1).
2. Including 'smart power' as advocated by Professor Joe Nye of Harvard University.
3. UK Government, *Central Government Arrangements for Responding to an Emergency*, London: Cabinet Office, March 2005, available at http://www.cabinetoffice.gov.uk/media/132685/conops.pdf.
4. Rupert Smith, *The Utility of Force*, London: Allen Lane, 2005, p. 278.
5. UK Government, *The Role of Lead Government Departments in Planning for and Managing Crises*, London: Cabinet Office, 2008, available at http://www.cabinetoffice.gov.uk/media/132847/lgds_framework.pdf.
6. HM Government, *UK Cyber Strategy*, London: Cabinet Office, June 2009.
7. London Chamber of Commerce and Industry, *Disaster Recovery, Business Tips for Survival*, London, 2003.

8. David Omand, 'Reflections on Secret Intelligence' in Peter Hennessy (ed.), *The New Protective State*, London: Continuum Books, 2007.

9. Alex Evans and David Steven, 'Risks and Resilience in the New Global Era', *Renewal*, Feb 2009, pp. 44–52.

10. UN/ISDR 'Disaster reduction and sustainable development: understanding the links between vulnerability and risk to disasters related to development and environment', background paper for the World Summit on Sustainable Development, Johannesburg, 26 Aug-4 Sept 2002, p. 24.

11. Geoff Mulgan, *Connexity*, Harvard: Harvard Business School Press, 1998.

4. CIVITAS: THE PUBLIC VALUE OF CIVIC HARMONY

1. Charles Farr, Home Office Director-General of the Office for Security and Counter-Terrorism in his Colin Cramphorn Memorial Lecture, London: Policy Exchange, April 2009.

2. A distinction introduced by Gerges, *The Far Enemy*, Cambridge: Cambridge University Press, 2005, p. 1.

3. See the speeches by Dame Eliza Manningham-Buller of 10 Nov 2006, and Jonathan Evans of 5 Nov 2007 and 7 Jan 2009, accessed on 18 April 2009 at http://www.mi5.gov.uk/output/news-speeches-and-statements. html.

4. *Human Rights Act 1998* (Designated Derogation) Order 2001, No 3644, which came into force on 13 Nov 2001.

5. House of Lords SESSION 2004–05[2004] UKHL 56 Judgments—A (FC) *and others* (FC) (Appellants) v. *Secretary of State for the Home Department* (Respondent).

6. UK Government, National Security Strategy for the UK, Update 2009.

7. Louise Richardson, *What Terrorists Want*, New York: Random House, 2006.

8. President Clinton, speech at Yale University, October 2003 cited in *Yale Alumni Magazine*, Jan/Feb 2004.

9. European Council Common Position, *The application of specific measures to combat terrorism*, Brussels: 2001/931/CFSP, 27 Dec 2001.

10. Alex P. Schmid and Albert J. Jongman, *Political Terrorism: a new guide to actors, authors, concepts, data bases, theories, and literature*, Amsterdam: North Holland, Transaction Books, 1988.

11. UK Government, *Preventing Violent Extremism*, London: Home Office, 2008.

12. UK Government, *Counter-Terrorism Strategy (CONTEST 2)*, London: Home Office Cm 7547, 24 Mar 2009.

13. Eliza Manningham-Buller, speech at Queen Mary College, London, 9 Nov 2006, available at www.mi5.gov.uk.

14. Culminating in the House of Lords vote against the extension of the time limit to forty-two days, http://news.bbc.co.uk/1/hi/uk_politics/7666022.stm accessed 18 Apr 2009.

15. Home Office Consultation Paper, April 2009, http://www.homeoffice.gov.uk/documents/cons-2009–ripa accessed 29 Apr 2009.
16. House of Lords Constitution Committee, *Surveillance: Citizens and the State*, London, 2008. UK House of Commons, Home Affairs Committee, *A Surveillance Society?* London: HC 58, 2008. Richard Thomas and Mark Wallport, *Data Sharing Review Report*, London, 2008. UK Information Commissioner, Surveillance Studies Network, A Report on the Surveillance Society, 2006.
17. Bentham, Jeremy, *The Panopticon* (Preface).
18. Michel Foucault, *Discipline and Punish: the Birth of the Modern Prison*, London: Allen Lane, 1977.
19. J. E. Butler, *Government by Police*, London 1888, cited in David Vincent, *The Culture of Secrecy*, Oxford: OUP, 1999.
20. Henry Porter, *The Guardian*, 28 April 2009, p. 31.
21. John Reid, *The Guardian*, 28 April.

5. THE INTELLIGENCE CYCLE: FROM WHENCE OWE YOU STRANGE INTELLIGENCE?

1. See the description of the production process in Michael Herman, *Intelligence Power in Peace and War*, Cambridge: CUP, 1996.
2. Richard Dearlove and Tom Quiggin, *Contemporary Terrorism and Intelligence*, IDSS Commentaries, 7 Aug 2006, accessed at http://www.rsis.edu.sg/publications/Perspective/IDSS0782006.pdf
3. General Sir David Richards, *Future War*, London: Chatham House, 2009.
4. Tom Fingar, Speech to the Council on Foreign Relations, Washington, 18 Mar 2008, accessed at www.dni.gov/speeches/20080318_speech.pdf.
5. The so-called Control Principle, discussed in the Court of Appeal (Civil Division) judgment in the case of Binyam Mohammed [2010] EWCA Civ63 Case T1/2009/2331.
6. The concept was pioneered by Colonel John Boyd (1927–97), a United States Air Force fighter pilot and military strategist.
7. Butler Review, 2004, p. 153.
8. John P. Sullivan and James Wirtz, 'Terrorism Early Warning and Counterterrorism Intelligence', *International Journal of Intelligence and Counter-Intelligence*, Vol. 21, No. 1, Spring 2008.
9. For example under the International Regulations for Signals Intelligence, IRSIG, see Jeffrey T. Richaelson, *The US Intelligence Community*, New York: Ballinger, 1989, chapter 12.
10. The phrase comes from T. S. Eliot's 'Gerontion', *Poems*, 1920 and was used by Angleton to describe the world of double and triple agents of the Cold War. The poem also expresses the counter-intelligence officer's dilemma: 'What will the spider do, suspend its operations, will the weevil delay?'
11. Gordon Corera, *Shopping for Bombs*, London: Hurst, 2006.

6. ELUCIDATION: YE SHALL KNOW THE TRUTH, AND THE TRUTH SHALL SET YOU FREE

1. http://watergate.info/sussman/25th.shtml, accessed 25 April 2009.
2. Reported by the BBC at http://news.bbc.co.uk/1/hi/entertainment/tv_and_radio/3831831.stm, accessed 26 April 2009.
3. Carmen Medina, What to do when traditional models fail, Studies in Intelligence, Vol. 14, No. 3, 2002.
4. Francis Bacon, *De Augmentis Scientiarum*, 1623.
5. *The Sunday Times*, London, 2 April 2006.
6. R. V. Jones *Reflections on Intelligence*, p. 48.
7. Opening words of L. P. Hartley, *The Go-Between*, London: Hamish Hamilton, 1953.
8. David Deutsch, *The Fabric of Reality*, London: Allen Lane, 1997.
9. Crabtree appears to have been an elaborate pre-war academic joke involving spoof 'Crabtree orations' at major universities.
10. John Buchan, *The Three Hostages*, London: Hodder & Stoughton, 1924.
11. John Le Carré, *Tinker, Tailor, Soldier, Spy*, London: Hodder & Stoughton, 1974, pp. 216–18.
12. Georg Polya, *How to Solve It*, Princeton: Princeton University Press, 1957.
13. Richards J. Heuer Jr, *Psychology of Intelligence Analysis*, Washington DC, Center for the Study of Intelligence, CIA, 1999.

7. ANALYSTS AND POLICY-MAKERS: IDEALISTS AND REALISTS

1. Norman E. Dixon, *On the Psychology of Military Incompetence*, London: Jonathan Cape, 1976.
2. Robert Jervis, 'Reports, Politics and Intelligence Failures: The Case of Iraq', *Journal of Strategic Studies*, 29/1, 2006, pp. 3–52.
3. George Tenet, *At the Centre of the Storm*, London: HarperCollins, 2007, p. 149.
4. Michael F. Scheuer, 'Tenet Tries to Shift the Blame. Don't Buy It', *Washington Post*, 29 April 2007.
5. *Report of the Commission on the Intelligence Capabilities of the United States Regarding Weapons of Mass Destruction*, Washington DC, 2005 p. 6, accessed at http://govinfo.library.unt.edu/wmd/about.html 30 July 2009.
6. Record of the Prime Minister's meeting of 23 July 2002, accessed at *The Times* Online, 1 May 2005, http://www.timesonline.co.uk/tol/news/uk/article387374.ece.
7. Robert Jervis, 'Reports, Politics and Intelligence Failures: The Case of Iraq', *Journal of Strategic Studies*, 29/1 (2006) pp. 3–52.
8. Lord Hutton, *Report of the Inquiry into the Circumstances Surrounding the Death of Dr David Kelly CMG*, London: House of Commons HC 247, Jan 2004.
9. Sir William Macpherson, *The Stephen Lawrence Inquiry*, London: HMSO CM 4261, Feb 1999.

10. For example, Sir David Omand, oral evidence to the Chilcot Inquiry, 20 Jan 2010, available at http://www.iraqinquiry.org.uk accessed 18 Feb 2010.
11. Michael Handel, *War Strategy and Intelligence*, London: Frank Cass, 1989.
12. UK Cabinet Office, *Central Intelligence Machinery*, London: Cabinet Office, 2004.
13. Michael Handel, 'Intelligence and the Problem of Strategic Surprise', *Journal of Strategic Studies* 7, no. 3, Sept 1984, pp. 229–81.
14. Michael J. Goodman, 'Learning to Walk: The Origins of the UK's Joint Intelligence Committee', *International Journal of Intelligence and CounterIntelligence*, Vol. 21, Issue 1, March 2008, pp. 40–56.
15. Thomas Lowe Hughes, *The fate of facts in a world of men: foreign policy and intelligence-making*, New York: Foreign Policy Association, 1976, p. 22.
16. Percy Cradock, *Know your Enemy: How the Joint Intelligence Committee Works*, London: John Murray, 2002.
17. Butler Review, p. 159.
18. Cited in Hayden M., Evidence to Joint Committee of Congress, 17 Oct 2002, https://www.cia.gov/news-information/speeches-testimony/2002/dci_testimony_10172002.html accessed 1 Nov 2009.
19. Carmen Medina, 'What to do when traditional models fail', *Studies in Intelligence*, 46/3(2002), pp. 23–9.
20. http://www.businessdictionary.com/definition/marketing.html accessed 26 July 2009.
21. Theodore Levitt, *Marketing Myopia*, Harvard: Harvard Business Review, July-Aug 1960.
22. R. V. Jones, *Reflections on Intelligence*, p. 200.
23. Cabinet Office, *Central Intelligence Machinery*, 2005.
24. K. L. Gardiner, 'Squaring the Circle: Dealing with Intelligence-Policy Breakdowns', *Intelligence and National Security*, 6/1 (1991), pp. 141–52.
25. Winston Churchill, *The Second World War, Vol. III: The Grand Alliance*, London: Cassell, 1949, p. 319.
26. Gill Bennett, *Desmond Morton, Churchill's Man of Mystery*, London: Routledge, 1997.
27. John L. Helgerson, *Getting to Know the President: CIA Briefings of Presidential Candidates*, Washington DC: CSI, 1994.
28. US Department of Defense, 'Review of the Pre-Iraqi War Activities of the Office of the Under Secretary of Defense for Policy', Washington DC: DOD, Feb 9 2007, now de-classified at http://levin.senate.gov/newsroom/supporting/2007/SASC.DODIGFeithreport.040507.pdf
29. Tenet, *At the Center of the Storm*, 2007, p. 348.
30. Helgerson, *Getting to Know the President*, pp. 19, 94.
31. Tenet, *At the Center of the Storm*, 2007, p. 232.

32. Gardiner, 'Squaring the Circle', 1991, pp. 141–52.
33. Dixon, *The Psychology of Military Incompetence*.
34. Helgerson, *Getting to Know the President*, p. 163.
35. Cited in Cradock, *Know Your Enemy*, 2002.
36. NIE, *Estimative Products on Yugoslavia, 1948–1990*, Washington DC: National Intelligence Council, 2007.
37. Cited in Daniel McNeil and Paul Freiberger, *Fuzzy Logic*, New York: Simon and Schuster, 1993.
38. Jack Davis, 'Why Bad Things Happen to Good Analysts' in Roger Z. George and James B. Bruce (eds), *Analyzing Intelligence*, Washington, DC: Georgetown University Press, 2008, pp. 157–70.
39. Irving L. Janis, *Victims of Groupthink*, Boston: Houghton Mifflin, 1972, p. 9.

8. INTELLIGENCE FAILURES: ON NOT BEING SURPRISED BY SURPRISE

1. Edgar Wind, *Pagan Mysteries of the Renaissance*, London: Peregrine Books, 1967.
2. Roberta Wohlstetter, *Pearl Harbor: Warning and Decision*, Stanford: Stanford University Press, 1962 was the pioneering text in post-war analysis of surprise.
3. Machiavelli, *The Art of War*, 1520.
4. Clausewitz, *On War*, Princeton: Princeton University Press, 1984, Book VI, chapter 3.
5. Charles Perrow, *Normal Accidents: Living with High-Risk Technologies*, Princeton: Princeton University Press, 1999.
6. M. Betts (ed.), *Paradoxes of Secret Intelligence: Essays in Honor of Michael Handel*, London: Frank Cass, 2003.
7. Richard Pipes, 'Team B: The Reality Behind the Myth', *Commentary*, Oct 1986, p. 29, cited in Betts, 2003, p. 86.
8. HMG, *Security for the Next Generation*, London: Cabinet Office, June 2009.
9. Carmen Medina, 'What to do when traditional models fail', *Studies in Intelligence*, 46/3(2002), pp. 23–9.
10. Woodrow Kuhns, *Intelligence Failures: Forecasting and the Lessons of Epistemology* in Betts, 2003.
11. Richard K. Betts, 'Surprise Despite Warning: Why Sudden Attacks Succeed', *Political Science Quarterly*, 95/4, 1980, pp. 551–72.
12. Michael Handel, *Perception, Deception and Surprise: The Case of the Yom Kippur War*, Jerusalem: The Leonard Davis Institute, 1976, p. 16.
13. Reproduced in Michael S. Goodman, 'The Dog That Didn't Bark: The JIC and Warning of Aggression', *Cold War History*, Vol. 7, Issue 4, Nov 2007, pp. 529–51.

14. Lawrence Freedman, *The Official History of the Falklands War*, London: Routledge, 2005, Vol. I, pp. 219–21 and Vol. II, p. 720.
15. MC 48/2 (Final Decision), NATO Brussels, 23 May 1957, http://www.nato.int/docu/stratdoc/eng/a570523b.pdf accessed 3 Aug 2009.
16. Betts, 'Surprise Despite Warning: Why Sudden Attacks Succeed', 1980.
17. Gordon Barrass, *The Great Cold War*, Stanford: Stanford University Press, 2009, pp. 298–9.
18. Daniel Franklin, 'The World in 2009', London: *The Economist*, 19 Nov 2008, http://www.economist.com/theworldin/displayStory.cfm?story_id=12494578 accessed 15 July 2009.
19. Perrow, *Normal Accidents*, 1999, p. 7.
20. John Adams, *Risk*, London: Routledge, 2001.
21. Gregory F. Treverton, *Reshaping National Intelligence for an Information Age*, Cambridge: CUP, 2003.
22. Freedman, *Official History of the Falklands Campaign*, 2005.
23. Cited in Wesley Wark, *The Ultimate Enemy: British Intelligence and Nazi Germany, 1933–1939*, Ithaca, New York: Cornell University Press, 1985.
24. Warren Buffet quoted in *New York Times*, article by Steve Lohr, 2008, http://www.nytimes.com/2008/10/06/business/06buffett.html accessed 21 Feb 2009.
25. HMG, *National Security Strategy: Security in an Interdependent World*, London: Cabinet Office, March 2008, p. 7.
26. Walter Bagehot, *The English Constitution*, London: Fontana, 1963, p. 205.
27. Clausewitz, *On War*, Book One, chapter 6.

9. *IN MEDIAS RES*: SECURITY AND INFOTAINMENT

1. Speech by Sir Rodric Braithwaite, Chairman, Joint Intelligence Committee 1992–3, The Royal Institute of International Affairs, Chatham House, Friday 5 Dec 2003.
2. US Government, *US Info*, http://usgovinfo.about.com/library/weekly/aa100200a.htm accessed 5 Dec 2009.
3. Christopher Andrew, *The Defence of the Realm*, London: Allen Lane, 2009.
4. Harold Laski, Foreword to J. P. W. Mallallieu, *Passed to you, Please*, London: Victor Gollancz, New Left Book Club, 1942.
5. Sir Compton Mackenzie, *Water on the Brain*, London: Cassell, 1933.
6. Sir Compton Mackenzie, cited in John F. Naylor, *A Man and an Institution*, Cambridge: CUP, 1984.
7. Nicholas Wilkinson, *Secrecy and the Media—the Official History of the D Notice System*, London: Routledge, 2009.

10. ETHICAL ISSUES: THE GOOD OF THE CITY AND THE CITY OF THE GOOD

1. David Omand, 'The Dilemmas of Using Secret Intelligence for Public Security' in Hennessy (ed.), *The New Protective State*, London: Continuum, 2007.
2. Anthony Glees, Philip H. J. Davies, and John N. L. Morrison, *The Open Side of Secrecy*, London: Social Affairs Unit, 2007.
3. Under the so-called Osmotherley Rules, a widely observed convention followed by successive UK governments, available at http://www.cabinetoffice.gov.uk/propriety_and_ethics/civil_service/osmotherly_rules.aspx.
4. For example, in the UK, Peter Oborne, *The Use and Abuse of Terror: The Construction of a False Narrative on the Domestic Terror Trail*, London: Centre for Policy Studies, 2006 and for the US, John Mueller, *Overblown: How Politicians and the Terrorism Industry Inflate National Security Threats and Why We Believe Them*, New York: Free Press, 2006.
5. Cited in the blog of the self-named '7th of July Truth Campaign', http://j7truth.blogspot.com/2007/05/imran-khans-post-crevice-trial.html, accessed 18 Apr 2009.
6. Channel 4 website, 4 June 2007, http://www.channel4.com/news/articles/society/religion/survey+government+hasnt+told+truth+about+77/545847 accessed 18 Apr 2009.
7. See the report in Haaretz of 30 Nov 2008, http://www.haaretz.com/hasen/spages/1041318.html accessed 24 Sept 2009.
8. Philip Bobbitt, *Terror and Consent*, New York: Random House, 2008.
9. Statement of Michael F. Scheuer: 'Extraordinary Rendition in U.S. Counterterrorism Policy: The Impact on Transatlantic Relations', Joint Hearing Before the Subcommittee on International Organizations, Human Rights, and Oversight and the Subcommittee on Europe of the Committee on Foreign Affairs House of Representatives, One Hundred Tenth Congress (First Session), 17 Apr 2007, p. 14. http://foreignaffairs.house.gov/110/34712.pdf.
10. In General McChrystal's 66–page report submitted in Aug 2009 to Defense Secretary Bob Gates, see http://www.nytimes.com/2009/09/21/world/asia/21afghan.html accessed 24 Sept 2009.
11. The five techniques of hooding, sleep deprivation, wall standing, restrictions on food and water and white noise were banned by the UK government following the adverse finding of the European Human Rights Court: *Ireland* v. *United Kingdom*, 25 Eur. Ct. HR (ser. A)(1978).
12. Intelligence and Security Committee, *UK Agencies and Rendition*, London: Cabinet Office, July 2007.
13. UNSC Resolution 1456 (2003).
14. Full Judgment of the Court of Appeal (Civil Division) on Appeal from the Divisional Court in the case of Binyam Mohammed, [2010] EWCA Civ 65, 10 Feb 2010, paras. 43–44.

15. [2010] EWCA Civ 65, para. 10.
16. David Vincent, *The Culture of Secrecy*, Oxford: OUP, 1999, p. 29.
17. The United Nations, previously unwilling to be thought of as recognizing the right of one member state to spy on another, accepted the value of intelligence in combating terrorism in UNSC Resolution 1373 passed immediately following 9/11, and the European Court of Human Rights has accepted in its judgments that nations have the right to protect their economic well-being and national security.
18. Professor A. John Radsan, 'The Unresolved Equation of Espionage and International Law', *Michigan Journal of International Law*, Vol. 28:595, pp. 595–623, available at http://students.law.umich.edu/mjil/article-pdfs/v28n3–radsan.pdf accessed 24 Sept 2009.
19. Daniel B. Silver, 'Intelligence and Counterintelligence' in John Norton Moore and Robert F. Turner (eds), *National Security Law* 935, 965, 2nd edn 2005 (updated and revised by Frederick P. Hitz and J. E. Shreve Ariail).
20. Radsan, *Michigan Journal of International Law*.
21. Tony Blair, speech to the Economic Club, Chicago, 24 Apr 1999, http://www.number10.gov.uk/Page1297 accessed 4 Aug 2009.
22. David Omand, CIISS Annual Lecture 2007, *Intelligence and National Security*, Vol. 23, No. 5, Oct 2008.
23. *Malone v. United Kingdom*, 7 Eur. Ct. H.R. 14 (1985).
24. David Bickford, lecture to Harvard Law School Forum, 15 Apr 1997.
25. Bickford, 1997.
26. Sir Stephen Lander, The Hinsley Lecture 1993, St John's College, Cambridge.
27. The operation of the RIPA 2000 Act is described in detail on the Home Office website, www/security.homeoffice.gov.uk/riparabout-ripa.
28. One of the conclusions reached by Peter Gill regarding the UK Intelligence and Security Committee: Peter Gill, 'Evaluating Oversight Committees: The UK ISC and the War on Terror', and Mark Pythian, 'The British Experience with Intelligence Accountability', both in *Intelligence and National Security*, 22, Feb 2007.
29. Evidence, General Hayden, http://www.q-and-a.org/Transcript/?ProgramID=1123, April 2007.
30. David Omand, 'Ethical Guidelines in Using Secret Intelligence for Public Security', *Cambridge Review of International Affairs*, 19/4, Dec 2006, pp. 613–28.
31. Admiral Stansfield Turner, *Secrecy and Democracy*, London: Sidgwick & Jackson, 1986. [PEQ1]AU: necessary to capitalize? Yes, better left with capitals.

11. INTELLIGENCE DESIGN: BUILDING INTELLIGENCE COMMUNITIES

1. David Omand, Ken Starkey, Victor Adebowale, *Engagement and Aspiration: Reconnecting Policy Making with Front-Line Professionals*, London: Cabinet Office (2009).
2. Robert Fludd, 'Utriusque Cosmi Maioris' in Vol. 1 of his *Macrocosmi Historia Oppenheim: Johann Theodore de Bry*, 1617, cited in Joscelyn Godwin, *Robert Fludd*, London: Thames and Hudson, 1979.
3. Michael Warner, 'The Creation of the Central Intelligence Group', *Studies in Intelligence*, 39(5), pp. 4–10, https://www.cia.gov/library/center-for-the-study-of-intelligence/kent-csi/pdf/v39i5a13p.pdf accessed 25 Sept 2009
4. Thomas R. Johnson, *American Cryptology during the Cold War, 1945–1989*, Book I: *The Struggle for Centralization, 1945–1960*, National Security Agency, Center for Cryptological History, Redacted copy, 1995.
5. Private information.
6. John Helgerson, *OIG Report on CIA Accountability with respect to the 9/11 Attacks*, Langley: CIA, 2009, https://www.cia.gov/library/reports/ Executive%20Summary_ OIG%20Report.pdf.
7. Amy Zegart, *Flawed by Design*, p. 166.
8. Michael Howard, *The Central Organisation for Defence*, London: RUSI, 1970.
9. HMG, Cmnd 124, *Defence: Outline of Future Policy*, London: HMSO, April 1957.
10. Christopher Andrew, 2009.
11. Helen Fessenden, 'The Limits to Intelligence Reform', *Foreign Affairs*, 84(6), 2005, pp. 106–20.
12. HMG, *Improving the Central Intelligence Machinery*, London: Cabinet Office 2009, http://www.cabinetoffice.gov.uk/media/300268/improving-the-central-intelligence-machinery.pdf accessed 1 Nov 2009.
13. Michael Goodman and David Omand, 'Analyst Training', *CIA: Studies in Intelligence*, 52(4): 2008, pp. 1–12.
14. Jones, 1989, p. 156.

12. A FRESCO FOR THE FUTURE

1. Matthew Arnold, *Baccanalia*.
2. The phrase is derived from an interview with the magazine *Vanity Fair*; see Deputy Secretary Wolfowitz interview with Sam Tannenhaus, *Vanity Fair*, 9 May 2003, http://www.defenselink.mil/transcripts/transcript.aspx?transcriptid= 2594.
3. In a BBC interview with Fern Britton broadcast on 13 Dec 2009, http://www.guardian.co.uk/uk/2009/dec/12/tony-blair-iraq-chilcot-inquiry accessed 13 Dec 2009.
4. Secrétariat Général de la Défense Nationale, *Livre blanc sur la securité intérieure face au terrorisme*, Paris: La Documentation Française, 2006.

5. See the ministerial statements by Tom Ridge and David Blunkett, at US Department of State, International Information Programmes, http://www. iwar.org.uk/news-archive/2003/04–01–2.htm.

6. The plans for London are described at http://www.londonprepared.gov.uk/ londonsplans/emergencyplans/massfatality.jsp.

7. David Omand, 'Using Secret Intelligence for Public Security' in *The Protective State*, 2007.

INDEX

Afghanistan: border with Pakistan, 89, 271; CIA intervention in, 174–5; Conflict, 186, 273; Invasion of (2001), 101; Kandahar Province, 238; Soviet Invasion (1979), 229, 255; Taliban, 271

Al-Qa'ida, xvii, 52, 89, 150, 192, 241, 271, 315; 9/11 attacks, 10, 16, 41, 54, 64–5, 86, 91, 95–6, 102, 122, 124, 160, 171, 193, 223, 270, 273, 281, 304; and al-Zawahiri, Ayman, 87; 'dirty bomb' rumour, 95; formation of, 16; havens of, 101; ideology of, 16, 87, 89, 93, 96, 101, 103, 105, 270, 313–14; lack of sufficient intelligence on, 174; Operation Overt, 21, 111, 266; waning of, 104

al-Zawahiri, Ayman: and Al-Qa'ida, 87; and bin Laden, Osama, 87, 314

Baginski, Maureen: Director of SIGINT of NSA, 181

Bali: Terrorist Bombing (2002), 264, 276

Bayes, Reverend Thomas: theorem of, 153–4, 156

Beveridge, William, xix

bin Laden, Osama, 74; and al-Zawahiri, Ayman, 87, 314; as high priority target, 174; leadership figure, 102–3

Blair, Tony: Prime Minister, 154, 171, 179, 281; and Dearlove, Sir Richard, 176; and Invasion of Iraq (2003), 175, 257, 314; Dossier Presentation to Parliament (2003), 171–2

Braithwaite, Sir Roderick: Chair of JIC, 28, 251

British Security Service (MI5), 30, 50, 131, 282, 292; and CIA, 297; established (1909), 36, 113; Director-Generals of, 90, 92, 100–1, 263; structure and function of, 30; Maxwell-Fyfe Directive (1952), 54; Security Service Act (1996), 54; Wilson, Harold conspiracy theory, 252

Burgess, Guy: Soviet agent, 166

Bush, George H.W.: former US President, 178

Bush, George W.: administration of, 270, 273; and Invasion of Iraq (2003), 175; authorisation of CIA intervention in Afghanistan, 174; authorisation of rendition and interrogation procedures, 273; 'War on Terror', 90

Callaghan, James: Prime Minister, 62

Campbell, Alistair: Director of Communications, 32; 'Dodgy Dossier' Incident (2003), 32, 47, 130, 144, 158, 179

Canada, 94, 123; Canadian Security Intelligence Service (CSIS), 52; Royal Canadian Mounted Police (RCMP), 52

Canberra, 16

Central Intelligence Agency (CIA), 33, 134, 162, 191, 278, 285, 297; and MI5, 297; and Vietnam War (1959–75), 202; Counter-Terrorism Center, 174, 270; established (1949), 51, 210; Directors of, 149; failure to find link between Al-Qa'ida and Hussein, Saddam, 192; formerly Office of Strategic Services (OSS), 51; headquarters of, 164; intervention in Afghanistan, 174; rivalry with NSA, 297; surveillance activities of, 53, 121, 241; 'threat matrix', 193

China: military of, 24–5

Churchill, Winston, 153, 193, 298; and Morton, Desmond, 190–1; interest in reading intelligence, 189–90

von Clausewitz, Carl: *On War*, 250; writings of, 116, 133, 151, 212, 214

Clinton, Bill: Former US President, 98

Cold War, xix, 9, 62, 102, 113, 118, 126, 252, 280–3, 312, 320; and NATO, 117, 169, 230; and USSR, 66, 186, 216, 243–4; 'Domino Theory', 200; effect on approach to national security, 9, 16–17, 19, 132, 182, 221, 230, 243, 268; end of, 10, 63, 124, 131, 291; ideological conflict of, 11, 160; National Technical Means, 115; Warsaw Pact, 186, 226

Committee for State Security (KGB), 35, 134; Operation RYAN, 214

Counter Terrorism Strategy (CONTEST), 2, 64, 86, 91, 93–4; origin of, 101; redrafting into CONTEST 2 (2009), 103

Cradock, Sir Percy: chair of JIC, 28, 180; foreign policy advisor to Thatcher, Margaret, 28

Cuban Missile Crisis (1962), 217–18, 230; and Khrushchev, Nikolai, 169, 216; Soviet presence, 213

Dean, Sir Patrick: and Suez Canal Incident (1956), 199

Dearlove, Sir Richard: and Blair, Tony, 176; former Chief of MI6, 121, 176

Distributed Denial of Services (DDOS), 72

Duff, Sir Anthony: appointed JIC Chair (183), 28; background of, 27–8

Egypt: Invasion of Israel (1972–3), 233–4; Luxor Massacre (1997), 97

Eisenhower, Dwight D.: Supreme Allied Commander, 297; US President, 297

Electronic intelligence (ELINT), 29, 120

Ethics: principles of in intelligence work, 286–7, 324–5

Europe, 81; and USA, 15; Court of Human Rights, 272, 283

European Union (EU), 125; and NATO, 319; and UK, 126; counter-terrorism policy of, 99; governments of, 34, 102

Falkland Islands Invasion (1982), 232, 244–5, 248; and JIC, 214, 229, 282; and Thatcher, Margaret, 18, 26–7, 48, 215

Federal Bureau of Investigation (FBI), 53–4; led by Hoover, J. Edgar, 51–2; role in Watergate Scandal, 143

Fingar, Tom: Chairman of US National Intelligence Council, 124

First World War, 113, 210, 254; and GCHQ, 50; and Germany, 21; decryption of Zimmermann telegram, 21; outbreak of, 282

Florence: Medici, 6; power of, 5

France: banning of public display of conspicuous religious symbols, 102; jihadists of, 89

Gates, Robert: US Defence Secretary, 178

Germany: and First World War, 21: and Second World War, 133–4; Berlin, 16: Fall of Berlin Wall (1989), 26; Federal Intelligence Service (BND), 145, 168; jihadists of, 89; Morgenthau Proposal (1944), 58

Gorbachev, Mikhail: meeting with Thatcher, Margaret, 128, 135

Gordievsky, Oleg: double agent in KGB, 35, 135, 235–6; report on Operation RYAN, 214; SIS Agent, 35, 128, 136

Government Communications Headquarters (GCHQ), xvii, xx, 36, 182, 224, 284, 294, 303; and First World War, 50; and NSA, 298; formerly Government Code and Cypher School, 37, 50, 191; location of, 186; staff of, 115, 228; structure of, 30;trade unions banned by Thatcher, Margaret (1984), 282; trial of Prime, Geoffrey (1982), 282

Grand Understanding, 323–4

Heath, Edward: Prime Minister, 272

Homeland Security: bilateral UK/US Group, 319; threat advisories, 231; US concept of, 65

Hoover, J. Edgar: FBI Director, 51–2

Human sources of intelligence (HUMINT), 29, 108, 120, 143, 146, 153, 167, 176, 185, 233, 284, 295, 300, 307; agencies of, 51, 121, 145, 234, 244; and MI6, 148

Hussein, Saddam, 192, 255; and First Gulf War, 215, 226; and Invasion of Iraq (2003), 197; illegal weapon programmes of, 141, 162, 175–7, 207, 219, 313; capture of (2003), 176

Intelligence and Security Committee (ISC): aims and output of, 264–5, 267, 276; and 7/7 attacks, 264; established by Intelligence Services Act (1994), 264, 279, 284; Parliamentary Intelligence and Security Oversight Committee, 273

International Monetary Fund (IMF): and National Security Strategy, 246

Iran, 207; and Iraq, 141, 229; (ian) Revolution (1979), 26; Soviet attack on (1980), 229

Iraq: and Butler Inquiry, 130, 144, 164, 168, 178–9, 181, 186, 201, 204, 206, 257–8, 294, 305, 312–13; and Hutton Inquiry, 144, 177; and Iran, 141, 229; Conflict, xvii, 28, 47, 89, 103, 178; Invasion of (2003), 49, 86, 130, 135, 150, 162, 281, 294, 313; Muslims of, 89

Islam: interpretations of, 87, 96; perceived threats to, 104; tenants of, 87; Shia, 89; Sunni, 89

Israel: alleged cyber-attacks on Syria, 72; Egyptian/Syrian

Invasion of (1972–3), 227, 229, 233–4; hostility toward, 87, 96, 314; Israeli Defence Force (IDF), 233; Supreme Court, 269; Tel Aviv, 233

Japan, 199
Joint Intelligence Committee (JIC), 27, 36, 48, 124, 147, 168, 177, 184–5, 205, 215, 229, 294, 298–9, 303; aims and output of, 37–8, 40, 44, 128–9, 144, 150, 152, 164, 167, 179, 195–6, 204, 206, 210, 224, 230, 237, 245, 249, 257–8; and 7/7 attacks, 42; and Falkland Islands Invasion (1982), 214, 229, 282; and NIE, 43; and Operation Barbarossa, 189; chaired by Braithwaite, Sir Roderick, 28, 251; chaired by Cradock, Sir Percy, 28; chaired by Duff, Sir Anthony (1983), 28; established (1936), 37; Iraq War intelligence failure (2002), 28, 37, 234; members of, 39, 151; position in UK Central Intelligence community, 38, 228; relationship with Current Intelligence Groups (CIG), 38–9, 127, 182, 232, 317; role in Second World War, 37; threat level system, 42
Joint Terrorism Analysis Centre (JTAC), 241, 263, 305, 311, 318; aims and output of, 41, 44, 124–5, 225, 231; and NCTC, 43; change of threat level, 104, 220; established (2003), 41, 231; location of, 147; model of, 302; staff of, 181

Karachi, 33
Keynes, John Maynard: and Great Depression, 153; *General Theory of Employment, Interest and Money*, 25

Khrushchev, Nikolai, 243; and Cuban Missile Crisis (1962), 169, 216
Kissinger, Henry: National Security Adviser, 195; US Secretary of State, 233
Korea: cyber conflict between North and South, 72; proliferation in, 207; (n) War (1950–53), 135

Leach, Admiral Sir Henry: First Sea Lord, 18
Lorenzetti, Ambrogio: *Allegory of Good Government*, xxi, 1–6, 20, 57, 92–3, 209, 309; philosophical beliefs of, 5, 10, 92–3

Macchiavelli, Niccolo, 55–6, 270; *The Prince*, 6–7, 210
Macpherson, Sir William: Inquiry, 177–8
Major, John, 86
Manningham-Buller, Baroness Eliza: former Director General of MI5, 92, 104
Meir, Golda; Israeli Prime Minister, 233
Menzies, Sir Stuart: former head of MI6, 191
Ministry of Defence, xvii, 30, 35, 86, 143, 151, 154, 214, 231, 233, 305, 316; Defence Intelligence Staff, 30, 38, 43, 44, 201; unification (1964), 37
Morton, Desmond: and Churchill, Winston, 190–1; background of, 190
Mulgan, Geoff, 78
Munich Olympics Incident (1972): effect on UK counter-terrorism policy, 61

National Counter-Terrorism Center (NCTC), 318; and JTAC, 43
National Intelligence Estimate (NIE), 164, 169, 179, 195, 205,

256–7, 313; and JIC, 43; methods of, 198; view on Balkan Wars (1990), 199–200

National Security Agency (NSA), 297; and Baginski, Maureen, 181; and GCHQ, 298; rivalry with CIA, 297; SIGINT, 181

National Security Strategy (2009), 119, 125, 133, 218, 246; and financial crisis, 246; British approach to, 10; demands in intelligence community, 123; requirements of, 290; UK, 14; Western, 16

Netherlands: jihadists of, 89

Nixon, Richard M.: US President, 298

'Normal accident': definition, 212; avoiding, 242; and secret intelligence, 324

North Atlantic Treaty Organization (NATO), 220, 320; Able Archer Exercise (1983), 235; and Afghanistan, 273; and Cold War, 117, 169, 230; and EU, 319; and Ismay, Major General, 189; and UK, 9–10, 15, 63, 67; and USSR, 136, 217; Intelligence Warning System (NIWS), 231; members of, 19; Nuclear Planning Group (NPG), 27; nuclear posture of, 10

Northern Ireland, 232; The Troubles, 10, 98, 106, 272, 303

Obama, Barack: administration of, 61; election of, 89

Organization of Petroleum Exporting Countries (OPEC), 238

Pakistan: border with Afghanistan, 89, 271; intelligence provided by, 274–5; terrorist presence, 94

Paris, 16

Penkovsky, Oleg: and Wynne, Greville, 278

Permanent Joint Headquarters (PJHQ), 35

Philby, Kim: Soviet agent, 166

Powell, Colin: presentation to UN Security Council (2003), 171, 313; Secretary of State, 313

Provisional Irish Republican Army (PIRA), 67, 98, 100, 103; mortaring of Downing Street (1991), 85–6; Siege (1975), 61, 69–70; Sinn Fein, 254–5

RAND Corporation, 32

Reagan, Ronald: 'Evil Empire' rhetoric, 235; US President, 235

Reid, John: former Home Secretary, 110

Rice, Condoleezza, 174

Rumsfeld, Donald, 156, 227

Russia: Mafia, 95; Moscow, 134; South Ossetian Conflict (2008), 72, 238

Scheuer, Michael: former Director of CIA Counter-Terrorism Center, 270; testimony of, 270–1

Scotland Yard, 35, 100

Second World War, 21, 50, 62, 113–14, 150, 184, 191, 253, 279, 299; and Germany, 133–4; and JIC, 37; cracking of Enigma Cipher, 35, 114, 146–7, 190; Molotov–Ribbentrop Agreement, 135; Normandy Beach Landings, 239, 297; Operation Barbarossa, 153, 189, 213, 218; Operation Fortitude, 213; Pearl Harbour Incident (1941), 21, 210, 213, 216, 218, 297, 304

Secret Intelligence Service (MI6), 30, 50, 134, 182, 186, 190, 224, 284; activities of, 137, 144–5; and HUMINT, 148; established (1909), 36, 113; headquarters of, 256; led by Menzies, Sir Stuart,

191; Security Service Act (1996), 54; structure and function of, 30, 51, 54

'Secrets and Mysteries': and complexities, 47–8; and R. V. Jones, 244; and surprise, 243; example of, 199

Serious and Organized Crime Agency (SOCA), 44

Siena, 1, 7: governing council of, 3–4, 57; Palazzo Pubblico, 1; population of, 1–3; power of, 5

Signals intelligence (SIGINT), 29, 44, 54, 108, 120, 123, 143, 146, 152, 162, 167, 234, 282, 297, 300, 307; and NSA, 181; satellites, 115, 297

Singapore, 16

Single Intelligence Account (SIA), 30; established (1689), 50

Soviet Union (USSR), 10, 268; and Cold War, 66, 186, 216, 243–4; and Cuban Missile Crisis (1962), 213; and NATO, 136, 217; attack on Iran (1980), 229; Invasion of Afghanistan (1979), 229, 255; Invasion of Czechoslovakia (1968), 21, 226, 228; GRU, 135; military of, 282; Polish intervention (1980–81), 229; *Spetznatz*, 67

Special Air Service (SAS): and Munich Olympics Incident (1972), 61; Iranian Embassy (1980), 61

Special Boat Service (SBS): and Munich Olympics Incident (1972), 61

'Strategic Notice' definition, 221; examples, 12, 20, 173, 175, 215, 219, 239; JIC papers 224; financial crash 246

'Strategic Surprise': and 'Strategic Notice', 173; and terrorism, 219; counter-surprise, 220; in intelligence, 210–12; reducing surprise, 249

Strong, Sir Kenneth: UK Director-General of Defence Intelligence, 26

Switzerland: banning of mosque minaret construction, 102

Thatcher, Margaret: and Falkland Islands Invasion (1982), 18, 26–7, 48, 215, 283; banning of trade unions at GCHQ (1984), 282; meeting with Gorbachev, Mikhail, 128, 135

The Hague, 16

Truman, Harry S.; US President, 193, 297

United Kingdom (UK), 7, 63, 306; 21/7 attacks, 109; 7/7 attacks, 42, 94, 97, 109, 264, 266; allies of, 123; and Cold War, 9; and EU, 126; and US, 16; Cabinet Office, xvii, xix, 14, 62, 85, 184, 194–6, 303–5; Cabinet Office Briefing Room (COBRA), 61, 63, 65; Cabinet Office Strategy Unit, 80; Centre for the protection of National Infrastructure (CPNI), 67; Civil Contingencies Committee, 62–3; Critical National Infrastructure (CNI), 66–7, 69–70, 73, 76, 80–2; Cyber Security Operations Centre (CSOC), 71; derogation of Human Rights Act (2000), 91–2; economy of, 69–70, 73, 83, 246–7; empire of, 23; Foreign and Commonwealth Office, 35, 37, 41, 50, 126, 155, 179, 221, 231, 305; Freedom of Information Act (2000), 253; Glasgow Airport Incident (2007), 91; Government of, xx, 12, 17–19, 23, 45–6, 62, 65, 68, 102, 106, 197, 259, 270, 313; Home Office, 35, 41, 64–5, 73, 87, 110, 151, 224; House of Lords, 92, 106; legal system of, 279–80;

London, 16; military of, 27; Metropolitan Police, 41, 71, 97, 100; member of NATO, 9–10, 15, 63, 67; military of, 98, 102, 272; Muslim population of, 101, 150; Office of Cyber Security (OCS), 71; Operation Crevice and trial (2007), 92, 94–5, 105, 111, 266; PIRA Terrorist Siege (1975), 61, 69–70; Regulation of Investigatory Powers Act (2000), 107, 109–10, 284; Resilience Industries Suppliers Council (RISC), 82; Security Service Act (1989), 100, 284; threats to, 10, 14

United Nations (UN), 175, 219, 280; Charter, 257; Convention on Torture, 287; General Assembly, 99; International Strategy for Disaster Reduction (UN/ISDR), 76; Security Council, 171, 273, 275, 313

United States of America (USA), 306; 9/11 attacks, 10, 16, 41, 54, 64–5, 86, 102, 122, 124, 160, 171, 173–4, 270, 281, 302, 304; and Europe, 15: and UK, 16; Congress of, 51, 302; Constitution of, 272; DEFCON Alert system, 220, 230, 233; Defence Intelligence Agency, 165; Detroit Incident (2009), 171; Director of National Intelligence (DNI), 43; Drug Enforcement Agency (DEA), 122; entry into First World War, 21; foreign policy of, 104; government of, 46, 270;

Homeland Security Department, 32 65, 122, 220, 231; hostility toward, 87; intelligence community of, 31, 55, 107, 174, 188, 296; Intelligence Reform and Terrorism Prevention Act (IRTPA) (2004), 302; Invasion of Iraq (2003), 49, 86, 135; Iran-Contra Affair (1986), 255; McCarthy era, 102; military of, 25, 174, 243; National Security Act (1947), 297; New York, 33–4, 64, 86, 171; Oklahoma City Bombing, 88; Pearl Harbour incident, 21; Pentagon, 43, 121, 145, 192; President's Foreign Intelligence Advisory Board (PFIAB), 217; Senate 'Church Commission' of Inquiry (1975), 53–4; Three Mile Island Incident (1979), 212; Washington, 16, 64, 86, 171

Vietnam: War (1959–75), 158, 202; US Military Assistance Command in Vietnam (US MACV), 202

Wilson, Harold: MI5 conspiracy theory, 252; Prime Minister, 252
World Bank: and IMF, 246; and National Security Strategy, 246
Wynne, Greville: and Penkovsky, Oleg, 278; exchanged for Lonsdale (1964), 278

Yom Kippur War (1973), 26, 245; outbreak of, 233–4